The awesome sweep of the Rainbow Slab with climbers on **Red and Yellow...** E1 5a and **Pull My Daisy** E2 5c photo: Adrian Trendall
Cover: Pete Robins pressing his way up the stunning F8a groove pitch of Johnny Dawes' slate masterpiece, **The Quarryman** E8 7a, Twll Mawr photo: Ian Parnell

Llanberis Slate

Authors: Pete Robins, Mark Dicken, Martin Crook, Simon Panton

Editor: Simon Panton

Design: Al Williams www.50folds.tumblr.com

Printing: C & C Offset Printing Company, Shenzhen, Guangdong, China

Distribution: Cordee www.cordee.co.uk

Publisher: Ground Up Productions Ltd

August 2011

ISBN 978-0-9554417-6-9

© Ground Up Productions Ltd

All rights reserved. No part of this publication may be reproduced, stored in a retrieval system, or transmitted in any form or by any means, electronic, mechanical, photocopying or otherwise without written permission of the copyright owner.

A CIP catalogue record is available from the British Library

Guidebook Disclaimer
The writer and publisher of this book accepts no responsibility for the way in which readers use the information contained therein. The descriptions and recommendations are for guidance only and must be subject to discriminating judgement by the reader. Advice and training should be sought before utilising any equipment or techniques mentioned within the text or shown in any of the photographic images.
Climbing and bouldering are activities with a danger of personal injury or death. Participants in these activities should be aware of, and accept, these risks and be responsible for their own actions and involvement.

www.groundupclimbing.com

Contents

Introduction 7	Colossus Wall 192
Getting there 8	Rainbow Slab 200
Access and Conservation 9	Rainbow Walls Lower 210
Local accommodation and facilities ... 10	Rainbow Walls Upper 226
Safety on the crags 11	Vivian Lower 240
Grades/Graded list 15	East Face of Vivian 258
Venue Table 25	Vivian Upper 260
Bus Stop Quarry 26	Fachwen Quarries 282
Australia Lower 38	Nant Peris Quarry 283
A Grand Day Out 64	Glyn Rhonwy 286
Australia Upper 66	Slate Walks and Adventures 315
Australia East Braich 88	Addendum 320
Dali's Hole 98	History 322
California 114	Route Index 364
Serengeti 124	Acknowledgements 374
Never Never Land 140	Bibliography/Advertisor's Directory ... 375
Twll Mawr 158	
Mordor and Lost World 174	A winding tower high up in the quarries photo: Adrian Trendall ∧

Introduction

Slate is a truly radical medium upon which to climb. It confounds all notions of 'normal' movement. The combination of a (typically) 'less-than-vertical' angle and a curiously frictionless surface dictates a peculiar style; high-stepping, improvised, tenuous and sometimes bizarrely powerful. The tiniest of holds must be trusted, pulled upon and weighted with confidence. It is rarely pumpy, at least not in the arms; although your calves will get a good working. There are many bold and soul searching leads, yet there are also numerous intense, technical clip ups where the next bolt is never far away.

There is, of course, adventure here: big, loose lines where an instinct for survival will serve you better than wall trained finger strength. There is also fun and much 'surreality' amongst these strange holes in the ground. Whatever you get up to, a day spent in this science fiction landscape will stay with you forever.

The Dinorwig and Glyn Rhonwy slate quarries sprawl across the hillsides above the mountain village of Llanberis. The vast spoil heaps and massive quarried holes sit in acutely contrasting juxtaposition with the more traditional landscape of this beautiful area. Despite Llanberis' emergence as one of the key Snowdonia tourist destinations, the history of the quarries defines its cultural base. The Dinorwig Quarries ceased working in 1969, yet their impact upon the local community still resonates to this day. After the closure the quarries seemed destined to drift back into neglect and obscurity, that is, were it not for the intervention of certain maverick elements of the local climbing community.

During the 1960s a post war generation of working class English climbers had moved into the area, buying up and renovating neglected rural properties that were being sold off (often for ridiculously cheap prices) by the Vaynol Estate. The following decades saw more climbers settling in the area, many staying on after completing courses at Bangor University. By the start of the 1980s Llanberis had become a thriving hub for an increasingly intense climbing scene. This new generation of full time – dole sponsored climbers set about developing this fascinating industrial wasteland into a

 Memorial for the quarrymen at Bus Stop photo: Si Panton
 A rusting relic above Lost World photo: Si Panton

premier climbing venue. By the mid 80s the quarries were 'the' place to be and new routes occurred almost on a daily basis. The legacy of this frenetic period of development is a rich and diverse collection of exquisitely technical and often fiercely bold routes.

During the 90s and early 00s the quarries sunk back into a state of neglect, with only a handful of classic routes receiving any attention. All that changed in 2006/7 when a re-equipping campaign was kick started by a group of local climbers operating with the support of the North Wales Bolt Fund. In particular, Mark Reeves, Mark Dicken, Pete Robins and Chris Parkin played a key role in the campaign, each putting in enormous amounts of time and effort to replace rotting bolts and belays with modern high quality hardware. The enthusiasm spilled over into an equally energetic new routes campaign, which crucially saw the establishment of several instantly popular low grade sport climbing areas.

Suddenly the quarries were buzzing again – five years previous, who could have predicted that?

The Llanberis Slate guide has had an unusually long inception, granted not as long as some guidebooks out there, but nonetheless it has not come easily. Part of the reasons for this are external factors (Ground Up getting drawn into the production of other guidebooks for example), part was the need to wait for an access agreement to Dali's Hole area to be sorted out, but mostly it has been down to the seemingly never ending surge of new routes which has occurred over the last three years. There is still much potential in the quarries for good quality routes so this trend is likely to continue. However there comes a time when you have to a draw a line, and that time is now.

So here it is the 'slate' of the art as it stands in the summer of 2011. Dive in and have a look around – you won't be disappointed!

8 Introduction

Getting there

Access to the quarries is made either from the Slate Museum car park (Gilfach Ddu) at the base of Vivian Quarry, or from the Bus Stop Quarry turning circle on the outskirts of the village of Dinorwig. Dinorwig is reached either by driving up the Fachwen road, or across from Deiniolen, both of which are signposted from the B4547 Llanberis-Bangor road.

There are also two other less used access points; the first being the Pen Garret road which runs above Bus Stop Quarry (and gives access to Australia Upper) and the second is the main quarry path which runs from the outskirts of Nant Peris right through the quarries to connect with Bus Stop Quarry.

The Glyn Rhonwy Quarries can be accessed from the Clegir road which continues up from Goodman Street (opposite Pete's Eats) in Llanberis.

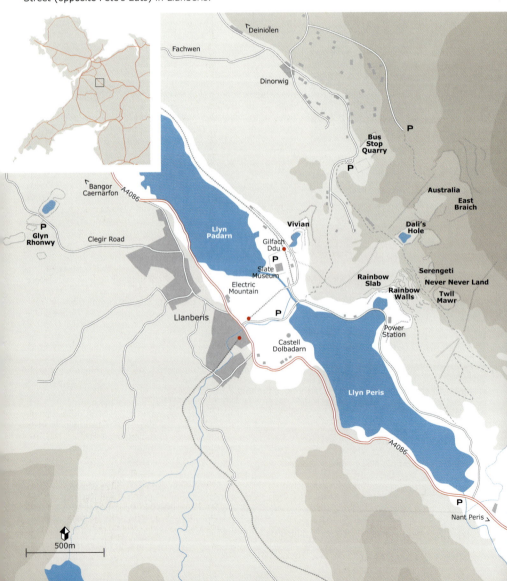

Introduction 9

Access and Conservation

Although there are public footpaths networking through and around most of the areas described in this guide there is no official sanction of climbing by the landowners, Gwynedd Council and First Hydro. Our presence in the slate quarries has thus far been tolerated, but only on the proviso that we keep a low profile, avoid damaging any fences or gates (always climb over at the hinged end) and keep dogs under control and away from sheep.

In the Dinorwig Quarries it is imperative that all climbers avoid the power station area and under no circumstances climb upon the walls below the Rainbow Slab and Rainbow Walls Lower area. The Trango Tower, situated directly above the power station offices should also be considered out of bounds.

Vivian Quarry is part of Parc Padarn and is owned by Gwynedd Council. Here there are a few specific requests: use the obvious fence crossings, and avoid the central areas of the levels with re-established vegetation; respect the trees on, or near, the climbs. Do not lower off directly from any trees; always use a sling and krab. Do not abseil into the quarry from its right hand side.

On no account whatsoever should routes be prospected, or attempted, anywhere above the tourist path track on the Pool level.

The Pool Wall area is subject to a specific climbing ban: during the opening hours of the diving centre do not climb in this area.

As for parking – use the Gilfach Ddu car park (taking note of the seasonal closing times), or walk over from the Castell Dolbadarn car park, or indeed the village of Llanberis itself.

The Glyn Rhonwy Quarries are owned by Gwynedd Council. Low key access to this area is tolerated but with the increasing development of the industrial park area below the Clegir road a sensitive approach would seem sensible. There is also a seasonal bird ban on a small section of Gideon Quarry – see the chapter for more details.

Bus Stop Quarry is also owned by Gwynedd Council. Access here is tolerated but please park sensibly and avoid damaging the fences.

Occasionally there will be changes to the access situation in the quarries, so it is recommended that prior to your crag visit, especially if you haven't been for a while, a quick reference is made to the British Mountaineering Council Regional Access Database **(thebmc.co.uk/bmccrag)**. This provides dynamic updates of any changes to access arrangements. For example, a temporary seasonal restriction may be applied if a rare bird is found nesting close to climbing routes. If you encounter any access problems, please contact the BMC immediately.

∧ The main path running past Twll Mawr photo: Si Panton   Access warning sign photo: Si Panton ∧

CRAG CODE
www.thebmc.co.uk

Access	Check the Regional Access Database (RAD) on www.thebmc.co.uk for the latest access information
Parking	Park carefully – avoid gateways and driveways
Footpaths	Keep to established paths – leave gates as you find them
Risk	Climbing can be dangerous – accept the risks and be aware of other people around you
Respect	Groups and individuals – respect the rock, local climbing ethics and other people
Wildlife	Do not disturb livestock, wildlife or cliff vegetation; respect seasonal bird nesting restrictions
Dogs	Keep dogs under control at all times; don't let your dog chase sheep or disturb wildlife
Litter	'Leave no trace' – take all litter home with you
Toilets	Don't make a mess – bury your waste
Economy	Do everything you can to support the rural economy – shop locally

BMC Participation Statement — Climbing, hill walking and mountaineering are activities with a danger of personal injury or death. Participants in these activities should be aware of and accept these risks and be responsible for their own actions and involvement.

Local Accommodation and facilities

Dyffryn Peris, or the Llanberis valley as it is known in English, is a popular tourist destination, and as such it is well served with accommodation to suit the weary traveller. All tastes are catered for: campsites, bunkhouses, youth hostels, bed and breakfasts and hotels. The choice is huge, but a traditional campsite base popular with climbers sits opposite the Vaynol Arms pub in Nant Peris
There are numerous cafes (for example: Caban in Brynrefail, Pete's Eats and the Electric Mountain in Llanberis), pubs, restaurants (The Heights and the Pizza 'n' Pint night at the Gallt y Glyn are popular options), takeaway food establishments and even an excellent ice cream parlour in Llanberis itself. Food shopping is well catered for too with various wholefood shops, bakeries, butcher shops and supermarkets in the towns and villages throughout the area.
Llanberis has two well established and well stocked climbing shops: V12 Outdoor and Joe Brown. The former even serves excellent coffee and delicious home made cakes.
The three main climbing climbing walls in the local area are the Beacon Climbing Centre in Waunfawr (but soon to be relocated to the Cibyn estate on the edge of the nearby town of Caernarfon - see their advert on page 3), the Indy Wall at Llanfair PG (see their advert on page 63) and the Plas y Brenin wall in Capel Curig (see their advert on page 109).
www.snowdonia-active.com provides a whole host of information about local guides, instructors and activity providers, accommodation and campsites, outdoor shops and cafes. Check out the Directory, a geographically specific database covering outdoor orientated businesses in the northwest Wales area. The site is also host to a whole range of downloadable activity and area guides and it has links to numerous weather forecasting websites.
The Slate Museum in Gilfach Ddu car park at the bottom of Vivian Quarry is essential viewing for all visitors. Be sure to spend a few hours learning about the fascinating history of the quarries.

Johnny Dawes in the **Gin Palace** F7b+, Vivian Quarry
photo: Adrian Trendall

Looking for wire placements on **Seams the Same** E1 5b
photo: Adrian Trendall

Climbing Equipment

On the majority of trad routes in the quarries it makes sense to use double ropes (normally 8 or 8.5mm x 50m); these will help to reduce drag and allow quick abseil descents where required. On certain big pitches (*Comes the Dervish* and routes on the Colossus Wall) up to 15 quick draws will be needed, however on most routes 10 will suffice. The nuts and cams required are often quite specific to a given route, but throughout a day's climbing you will need a good selection of both. Micro wires are particularly useful, as are Offsets. A couple of 120cm and 60cm slings and screwgates should be carried.

It is always a good idea to have a skyhook hanging from your harness when you're climbing on slate. Occasionally they will give you protection, albeit of a very marginal nature, but they can also provide a potential lower-off point if you get caught a long way out from your runners in a down pour.

On most sport routes a single 50m or 60m rope and 10 quickdraws will be enough, although it is common practice to carry some wires. Do bear in mind that some clip ups (for example: on Skyline Buttress) can have as many as 16 bolts, plus two further bolts on top for the belay. A telescopic 'stick clip' is a useful tool to have, especially if you are trying a harder sport route.

Stiffer, 'edgey' rock shoes are best for slate. On the harder routes some of the footholds are microscopic; only a new (ish) shoe will work on these types of holds. Don't expect to climb at your limit in a pair of worn out, bendy slippers! And lastly, a head torch is handy for some of the darker tunnel approaches.

Bolts and Pegs

There has been a fairly comprehensive re-equipping campaign over the last five years but many old bolts and pegs still form crucial protection on certain routes. These aging relics should be treated with suspicion, and the routes they adorn perhaps best avoided until further re-equipping has been carried out. Use your judgement; if a bolt looks suspect, treat it with caution.

If you find any hangers that are loose please tighten the nut up. Any 'wobbly' or suspect bolts should be reported on the slate wiki: **www.slate.wetpaint.com.**

Ivan Holroyd high stepping on **Where are my Sensible Shoes** F7b, Rainbow Walls photo: Adrian Trendall

New bolts, old bolts photo: Jethro Kiernan >

12 Introduction

Seasonal conditions

The quarries provide genuine opportunities for climbing throughout the year. The rock dries extremely quickly, making this a popular option in showery or changeable weather. There is nearly always an option of shade or sunlight, and so by picking the right area you can make the most of your visit.

Rockfall and other hazards

Large rockfalls do occur in the quarries from time to time. You may arrive at an area only to find that what you see doesn't match the topo image in this guide. Any routes within or close to fresh rockfalls should be avoided. If you discover any new rockfalls please report them on the slate wiki.
Loose holds are common in the quarries, even on relatively popular routes. This is especially a problem if there has been a harsh winter. Freeze-thaw action can turn previously solid routes into death traps, so tread carefully in the spring months.
Many of the climbing areas in the quarries consist of series of narrow levels stacked on top of each other. Care should be taken to avoid knocking slate pieces down onto the level below.
Slate often forms sharp edges; the type of edges that could cut a rope. Do take care to extend runners properly so that the rope is not forced to run over a sharp edge. Extra care should be taken to protect abseil ropes – if you have to jumar back up the rope think about how the rope will rub over any exposed edges.
Moving around the levels in the quarries often requires the use of the old quarry ladders. Many of these are in a perilous state – if in any doubt rope up or find a different route/method to reach the next level.

Helmets

Head injuries are common in climbing and abseiling accidents, so it seems sensible that all climbers, whatever grade they climb, should consider wearing a helmet. Luckily there is a wide range of lightweight designs currently available. If you haven't got one, go and try a few on at your local climbing shop, you'll be surprised how comfortable (and stylish) they are these days.

Introduction 13

First Aid

- If spinal or head injuries are suspected, do not move the patient without skilled help, except to maintain breathing or if this is essential for further protection.
- If breathing has stopped, clear the airways and start artificial respiration. Do not stop until expert opinion has diagnosed death. However it is recommended that the First Aider should give due consideration to their own well being in view of the physical demands of this method of treatment.
- Treat major bleeds as the second priority to breathing.
- Summon help as quickly as is compatible with safety.
- If Hypothermia is suspected treat the sufferer – assuming they are still conscious – with food, drink, warm clothing, and if possible get them into a bothy tent/shelter or down off the hill.

Rescue

In the event of an accident where further assistance is required dial 999 and ask, for Police Mountain Rescue. Give as many details as possible including a grid reference if this is known – each chapter heading has a grid reference. (NB. Do bear in mind that mobile phones cannot always be relied upon to work; signal quality will be found to vary considerably, especially in mountain areas. It is worth registering with www.emergencysms.org.uk which will allow you to send emergency texts when signal quality is poor.)

In the event of a helicopter evacuation secure all loose equipment, clothing, rucksacks etc. All climbers in the vicinity should try to make themselves safe. Do not approach the aircraft unless told to by the crew.

Mountain Rescue teams

The local Mountain Rescue teams are manned by volunteers and funded almost entirely by donations. Please help to support their valuable work by making a donation. Details of how to donate can be found on the following websites:

www.llanberismountainrescue.co.uk
www.ogwen-rescue.org.uk
www.aberglaslyn-mrt.org

1 Old quarry ladder dropping down from the G'Day Arete Level on the Australia East Braich photo: Si Panton
2 Get yourself a helmet! photo: Adrian Trendall
3 Watch out for sharp edges! photo: Andy Newton
4 Pete Robins shows the perils of slapping a sharp slate edge photo: Si Panton
5 Helicopter rescue photo: Adrian Trendall

14 Introduction

Style and ethics

In terms of style and ethics the slate quarries have gone through two distinct phases. Firstly during the original new route boom in the mid 80s came the notion of 'designer danger'. Bolts were often used, but usually in a sparing fashion. This happened partly through a desire to create routes with a bold character, but also because of the relative poverty of the 'dole-sponsored climbers of that era who could little afford the cost of the hardware.

Towards the end of the 80s more fully bolted sport routes were done especially in the harder grades, but low grade clip ups were unknown. When the re-quipping program kicked off in 2006/7 there was a corresponding surge of low grade sport routes established. These have proved to be extremely popular and now we have the happy position of a wide variety of route styles existing often right next to each other. Current thinking is that a first ascencionist should aim to create the best possible route; some lines suit the full bolted treatment, but others, particularly where the rock quality is good, may be better with some carefully considered run outs.

Because unclimbed slate is often loose, onsight first ascents are quite rare, although climbers such as Ray Kay have climbed some difficult lines in this admirable, if somewhat dangerous style. Abseil inspection and cleaning are the norm and in most cases will give better routes. Cleaning slate is an activity during which the boundary between loose rock removal and hold creation is often blurred. Indeed many of the harder routes in the quarries have been carefully sculpted to give moves of a particular standard, often suiting the reach of the creator!

Anybody considering bolting a new route should take note of the following advice: firstly abseil the line and decide if it really is as good as you think it might be. If it is, give it a rudimentary clean and if you are still convinced of its worth place a belay at the top and top rope the line. This will give you final confirmation that the route is worth pursuing any further. If it is then work out the bolt positions, taking care to consider the onsight climber who will not have the quickdraws in place and won't know about any hidden holds or sneaky tricks. Badly positioned bolts can make the difference between a good climb and a poor one.

It is also important to ensure that the bolts used are the best quality available (i.e. stainless steel) and that you are well versed in bolt placement best practice as advocated by the BMC. There is a wealth of information accessible online, for example: **www.thebmc.co.uk/Download.aspx?id=8**. If you are in any doubt how to place bolts properly please contact Chris Parkin who runs the North Wales Bolt Fund.

Re-equipping the quarries

Although an enormous amount of re-equipping has already occurred, there is still more to do. If you would like to contribute to the ongoing project of re-equipping the quarries then please support the North Wales Bolt Fund, either by getting involved in the actual re-equipping work or by making a donation. Contact Chris Parkin at **northwalesboltfund@googlemail.com** for more details, or look out for collection jars in the local climbing shops and climbing walls.

Grades

This guide uses the standard British grading system for non sport climbs. This runs in ascendance through the full range of difficulty, from straightforward climbs suitable for beginners, right up to state-of-the-art test pieces: Very Difficult, Severe, Hard Severe, Very Severe, Hard Very Severe, and Extremely Severe, an upper range which is subdivided into numbered E grades (E1 to E11, although the hardest climb described in this book is E8). This adjectival grade gives an overall impression of the difficulty of the climb, taking into account factors such as how serious it is, how physically sustained it is and how technically difficult the climbing is. There is also an additional technical grade (4a, 4b, 4c, 5a, 5b, 5c, 6a, 6b, 6c, 7a), which gives an indication of the hardest single move on a given pitch.

Sport climbs are described with the simple linear French system: F3, F4, F5, F5+, F6a, F6a+, F6b, F6b+ etc, right up to F8b+, the hardest featured route in this guide. On some routes the first ascensionists have offered a further clarification in the F3-F5 range expressed as, for example, F4a, F4b or F4c.

There is an approximate parity between a given sport grade and a well protected traditional route, however there are so many other factors governing the difficulty of a slate traditional route - beyond the physical and technical difficulty, which are covered by a sport grade - that any comparisons should be treated as no more than very rough guides. For example, F6a would be similar to a well-protected E1, but only to someone familiar with placing natural protection and dealing with the myriad challenges of a typical traditional route (e.g. boldness, loose rock, navigation of line etc.).

There aren't many boulder problems in the quarries, but those that are described are given a split grade of the American 'V' system, which runs from V0- to V16, and the Fontainebleau system, which runs from Font 3 to Font 8C+. There are also a few drytooling routes and aid routes which use the modern grading systems prevalent elsewhere in the world.

The intro sections to each of the crags gives a colour coded list of the featured routes. The grade ranges are as follows:

	UK (adjectival/technical)	French (sport)	American
E6 and above	E8 6c/7a	F8b,8b+	5.13d/5.14a
E3 – E5	E7 6b,c/7a	F8a,8a+	5.13b,c
HVS – E2	E6 6a,b,c	F7b+,7c,7c+	5.12c,d/5.13a
S – VS	E5 5c/6a,b,c	F7a,7a+,7b	5.11d/5.12a,b
	E4 5b,c/6a,b	F6c,6c+	5.11b,c
	E3 5b,c/6a	F6b+	5.11a
F7c and above	E2 5a,b,c/6a	F6a+,6b	5.10c,d
F7a – F7b+	E1 5a,b,c	F6a	5.10b
F6a+ – F6c+	HVS 4c/5a,b	F5,5+	5.9/5.10a
	VS 4b,c/5a	F4+	5.8
F5 – F6a	HS 4a,b,c	F4	5.6/5.7
	S 4a,b	F3+	5.5/5.6
F3 – F4+	VD	F2+,3	5.3/5.4
	D	F2	5.2

↑ Jeff McDonald on the lower crux of **Ride the Wild Surf** E4 6a, Colossus Wall photo: Rob Lamey
< Jon Ratcliffe blowing out a bolt hole on a project line photo: Si Panton

16 Trad Graded List

E8
Coeur De Lion
The Quarryman

E7
The Cure for a Sick Mind
Dawes of Perception
Blockhead
The Firé Escape
I Ran the Bath
Raped by Affection
Clap Please
Stairway to Silence
Breakdance
My Halo
The Spirit Level

E6
Split Decision
Naked Before the Beast
Windows of Perception
The Shark that Blocked the Drain
Prick up Urea's
The Faffer
Phil's Harmonica
DOA
Slip of the Tongue
The Big Sur
Prometheus Unbound
Menstrual Gossip
The Dwarf in the Toilet
Fat Lad Exam Failure
Wishing Well
Sombre Music
Order of the Bath
The Wonderful World of Walt Disney
Released from Treatment
For Whom the Bell Tolls
Drury Lane
Stiff Syd's Cap
Tribal Blow
Jai'a'n
Spider Pants
The Rainbow of Recalcitrance
The Dyke
North West Face of the Druid
The Gay Blade
Lob Scouse
Scare City
Love Minus Zero
Ringin' in Urea's
A Mere Trifle

E5
Glass Axe
The Mosquito
The Listening and Dancing
The Homicidal Hamster from Hell
Senior Citizen Smith
Cystitis by Proxy

Wedlock Holiday
Watching the Sin Set
The Spark that Set the Flame
Flashdance/Belldance
The Long and Winding Road
Fruity Pear in a Veg Shop Romp
Lost Crack
Midnight Flier
Marital Aids
Mildly Macho
Private Smells
Piper at the Gates of Dawn
Shame and Embarrassment
Light and Darkness
The Hobbit
Chewing the Cwd
Freak Yer Beanbag
Splitstream
The Machine in the Ghost
Big Wall Party
Simply Peach
Never Never Land
Dali's Dihedral
Return of the Visitor
Cuts like a Knife
Central Sadness
Josy Puss
The Bridge Across Forever
Black Daisies for the Bride
Poetry Pink
Young Men Afraid of Horses
Hysterectomy
Small Rusty Nail on a
   Large Mantelpiece
Over The Rainbow
Slip Sliding Away
Gay Lightweights and
   Hetro Stumpies
Flashdance
Broken Memories
Green Ernie
Unpaid Bills
Bathtime
Heinous Creature
1000 Tons of Chicken Shit
Shazalzabon
Out of Africa
Sanity Claws
Major Headstress
Where the Green Ants Dream
Swinging By the Bell
Wall of Flame
Salvador
Waves of Inspiration
The Book of Brilliant Things
In on the Kill Taker
Fool's Gold – Scare City
Hymen Snapper
Dark and Scary Stories
Dope on a Rope
Now or Never

E4
Putting on Ayres
Menai Vice
The Second Coming
Taith Mawr
Jack the Ripper
The Wow Wow
Liquid Armbar
Dwarf Shortage
Jaded Passion
Nostromo
The Bone People
Great Balls of Fire
Jack of Shadows
No Problem
Imperial Leather
Pitch Two
Ride the Wild Surf
The Sweetest Taboo
Short Stories
The New Salesman
Laund Arête
Slug Club Special
Esprit de Corpse
Manatese
Moving Being
Resurrection Shuffle
Twisted Nerve
The Gorbals
Caleduwlch
The Sneaking
Teliffant
The Reclining Bloon
Ancestral Vices
Tentative Decisions
Swan Hunter
Igam-Ogam
Monsieur Avantski
Working up a Lather
Crossville
I Don't Wanna Pickle
Menage a Trois
Y Rybelwr
Stump Rogers
The Color Purple
Sad Old Red
Far from the Madding Crowd
Yuk Hunter
Blah de Blah de Blah
General Odours
Celestial Inferno
Stack of Nude Books Meets
   the Stick Man
Gods Between Money
Mad on the Metro
Balance of Power
The Coming of Age
Silver Shadow
Virgin on the Ridiculous
The Mau Mau

V12
Rock Climbing Specialists

The largest selection of technical hardware, more than 40 rock shoe styles, plus the latest men's and women's crag gear

The best deals on the net:
www.v12outdoor.com

V12 OUTDOOR

Llanberis   01286 871534
Liverpool   0151 2074123
Stockport   0161 4946008

Rob Wilson and Katie Haston repeating Katie's dad's classic slate route, **Comes the Dervish** E3 5c, Vivian Quarry photo: Si Panton

Trad Graded List 19

Ari Hol Hi
Remain in Light
Young and Easy Under the Apple Boughs
Gideon's Way
Soap on a Rope
Four Wheel Drift
Shtimuli
Scarlet Runner
Meltdown
Sup 2
Men of Leisure
Sweetest Taboo Direct Start
Ultra Cricket Zone
On Shite
Foetal Attraction
Glurp
Memorable Stains
Lord of the Rings
Buffalo Smashed in Head Jump
The Chiselling
Two Steps to Heaven, Three Steps to Hell
The Wall Without
Pandora Plays Sax Direct Start
Wakey, Wakey, Hands off Snakey
The Coolidge Effect
Loved by a Sneer
Darkness Visible
Old Cow, New Cow
Here to Stay, Gone Tomorrow
Stretch Class
One Wheel on my Wagon
Spread'em
The Toms Approach
Khubla Khan
Watch Me Wallaby Wank Frank
Put it on the Slate, Waiter
As the Sun Sets in the West
Octopussy's Garden

E3

The Razors Edge
Gender Bender
Arthur Dali
Moth to the Flame
Beijqueiro
Feet Apart
Dali's Lemming Ducklings
Ladder Resist
Bushmaster
Captain Condom and the Mothers of Prevention
A Good Slate Roof
Dinorwig Unconquerable
See You Bruce
Good Crack
Purple Haze
Colossus
Cyclone B

Scarlet Runner Direct
Dali Express
First and Last
The Mancer Direct
Between Here and Now
Zzzooming the Tube
Ladybird Girl/Giddy One
Ya Twisting Ma Melon Man
Proliferation Bang On
The Golden Shower
Buzz Stop
Don't Look Back in Bangor
Cat Flaps of Perception
Night of the Hot Knifes
Down to Zero
Legal Murders
Hamadryad
Short Staircase to the Stars
Comes the Dervish
Astroman From the Planet Zzzoink
Geographically Celibate
Pain Killer
Loony Toons
Solitude Standing
Planet Zzzoink Arête
Unchain My Heart
Mark of Thor
Poetry in Motion
N.E. Spur
Goose Creature
Sesame Street Comes to Llanberis
Men at Work
The Mad Cap Laughs
Red Throated Diver
Reefer Madness
Off the Beaten Track
Long Distance Runner
Rycott
Jugs Mawr
Hasta La Vista Baby
Last Chance for a Slow Dance
The North face of the Aga
A Selfish Act of Loonacy
Maupin Ray Route
Fellowship of the Ring
The Hong Jagged Route of Death
Unsexual
Sabre Dance
Genital Persuasion
Primal Ice Cream
Youthslayer
The Richard of York Finish
Son of Rabbit
Ritter Sport
The Race against Time
Little Urn
Wild Horses
Solvent Abuse
Sanity Fair
The Wooley (or won't he) Jumper

E2

The East Face of the Vivian Womaninstress
Dangling by the Diddies
How Hot is Your Chilli?
Immac Groove
Uhuru for Mandela
Cracking Up (5c/6a)
Pull My Daisy
Lethal Injection
Hemulin
Two Tone
The Samba Drum
Solstice Direct
One Step Beyond
Pork Torque
Massambula
Is it a Crime?
Never as good as the First Time
German School Girl
Too Bald to be Bold/The Turkey Chant
Dyke Rider
The Great Curve
Blue Touch Paper
Holy, Holy, Holy
Eros
The Velociraptor
Stretched Limo
Sterling Silver
The Gnarly SPAR Kid
Ride of the Valkyries
Faulty Towers
2nd Class Passenger
Puff Puff
Bise-Mon-Cul
The Man Who Fell to Earth
Giddy Variations on a Theme
Dali Mirror
A Pair of Six
Harold Void
Bring me the Head of Don Quixote
Just For Fun
Sprint Finish
Tribulation of Bob Marley and Peter Tosh
Simion Street
Sylvanian Waters
F Hot
Single Factor
Aultimers Groove
Wobbly Variations on a Slab
Eric the Fruitbat
Friendly Argument
Heaven Steps
The Rothwell Incident
Chariots of Fire
Slippery People
Blades of Green Tara
Legs Akimbo

20 Trad Graded List

Pruning the Tube
Psychotherapy
Cabbage Man meets the Flying
  Death Leg
Genevieve
Toilet Trouble
Stinky Boots
Legs Together
Layed Back Boys
Midnight Drives
Tennent's Creek
Grandad's Rib
Fetzer
Franzia
Throttle With Bottle
Abattoir Blues
Abus Dangereux
Rhyfelwr
The Stick Up
Rosen Chosen
Turn of the Century
Catrin
Angel on Fire
Slate's Slanting Crack
Walrus Wipeout
Ronald Reagan meets Doctor
  Strangelove
Near Dark (After Dark)
Malice in Wonderland
Rock Video
The Skyline Club
Captain Black and the Mysterons
Satires of Circumstance
Stairlift to Heaven
Rastaman Vibration
Scratching the Beagle
Silent Homecoming
Proless Cliff Arête
The Blind Buddha
Classy Situation
So this is Living
Brain Death
Wendy Doll

E1

Sup1
Last Tango in Paris
The Colour Purple
The Barrel of Laughs
Patellaectomy
The Monster Kitten
Home Run
Stuck up Fruhstuck
Rodent to Nowhere
Way Down in the Hole
Zippies First Acid Trip
Lord of the Pies
Tongue in Situ
Making Plans for Nigel
Red and Yellow and Pink and
  Green, Orange and Purple and Blue

Coy Mistress
Bella Lugosi is Dead
Surfin' USA
Brief Encounter
Bungle in the Jungle
Hooded Cobra
Combat Rock
Billy Two Tokes
The Christening of New Boots
Mu Hat Mu Ganja
Fool's Gold
Artichokes, Artichokes
The Dreaming
Nearly but Not Quite
M.I.L. Arête
Walls Come Tumbling Down
Arrampicata Speiligone
Jumping the Gun
The Madness
The Trash Heap Has Spoken
Top Gear
Carneddau Flash Goggles
Bar of Soap
California Arête
Launching Pad
Waiting on an Angel
Squashing the Acropods
Seams the Same
The Grey Slab
Theftus Maximus
Alpen
The Daddy Club
The Sponge that Walked Away
Wave Out on the Ocean
Youthanasia
Gnat Attack
At the Cost of a Rope
John Verybiglongwords
Demolition Derby
Occam's Razor
Arnie Meets the Swamp Monster
Antiquity
The Wriggler
Biggles Flies Undone
Nifty Wild Ribo
The Mancer Original Start
Brian Damage
Andy Pandy
Rest in Pete's Eats
Dried-Mouth Sesame Seed
Snap
Another Wasted Journey
The Moon Head Egg Monster
  from Allsup

HVS

Temple of Boom
Cracked Up
Looning the Tube
Is Marilyn Monroe Dead?

The Climbing Pains of
  Adrian Mole
Pop
Rock Athletes Day off
Le Cochon
Hot Air Crack
Pandora's Box Finish
The Methane Monster
Bonza Crack
Blue Bottle
Mental Lentils
Booby Building
Pandora Plays Sax
Lentil in a Stew
Lesser Mortals
Cross Eyed Tammy
Razorback
Medicine Show
....and a Pen Please
Gideon
Solstice
Skinning the Ladder
You Can Dance if You Want To
Damocles
Binman
Dolmen
Indiana Jasmine and the
  Topple of Doom!
Geronimo's Cadillac
Breaking Wind
Saved by the Whole
Silly on Slate
Werp
Cross Eyed Tammy
Pit and the Pendulum
Vivander
Lindy Lou
Pigs in Space
Frustrated Lust
Digital Deflection
Koala Bare
Flying Death Fin (or is it Dutch?)
Guillotine
U.B.L.
Above the Line
Greedy Girls
Clegir Arete

VS

Neat Arête
Tower of Power
Walking Pneumonia
Mental Block
Good Afternoon Constable
Fallout
Big Bendy Buddha
Zambesi
Vertigo
Pontiac Arête
Snuffler
Sad Man Who's Sane

Trad Graded List • Sport Graded List 21

Come off it Arfer
Under the Glass
Hole in One
Velvet Walk
Run for Fun
Act Naturally
Watford Gap West
Wond
Menhir
Antiquity
The Shining
Seamstress
The Trash Heap Speaks Again
Dog Day Dogfish
Old Fogies Never Die
Equinox
Mad Dog of the West
The Stick's Groove
Bong to Lunch
Stand to your Right
Crackle
Goblin Party
Arse Over Tit
Turkey Trot
A Swarm of Green Parrots
Emerald Eyes
Baby Nina Soils Her Pants
Second Thought
Kosciusko
Second's Chance
Binwomen
Gully
Breakdance
A Tourmegamite Experience
That Obscure Object of Desire
OM 69 Runner Bean

HS

Frogs
Up the Garden Path
Dried Mouth Frog
Mudslide Slim
Joie De Vivre
Little Mo
The Groovy Gang
Snowdon Lady
Lone Pine

XS

Fruit of the Gloom
Big Thursday
Buffer in a Crackhouse
Stannah to Hell
The Dude in the Orange Hat
Scorpion
If You Kill People They Die
Opening Gambit
The Dunlop Green Flash
A Big Wall Climb

F8b+

The Very Big and the Very Small

F8b

The New Slatesman
Sauron
The Serpent Vein
Bungles Arête

F8a+

Menopausal Discharge

F8a

Bobby's Groove
The Medium
Cwms the Dogfish
The Untouchables
Manic Strain
Tambourine Man
Forsinain Motspur Super Direct
The Dark Half
Concorde Dawn

F7c+

The Master Craftsman
The Mu Mu
Running Scared
Forsinain Motspur Direct
The Dark Destroyer
Shoreline
The Wall Within
Wish You Were Here
Chitra

F7c

Rowan
Forsinain Motspur
Spong
Doggy Style
Sucked Away with the Scum
Le Voleur
Heatseeker
Psychodelicate

F7b+

Slabs 'R' Us
Gin Palace
Satisfying Frank Bruno
Pas de Chevre
Jepp the Knave
Colditz
True Clip
Artichokes, Artichokes
Two Bolts or Not to Be
Glasgow Kiss
Beltane
Raisin Frumpsnoot
Birthday Girl

F7b

Nick the Chisel
Vermin on the Ridiculous
Toe be or not Toe be
Race Against the Pump
Song of the Minerals
Con Quista Dors
Cig-Arête
A Room With a View
Diagonal Dilemma
Jai'a'n
Beating the Raine
Mfecane
Pulverised
Ziplock
Where are my Sensible Shoes?
Child's Play
Time Bandit
My Secret Garden

F7a+

Cirith Ungol
Geordie War Cry
Synthetic Life
The Rock Dancer's Daughter
Heading the Shot
Coming up for Air
Black Hole Sun
Full Metal Jack Off
Narcolepsy
Pocketeering

F7a

De Nouement
Impact Zone
Dragon Slayer
Toad in Toad Hall
Fruity Pear gets Just Deserts
Saruman
Rock Yoga
Scheherezade
Smokeless Zone
Great Bores of Today
Beyond the Pail
Dekophobia
Road to Botany Bay
The Beanstalk
Y Gwaedlyd
L'Allumette
Gerbil Abuse
The Take Over by Dept C
Supermassive Black Hole
Slatebite
Shorty's Dyno
Mister Blister
Suspension of Disbelief
When the Wind Blows

22 Sport Graded List

F6c+
The Spleenal Flick
Escape from Coldbitz
Walk This Way
The Stream of Obscenity
State of the Heart
Minder
The Weetabix Connection
Gymnastic Fantastic
Pail Rider
Hand of Morlock
The Carbon Stage
The Porphyry Chair

F6c
Steps of Escher
Swiss Air
Sleeper
Her Indoors
Sleight of Hand
Wave Rock
Slabology
Wizz Bang
G'Day Arete
Atticus Finch
Penblwydd Hapus (i fi)
Donald Duck
Crazy Train
Paradise Lost
Monster Hamburger Eats the Alien Baby
Finatic

F6b+
Release the Kraken
Ride Like the Wind!
The Manimal
My Hovercraft is full of Eels
Slab Rog
Yossarian
Truffle Hunter's Roof
The Telescopic Stem Master
Autocrat
A Little Pail
Y Raffwr
Back in the Saddle
Freezer
Fridge

F6b
Mister, Mister
The Drowning Man
To Infinity and Beyond!
The Koala Brothers
The Burning
A Grand Day Out
Maximum Tariff
Scarface Claw
Clipapotamus

Tower of Laughter
Harvey's Brassed Off Team
Sans Chisel variation
The Fat Controller
Gadaffi Duck
The Australian
In Loving Memory
Offa's

F6a+
Hogiau Pen Garret
Feeling Rusty?
Peter Pan
Horse Latitudes
Alive and Kicking
Cyber World Sl@te Heads
Orangutang Overhang
Home Run
Gargoyle
Pas the Duchie
Birdsong
Slab Slayer
Zeus
XXXposure
Shock the Monkey
Bish Bash Bosch
Gwion's Groove
Journey to the Centre of the Earth
Le Gendre
In Loving Memory
Bosch Stop Quarry

F6a
Harri Bach Llanrug
Overtaken by Department C
Le Petit Pois
Sprint Finish
The Full Monty
Ruby Marlee Meets Dr Holingsworth
Plastic Soldier
The Railway Children
Tomb Raider
Clash of the Titans
Cartoon Lesbians
Pour Tout le Monde
Mini Bus Stop
Fresh Air
We No Speak Americano!
Surprise, Surprise

F5+
Aardman Productions
Septuagenarian
Cabin Fever
Dried Mouth Sesame Seed 'N' Gauge
Easy Routes Can Have Bolts Too
Kenny's Wall

Sodor
Le Grandpere
Hawkeye
362
The Mallard
Hogwarts Express
The Level Crossing
Fuck Les Clotures
Those who climb...

F5
The Lost Tomb
The Deceptive Dyke
Kinder Surprise
Steps of Glory
Sport for All
Tolerance
La Grandmere
My Wife's an Alien
As Yet Unnamed
First Step
Comfort Zone
Mon Amie
Rack and Pin
Polar Express
Choo Choo
Ivor the Engine

F4+
Slate Arrivals
Side Line
Quelle Surprise
All for One
Titan
Captain Slog
La Famille

F4
U.B.L.
Derailed
Jenga
The Big Easy
The Garret Slide
Exploding Goats
Jagged Face
Emerald Dyke
Thomas the Tank
Binky Bonk Central
Kinder Sport
Gordon

F3
Aliens Stole My Bolt Kit/ Departure Lounge
The Californian Express

Venue	D-VD	S-VS	HVS-E2	E3-E5	E6-E8	XS/ABO	F3-F4+	F5-F6a	F6a-F6c+	F7a-F7b+	F7c-F8c	Aid Dry Tool	Sun am	Sun pm
Bus Stop	6		11	10	1	1	3	4		7	4	3		
Australia Lower	7		15	26		4	5	20	17	5	1			
Australia Upper	12		33	12	1			7	4	12	1	1		
Australia East Braich		1	1	3		2	1		9	4	1			
Dali's Hole	4		15	17	2	1	5	7	7	4				
California		6	4	4	4	1	1	1	2	1	4			
Serengeti		6	8	16	3		3		2	5	1			
Never Never Land	1	1	14	13	1	2	1	4	16	2	2	2		
Twll Mawr		1	9	12	14	2			3	3	1			
Lost World and Mordor		2	6	16	2				2	2	2			
Colossus Area		2	4	10	11					3				
Rainbow Slab		2	7	10					6		3			
Rainbow Walls Lower		5	10	7					2	9	5			
Rainbow Walls Upper		5	18	10	1				2	4				
Vivian Lower		1	18	29	8	1			2	3	3			
Vivian Upper		5	27	26	5	1		1	5	4	2			
Glyn Rhonwy		4	25	19		1		2	3	2		1		

Bus Stop Quarry

Style: Trad/sport
Aspect: Varied
Approach: 5 minutes
Altitude: 350m
OS grid Ref: 593612

Bus Stop Quarry

A popular and accessible venue home to surefire slate classics. Perfect for an evening session, but enough to keep you busy all day. There is a good mix of routes throughout the grades and a lot of recent low grade sport additions. The rock needs care in places.

Conditions: The general southerly aspect ensures that most parts of the crag will receive the sun at some point during the day. The Rippled Slab is particularly pleasant in the evening sun. The routes mostly dry quickly, however sections of the Rippled Slab and the Macho Wall are plagued by drainage after rain.

Approach: The crag is situated just by the end of the Dinorwig road. To reach it, take the main road through Deiniolen and continue along through Dinorwig until you arrive at the turning circle. The cirque of walls can be clearly seen on the left. Park just before the turning circle by a stile on the left. Follow a path from the stile into the quarry.

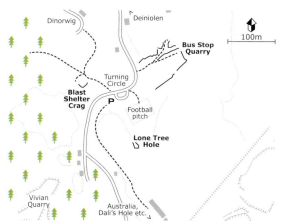

Scare City	E6
Mildly Macho	E5
1000 Tons of Chicken Shit	E5
Crossville	E4
Virgin on the Ridiculous	E4
Scarlet Runner	E4
Meltdown	E4
Scarlet Runner Direct	E3
Buzz Stop	E3
Hasta La Vista Baby	E3
Solstice Direct	E2
Massambula	E2
Sterling Silver	E2
Fool's Gold	E1
Gnat Attack	E1
Biggles Flies Undone	E1
Solstice	HVS
Equinox	VS
Forsinain Motspur Super Direct	F8a
Shoreline	F7c+
Forsinain Motspur	F7c
Beltane	F7b+
Raisin Frumpsnoot	F7b+
Race Against the Pump	F7b
Geordie War Cry	F7a+
My Hovercraft is Full of Eels	F6b+
Fridge	F6b+
Bish Bash Bosch	F6a+
Bosch Stop Quarry	F6a+

< George Smith heading into steep ground on the brilliant **Race Against the Pump** F7b photo: Si Panton

28 Bus Stop Quarry • Upper Level

A recently developed area on the left provides the first routes.

1. First Step F5a 16m
The obvious line up the grey buttress. 3 bolts lead to a lower-off. [C Goodey, S Trainer 14.10.09]

2. Septuagenarian F5+/6a 20m
The central line on the slab gains the rightward leading ramp (some loose rock) and follows it for a few metres before breaking directly up the upper slab to reach a lower-off.
[C Goodey, S Goodey, D Kelly 11.08.09]

**3. Mudslide Slim
(aka: Ferrero Roche) HS 4a** 20m
The once scruffy corner line has been re-ascended after a major clean up, and the addition of a lower-off. [F Ferrero, D King 05.09.86/C Goodey, S Goodey, D Kelly 08.08.09]

4. Wizz Bang F6c 10m
A popular, yet very contrived line which gives some intense moves if taken direct. Unfortunately it is far easier and more natural to stray slightly to the left. [C P Smith, P Doyle 28.01.94]

Upper Level

A number of short sport routes have been established on a series of craglets running up behind the Dinorwig Needles. Access is via a broken path zig zagging up the scree slope.

5. The Big Easy F4 7m
A nifty line up the short slab left of the initial section of the path. [P Targett 02.03.08]

6. Jagged Face F4 7m
Start just right of *The Big Easy* and climb to a shared lower-off.
[M Hurst, B Wedley, T Muller 21.05.08]

7. Comfort Zone F5b 12m
30m further up the scree is a square cut recess on the left side of a buttress. Steep moves precede a pleasant saunter up to the lower-off.
[C Goodey, S Goodey 08.10.09]

8. Finatic F6c 7m
Obvious clean plinth of rock on the left; take a line between the 2 fins of rock to reach a lower-off. [I Lloyd-Jones, P Targett 15.12.07]

9. Jenga F4 7m
Up on the right, close to the edge of the *Solstice* face below is a well cleaned corner; climb it to a lower-off. [I Lloyd-Jones 13.12.07]

10. Bosch Stop Quarry F6a+ 8m
The shallow groove left and around the arete from *Jenga* leads to a lower-off.
[I Lloyd-Jones 13.12.07]

11. Bish Bash Bosch F6a+ 8m
Start on a sloping ledge and follow the bolts up to a lower-off which can't be seen from the last bolt; keep climbing and it soon appears.
[I Lloyd-Jones 14.12.07]

Upper Level • **Bus Stop Quarry 29**

30 Bus Stop Quarry • The Dinorwig Needles

The Dinorwig Needles
Back in the 80s this ridge of rock was capped by a narrow tower of rock. This fell down and left an attractive wall where the rock quality varies from superb, to frankly worrying.

▶ **12. Guillotine HVS 4c** 18m
The crack line 3m left of *Fool's Gold* has been blighted by rock fall and is best avoided.
[T Taylor, A Whittall 18.06.85]

▶ **13. Wusty Woof XS** 26m
Another unstable route hit by rock fall and best avoided in its current state.
[A George, T Taylor 23.06.85]

▶ **14. Fool's Gold E1 5c** *** 26m
A contender for the most popular E1 in the quarries, and the polish really shows on the crux! Climb the groove to an obvious step right into the upper crack. Hard moves lead to an easier but still interesting finish. Bolt belay.
[P George, A George 24.06.85]

▶ **15. 1000 Tons of Chicken Shit E5 6a** * 28m
The eye-catching flake feature provides a serious alternative start to *Fool's Gold*. [S Haston 10.06.86]

▶ **16. Scare City E6 6a** ** 24m
A bold lead linking the *1000 Tons* start into some superb, open wall climbing. From the top of the flake step right and climb carefully up to good cam placements in a horizontal slot level with the upper overlap on *Raisin Frumpsnoot*. Continue up left and keep it steady on a direct line to the top. A less mortally bold version of the route can be done by starting up *Fool's Gold* until just past the crux, and traversing rightwards along the *1000 Tons* flake. This goes at about E5 6a.
[T Kay, P Pritchard 28.10.87/E5 start: P Rowlands 12.08]

▶ **17. Raisin Frumpsnoot F7b+** * 22m
An intense and sustained challenge which will keep you on your toes (quite literally) all the way. Start just right of *Scare City*, moving straight into an initial crux passing the small overlap. Continue up, moving right into the difficult finish of *Forsinain Motspur* at the top overlap.
[A Wainwright 05.05.07]

▶ **18. Forsinain Motspur F7c** *** 22m
Strange name, awesome route. Follow the snaking line past the overlaps and onto the thin upper wall. Sustained and fierce wall climbing? Oh yes!

There are 2 harder variations:
FM Direct F7c+ A hard (V6/7/7A/+) boulder problem start up the wall a few metres left of the original start.
FM Super Direct F7c+/8a Link the previous variant into the top of *Beltane*.
[T Hodgson 28.03.88 *FM Direct*: C Muskett 05.10 *FM Super Direct*: C Muskett 16.06.10]

Slatehead • Trevor Hodgson

▶ **19. Beltane F7b+ ** 22m**
Great climbing up the blank wall left of *Solstice*. Climb up through the overlap and move horizontally left for 2m from the flat hold level with the 3rd bolt. Continue up to a final crux section gaining, and stepping left past, the last bolt. The top couple of moves are easier.
[A. Wainwright 30.05.07]

▶ **20. Solstice HVS 5b ** 26m**
An attractive line which has become harder since the departure of a suspect flake at the bottom. Follow the line of flakes and take the right hand exit near the top.

Variation Finish: E2 5c The obvious thin groove leading up from the curved flake.
[A George, T Taylor 23.06.85]

▶ **21. Equinox VS 4c * 26m**
A steady and popular route striking a counter diagonal to *Solstice*. Follow the flakes and ledges trending leftwards to the sanctuary of the big flake runner on *Solstice*. Continue up diagonally leftwards to finish.
[T Taylor, A George 24.06.85]

▶ **22. Sterling Silver E2 5c * 28m**
A good route climbing the slightly alarming line of creaking flakes. Follow the flakes - none of which seem to inspire confidence - to a hard move to gain the final flake and thus the top.
[J Banks, L Naylor, D Clark 04.07.86]

▶ **23. Demolition Derby E1 5a 20m**
Start 8m right of *Sterling Silver*. Pick your way up the solid bits between the rubble to the ledge and then ponder the thin air where once a tower of rock sat. [P Jenkinson, M Boniface 23.03.88]

Although Trev (or Carlos as he was known on account of his trademark moustache) did not climb that many first ascents, he was most definitely a key figure in the emerging 80s slate scene. Sharing a legendary 'party' house in Llanberis with other dole sponsored slateheads such as Paul Pritchard and Gwion Hughes, he embodied the spirit of the times: namely a reckless devotion to partying and a ballsy acceptance of the designer danger style. Memorable shots of him running it out on Rainbow Slab in garish tights cast him as perhaps the definitive slatehead. In hindsight his greatest achievement in the quarries was perhaps *Forsinain Motspur*, a fiercely technical F7c in Bus Stop Quarry, but he also climbed notable routes such as *The Listening and Dancing* E5 6b on the Rainbow Walls and the *NW Face of the Druid*, a bold E6 in the Lost World climbed onsight.

Trev and JD on **The Quarryman**
photo: Paul Williams

Trev on, then off **The Rainbow of Recalcitrance**
photo: Paul Williams

Diary of a Slatehead

The Council Strikes Back

In 1984 Dinorwig's bus stop turnaround featured mainly in school children's lives and those without transport living in or around Blue Peris's tiny hamlet. It was they who embarked, or were disgorged there fulfilling daily rituals overseen without apparent ceremony by Crossville drivers long since contracted to stoicism.

The freshly landscaped and grass seeded Bus Stop Quarry, back in 1984 photo: Paul Williams

The bus stop also provided an access point for heads wishing to explore the upper quarries. The area itself, although topographically interesting did not appear to host great climbing possibilities. A kind of slate peninsula allowed anyone without vertigo to peer vertically down shattered walls into deep green pools which had they not contained a number of fly tipped household objects and other impalers may have provided a challenge similar to Nikki's Leap in Vivian Quarry. Nevertheless in May 1984 the Captain (Cliff Phillips) soloed five new routes including the elegantly named Gutter Slut Strut in the vicinity which had been severely developed by Gwynedd Council. Precise location and lines taken were alas tutenkhamuned by sir Alfred McAlpine bulldozers the same autumn, entombed forever in a thousand tonne lament with fake pine and splintered formica, shattered tv tubes, breezeblock bag cats, discarded motorbikes and burnt out cars pushed over the hole's perimeter at dead of night by persons unknown.

By the following spring work finished resulting in an equally bizarre landscape as its predecessor, still overlooked by giant steps each one composed of slate waste sloping hundreds of metres towards the upper quarries which sealed off a kind of cirque surrounded on one side by 20m high pinnacles forming a sleight shark toothed ridge whilst opposite lay a steeply inclined mossy slab above a slate bouldered slope equally as high, somewhat fish scaled and 30m or so in width. Between these two, forming a back wall, came a steep sometimes overhanging, black streaked wall with roofed grooves at its right side before it met the slab at a botanically interesting gutter like corner, its base partially obscured by determined trees, saplings and brambles.

This cirque could be approached via a fence bordering the road which once negotiated proved the only impediment on open ground leading in a few hundred metres easy walk to further horizontal territory beneath jagged pinnacle topped walls resembling in certain lights phoney Chamonix Aiguilles. These the council had produced by accident, their extant thrust only appearing as a side effect after filling in the space rocket size silos that now appeared never to have existed or were at least as difficult to imagine as gazing on Mount Fuji from Glossop.

The Captain hardly laboured under great emotion at the loss of his now subterranean routes, nor did he confide a desert solitaire lament, but turned his attentions elsewhere towards less public arenas than the new bus stop archipelago.

Gustard Paul Williams, the George twins and Billy Wayman as if decreed by a town crier stepped in to provide a coup of easily accessible, ready mix classics almost entirely paid for by local tax payers.

Martin Crook

Macho Wall

Between the Dinorwig Needles and the Rippled Slab, there is a steeper water streaked area which is home to some excellent routes.

▶ **24. Hasta La Vista Baby E3 6a** * 10m
A nifty little route, worth seeking out. Reach the crack via the arête at the very toe of the buttress. Follow the crack/groove to a big ledge. Bolt lower-off. [F Haden, M Davies 18.07.94]

▶ **25. Race Against the Pump F7b** ** 15m
A pumpy and sequential route with a flamboyant crux sequence; superb stuff! Follow *Hasta La Vista Baby* (wires and cams needed) until level with the 1st bolt on the right. Step right just below this and move up to a hang a ledge on the right. The next clip up left is tricky (try a kneebar – it works for some), but essential as it protects the powerful and unlikely crux. Continue up on pinches and side pulls, moving briefly left to the arête before gaining the lower-off. [F Haden 21.07.94]

▶ **26. Shoreline F7c+** ** 25m
A neglected line which suffers from seepage. Shame, it looks good and would be worth re-equipping in a dry period. [S Haston 04.90]

▶ **27. Geordie War Cry F7a+** *** 22m
One of the best clip ups in the quarries, but notoriously tricky. A 'locky' crux might get you onto the headwall, but avoid the perma-chalked direct line above (as it's desperate); instead trend rightwards to reach a sneaky rest. Once composed head up left then direct to the lower-off. Don't forget to let out a celebratory 'Why aye man!' at the chains. There is a steeper right hand start passing a single bolt which is useful when the slab is wet. [B Wayman, D Kirton, M Barnicott 11.10.87]

▶ **28. Mildly Macho E5 6b** ** 25m
A seriously macho leader is required for this little number. An open corner is formed just to the right of *Geordie War Cry*. Start 5m to the left of the damp corner where Rippled Slab meets the *Macho Wall*. Climb a groove until it is possible to hand traverse right on to a ledge. Follow the loose groove above to reach a roof; a large loose flake resides here. The finger crack above is problematic and is followed to another detached flake. A few scary moves above on slate fins attain easier ground leading to the top.
[S Haston, G Jones 05.87]

34 Bus Stop Quarry • The Rippled Slab

The Rippled Slab

The attractive, light coloured slab on the right side of the quarry has a trio of classic designer danger routes. *Gnat Attack*, *Massambula* and *Scarlet Runner* are rites of passage for all aspiring slateheads and shining examples of the slate slab genre: partially bolted, but still packing in plenty of drama. Drainage and creeping vegetation is a problem on certain routes.

Access to the slab is made via a pair of rough paths which pick a line through the scree from either end of the slab.

▶ **29. Breakdance VS 4a** 43m
The strong visual line sweeping across the slab gives a serious and chossy route which can't be recommended. From the base of *Scarlet Runner* move up and follow the rising line across the lower part of the slab, passing *Gnat Attack* to reach a large rowan tree.
[F Ferrero, D King 12.09.86]

▶ **30. Scarlet Runner Direct E3 6a** * 25m
An alternative start to the parent route. Technically harder, but better protected, although there are some friable holds.
[F Haden, M Davies 22.07.94]

▶ **31. Scarlet Runner E4 5c** *** 25m
An excellent route with a bold start and a well protected crux. The climbing is sustained and technical, but an insecure rock up to gain the 1st bolt will test most leaders. From the left side of the slab climb the centre of the clean streak with 5 bolts to aim for. (Clip Sticks are cheating!) [B Wayman, P Williams 28.06.85]

▶ **32. Buzz Stop E3 6a** * 25m
A good route, when dry. A line of bolts running up the obvious drainage streaks lead to a chain lower-off. [B Jones, P Trewin 20.06.02]

▶ **33. Virgin on the Ridiculous E4 6a** * 28m
This line is currently heavily vegetated, but could be restored to its original state without too much effort. There are 2 bolts but no lower-off, so pull over the top to belay.
[B Wayman, P Williams 03.07.85]

The Rippled Slab • **Bus Stop Quarry** 35

▶ **34. Massambula E2 5b** ∗∗ 26m
"Bolder than life itself" as Paul Williams once opined so elegantly. A more sustained alternative to *Gnat Attack*, with a hard move to reach the 1st bolt and some long runouts. The route climbs the middle clean streak of the slab with 2 bolts to mark the way. The upper section is bold, but steady. (Do not attempt if the top section looks at all wet). Climb up and right and make a bold mantel onto the ledge system of *Breakdance*. Step left and clip the 1st bolt with relief. Head up to the next bolt then climb carefully to the top with a growing sense of exhilaration.
[P Williams, B Wayman 03.07.85]

▶ **35. Meltdown E4 6a** ∗ 21m
A fine route slightly drowned out by the fuss over its more famous neighbours. Start just left of *Gnat Attack* and climb boldly up to the 1st bolt. Make crux moves with the comfort of close protection and continue up passing 2 more bolts and trending rightwards to reach the lower-off of *Gnat Attack*.
[T Taylor, A Barton 28.04.91]

▶ **36. Gnat Attack E1 5c** ∗∗ 21m
A popular excursion with a fierce little crux and an airy finish. Climb carefully up left of the diagonal break to the 1st bolt on the slab. Shorties can now show off their technical prowess, whilst giants can casually span to the good holds and so reach the 2nd bolt. Pleasant and thankfully easier climbing leads a long way up to a lower-off.
[A Newton, R Newton original start up *Massambula*: 31.07.85/direct start: 04.04.86]

▶ **37. Blue Horizon S** 22m
A manky, vegetated line 10m right of *Gnat Attack*. Climb direct to the Rowan Tree at the end of *Breakdance* passing a lone bolt at half height. [F Ferrero, D King 12.09.86]

▶ **38. Crossville E4 6a** ∗ 45m
Another neglected route following the rising line of weakness running across the middle of the slab. From the 1st bolt of *Gnat Attack* head across *Meltdown*, *Massambula*, *Virgin*... to a finish up *Scarlet Runner*.
[A Moss, K Neal 03.87]

In sustained cold periods a thin ice smear forms down the centre of the Rippled Slab in the *Virgin on the Ridiculous* and *Buzz Stop* area. This gives a rather unique climbing experience: an ice route partially protected by bolts! It goes at about V 6, provided you can find the bolts under the ice. The first known ascent was a solo by Stevie Haston back in the 80s. In the early 80s before any rock routes had been established on the slab Paul Trower and Ken Toms climbed a bold line on the left side. The Tube went at about grade V, but was protectionless. The drainage line down the slab subsequently shifted to a more central position.

Adam Wainwright heading for the belay at the top of **Buzz Stop** photo: Ray Wood

30m down and right of the Rippled Slab is a short wall gradually decreasing in height towards its right side. This is all that remains of a 20m wall that marked the edge of the old quarry and pool which was filled in and landscaped in the mid 80s. The next route climbs the left most and highest part of the wall.

▶ **39. My Hovercraft is Full of Eels F6b** * 10m
The steep blocky arete has 4 bolts and a lower-off. Care required with some loose rock.
[R Mirfin 22.08.06]

▶ **40. Mini Bus Stop F6a** 8m
A tough little cookie. The groove feature right of *My Hovercraft*... turns tricky at the 3rd bolt which is very awkward to clip.
[I Lloyd-Jones, L Body, I Martin 22.05.07]

▶ **41. Fridge F6b+** * 6m
The nifty little groove 20m right of *Mini Bus Stop* leads to a lower-off.
[P Doyle, C P Smith 26.02.93]

▶ **42. Freezer F6b+** 6m
Another short and sweet addition. Climb up and then move right under the overlap before breaking through on to the head wall. Lower off.
[P Targett 26.05.07]

Lone Tree Hole

This dirty hole has all but returned to nature; a sizable tree in the middle ensures that the routes stay both dirty and damp. It might just be worth a look in a sustained dry period.

The hole is situated on a rounded ridge that lies in between Bus Stop Quarry and the main footpath into the quarries. It is best reached from a gate in the bottom of the field with the football pitch in it. At the left side of the ridge is a quarried hole with a tree.

▶ **43. So this is Living E2 5a** 8m
Just around the apparently unclimbed, but attractive looking arête, is slabby corner choked with copious greenery. Climb this to a tricky finish. [C Phillips 08.05.84]

▶ **44. Malice in Wonderland E2 5b** 8m
The unprotected slab to the right. [W Perrin 90s]

▶ **45. As the Sun Sets in the West E4 5c** 8m
The right hand corner bordering the *Malice in Wonderland* slab is also very overgrown.
[C Phillips 08.05.84]

▶ **46. Wond VS 4c** 10m
The obvious blocky arete on the right side of the quarry. [C Phillips 08.05.84]

Blast Shelter Crag • **Bus Stop Quarry** 37

Blast Shelter Crag

A small crag with a very open and pleasant aspect, situated on the downhill side of the bus stop turning circle. From the dead end sign at the turnaround a small gravel track leads down into a field. 50m along this track on the left is a small quarried face with a blast shelter. Whilst only 2 routes are described here the imaginative can make up seemingly endless eliminates and variations.

▶ **47. Biggles Flies Undone E1 5b** ∗ 12m
A cracking little slab route. Climb the left edge to a ledge and peg at 5m (or go direct at 5c). Move up and right to footholds and then follow a thin left slanting crack to the top; belay off metal spikes.
[C Phillips 15.05.85]

▶ **48. Stand to your Rights VS 4c** 13m
Climb the right-hand corner of the slab, and then take the slab/groove to the top.
[C Phillips 08.05.84]

photo: Susan Hatchel

An impressive and seemingly vast ampitheatre, visually dominated by the massive rubble slope (the Oil Drum Glacier) which fills the back of the quarry. Confusingly it was wrongly named by climbers and in fact should be referred to as 'Garret', Australia actually being the name the quarrymen gave to what climbers now refer to as the Far Out Level. Such is the scale of Australia it is best viewed as 3 separate, albeit closely related areas, and thus there are 3 chapters: Australia Lower, Australia Upper and Australia East Braich.

∧ Anne Vowles on the classic **Looning the Tube** HVS 5b
photo: Ray Wood

Australia is the largest excavation of the Dinorwig quarries, and correspondingly there is a huge volume of routes to go at. Quantity does not always equate with quality, however, but hidden among the numerous levels and slabs are some great routes well worth seeking out. Initially developed with an 80s style minimal bolting ethic, in recent years there has been a strong trend towards intense, bolt protected climbs. In particular there are now a large number of low grade sport routes; and for those operating in the sub F6a level this is arguably the best place to visit in the quarries.

Australia Lower

Style: Trad/sport
Aspect: South-East
Approach: 15-30 mins
Altitude: 330-400m
OS Grid ref: 597 608

Big Thursday	XS
If You Kill People They Die	MXS

Glass Axe	E5
Hysterectomy	E5
Menai Vice	E4
The Wow Wow	E4
Ancestral Vices	E4
Swan Hunter	E4
Mad on the Metro	E4
Zzzooming the Tube	E3
Loony Toons	E3
Off the Beaten Track	E3
Goose Creature	E3

2nd Class Passenger	E2
Single Factor	E2
Turn of the Century	E2
Abattoir Blues	E2
Brief Encounter	E1
Looning the Tube	HVS

Kosciusko	VS

Psychodelicate	F7c

My Secret Garden	F7b
Great Bores of Today	F7a
Dekophobia	F7a

The Stream of Obscenity	F6c+
Sleeper	F6c
Donald Duck	F6c
Crazy Train	F6c
Y Rhaffwr	F6b+
The Burning	F6b
Maximum Tariff	F6b
Gadaffi Duck	F6b
The Australian	F6b
In Loving Memory	F6b

Sodor	F5c
The Mallard	F5c
The Level Crossing	F5c
Those Who Climb...	F5c
The Deceptive Dyke	F5b
Steps of Glory	F5b
Rack and Pin	F5b
Polar Express	F5b

Thomas the Tank	F4a
Gordon	F4a

40 Australia Lower • Approach

View fron the 'Col'

Approach: From the turning circle by Bus Stop Quarry, walk into the quarries along the main track passing a large disused quarry building on the left. Go left through the gate, viewing the massive quarried cwm of Australia above. 50m from the gate the track turns right and dips down hill, a gate is seen on immediately on the left. Beyond this it is possible to walk diagonally right for a further 100m before steps lead up one level. Cut back left and ascend a further 2 levels to arrive at the 'Col', in front of the massive amphitheatre of Australia. On your left is a promontory with a tunnel running through its base and to the right of this on the left side of the quarry is a slab with a tube hanging across it – this is the *Looning the Tube* slab.
This vantage point provides a good place for 1st time visitors to orientate themselves. This part of Australia is described from the bottom up and individual approach notes can be found in each section introduction.

Warning: because the successive levels in Australia Quarry are so tightly racked there is a risk of dislodging rocks onto climbers on the level below. Great care should be exercised at all times, but especially when close to the edge of a level.

Conditions: The majority of routes on the west side of the excavation get the sun from the morning until early afternoon. Parts of the *Looning the Tube* area stay in the sun until the sun sets, yet the sun does come off other parts earlier in the day. Most routes are quick drying and seepage is rarely a problem, however Railtrack Slab and the Rognon do suffer after rain. The lowest levels (Tasmania and Billabong) don't receive much sun at all, but even down here seepage is limited.

Approach • **Australia Lower 41**

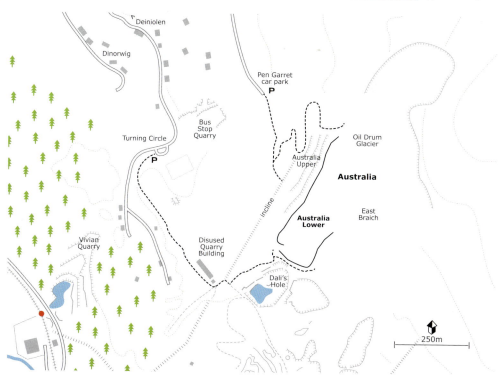

42 Australia Lower • Tasmania

Tasmania

This obscure and little visited slab is found at the lowest point in the vast working that is Australia.

It can be approached in a number of ways; the easiest from the Looning the Tube Col is to descend 1 level and take the right hand of 3 tunnels, and then the right fork where it splits. From the tunnel mouth make a mad dash, down and out of the 'fall out zone' from the dangerous looking scree/rock pile above. A tedious scramble across the debris strewn floor to the far side of the hole leads to a hidden slab in the depths. Other alternatives are to abseil off the pipe of *Looning the Tube*, or by walking along the base of Dali's Wall till below the corner of *Dali Express* - if you hunt around the blocks you will find a squeeze that will lead you down into a tunnel, which leads out directly below the Billabong Wall and *Darkness Visible* (head torch advisable).

▶ **1. Arnie Meets the Swamp Monster E1 5a** 30m
From the centre of the slab head up left over some loose blocks to the arête and a large layaway (the 1st gear). Climb the large crack to a series of mantels which lead up to a leftward hand traverse to the arete and a ledge. Continue up the arete to the top. There is a block belay well back from the edge.
[C Jex, N Manning 03.07.90]

▶ **2. Toilet Trouble E2 5c** 30m
Climb directly up the centre of the slab to a bolt. A hard section passing the bolt leads to a crack which is followed to the top. Belay as for *Arnie*... [N Butterworth, C Jex 03.07.90]

▶ **3. Stinky Boots E2 5b** 30m
The right hand line on the slab starts 3m left of the unappealing corner. A scar is followed up to some ledges where a bolt protects some hard moves leading to further ledges. The original line stayed right of the top crack of *Toilet Trouble* and placed protection in the corner. Given the loose nature of the corner it might be prudent to stay in the crack.
[N Manning, N Butterworth 03.07.90]

Jon Ratcliffe on the 1st ascent of
The Wow Wow E4 6a photo: Si Panton

Billabong

The main quarry walls at the base of Australia (and situated 2 levels directly below *Looning the Tube*) has a number of excellent routes situated in an atmospheric position.

Approach: Follow the Tasmania approach, and once past the 'mad dash', walk leftwards into the quarry. (Alternatively take the hidden tunnel from Dali's Wall to arrive below *Darkness Visible*.)

The routes are described from left to right looking at the wall. Walk down a slight path following the left edge of the scree for about 20m and behold a steep slab with a line of 12 bore holes running up its centre, forming the right wall of a V groove. This is:

4. Great Bores of Today F7a ** 15m
A superb, quirky pitch – well worth seeking out. Start by climbing the metal pipe (be gentle); a stiff pull allows one to meander up the lower wall until a hard move left gains access to the line of bore holes. Yard up these with glee to a tricky rockover before the lower off. (NB. The bore holes fill up with water after rain, but if you take a few rags with you and clean them out first on abseil, by the time you've warmed up/done some other routes elsewhere they'll be dry enough to climb.) There is a single access bolt above the route: walk right (facing into the hole) along the lip of Australia for about 30m or so from the building on *Looning the Tube* Level; the bolt is on the wall just above the 'path'. From here you can get to the double lower-off (visible) and down to the base. Be careful not to dislodge slates with your rope. [J Ratcliffe 23.07.08]

5. The Wow Wow E4 6a ** 45m
The striking rightward diagonal crack 20m right of *Great Bores of Today* yields a great route. An ample rack of cams (# 00-4) with some double ups is essential.
P1 6a 27m Tackle the crack above the small alcove, via some hard moves, to reach a decent hold. Continue with sustained difficulties, passing a brief respite, before a good ledge is reached. Above, easier climbing remains, albeit with interest as the crack widens (cam #3.5/4 handy at this point). Double bolt belay a few metres back.
P2 5b 18m Follow the continuation crack, but before it deteriorates head off to good holds on the left wall and follow these to a bolt. Mantel in to the groove above, and move up to a tree. Belay bolt on boulder 3m back.
[J Ratcliffe, S Franklin 09.06.09]

6. The Dunlop Green Flash MXS
Born from a moment of stupidty, this reckless challenge follows the line of least resistance up a series of vegetated ledges to a steep finish. [Mark Dicken 2003]

7. Darkness Visible E4 6a 15m
The slab down below the *Looning the Tube* area is split by a narrow crack. Climb the crack to a bolt near the top of the crag. Belay way back on blocks and a new bolt over to the right. [G Smith, D O'Dowd 1986]

Project Arete: The obvious line just to the right of *Darkness Visible* has a lower-off. Sadly it doesn't climb how you would hope it too.

44 Australia Lower • Temple of Boom

Temple of Boom (Under the Rails)
Down below the Railtrack Slab a large boulder is embedded in the scree. Use the Tasmania approach to reach it. The name comes from the unexplored chasm/crevasse behind the block; the area also has unusual acoustic properties.

▶ **8. Dekophobia F7a** ∗ 15m
An intense sport route with a hard, dynamic crux passing the small overlap on the lower wall. There is a lower-off on the upper slab.
[M Dicken, M Turner 08.06]

Project: Holes drilled and a lower-off in place to the right of *Dekophobia*. This is open for anybody to try.

▶ **9. Son of Rabbit E3 5c** 12m
Crack line to the right of *Dekophobia*. Climb up to the wobbly block with difficulty (apparently sound), then follow the crack rightwards to the scree above. [M Dicken 2006]

▶ **10. Temple of Boom HVS/5.9** 12m
Character building offwidth to the right of *Son of Rabbit*. Kit: a car jack (placed on lead on the FA) is required, otherwise you are soloing!
[M Dicken, R Huws 2006]

On the pyramid boulder beyond *Dekophobia* block is:

▶ **11. My Secret Garden F7b** ∗ 9m
Slab test piece with an exciting finale. Step off Rodin's podium onto the initial slab, turn the roof, and pad tenuously up the centre of the upper slab to slap for the summit. Lower off.
[M Dicken, G Owen 04.5.07]

The Rognon
This obscure buttress juts out from the scree below the Salt Pans, and will no doubt remain a back water of the quarry, as much as a consequence of the difficult access as the quality of the climbing (*Single Factor* and *Abattoir Blues* excepted).

Approach: Not the easiest of places to reach – there is a choice of approach routes though. Either come through the tunnels as if approaching Tasmania but scramble across the quarry base and up the scree, or traverse round on the Fruitbat Level (Australia Upper) and drop down to the Salt Pans and descend steep scree to reach the double tier of the Rognon which sits just above the slab of Tasmania. The bottom tier is host to:

The Rognon • **Australia Lower** 45

▶ **12. Joie De Vivre HS 4a** 13m
2m left of *Theftus Maximus* is an indistinct line of edges leading up to a difficult move at the top. [09.06.90]

▶ **13. Theftus Maximus E1 5b** 13m
Start 3m left of the broken corner. Ascend the slab which may contain some friable holds.
[K Strange 15.05.86]

▶ **14. Little Mo HS 4a** 13m
2m right of *Theftus Maximus* and just left of the corner. Ascend direct with a hard move near the top. [09.06.90]

The next routes are on the upper tier:

▶ **15. Abattoir Blues E2 5b** * 17m
A fine and exposed arête climb with 3 bolts (but no other runners). Step off the boulders to gain the 1st bolt then climb the arete a cheval. The 2nd bolt is a tricky clip, move onto front face above it and follow good holds to the top.
[M Dicken 2007]

▶ **16. Genital Persuasion E3 5c** 17m
Start below a groove (which sports a bonsai-esque rowan tree) near the top of the cliff. Climb up via a shot hole past 3 bolts directly up the groove to the top.
[A Jackson, N Biven 26.04.86]

▶ **17. Single Factor E2 5c** * 17m
Classic slate edge climbing. Start just right of *Genital Persuasion* and ascend directly to the bolt at 10m, then take the crack on the right to a good foothold. Finish straight up the wall passing another bolt.
[N Biven, A Jackson 26.04.86]

▶ **18. Second Thoughts VS 4b** 16m
This route tackles the blunt right hand arete situated some 15m to the right; an unprotected, friable and alarming pitch. You might just have... [09.06.90]

46 Australia Lower • Looning the Tube Area

Looning the Tube Area
An intensely developed and popular area with numerous good routes. See the main introduction for approach details.

▶ **19. Puddy Kat F5** 10m
A poor route. Climb the cleaned flake/groove up to the central ledge. Make a tricky move up the cleaned slab above. 2 bolts to a lower-off.
[Jim Kelly, Julia Kelly 14.05.09]

▶ **20. Just For Fun E2 6a** 11m
An eliminate line avoiding the corner. Climb the narrow slab left of the tunnel. It is possible to back up the top bolt with some medium/large cams in the crack on the right. [I Lloyd-Jones, C Davies 21.04.91]

▶ **21. The Burning F6b** ** 15m
A good route which climbs the steep groove 5m right of the tunnel. The crux is between the 3rd and 4th bolt. Lower off. [P Targett, M Turner 08.08.91]

Looning the Tube Area • **Australia Lower 47**

The Burning • Looning the Tube →

The Deceptive Dyke → • Donald Duck →

▶ **22. The Deceptive Dyke F5b** * 15m
An enjoyable route on clean rock. It lies round to the right of *The Burning*. After the initial scramble up the green stone pillar to a ledge the climbing improves. From the ledge make a move up the right hand side of the pillar past a bolt, move slightly left past another bolt and climb direct past a final bolt to a lower-off.
[M Reeves, B Wills 09.06]

▶ **23. 1066 F6b** 15m
A sustained route tackling the crack in the wall to the right of *The Deceptive Dyke*. 3 bolts to a lower off. It is hard to stay on line unless you keep the blinkers on, in fact the more logical line on the left is probably F6a.
[P Targett, T Hughes 27.08.08]

▶ **24. N.E. Spur E3 5c** 20m
A bold committing climb which has some loose rock. Climb the arete directly to a bar and then a blind hex 2 placement.
[C Parkin, W Rees 13.07.86]

▶ **25. Loony Toons E3 6a** * 20m
A surprisingly good, albeit slightly bold climb. Move up past a metal spike to reach the 1st bolt; continue via a sustained sequence of technical moves passing a further 2 bolts to join the same ledge as for *Brief Encounter*. Finish direct to the lower-off. [S Puroy, C Fowler, E Thomas 13.09.90]

< The shoulder of the NE Spur photo: Ray Wood

▶ **26. Brief Encounter E1 5b** * 20m
Despite the mossy appearance, this is a good route with much character. Start at the base of a flake crack (3m left of the tunnel) and ascend this to a ledge, reaching left to clip the 1st bolt. Step up and move into the groove passing a 2nd bolt; some sustained run out climbing leads to a 3rd bolt and a direct finish to a lower-off.
[I Lloyd-Jones, B Lleywelyn 20.04.91]

The following trio of climbs are dirty, the bolts dangerous, or non existent. They are all probably best avoided until they have been re-equipped.

▶ **27. Astroman from the
Planet Zzzoink E3 6a** 15m
Start just right of the tunnel, and move up and right to a ledge. Ascend the dirty corner above to a lower-off.
[N Manning 05.07.91]

▶ **28. Planet Zzzoink Arete E3 5c** 15m
An eliminate on *Astroman...*, climbing the arete of the dirty corner to the same lower-off, and clipping the same bolts.
[I Lloyd-Jones 06.07.91]

▶ **29. The Man Who Fell to Earth E2 5c** 15m
Another dirty, neglected route tackling the slab, groove and arete to the right of the *Zzoink* routes. Finish leftwards to the same lower-off.
[I Lloyd-Jones 29.06.91]

48 Australia Lower • Looning the Tube Area

▶ **30. Donald Duck F6c** * 17m
A bouldery test piece; E3 6b in old money. The narrow corner immediately left of *Gadaffi Duck* has a hard start and a tricky 2nd clip. The upper section is easier and leads to a tree lower-off.
[I Lloyd-Jones 10.90]

▶ **31. Gadaffi Duck F6b** ** 17m
The large left facing open corner yields a fine route with an intense, but reachy crux low down and more good climbing above. Lower off.
[R Deane, P Hawkins 05.08.86]

▶ **32. Sad Man Who's Sane VS 4c** 15m
Climb the line right of *Gadaffi Duck* passing 2 bolts and trending slightly right to a lower-off.
[M Reeves, B Wills 09.06]

▶ **33. U.B.L. F4/VS 4b** 14m
The slab left of *Hyperfly* gives a rather forgettable route. Lower off. [M Reeves, B Wills 09.06]

▶ **34. Hyperfly F6b** 14m
Arete left of *Turn of the Century* lacks independance and is much easier (F6a) if the arete to the left is used. 4 bolts to a lower-off.
[P Targett, I Lloyd-Jones 23.08.07]

▶ **35. Turn of the Century E2 5c** ** 15m
The steep right facing corner/groove gives an interesting and sustained route. Lower off.
[P Hawkins, G Smith 12.08.86]

▶ **36. Maximum Tariff F6b** * 15m
A good pitch up the obvious crack slightly spoilt by the escapable upper section. A tricky layback sequence low down leads into a series of reachy manoeuvres. Scuttle right at the very top to reach the lower-off.
[P Targett, I Lloyd-Jones, P Walley 07.09.07]

▶ **37. Buffalo Smashed in Head Jump E4 5c** 15m
A bold and technical route, more commonly top roped these days. Start by a large boulder below the square cut groove. Climb the groove to the overlap, place poor protection on the left and make difficult moves over to reach a ledge system and easier ground leading to the *Maximum Tariff* lower-off. [07.87]

▶ **38. Dried Mouth Sesame Seed F5c** 10m
The short corner leading to a lower-off.
[K Turner, L Dow 28.08.91]

▶ **39. Technical Hamster F6c** 10m
A bouldery eliminate line up the left side of the arete just right of *Dried Mouth Sesame Seed*. It is also possible to climb the arête on its right side (**Technical Hamster Dance HVS 4b**, Eric T 24.08.07) [P Targett, T Hughes 06.08.07]

▶ **40. Dried Mouth Frog HS** 8m
The slabby corner just to the left of the arete of *Swan Hunter*. Take some micro wires and slings.
[K Turner, L Dow 28.08.91]

Looning the Tube Slab • **Australia Lower** 49

The Burning F6b, a popular clip up.   photo: Ray Wood

50 Australia Lower • Looning the Tube Slab

Looning the Tube Slab

An excellent venue for the mid grade climber and a great way to prepare for some of the harder/bolder routes that the quarries have to offer.

▶ **41. Swan Hunter E4 6b** * 15m
A quality climb with a bold finish. Ascend the left arête of the slab to a ledge at half height. Make a brief detour right to clip the bolt on *Goose Creature* before stepping back left and tackling the bold upper section of the arete (Try not to think too hard about the sweeping fall potential!). [N Yardley and party 20.04.86]

▶ **42. Goose Creature E3 6a** ** 15m
A great, technical route with a well protected but hard crux. Climb the slab and crack just right of the left arête of the slab. The 1st bolt on *Menai Vice* protects the moves up to the 1st bolt proper. Hard moves above this lead to a lower-off. [A Swann and party 20.04.86]

▶ **43. Menai Vice E4 6c** ** 17m
An intense pitch destined to stop all but the sharpest of slab ninjas. The crux, which is desperate, is near the 2nd bolt; thereafter the climbing eases but is still very thin and feels quite bold. Absolute top of the grade. Climb up to the 1st bolt (shared with *Goose Creature*), then break out right passing a further 2 bolts with extreme difficulty. Bolt and spike belay well back. [G Smith, W Rees 12.07.86]

▶ **44. Hysterectomy E5 5c** * 18m
A very serious lead. Start as for *Looning the Tube* but forge a lonely line up the slab between this and *Menai Vice*. A lone skyhook below half height provides dubious comfort. Finish past an old bolt at the very top.
[A Swann, D O'Dowd 20.04.86]

▶ **45. Looning the Tube HVS 5b** *** 20m
A classic for the grade; the airy traverse out across the slab gives it the character of a much larger route. Traverse out across the slab where the tube once resided (bolt). Reach the obvious ironmongery at the base of the crack out right and climb this to the top passing a 2nd bolt (crux). Medium cams useful. [C Phillips 19.06.84]

▶ **46. Zzzooming the Tube E3 6a** * 22m
Some great climbing and a touch of designer danger. Start as for *Looning the Tube* to the spike, then traverse right and make a bold move up to clip the 1st bolt; pass a 2nd bolt to a lower-off left of the tree (note: when lowering off aim for the Tube where you can shuffle back to your belayer). [I Lloyd-Jones, T Hughes 21.08.07]

▶ **47. Pruning the Tube E2 5c** 25m
A somewhat loose route making the best use of the space once occupied by the tube tip-toeing route: *Tubing to Loon*. Climb *Looning the Tube* to the iron mongery. Traverse further right to a bolt at foot level. Move slightly right then climb direct to finish just right of the hanging tree.
[N Walton 26.04.86]

The Railtrack Slab • Australia Lower 51

The next 2 routes can be gained by a short abseil off the tube and a careful traverse to a pile of rubble and stacked blocks. Alternatively approach as for the other routes on Railtrack Slab and descend the rake to them.

▶ **48. Mad on the Metro E4 5c** ∗ 22m
Start at the top of the rubble pile below 1 new bolt and a ring bolt left for posterity. A good climb which is bit loose, a bit run out and quite sustained. Climb carefully up to the 1st bolt and continue on slightly better rock passing 2 more bolts until jugs and a lower-off are reached at the top. [C Davies, M Wells 06.93]

▶ **49. Gerboa Racer E4 5c** 23m
Even though this has 4 bolts the looseness of the rock dictates that it be treated with respect. Follow the line of bolts up the slab starting 5m right of *Mad on the Metro*. At the 3rd bolt swerve right to climb a broken groove and a final bolt on the way to the top. Lower off.
[R Mirfin, B Crampton 2002]

The Railtrack Slab

This is actually a continuation of the Looning the Tube slab, stretching rightwards and increasing in height. It is normally reached by abseiling in from the Sidings level down the line of *Off the Beaten Track* (which tops out where the railway tracks hang over the slab).

The next routes are reached by scrambling down along the base of the slab:

▶ **50. Patio Door of Perception E3** 17m
3 bolts mark the line of this neglected route which starts just right of the loose pillar. Lower off or top out. [B Crampton, R Mirfin 2002]

▶ **50a. Cartoon Lesbians F6a** 17m
A sustained line up the slab right of *Patio Door of Perception*. 5 bolts lead to a lower-off.
[Jim Kelly, Julia Kelly 10.10.10]

▶ **51. The Fat Controller F6b** 17m
The next line of 5 bolts to the right of *Cartoon Lesbians* gives a harder route.
[P Targett, I Lloyd-Jones 22.06.07]

▶ **52. Scarface Claw F6b** 17m
The line of 6 bolts and lower off left of *Red Throated Diver* mark the line of this route.
[I Lloyd-Jones, P Targett 23.08.07]

▶ **53. Red Throated Diver E3 6a** ∗∗ 17m
A good route with a hard finish. Start approximately 10m right of *Patio Door...* at a line of 4 bolts leading to a lower-off. Climb up past the 1st bolt then trend up leftwards before following the bolts up to a cruxy section below the lower-off. [P Hawkins, R Deane 03.08.86]

▶ **54. 2nd Class Passenger E2 5c** ∗ 17m
Another worthwhile route starting just right of *Red Throated Diver* and marked by 3 bolts and a lower-off. A bouldery start guards access to a ledge and the 2nd bolt. Continue up heading slightly right before going left to the final bolt and making hard moves to gain a ledge and lower-off. [C Parkin, P Hawkins 03.08.86]

52 Australia Lower • The Railtrack Slab

▶ **55. Sleeper F6c** ∗ 17m
Just before the top of the slab kicks up to The Sidings Level there is another line of bolts (6) leading to a belay/abseil bolt.
[I Lloyd-Jones, P Targett 04.06.07]

▶ **56. Crazy Train F6c** ∗∗ 26m
A fine sustained route. Start 4m left of *Ancestral Vices*; follow a curving line of bolts (8 in total) to top out or make a short and easy traverse to the lower-off on *Ancestral Vices*.
[I Lloyd-Jones, P Targett 22.06.07]

▶ **57. Ancestral Vices E4 6b** ∗ 24m
Another sustained pitch with 5 bolts and a difficult but avoidable crux at the top. Start directly below the rails on *Off the Beaten Track* and a few metres left of its start. Head up slightly leftwards, following the bolts to a lower-off. [P Williams, N Carson, D Carson, S Kerr 05.04.88]

▶ **58. Off the Beaten Track E3 5c** ∗∗ 24m
A great route, the best hereabouts. Another line marked by 5 bolts. A bold start leads to the 1st bolt; continue up passing a goey mantel (possible sling protection on a spike) and more bolts until a swerve right gains the last bolt. Move up and grab the hanging rail tracks to finish.
[C Parkin, P Hawkins, G Smith 02.08.86]

▶ **59. Here to Stay, Gone Tomorrow E4 6b** 24m
Climb the flake to the right of the 5 bolt line of *Off the Beaten Track* and continue up for a further 7m to a small spike, bear right to a flake and so to another larger spike. Finish straight up past a bolt. It is possible to start up *Between Here and Now* and traverse into the route; E3 if done this way. [G Smith, C Parkin, P Hawkins 02.08.86]

▶ **60. Between Here and Now E3 5c** 24m
The less than obvious bolted line left of diagonal crack of *The Toms Approach* gives a worthwhile route. Lower off.
[G Smith, P Hawkins, R Deane 04.08.86]

▶ **61. The Toms Approach E4 5c** 24m
The striking leftward slanting crack is a good point of reference for first time visitors. Ironically the crack offers scant protection, a Wallnut 1, cam # 1.5 and a Wallnut 8; all are said to be poor. [R Drury, M Ingle, K Toms 07.09.86]

▶ **62. Now or Never Never E5 5c** 27m
Another lonely, bold lead, starting just to the right of *The Toms Approach* crack. Climb the cleaned ledges firstly rightwards then back left to reach the final right-slanting finishing holds. A single skyhook for protection?!
[G Smith, P Hawkins 12.08.86]

Further right a detached slab of rock leans against the main slab. To the right of this is:

▶ **63. Psychodelicate F7c** ∗∗ 37m
A fantastic route with 2 distinct cruxes. Originally graded E5 6c, a rock fall on the lower section left it unrepeated for many years until it was re-climbed in 2010 at the harder sport grade. Follow the bolted zig-zag line; a difficult passage between the 4th and 5th bolts is sure to test your problem solving skills. There is also a very thin section near the end of the route.
[G Smith, C Parkin 06.12.86/re-climbed after rockfall by C Muskett 07.04.10]

Project: The impressive and partially bolted line right of *Psychodelicate* awaits an ascent.

Slatehead • Cliff Phillips

Back in the day, The Captain taking a break with Nick Thomas
photo: Martin Crook

With nearly 50 routes to his name, 'The Captain' was one of the most prolific activist in the quarries during the 80s. Blissfully stoned and wandering round the levels, he nonchalantly soloed through loose 5c territory as if it was just an extension of the footpath. His many bold and esoteric routes are left for us to rediscover, but he also established his fair share of classics, including the amazing *Looning the Tube*. Sadly this has lost much of the hanging tube which graced its lower traverse, but the principal of using tubes and other such old quarrying detritus remains alive and well today. For example, the recent addition *Great Bores of Today* in the bottom of Australia was made possible by leaning an old pipe tube against the initial blank section.

An early ascent of **Tubing to Loon**, with the full tube still in position. Sadly the tube was vandalised and destroyed in early 1986. photo: Paul Williams

54 Australia Lower • The Salt Pans

The Salt Pans

The flat, water logged area that runs across the Oil Drum Glacier provides a convenient crossing point leading to the bottom of the East Braich. It is also home to a small number of interesting routes on the levels right of the Railtrack Slab. Approach via the Fruitbat Level (see Australia Upper chapter) and drop down to the Salt Pans and then head back along the level towards the right edge of Railtrack Slab.

▶ **64. The Australian F6b** ∗∗ 12m
At the very far end of the Railtrack Slab is a corner. This route lies just to the right of the corner, up a slab in the arete. From a bolt belay on the right move out left and climb the crack past a bolt (the short will need to improvise a clip stick or be brave) to a ledge and bolt. Move left to the arête and pass another bolt on the way to the top. Lower off or climb up to a bolt belay.
[C Davies, P Targett, M Wells 21.10.89]

The Salt Pans • **Australia Lower 55**

▶ **65. The Stream of Obscenity F6c+** * 10m
A frustratingly technical challenge situated halfway between *Kosciusko* and *The Australian*. Start under a small overhang; gymnastic moves up its left arête allow you to enter a rightward facing groove above leading to a bivy ledge. All that remains is some teetering up the diagonal bore hole above. Lower off. [M Dicken 2007]

▶ **66. Kosciusko VS 4b** * 12m
The attractive curving arete by a stream. Ascend the arete and hand traverse the upper section. Finish at a perched block. [25.03.91]

The level below has a couple of lines. If you carry on walking right past the corner at the right hand end of Railtrack Slab, and continue for another 50m you get to the bolted line of *Narcolepsy*. This can also be accessed by scrambling down from the Salt Pans.

▶ **67. Narcolepsy F7a+** 20m
A friable line with 5 bolts marking the way up the steep slab. Pass the 1st bolt with a slap to the ledge above and continue above with some technical climbing and a leftwards kink. Finish directly to a lower-off. [R Mirfin 2002]

▶ **67a. Y Rhaffwr F6b+** * 15m
Good quality slate and some great moves make this arete well worth seeking out. Tackle the clean arete further left of the *Narcolepsy* slab, passing 5 bolts to a lower-off.
[I Lloyd-Jones, C Davies 18.12.09]

< Ian Lloyd-Jones on the first ascent of **Y Rhaffwr** F6b+
Photo: Chris Davies

56 Australia Lower • Upper Dinorwig

Upper Dinorwig
The vast expanse of rock perched above the right edge of the Oil Drum Glacier provides some extremely adventurous undertakings. The cliff is split into a series of rubble strewn tiers and is approached from the Salt Pans, or in the case of *Big Thursday*, by dropping down from the upper levels of Australia.

▶ **68. Big Thursday XS ABO ★★★** 230m
The route links the obvious series of green pillars that run up the left side of the cliff. Harrowing in places, but a fine expedition in total. The description is kept in the Crook vernacular.
P1 4c The pillar, greasy and loose, then scramble to the belay.
P2 4c Move easily up the groove and slabby green pillar.
P3 5c The Wrist Cutter Crack. Step off block; loose and serious.
P4 5a The next 1, hardly any pro on terminal rock.
P5 5b Overhanging suspect flakes to corner, loose pillar, very fine.
P6 5b (The Crux) Assemble on the rim of the slate crevasse, step on, get into groove then grim rock and razor fins. To easier slab. Ace.
P7 4c The remains of the day. Easier looking remains of the pillar with 1 or 2 weird moves. Great. [M Crook, N Walton 05.94].

▶ **69. Project XS 5c?**
Another deeply adventurous prospect, albeit on mainly solid rock. P1 was completed by M Dicken and J Redhead in 2004. Start from the mass of boulders at the base of the prominent overlapping slab. Follow the slab to a leaning corner which is tackled on the left. Step airily back right to gain an overlap which allows an escape right to easier ground. Continue up to a ledge with a single rock 2 belay.
The rest of the line above remains unclimbed – the original idea was to follow the slab to its terminus, but child care responsibilities forced a scramble retreat. *"The most scared I've been in recent times, youth!"* commented JR after the aborted attempt.

▶ **70. If You Kill People They Die MXS**
approx 200m (including a scramble finish)
The odds are you will fulfil the promise of the name if you attempt this route; a route for keen alpinists and extreme explorers only. Approach from the Salt Pans to the big boulders at the lowest point of Upper Dinorwig, go round the arete to the right and up and over a green boulder to a right diagonal groove.
P1 60m Follow the groove to a vertical shale band, cross this to solid rock then follow the most solid rock to the next level.
P2 5b 12m To the left of a prominent smooth brown overhanging wall is an arete/groove thing. Follow this on interestingly wobbly holds to an arete below a decaying hut.
P3 4c 12m The V groove in the right of the arete of the small wall with a chain draped over the buttress, just behind the hut. A great pitch (one of the best VS pitches in the quarries).
P4 4c 30m The blocky arete left of the big bay behind the groove. Climb this until it is possible to traverse rightwards to easy ground at the back of the bay.
P5 4c 30m The prominent arete split by a chimney. Climb the right arete until it is possible to traverse into the chimney. Scramble up to the next level and the hanging pipe and walk off.
[M Dicken 14.10.02]

▶ **71. Conquistadors of the Useless ABO** 150m
Winter line up the rubble gully at the right side of Upper Dinorwig. [M Crook 1994]

Above the Rails • **Australia Lower 57**

Above the Rails
(aka: Level above *Looning the Tube*)

A recently developed area with several pleasant, albeit short sport routes. It is reached by walking up 1 level from the Looning the Tube Col.

▶ **72. Sport 4 All F5** 8m
Climb the groove left of *Kinder Surprise*; 2 bolts lead the way to a lower-off above the square roof. [I Lloyd-Jones 02.10.07]

▶ **73. Kinder Surprise F5** 9m
Climb the rightwards slanting line just above the *Looning the Tube* belay bolt; 3 bolts and a hard move to reach the lower-off.
[I Lloyd-Jones, P Targett 07.09.07]

▶ **74. Surprise Surprise F6a** 9m
A slightly tricky start leads to a final testing mantel. 3 bolts lead to a lower-off.
[I Lloyd-Jones 11.09.07]

▶ **75. Shorty's Dyno F7a** 10m
Gain the overlap with some difficulty and make a desperate/dynamic move up to good holds before finishing more easily. Lower off.
[I Lloyd-Jones, P Targett 13.09.07]

▶ **76. Orangutang Overhang F6a+** ✶✶ 12m
The superb technical groove left of *Cyber World Sl@te Heads* leads to an entertaining series of swings through the steepness. Lower off.
[I Lloyd-Jones, T Hughes, P Targett 28.08.07]

▶ **77. Cyber World Sl@te Heads F6a+** 13m
A little loose at the top but still a worthwhile route. Climb the groove up to the right hand side of the large roof and escape up right on suspect rock to reach the lower-off on the large flake. [I Lloyd-Jones, P Targett, T Hughes 27.08.07]

There is an unknown, but presumably climbed line between routes 77 and 78.

▶ **78. Steps of Glory F5b** ✶ 15m
Climb the slabby wall to the right of *Cyber World Sl@te Heads*. 2 bolts lead to a ledge; 3 further bolts and some nice stepped edges run up to a lower-off. [M Chambers, C Roots, I Pagano 02.03.08]

▶ **79. The Groovy Gang HS** 7m
Tackle the obvious groove in the corner over to the right of the broken slabs. Nice moves but no protection. [P Targett 04.06.07]

NB. A last minute F6c+ has been climbed between routes 75 and 76.

58 Australia Lower • The Sidings

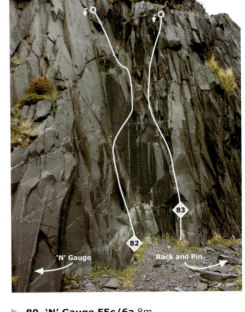

The Sidings
This level has recently been developed as a low grade sport climbing venue. Although the routes are short the rock is of good quality and there is plenty to go at. To reach it go up 2 levels from the *Looning the Tube* Col.

A number of low grade boulder problems have been climbed at the left end of the level:

Gentle LayBack V0-//Font 3+ To the left of Shothole Arete using the last obvious slab feature, layback from a sitting start. [E Russell 03.04.09]

Shothole Arete V0/Font 4 Climb the arete with a shothole in it! [E Russell 03.04.09]

Loose Block Corner V0/Font 4 Pull on the loose block tentatively then continue up the dirty corner. Could be worthwhile after lots of traffic. [E Russell 03.04.09]

Puffing Billy V0+/Font 4+ 10 paces to the left of *'N' Gauge* there is a small tree growing out of the slate. To the left of this is a corner. Climb the corner with a couple of nice moves. [C Jordan 30.08.08]

With a Little Help From a Tree V2/3/Font 5+/6A Gain the tree with difficulty, thereafter continue upwards with assistance from left hand arete. Highball! [E Russell 03.04.09]

▶ **80. 'N' Gauge F5c/6a** 8m
It is possible to climb the centre of the pillar at F6a, but only if you keep the blinkers on. Use the obvious holds out right and it is only F5c. [J Ball 11.07]

▶ **80a. Glass Axe E5 7a** ∗ 8m
The attractive left facing groove just to the left of *'N' Gauge* gives an extremely technical challenge. Can be soloed direct or starting on the right with protection from the *'N' Gauge* bolts. [A Woodward 1986]

▶ **81. Side Line F4c** 8m
Climb out right from 1st bolt of *'N' Gauge* and continue up the flakey groove. 5 bolts to a lower-off. [J Ball 27.01.08]

8m to the right is another pair of routes:

▶ **82. Derailed F4b** 8m
Climb the corner just left of *Thomas the Tank* start direct, then move right. 3 bolts to a lower-off. [J Ball 27.01.08]

▶ **83. Thomas the Tank F4a** ∗ 9m
The grooved ramp feature yields a good slabby route with a 'faith in friction' crux at the top. 4 bolts to a lower-off. [A Ball 16.12.07]

Jon Ratcliffe plugged into the superb **Great** > **Bores of Today** F7a photo: Ray Wood

The Sidings • **Australia Lower 61**

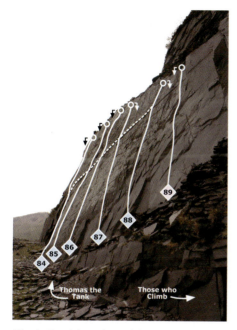

15m to the right a clean slab is reached:

▶ **84. Rack and Pin F5b** ✶ 11m
The corner and slab line on the left, with the crux passing the top bolt. 4 bolts to a lower-off. [J Ball 16.12.07]

▶ **85. Sodor F5c** ✶ 11m
Follow the hairline crack left of the centre of the slab; when the crack terminates at the horizontal feature continue straight up to a lower-off. [J Ball 13.10.07]

The original route here: **Above the Line HVS 4c** [C Parkin 2.8.86] has been superseded by the following 2 routes:

▶ **86. The Mallard F5c** ✶ 11m
The next obvious hairline crack 2m right of *Sodor* gives another good route. 4 bolts to a lower-off. [J Ball 16.12.07]

▶ **87. Polar Express F5b** 9m
Utilises the alternative start to *Above the Line*, but continues direct. 4 bolts to a lower-off. [J Ball 13.10.07]

▶ **88. Ivor the Engine F5a** 8m
Climbs the slab to the right of *Polar Express*, with the crux at the top. 3 bolts to a lower-off. [J Ball 27.01.08]

▶ **89. Gordon F4a** 8m
The slab and corner at the right hand side of the slab. 3 bolts to a lower-off. (A Ball 16.12.07)

▶ **90. The Level Crossing F5c** ✶ 20m
An entertaining traverse of the slab following the distinct break at half height. Start up *Rack and Pin* then follow the break to finish at *Ivor the Engine*. 7 bolts to a lower-off. [J Ball 27.01.08]

10m right of *Gordon* is the next trio of routes:

▶ **91. Those who climb clearly marked projects are the kind of people who would steal the chocolate bar from a kid's lunch box - selfish tossers, who owe the bolt fund cash F5b/c** ✶ 8m
A not so new route, soloed in August 1986 at the same time as *Above the Line*, but never claimed at the time. The obvious groove/niche line. 4 bolts to a lower-off. [C Parkin 02.08.86 retro bolted 02.08]

▶ **92. Choo Choo F5a/5b** 8m
Arete and groove right of *Those who climb...* 4 bolts to a lower-off. There is a loose jug at the top - not using it makes the route harder but safer. [J Ball 28.02.08]

▶ **93. Hogwarts Express F5c** 8m
The stepped corner with the crux at the top. 3 bolts to a lower-off. [J Ball 27.01.08]

Right at the end of the level are 2 final routes:

▶ **94. The Railway Children F6a/+** 10m
The bouldery wall to some good jugs, then move right onto the clean headwall. Height dependant move at top, thus the split grade. 5 bolts to a lower-off. [J Ball 15.02.08]

▶ **95. In Loving Memory F6a+** 10m
A question mark shaped line to the right *The Railway Children*; 5 bolts to a lower-off. [J Ball 14.4.08]

ERYRI MOUNTAINEERING
Driven by Adventure

Professional, independent provider of high quality courses, adventure activities and guided instruction in the outdoors.

- SPA, CWA, ML Courses
- All aspects of summer and winter mountaineering
- Corporate team building and development
- Coasteering and Gorge adventures
- Bouldering tours

ERYRI
MOUNTAINEERING AND ADVENTURE ACTIVITIES

website: www.eryri-mountaineering.co.uk
email: enquiries@eryri-mountaineering.co.uk

Charlotte Jelleyman being coached by Darren Williams on a lead of **Equinox** VS 4c, Bus Stop Quarry photo: Jon Ratcliffe

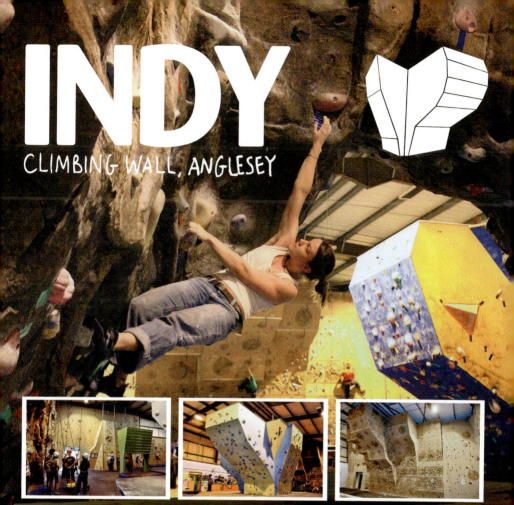

64 Australia • A Grand Day Out

The succession of levels on the west side of Australia, that run up from the Lower area to the Skyline Level, provide an opportunity for a superb multi pitch link up.

▶ **A Grand Day Out F6b** ∗∗
This route was first done as a 3 pitch trip but is described here with a logical extension up to a dramatic finish on the Skyline Level. It has a similar feel to the *East Face of Vivian* route and is best tackled with the same tactics (i.e. take a small rucsac to carry your trainers, a spare top, snacks and drink).
There are a number of ways of reaching the start of the route on the far right side of the Railtrack Slab. The best 2 options are as follows:

1. From the Looning the Tube Col descend 1 level and take the right hand of 3 tunnels, and then the right fork where it splits. From the tunnel mouth make a mad dash, down and out of the 'fall out zone' from the dangerous looking scree/rock pile above. Cross the quarry floor and scramble up the broken blocks and scree left of *Temple of Boom* to reach the left side of the Railtrack Slab. Walk up rightwards along the base of the slab to a large detached block leaning against the slab.
2. Abseil off the pipe of *Looning the Tube* and follow the base of the Railtrack Slab up rightwards.

P1 F6b Climb the crux slab past 2 bolts to the top of block, then head up the right trending ramp past 3 more bolts to top out with care onto the right hand end of The Sidings level and a twin bolt belay.

P2 F5a An excellent pitch in a great situation. Climb up and out onto the obvious traverse line crossing the top left hand section of the *Psychodelicate* slab to a crux move to gain the top and a twin bolt belay.
P3 F6a Tackle the 'harder than it looks' wall behind the twin bolt belay (left of *M.I.L. Arete* on the Fruitbat Level) past 3 bolts to twin bolt belay, taking care when gaining the top.
P4 *Feeling Rusty* (F6a+/b) Walk rightwards along the Zippy Level to reach the bolted line on the right side of the smooth rust stained slab. A bit of an eliminate, but good moves if you avoid the ledges to the right.
P5 *Plastic Soldiers* (F6a) Walk rightwards along the Skyline Level. At the right side of the highest part of the cliff there are 2 bolted lines; take the left hand line, which is protected by 13 bolts. Top out to a gloriously positioned belay.
[P1-3: F Ball, A Ball, J Ball 21.08.10]

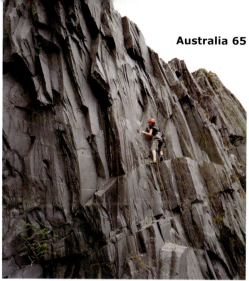

Josie Ball on **A Grand Day Out** P3 photo: Fraser Ball

Archie Ball on **A Grand Day Out** P2 photo: Fraser Ball

Other 'grand days out' can be concocted:

▶ **West Face of Australia E1 5b/F6a** ∗∗
A trad orientated link with great features.
P1 *Looning the Tube* (HVS 5b) A classic start.
P2 *Surprise, Surprise* (F6a) A neat little pitch, steady for the grade.
P3 *Sodor* (F5c) Short but sweet.
P4 *M.I.L. Arete* (E1 5b) The psychological crux of the route.
P5 *Razorback* (HVS 5a) A good crack pitch.
P6 *Act Naturally* (VS 4b) A b-i-g majestic pitch.
P7 *Goblin Party* (VS 4b) A striking line to finish the day.

▶ **West Face of Australia Direct E3 6a/F6a+** ∗∗
A varied and interesting trip.
P1 *Goose Creature* (E3 6a) An intense start to the day.
P2 *Orangatang Overhang* (F6a+) One of the best of the new wave of sport routes.
P3 *Sodor* (F5c) Up you go...
P4 *Stretched Limo* (E2 5c) to snake up the attractive groove line...
P5 *The Samba Drum* (E2 5c) and attack the crack...
P6 *Harri Bach Llanrug* (F6a)...to a slabby clip up...
P7 *See You Bruce* (E3 5b)...before the final big, bold pitch.

▶ **West Face of Australia
Super Direct F7a/E4 6a** ∗∗
The slab connoisseur's dream come true.
P1 *Crazy Train* (F6c) Superb and sustained.
P2 *Sodor* (F5c) Probably the best here so you may as well do it again.
P3 *Slatebite* (F7a) An excellent pitch...
P4 *The Beanstalk* (F7a)... and another corker.
P5 *Rock Yoga* (F7a) Then the crux...
P6 *Slabology* (F6c)...before more slabtastic fun.
P7 *Men of Leisure* (E4 6a) And finally, an optional trad pitch for those carrying the right gear.

Josie Ball on **A Grand Day Out** P1 photo: Fraser Ball

Australia Upper

Style: Trad/sport
Aspect: South-East
Approach: 10-30 minutes
Altitude: 400-500m
OS Grid ref: 598 610

The Faffer	E6
In on the Kill Taker	E5
Putting on Ayres	E4
Resurrection Shuffle	E4
The Gorbals	E4
Men of Leisure	E4
Put it on the Slate, Waiter	E4
See You Bruce	E3
Captain Condom and the Mothers of Prevention	E3
Don't Look Back in Bangor	E3
Men at Work	E3
The North Face of the Aga	E3

The Samba Drum	E2
Stretched Limo	E2
Eric the Fruitbat	E2
Genevive	E2
The Skyline Club	E2
Ronald Reagan Meets Doctor Strangelove	E2
Rastaman Vibration	E2
Zippies First Acid Trip	E1
M.I.L. Arete	E1
Antiquity	E1
Razorback	HVS
Indiana Jasmine and the Topple of Doom!	HVS
Digital Delectation	HVS

Act Naturally	VS
Mad Dog of the West	VS

Wish You Were Here	F7c/+
Jepp The Knave	F7b+
Glasgow Kiss	F7b+
A Room With A View	F7b
Pulverised	F7b
Ziplock	F7b
Mister Blister	F7a
Slatebite	F7a
The Beanstalk	F7a

Gymnastic Fantastic	F6c+
Slabology	F6c
Slab Rog	F6b+
Slab Slayer	F6a+
Harri Bach Llanrug	F6a
Ruby Marlee meets Dr Holingsworth	F6a
Plastic Soldier	F6a
Clash of the Titans	F6a

The Very Old and the Very New	C2+/C3

The upper part of Australia has many fine routes situated in impressive surroundings. The lofty position allows dramatic views both of the quarry levels stretching out below, and across to Snowdon, Cloggy and the Moel Eilio range.

There is a wide spread of quality traditional routes in the VS to E4 range, interestingly with several of the best VSs in the quarries. On the sport side there are some rather unique 40m F6as and a fine collection of grade 7 test pieces which includes a contender for the best sport route in the whole of the quarries: Jon Ratcliffe's brilliant *Wish You Were Here* F7c/+.

Martin Dale enjoying an evening ascent of **Plastic Soldier** F6a
photo: Si Panton

68 Australia Upper • Approach

Australia Upper Layout

Warning: because the successive levels in Australia Quarry are so tightly racked there is a risk of dislodging rocks onto climbers on the level below. Great care should be exercised at all times, but especially when close to the edge of a level.

Conditions: As with Australia Lower, the majority of routes get the sun from the morning until early afternoon. Most routes are quick drying and seepage is rarely a problem, with the following notable exceptions: *In on the Kill Taker* and around *Zippy's First Acid Trip* on the Zippy Level, the *Men at Work* slab on The Gorbals Level and the start of *Wish You Were Here*.

Approach: There are 2 possible approach routes, but 1st time visitors are probably best to use the following as it allows for a greater degree of orientation:

From the turning circle by Bus Stop Quarry, walk into the quarries along the main track passing a large disused factory unit on the left. Go left through the gate, viewing the massive quarried cwm of Australia above. 50m from the gate the track turns right and dips down hill, a gate is seen on immediately on the left. Beyond this it is possible to walk diagonally right for a further 100m before steps lead up one level. Cut back left and ascend a further 2 levels to arrive at the 'Col', in front of the massive amphitheatre of Australia. The upper levels are reached by walking up a series of rough paths on the end of each of the successive levels.

The 2nd approach route, from the Pen Garret car park involves less ascent/descent, but the layout of the quarry is less obvious from this perspective. The car park is also quite small, with room for only 4 or 5 vehicles. Under no circumstances should the gate be blocked – if you find all the places taken please drive back down to the Bus Stop area and use the 1st approach route instead. If there is an accident on the Upper Australia levels access to the gate will be vital for the Mountain Rescue team.

To reach the Garret car park retrace your steps from the Bus Stop turnaround and take the 1st right (at the crossroads) turn up a hill, and then turn right again after 150m and follow the narrow road up the hill to reach the car park at its end. At this point you are directly above Bus Stop Quarry. Go past the gate and follow the continuation track up and round into the top levels of Australia. If you walk across to the edge of the quarry a tunnel on the left will be seen – this leads through the top of The Skyline Buttress and onto The Gorbals Level.

The view into the quarries and Snowdon beyond from the Pen Garret car park approach photo: Si Panton

Australia Upper 69

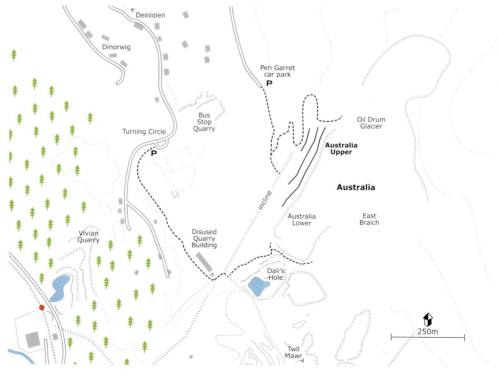

Australia Upper • The Fruitbat Level

The Fruitbat Level
If you come up 3 levels from Looning the Tube Slab you get to the 1st terrace that can be followed all the way round to the winding house above the Salt Pans, the flat area below the immense Oil Drum Glacier. The first route is about 30m along the terrace.

▶ **1. Solitude Standing E2 6a** 13m
6m left of *Eric the Fruitbat* is short inverted V groove. Ascend the groove which is hard to start, to an overlap at 8m. Continue up and belay on a block to the left. A lonely skyhook protects.
[P Targett, D Dutton, C Stephenson 25.11.89]

▶ **2. Eric the Fruitbat E2 5c** * 13m
A strenuous little number. Scale the slab mindful of the poor protection until an overhanging wall is reached. Step right to a bolt and climb past it with difficulty before moving up to the Silver Birch tree above.
[L Dutton, P Targett, C Stephenson 25.11.89]

20m right of *Eric the Fruitbat* a broken slabby area, marked by 'HIW' and 'RR' carved into the rock, provides a number of friable lines. 20m right again there is a compact slab; 5 lines have been squeezed onto this, most at VS or easier. The best is:

▶ **3. M.I.L. Arete E1 5b** * 11m
The left side of the slab passing the droopy metal bar on the easier but bold upper section.
[P Targett, C Davies 21.10.89]

Continue to the right of these crossing a loose and exposed section of the level with care; 30m beyond this awkward bit is a groove.

▶ **4. Genevive E2 5c** * 13m
Climb the corner groove, passing a ledge on the right at 3m, and a peg higher up.
[C Allen, R Wight 16.02.91]

▶ **5. Pontiac Arete VS 4c** 13m
The obvious green stone cracked arete 3m right of *Genevire*. Good climbing but some care needed with the rock towards the top.
[C Allen, R Wight 16.02.91]

▶ **6. Stretched Limo E2 5c** * 13m
The attractive looking groove 3m to the right of *Pontiac Arete* has a small ledge on the right at 5m. Climb the groove with a series of long reaches, and clipping a peg on the way. [C Allen, R Wight 16.02.91]

▶ **6a. Gymnastic Fantastic F6c+** * 11m
The obvious bolted line just right of *Stretched Limo* gives a good route. A reachy start leads right to a text book slate move, followed by either a difficult stretch back left into the flake or straight up. Trust the smears, go for the top of the flake and continue up to the lower-off.
[N Sharpe, G Jones 20.09.10]

The Fruitbat Level • **Australia Upper 71**

▶ **6b. Slatebite F7a** ** 15m
A fun route up the left side of the clean wall 10m right of *Stretched Limo*. Start up the groove, then make a thin move right at the 2nd bolt to gain the tall pocket. Rock up into this then make a hard lock above the 3rd bolt and continue up to the lower-off. The line of bolts to the right is a good project: F7a+ish if you stay to the left on the lower crux; F7bish if you stay on the right. [C Davies 06.02.10]

The next 2 routes can be found about 20m before you reach the main huts of the winding shed, at a smooth corner near the end of the pipe.

▶ **7. The Christening of New Boots E1 5b** 15m
Start 1m left of the corner. Move up right into the corner before climbing up left to a small overhang; climb this direct and finish up the crack to the top.
[A Nother, M Wells, I Hill 05.06.93]

▶ **8. Rock Athletes Day Off HVS 5b** 15m
From the smooth corner and move up right to join the arete. Follow this up on the right hand side until near the top then finish out left.
[I Hill, A Nother 05.06.93]

Chris Davies on his own route **Slatebite** F7a, Australia
photo: Glyn Davies

The Zippy Level

The next level up from the Fruit Bat Level is the 2nd level that can be followed all the way along to the Oil Drum Glacier 2 levels above the Salt Pans. This level has some great slate.

The first section of rock on the level is steep; a rare thing hereabouts.

▶ **9. Jepp the Knave F7b+** ** 12m
An intense pitch with a sustained mid section. Start up the lower slabby shield: a hard rockover leftwards passing the 1st bolt leads to good holds. Layaway up the steep rib to the obvious sloper. Another couple of difficult moves allow you to stand on this to gain the ledge and the lower-off above. [P Targett, C Davies 28.10.09]

▶ **10. Project**
A steep line with a wild sideways dyno crux.

▶ **11. Last Chance for a Slow Dance E3 5b** 20m
The curving flake line yields a creaky and potentially serious climb. Climb direct to the start of the flake line and follow it rightwards with improving gear (some might like a skyhook on the initial section) to a blunt spike at its apex. From here traverse right into the bay and finish as for ...*and a pen please*. [M Dicken 02.11.07]

▶ **12. In on the Kill Taker E5 6b** * 16m
Start up *Last Chance for a Slow Dance* to the blunt spike. Stand on it and lean out for the bolt. Traverse onto the overlap and climb straight up the cleaned holds to the top. There is ample opportunity for 6m of clean-ish air if messed up. [M Dicken, M Reeves 08.08.08]

▶ **13. The Beanstalk F7a** * 16m
The hanging groove line which cuts through the *Last Chance for a Slow Dance* traverse provides a great route with 3 distinct hard sections. Start about 5m right of *LCFASD*; move up past a bore hole and then right beneath the 2nd bolt to a jug on the right. Step up and back left into the groove which leads with difficulty to the *LCFASD* traverse. Sling the spike and continue up past a 5th bolt to a lower-off. [C Davies, P Targett 07.10.09]

The open, clean slab to the right has a number of popular routes.

▶ **14. ...and a pen please HVS 5a** 13m
The slab, corner and headwall left of *Rastaman Vibration*. [P Woodhouse, K Archer 05.07.03]

The Zippy Level • **Australia Upper** 73

▶ **15. Rastaman Vibration E2 6a** ∗ 13m
The blind crack line just left of *Razorback* gives an intense little route. Difficult moves past the 1st bolt allow access to the thin crack above; continue up past the 2nd bolt to a ledge. Step right and finish as for *Razorback*. [M Boniface 1988]

▶ **16. Razorback HVS 5a** ∗ 13m
The obvious crack line provides a good climb.
[M Boniface 08.07.88]

▶ **17. Putting on Ayres E4 6c** ∗ 13m
The smooth slab right of *Razorback* provides a desperate challenge. Go up passing the 1st bolt on its left (the more obvious right hand line leads into a dead end, from which an optimistic jump seems to be the only solution); if you make it to the horizontal break, scuttle rightwards and rock up to gain the 2nd bolt. Continue straight up and finish by a rockover out left. [L Dutton 26.03.89]

▶ **18. Feeling Rusty F6a+/b** 13m
An eliminate line which gives great moves, provided you keep the blinkers on and avoid the temptation to drift into the easy groove on the right. Lower off. [I Lloyd-Jones, C Davies 24.09.09]

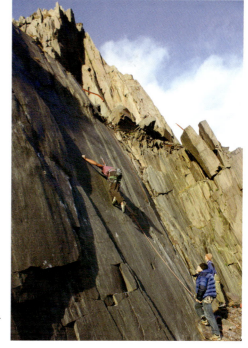

Jon Mathis on the utterly desperate **Putting on Ayres** E4 6c >
photo: Si Panton

74 Australia Upper • The Zippy Level

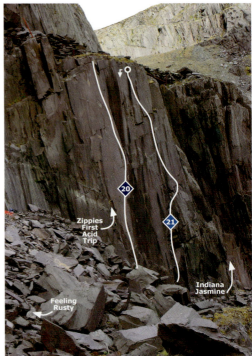

To the right of the slab, just beyond a jumble of boulders, is the narrow slab of:

▶ **19. Zippies First Acid Trip E1 5c** * 15m
Ascend the left edge of the slab, passing a bolt, and traverse right into the corner just below the top. [M Boniface 05.01.88]

▶ **20. Project**
The wall right of *Zippies First Acid Trip*, leading into the obvious upper crack.

▶ **21. Ziplock F7b** ** 15m
A good sport climb, similar in style to *Taken Over by Dept C*. An awkward lower groove leads into a hard crux section. Continue to the lower-off with less difficulty. [I Lloyd-Jones, P Targett 17.09.09]

5m right again is another slab/corner that terminates at a wall stacked up on railway tracks.

▶ **22. Indiana Jasmine and the Topple of Doom! HVS 5a/F5+** * 15m
Wall and arete about 5m right of the *Ziplock* wall. Nice solid climbing, passing 3 slightly spaced bolts, to a top out. Sling and metal post belays. [C Davies, I Lloyd Jones 24.09.09]

Owen Samuel leading **Indiana Jasmine and the Topple of Doom!** HVS 5a in glorious evening light photo: Si Panton

The Zippy Level • Australia Upper

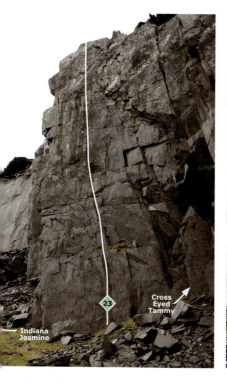

10m further along the level is another small bay which is home to the following routes:

▶ **23. Second's Chance VS 4b** 16m
Climb the slabby left wall of the bay via a slight overlap at half height.
[R Wright 13.10.89]

▶ **24. Cross Eyed Tammy HVS 5a** 16m
The series of bulging ledges leading to the corner right of *Second Chance*. Start below the lowest roof, surmount it on the right and continue up to the corner, before a traverse leads out to the arete. [M Dicken 16.11.02]

A little further along the level there is an attractive wall:

▶ **25. Resurrection Shuffle E4 6b** ✱✱ 16m
An excellent route, well worth seeking out. 3.5m right of the arête are a pair of parallel hairline cracks. Climb the left crack; moving up slightly left, then back right to reach the ledge at half height. The superb upper finger crack leads to the top. A harder (E5 6c/7a?) right hand start is possible up the lower wall. [THE Impostor, I Dutton 1987]

▶ **26. The Samba Drum E2 5c** ✱ 16m
A good route, quite stiff at the top. Climb the crackline 3m to the right of *Resurrection Shuffle* to reach the half height ledges. Finish via the obvious upper crack. [K Archer, P Woodhouse 05.07.03]

▶ **27. Pulverised F7b** ✱ 16m
The wall right of *The Samba Drum* is thin and vertical; a wiggy 3rd clip and an intense fingery crux at the 4th bolt provide the entertainment. 6 bolts lead to some funky rockovers on the upper section. Lower off. [I Lloyd-Jones 24.09.09]

▶ **28. De Nouement F7a/+** 16m
The obvious bolted line just left of the corner. Nice climbing, with hard moves at the 2nd and 5th bolts, but lacking independence from the corner. Lower off. [P Targett, O Jones 08.10.09]

Australia Upper • The Skyline Buttress Level

The Skyline Buttress Level

The next level up is easily identified by the large slab of Skyline Buttress, which runs through 2 seperate levels. A tunnel runs through the back of the cliff onto the Gorbals level from which it is possible to stand eye-to-eye with somebody climbing *Clash of the Titans*. Some of the rock on this level is particularly suspect, so take care.

▶ **29. Digital Delectation HVS 5a** * 27m
The left hand crack on the shorter section of the buttress. Climb the crack to the large ledge, step left and take another thin crack in the upper wall to finish. [L Hardy, G Parfitt 01.05.86]

▶ **30. Good Afternoon Constable VS 4c** 27m
A series of cracks right of *Digital Delectation* gives an okay route with sparse protection.
[I Wilson, T Downes 06.10.85]

▶ **31. Dolmen HVS 5a** 40m
To the right of *Good Afternoon Constable* is a rightwards slanting stepped groove with a peg. Climb this and continue directly to finish up *Menhir*. [J Brown, J Lyon 02.02.02]

▶ **32. Menhir VS 4c** 40m
7m to the left of *Act Naturally* there is a left trending groove that runs the full height of the buttress. [J Brown, J Lyon 02.02.02]

▶ **33. Antiquity E1 5a** * 40m
Climb the *Act Naturally* groove to the half way ledge, then a traverse out left, rising slightly past 2 bolts and an old peg. The original line finished up *Menhir*, but it is now done with an independent finish up the groove where a further bolt will be found. Quite nervy in the lower reaches until the 1st of the bolts is clipped.
[J Brown, J Lyon 26.02.02]

▶ **34. The Skyline Club E2 5b/c** * 40m
Another big pitch with great positions. Start just left of the *Act Naturally* groove. Climb the blunt rib/arete, passing 2 bolts until you get to the 1st bolt of *Antiquity*. Continue up and right following a line towards the upper hanging arete. Climb directly over the overlap and go straight up clipping another 3 bolts to a top out and double bolt belay. [C Davies, P Targett 01.10.09]

The Skyline Buttress Level • **Australia Upper 77**

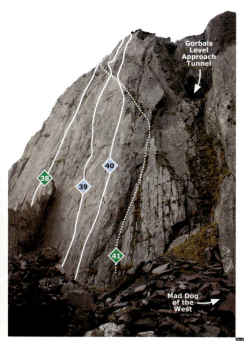

▶ **39. Plastic Soldier F6a** ✶ 40m
A long and airy pitch, perhaps the best of the trio of sport routes on this buttress. Move up carefully to the 1st bolt and continue following the line of 13 bolts, crossing the diagonal crack of *The Dreaming* and pulling onto the upper shield where an amusing adornment is sometimes found on the penultimate bolt. Top out and belay on 2 bolted blocks. Some loose rock, which should improve with traffic.
[I Lloyd-Jones, P Targett, S Beesley 15.04.09]

▶ **40. Clash of the Titans F6a** ✶ 40m
The parallel bolted line right of *Plastic Soldier* has a whopping 16 bolts and is a similarly fun outing, provided care is taken with the loose rock. Top out and belay on 2 bolted blocks.
[I Lloyd-Jones, C Davies 16.06.09]

▶ **41. The Dreaming E1 5b** 43m
An obsolete route? On the far right hand side of the buttress, above the quarrymen's hut, is a crack. Reach the crack from a scoop, and then follow it to a pinnacle level with The Gorbals Level tunnel. Thereafter a leftwards slanting crack leads across *Clash of the Titans* and *Plastic Soldier* to arrive at an arete near top of *Lindy Lou*. Move back right and up to reach the top.
[R Ebbs, S Parker 02.11.93]

▶ **35. Ruby Marlee meets Dr Holingsworth F6a** ✶ 40m
A big climb with much atmosphere and some suspect holds. Climb the *Act Naturally* groove to the half way ledge (wires/cams needed) and then follow the line of bolts up the slabby wall to a top out and double bolt belay. [C Davies, I Lloyd-Jones 16.06.09]

▶ **36. Act Naturally VS 4b** ✶✶ 43m
The striking diagonal groove line provides one of the best VSs in the quarries. Ascend the initial groove to reach a ledge system. From the right side of the ledge follow the continuation crack/groove to the top. [C Phillips 19.06.84]

▶ **37. Ronald Reagan Meets Doctor Strangelove E2 5b** ✶ 43m
The obvious line dissecting *Act Naturally*. Climb the scoop and crack 3m right of the *Act Naturally* start to reach the ledge system at half height. Finish up the crack line a few metres to the left of the final groove system of *Act Naturally*. [L Hardy, M Crook 23.04.86]

▶ **38. Lindy Lou HVS** 40m
Just left of the short tower, which leans against the main slab, is a shallow groove. Climb this and trend right to a ledge. Exit this on the right and climb up the right arete of the final groove of *Act Naturally* to the top.
[29.03.87]

Dennis Wong on **The Skyline Club** E2 5b/c photo: Jim Jones

78 Australia Upper • The Skyline Buttress Level

Just right of the quarrymen's huts at the right side of Skyline buttress is a small slab tucked in behind the next prominent buttress. The crack splitting the slab is:

▶ **42. Mad Dog of the West VS 5a** * 14m
A good little crack route; shame it isn't longer. Womble up the broken groove then surge up the crack plugging in ample protection as you go. Bolt belay on back wall of Gorbals Level. The left arete was once soloed (by Ivan Holroyd in 2007), but it can hardly be recommended.
[P Hawkins, J Elliot, R Caves 19.4.86]

The next 4 routes all share the same bolt belay.

▶ **43. The Methane Monster E1 5b** 17m
This route starts on the facet facing Llanberis and climbs the V groove, just left of the arete of the main slab. Climb the wall, then a finger crack past a small overlap to move right onto the left arete of the slab. Follow the arete up past ledges to the top. [C Davies, M Wells 23.09.89]

▶ **44. Binwomen VS 4b** 17m
Start at the left side of the front slab of the buttress. Climb friable rock up the left arete of the wall. [M Crook 06.05.86]

▶ **45. Up the Garden Path HS 4a** 17m
The 'cleaned' line up the scabby wall just right of *Binwomen*. [16.06.89]

▶ **46. Billy Two Tokes E1 5b** 17m
To the right of *Up the Garden Path*. After a grubby start climb directly past the peg and bolt on creaking holds to the top.
[M Crook, N Craine 06.05.86]

30m further along the level is a whitish slab.

▶ **47. Youthslayer E3 5b** 20m
Ascend the narrow crack in the whitish slab and finish up a crack for 5m. 3 or 4 IMP/RP #1s might help to calm your nerves. Lower off.
[L Hardy, G Parfitt, S Anderson 05.05.86]

At the far end of the level there is a steep smooth slab.

▶ **48a. Harri Bach Llanrug F6a** * 18m
The left hand bolted line on the slab. Start by the obvious flake crack. 6 Bolts lead to a lower-off.
[I Lloyd-Jones, C Davies 12.11.09]

▶ **48. Put it on the Slate, Waiter E4 5c** * 20m
A sustained route with long reaches for small holds. 3 old pegs mark the line.
[C Allen, R Wright 18.06.89]

▶ **48b. Toe be or not Toe be.... F7b** * 12m
A fiercely technical number up the clean slab to the right of *Put it on the Slate, Waiter*. Execute a '*Poetry Pink*' style mantel to get established on the slab; easier climbing leads to the stopper *Time Bandit/Menai Vice* like crux (possibly British 6c) by the 4th bolt. [I Lloyd-Jones 21.10.09]

The Skyline Buttress Level • **Australia Upper 79**

The Oil Drum Glacier

Slateheads • Chris Davies and Phil Targett

Chris and Phil, often in the company of Ian Lloyd-Jones, climbed numerous new routes in the late 80s and early 90s. *The Australian, Tentative Decisions, The Burning* and *M.I.L Arete* stand out, but they really kicked into gear again in recent years; Phil was quick off the mark with a number of excellent modern style clip ups: *Atticus Finch* F6c, *The Fat Controller* F6b, *Steps of Escher* F6c and *Yossarian* F6b in Australia and the Never Never Land areas. While Chris stepped back into the ring, initially with a pair of 40m pitches (*Ruby Marlee meets Dr Holingsworth* F6a and *The Skyline Club* E2 5b/c) on Skyline Buttress. And then, at a tougher level, they came up with a pair of corkers on the Zippy Level and one on the Fruitbat Level - *Jepp The Knave* F7b+ (by Phil), and *The Beanstalk* F7a and *Slatebite* F7a (by Chris) may prove to be their best new routes yet!

Chris Davies, and below Phil Targett
photos: Lloyd-Jones collection

Australia Upper • The Gorbals Level

The Gorbals Level
There are good routes to be found here, although the rock is of variable quality. The level is reached by walking through the tunnel in the upper part of the Skyline Buttress.

A short distance onto the level there are 2 minor routes up the small slab either side of the low buried tunnel: a HVS and an E1; each have a single bolt.

The 1st significant routes are located on the obvious drainage streaked slab reached via short scramble up broken ground.

▶ **49a. Slab Rog F6b+** * 17m
A typical thin slate route tackling the clean slab left of *The Shining*. 5 bolts lead to a lower-off.
[I Lloyd-Jones 04.12.09]

▶ **49. The Shining VS 4c** 18m
The obvious diagonal groove is quite loose.
[C Allen, R Wright 18.06.89]

▶ **49b. Mister Blister F7a** * 17m
Another thin slab climb with good quality slate and some entertaining rockovers. The black streak to the right of *The Shining* marks the line; 4 bolts lead to a lower-off.
[I Lloyd-Jones, C Davies 10.04.10]

▶ **50. Men at Work E3 6a** ** 17m
Make a bold start to reach the 1st of 4 old bolts on the slab right of the black streak of *Mister Blister*. Continue with interest to the top.
[P Hawkins, C Parkin 20.04.86]

▶ **51. The North Face of the Aga E3 6a** * 18m
Another bold - and perhaps unnecessary - start leads to some open slab climbing. From the large flake head up rightwards to clip the bolt on route 52 (or if that seems a bit silly just start as for 52). Either way trend back left to a 2nd bolt and continue more directly past a final bolt.
[K Simpson, S Winstanley, C Stephenson, R Pink 01.04.89]

▶ **52. Unnamed E3 6a** 18m
A zig-zagging hybrid line squeezed in between *The North Face of the Aga* and *Sprint Finish*. Step onto the slab from the right and reach the 1st bolt; head left to the 2nd bolt on *The North Face of the Aga* before swerving back right to the top bolt on Sprint *Finish*. Move leftwards to a final independent bolt and finish with difficulty.

▶ **53. Sprint Finish F6a** * 16m
This climbs the slab 4m right of *The North Face of the Aga*. Trend up left then back right to finish. 3 bolts lead to a top out and bolt belay.
[C Allen, R Wright 18.06.89]

Ben Slack on the top arete of **See You Bruce** E3 5b
photo: Ray Wood

▶ **54. As Yet Unnamed F5b** 12m
The right hand side of the slab. 3 bolts lead to a top out and bolt belay.

▶ **55. Youthanasia E1 5b** 15m
The groove in the left arete of *The Gorbals* slab is reached by scrambling up a broken groove to the ledge on the shoulder. Climb up to a peg below a small roof. Move left and then up to some good wires, step up and go rightwards to the top. [M Podd, L Lovatt 17.07.89]

▶ **56. See You Bruce E3 5b** ✱✱ 30m
The left arete of *The Gorbals* slab makes for a heady trip; despite the 5 bolts and the generally good, albeit occasionally suspect, holds this has quite a bold feel. Start 4m left of the large embedded boulder. The lower slab leads to the ledge on the shoulder; step out right and follow the arete up to a lower-off.
[L Lovatt, M Podd, P Warsop 09.89]

▶ **57a. Glasgow Kiss F7b+** ✱✱ 28m
An intense sequency climb that strikes an independent line up the slab between *See You Bruce* and *The Gorbals*. Straightforward climbing up the lower slab eventually leads to a sustained technical section passing the top 4 bolts. Take plenty of quickdraws as there are 11 bolts to clip before the lower-off is reached.
[I Lloyd-Jones, S McGuiness 22.04.10]

▶ **57. The Gorbals E4 6a** ✱✱ 27m
The original line on the slab has been tamed somewhat by the appearance of some new bolts, but it remains a bold lead with much character. Start by the large embedded boulder. Climb directly up clipping the 1st bolt with a degree of relief and continuing past a 2nd bolt before moving diagonally right to a large ledge. Continue up leftwards to the final bolt before following a crack up towards the lower-off. [C Parkin, P Hawkins 25.04.86]

▶ **58. Black Daisies for the Bride E5 6b** 27m
A neglected line perhaps due for a revival? Start just left of the gully. Climb direct passing 3 bolts, moving leftwards into a faint crack at the 3rd bolt. Finish with a precarious mantelshelf. [P Doyle, C Smith, B Smith 10.08.93]

▶ **58a. Slabology F6c** ✱ 25m
The bolted line on the far right side of the slab should satisfy the slabaholic in the team, or failing that anybody who enjoys a good rockover. Climb out of the gully and follow the line of bolts (7 in total) to a lower-off.
[I Lloyd-Jones, S Beesley 11.03.10]

82 Australia Upper • The Gorbals Level

The next set of routes tackle the loose looking 2 tiered buttress to the right of The Gorbals Slab.

▶ **59. Tennent's Creek E2 5b** 33m
Follow the crack, with marginal protection, to the base of the upper tier. Finish up the top arête of *Fetzer*. [I Hassell, J Smithies 18.09.88]

▶ **60. Fetzer E2 5b** 33m
Start as for *Tennent's Creek*; after 2-3m trend right to clip the lone bolt, and then continue more directly to the ledge. Finish up the left hand arête passing a bolt on the way.
[I Hassell, J Smithies 18.09.88]

▶ **61. Franzia E2 5b** 33m
Start 1m to the left of the big flake that marks the start of *Turkey Trot* and climb direct to a sloping ledge and a bolt (shared with *Fetzer*); pass this to finish straight up. Top out to the next level via *Fetzer* or *Turkey Trot*.
[I Hassell, J Smithies 18.09.88]

▶ **62. Turkey Trot VS 4c** 33m
Start by the big flake. Follow the flake system up the middle of the of the bottom slab (poor protection). Then scramble across the 8m of scree to continue up an obvious blocky corner (which provides the 1st decent protection on the route), exiting left to finish. [P Williams 14.05.86]

The last route on this level, tackles the hidden wall rising from the edge of the Oil Drum Glacier.

▶ **63. A Swarm of Green Parrots VS 4c** 21m
A bold and no doubt loose route - proper esoterica! Climb the jagged crack to the highest point of the wall. [S Parker, R Ebbs 02.11.93]

Alice Springs Level

The level above The Gorbals Slab is a peaceful place. Although rarely visited these days it does have a few worthwhile routes.

▶ **64. Koala Bare HVS 4c** 20m
An indeterminate line just to the left of the centre of the stepped slab, situated just left of the *Men of Leisure* slab. Ascend the slab and finish up a shallow groove. [T Hodgson 39.11.87]

▶ **65. Men of Leisure E4 6a** ** 22m
An excellent pitch striking a line up the centre of the attractive triangular slab. Climb boldly (sky hook protection) up to the 1st bolt at 6m. Continue with difficulty to the 2nd bolt and run it out to the horizontal break which takes cams. Move out left before hand traversing back right to gain the lower-off.
[R Tompsett, P Dobbs, T Clements 28.09.93]

▶ **66. Flying Death Fin
(or is it Dutch?) HVS 4c** 20m
A serious pitch. Start at a thin crack just right of the unclimbed blocky groove which marks the right side of the *Men of Leisure* slab. Climb the crack and the flying arete above to join and finish as for *Goblin Party*. [26.11.87]

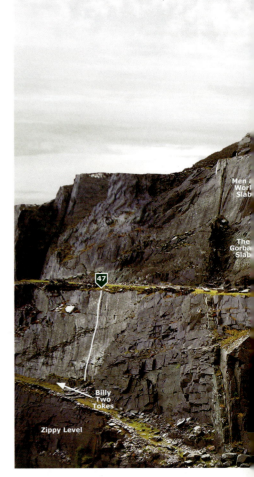

▶ **67. Captain Condom and
the Mothers of Prevention E3 6b** * 20m
A direct boulder problem start to *Flying Death Fin* which takes on the thin and technical challenge of the blunt arete just to the right. [N Harms 21.4.87]

▶ **68. Goblin Party VS 4b** 23m
The prominent dyke feature above the blast shelter gives an escapable but compelling route. There is only really one awkward move at about half height, but care should be taken with the rock which can be suspect in places.
[P Williams 10.05.86]

The final route (**Alice Springs E3 5c** 27m [D Holmes, E Wall 24.7.86]) was situated on a sweeping slab 50m beyond *Goblin Party*. Although it once gave its name to the level it has long since fallen down to join the scree below. A large but precarious looking roof remains - approach at your own peril!

The Gorbals Level • **Australia Upper 83**

Alice Springs Level

The Oil Drum Glacier

84 Australia Upper • The Darwin Level

The Darwin Level

Sitting at the top of the Oil Drum Glacier is the highest section of Australia. An atmospheric place to climb with a number of excellent routes and panoramic views across the valley.
To reach it turn off left from the Garret car park path and follow the ascending track through a number of zig-zags until it is possible to walk onto the level (15 minutes walk from the car park). For orientation purposes it is worth noting that there are 2 levels above (with no routes currently) before the open hill side of Elidir is reached.

The 1st route is found in the 1st bay encountered, to the right of the tunnel.

▶ **69. Another Wasted Journey E1 4c** 25m
Start on the right side of the large bay. Ascend the disposable arête, passing an iron spike runner. Belay well back on another spike.
[P Jenkinson, J McKim, G Howard 20.02.88]

Around the outcrop (or through the tunnel) is:

▶ **70. Easy Routes Can Have Bolts Too F5+** 10m
Wall to the right of the small through tunnel on the left as you enter the level proper. 2 bolts to a lower-off. [S Beal 31.03.07]

Further right a larger wall is seen.

▶ **71. Don't Look Back in Bangor E3 5b** ∗ 25m
An interesting excursion with a superb jamming section. Start below the right hand end of a large leftward sloping ledge with a big rock on it. Climb the pleasant corner/layback crack to the ledge and step left to below the left facing groove. Set off up this heading to the obvious blocky jugs below the hand crack; interesting moves into and up this lead to a small ledge below the final short corner. Good boulder belays behind wall.
[J Ratcliffe, S Franklin, A Scott 06.06.08]

▶ **72. A Room With a View F7b** ∗∗ 20m
A fine and intense clip up taking the line of weakness up the wall through an obvious rock scar. A French start allows access to a sustained, technical and pumpy lower wall. Execute the crux move left to a crack and move up to good holds below the rock scar. Finish by exiting rightwards out of the scar via a couple of long pulls. 7 bolts to a lower-off. [J Ratcliffe, R Lamey 14.06.08]

N.B There is an 'access' bolt on a small dolorite block above the next wall.

▶ **73. The Faffer E6 6b** ∗∗ 16m
A superb and forceful route tackling the obvious diagonal crack on the left hand side of the wall; well protected, but F7b+ish climbing. The lower half is both desperate and sequency and includes a crucial and hard to place small wire. At the break there is a slight easing and the gear improves. Lower off. [J Ratcliffe 11.06.08]

▶ **74. The Very Old and the Very New C2+/C3** ∗ 22m
A clean aid route taking the hairline crack to the left of *Wish You Were Here*. There are a couple of bolts to protect the fragile lower gear placements and a very thin finish. [S Beal 17.02.07]

▶ **75. Wish You Were Here F7c/+** ∗∗∗ 20m
An awesome route up the leftward facing flake line – a serious contender for the best clip up in the quarries. A hard bouldery start bars entry but above the difficulty kicks in again with a sustained and very powerful battle with the large flake feature. At 2/3rds height easier (i.e. F6cish) ground is reached. Run it out to the top lower-off and wipe that big smile off your face! The start is prone to seepage and a stick clip is useful for reaching the 1st bolt. [J Ratcliffe 31.03.07]

Jon Ratcliffe making three first ascents: **A Room with a View** F7b, **The Faffer** E6 6b and **Wish You Were Here** F7c/+ photos: Rob Lamey and Streaky Desroy

The Darwin Level • **Australia Upper 85**

Diary of a Slatehead

Instant Derek

At times various quarry areas were not only the preserve or focus for climbing activity, but also succumbed to sporadic quasi clandestine pilfering expeditions undertaken by opportunistic predators typically working in pairs, though solo excursions ingrained with the same planning and tenacity as a capsule style ascent on a big mountain were not uncommon. The booty in most instances was roofing slates which once removed from abandoned buildings enhanced a structural demise instigated years previously by constant exposure to bad weather, coupled with no maintenance. So that after being plundered by human locusts already derelict or semi derelict edifices although still extant, took on further skeletal aspect. Conceived under harsh economic imperatives such piracy succeeded since after the relatively easy roof stripping process aspiring black marketeers faced herculean weightlifting tasks followed by a sort of decathlon which often forced them to negotiate rusty barbed wire fences, unreliable slate inclines or dark hundred metre long tunnels, their uneven ankle turning floors immersed in water.

On one occasion I noticed a five strong gang which in distant profile appeared as a 19th century hunting party returning after an unsuccessful big game shoot since carriers at front and back were spanned three metres apart by a pole burdening their shoulders, which in quite different geographical locations at certain misguided times might have suspended a gazelle, onyx or lion. Close up and grainy, reality showed unemployed men, not without enterprise, staggering down hill, forlorn couriers in a handicapped raleigh team, their prize no more exotic than a solid pine beam the encumbrance of which they exchanged at intervals on the pitted track.

> These free market entrepreneurs seldom functioned in the lower quarries, preferring instead the relatively isolated and less publicly viewed areas in upper Dinorwig. Yet even here they maintained a cautious approach owing to the possible sudden appearance of 'Instant Derek', a local farmer who seemed to enjoy 'policing' the area in a generally unsuccessful attempt to discourage climbers and 'removal squads'. Thus laden it raised emergency levels to defcon six whenever he materialised, whilst climbers fared little better.

I first bumped into Derek during an early quarry sojourn in 1982, but as one of our crew answered his initial enquiry in Welsh, assumed that things would simmer down. They didn't. There followed an abrasive exchange conducted through North Walian Welsh which at times relies on certain Creole, the only part of which I could understand being 'bastard', pronounced: 'bastad', as if it were almost two words. Yet it seemed to me the conversation, although between intruders and a one man militia, was imbued with a certain gamesmanship which the social anthropologist Isabel Emmet observed in her book, A North Wales Village as long ago as 1964, as something common within many interactions whether or not they involved conflict.

An abrupt junction: traditional farmland meets the stark spoil heaps of the quarries on the Pen Garret track photo: Si Panton

Diary of a Slatehead

To the casual observer one thing that divided each party in this interlude, apart from an obvious age gap, was a conflicting garb which stood in so many ways to symbolize opposing positions. On the one hand, the ageing farmer, standing olive green cap in hand, white check shirt open at the neck, only visible because his 'Barbour thornproof' or a cheaper derivative, which all fall under the title 'wax jackets', was not fully buttoned. His kecks were dark grey and looked as if they had fallen from their initial lofty position as 'Sunday bests' before being demoted to comfortable slacks, thus ending up as work clothes. Completing this apparel in rural camouflage and peering out from lop sided one inch turn ups were blackened workman boots, worn with age and of the type made only for practical reasons: 'steel toes' and which if he'd been unfortunate enough to live in some parts of the United States, would have garnered him the title 'shitkicker'.

A collection of 80s climbing style gurus, including a young Stevie Haston
photo: Andy Newton

In contrast with Derek, whose attire suggested hard work and blended with an overall subdued tone common in slate quarries (until one explored them enough to become familiar with ever changing contrasts), Slateheads often stood out like easy targets on a shooting range or red crested grebes in mating plumage, though there was no one to attract and very little to command our choice of garb.

Nick for instance had a purple mohican so that whilst most of his head was shaved a three inch strip of hair ran from his neck over the crown before terminating abruptly above his forehead, giving the appearance of an upturned scrubbing brush with dyed purple bristles having been glued to his skull. A bum-starving black leather jacket with silver studs doubling as button fasteners furnished his torso setting off a gold cross ear ring and providing contrast with a set of leopard skin motifs tights before they disappeared tucked into ankle cuffs provided by a pair of twelve lace hole shiney Doc Martins 'airwair'.

Derek stood about five feet five, in a stance comparable with a chinese tai chi master, rooted on some imperceptible spot. Then all resemblance to those humble beings ended abruptly since his pallid round face topped with a bobby Charlton quiff was usually less than serene, whilst his general demeanour when confronting climbers either in the quarry or anywhere else near his land gave cause for concern since his usual greeting "What the hell do you think you're doing?" was uttered with such apparent malice that it was hard to respond without escalation into violent abuse, if only in a form of self defence.

Martin Crook

Australia East Braich

Style: Sport/trad
Aspect: North-West
Approach: 25-30 minutes
Altitude: 350-420m
OS Grid ref: 597 607

Far from the Madding Crowd	E4
Sylvanian Waters	E2

The Serpent Vein	F8b

Birthday Girl	F7b/+
Cirith Ungol	F7a+
Impact Zone	F7a
Road to Botany Bay	F7a

Walk This Way	F6c+
Wave Rock	F6c
G'Day Arete	F6c
Atticus Finch	F6c
Ride Like the Wind!	F6b+
To Infinity and Beyond!	F6b
The Koala Brothers	F6b
Hogiau Pen Garret	F6a+

The eastern wing of the immense cwm of Australia offers much quality and atmospheric climbing. It is also a good place to get away from it all; the steep approach stomp up the stairs of Cirith Ungol keeping most folk at bay. Most of the climbing is sport orientated, including one of the hardest routes in the quarries, *The Serpent Vein* F8b. There is of course the infamous *Buffer in a Crack House*, a 'classic' Martin Crook/Ray Kay XS adventure which may or may not have fallen down by the time you read this.

< James McHaffie on his own creation, **The Serpent Vein** F8b; an impressive and difficult route in the wildest of positions   photo: Gareth Aston

Slatehead • Ian Lloyd-Jones

Ian is perhaps 'the' most prolific new router that has ever operated in the quarries; only Cliff Phillips comes close to matching his output. During the early 90s he produced many new climbs, such as *Rhyfelwr* E2 5b, *Y Rybelwr* E4 6a, *Y Gwaedlyd* E4 6a and *Suspension of Disbelief* E4 6a.

More recently he spearheaded a frenetic wave of development, the like of which has not been seen since the heady days of the mid 80s. Stand out additions (so far) are: *Slabs R Us* F7b+, *Ziplock* F7b, *Plastic Soldier* F6a, *Cirith Ungol* F7a+, *Walk This Way* F6c+ and *Impact Zone* F7a.

Ian Lloyd-Jones on his own route **Ziplock** F7b, Australia Upper
photo: Chris Davies

Ian's connection with the quarries runs deeper than most as his grandfather, two of his great-grandfathers and his great-great-grandfather were quarrymen:

My great-great-grandfather Lewis Griffiths died in 1924 aged 70 whilst still working; he and another quarryman got blown over an edge in a quarry wagon. A huge funeral followed with hundreds of quarrymen attending. My great-grandfather, 'Harri Bach Llanrug', was apparently an expert Ropeman. He ran a team for many years on various levels, mainly lower Dinorwig I think. He was a respected quarryman training others; he was also a renowned musician/singer/conductor. He started at age 9 working for his education by making the school slates in exchange for lessons. He started formally as an apprentice at age 13 working a 6 day week until he was 67! He took on his son, my grandfather, as an apprentice, who also turned out to be a talented Ropeman (Rhaffwr). When the war came he was selected because of his climbing skills to go into the Engineers to build bridges (during the war he fell off one fracturing his spine)."

One would hope that Ian's forbears would approve of how the new generation have breathed life into this abandoned landscape. Aside from the fun and adventure aspect, the economic and social benefits of the latest slate boom cannot be underestimated. After all, visitors bring vital money, and by default, jobs to a deprived area. It seems quite fitting that the grandson of those who worked the quarries is now a key player in their revival.

˄ The quarry choir with Harri Bach Llanrug squatting at the front left of the group (circa 1920s). photo: Lloyd-Jones collection

˄ Harri Bach Llanrug and his son Rheinallt Roberts (Ian's grandfather) squatting in front of one of the quarry trains (circa 1930s). photo: Lloyd-Jones collection

Approach • **Australia East Braich**

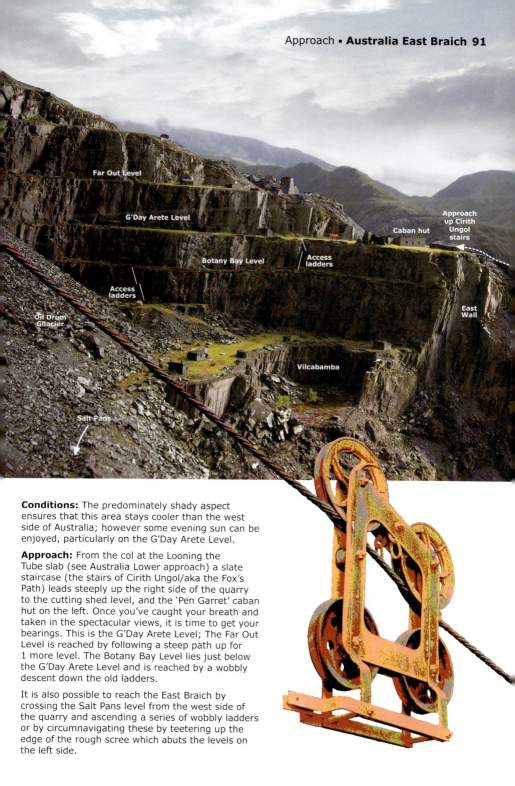

Conditions: The predominately shady aspect ensures that this area stays cooler than the west side of Australia; however some evening sun can be enjoyed, particularly on the G'Day Arete Level.

Approach: From the col at the Looning the Tube slab (see Australia Lower approach) a slate staircase (the stairs of Cirith Ungol/aka the Fox's Path) leads steeply up the right side of the quarry to the cutting shed level, and the 'Pen Garret' caban hut on the left. Once you've caught your breath and taken in the spectacular views, it is time to get your bearings. This is the G'Day Arete Level; The Far Out Level is reached by following a steep path up for 1 more level. The Botany Bay Level lies just below the G'Day Arete Level and is reached by a wobbly descent down the old ladders.

It is also possible to reach the East Braich by crossing the Salt Pans level from the west side of the quarry and ascending a series of wobbly ladders or by circumnavigating these by teetering up the edge of the rough scree which abuts the levels on the left side.

92 Australia East Braich • The Far Out Level • The G'Day Level

The Far Out Level
Peace and quiet is guaranteed on this remote level.

▶ **1. Atticus Finch F6c** * 20m
Climb the groove in the arete on the right hand side of the level. An easy stepped start leads to a unique finishing sequence best climbed like a duracell bunny. 4 bolts to a lower-off.
[P Targett, I Lloyd-Jones 04.05.08]

There is an unknown line just left of *Atticus Finch*, passing an old bolt low down and a peg higher up.

▶ **2. Cirith Ungol F7a+** ** 18m
Further along the level, just above a set of ladders leading up from the G'Day Arete Level, there is a prominent steep dolerite vein; this yields an intricate and sequency route. 5 bolts lead to a lower-off. [I Lloyd-Jones, P Targett 20.05.08]

The hanging groove left of *Cirith Ungol* is an old project line. The big slabby wall just to the left has 2 routes and a good V4/Font 6B+ left-to-right low level traverse finishing up to an obvious letterbox [Si Jones 05.10].

▶ **3. Ride Like the Wind! F6b+** * 30m
A sweeping line up the right side of the face. Follow *To Infinity and Beyond!* through its initial crux below the 2nd bolt, then continue rightwards and follow the line of 8 resin bolts to the lower-off.
[I Lloyd-Jones, P Targett 04.05.08]

▶ **4. To Infinity and Beyond! F6b** * 28m
A good pitch with a hard low crux and a thin headwall. Climb up and make a desperate move right beneath the 2nd bolt (which is very hard to clip). Continue up a flake line at a more steady standard until a series of thin moves lead to the lower-off. [I Lloyd-Jones, S Beesley 22.04.08]

▶ **5. The Curious Incident F6a+** 25m
The slabby side of the obvious arete left of *To Infinity and Beyond!* gives an awkward route. 7 bolts to a lower-off.
[I Lloyd-Jones, P Targett 02.05.08]

▶ **6. Far from the Madding Crowd E4 6a** * 23m
At the far end of the level, beyond the blast shelter and just past a pipe is a leaning wall. The striking layback flake on the right is a compelling but potentially fragile feature. Climb up just right of the ledge at the base of the main flake and rock up onto it (do not climb direct up the lower flake). Climb the flake crack to its top and finish up a short slab, moving slightly leftwards to a metal spike belay.
[P Jenkinson, P Hiscock 23.04.88]

The Far Out Level • The G'Day Level • **Australia East Braich** 93

The G'Day Arête Level

Aside from the fine climbing, this level has fantastic views across the quarry. It is also home to the Pen Garret hut; see the next page for more on this curious relic of life in the quarries.

▶ **7. Jack the Ripper** E4 6a 26m
Tackle the corner to the right of *G'Day Arete*, passing a peg on the way. [J Jackson 03.09.87]

▶ **8. G'Day Arete** F6c ✶✶✶ 26m
The clean cut 90 degree arête gives an excellent pitch. 6 bolts to a lower-off. [M Turner, C Goodey 24.8.87]

▶ **9. The Koala Brothers** F6b ✶ 25m
A dolerite route launching from the collapsing shed roof 30m left of *G'day Arete*. The start is the crux - go up and clip the 1st bolt then step back and climb up on the right - but the top section is also tricky. 8 bolts to a lower-off. The roof is unstable so be careful where you stand when accessing the route. [J Ball 19.05.08]

▶ **10. Hogiau Pen Garret** F6a+ ✶ 25m
The obvious line just right of the rusty pipe and cable with a hard move in the groove and more trickyness above 8 bolts to a lower-off. [I Lloyd-Jones, P Targett 21.04.08]

▶ **11. Walk This Way** F6c+ ✶✶ 20m
The narrow shield of clean rock gives a superb intricate route. Make tricky/reachy moves up the shallow groove to gain the ledge above. Foot traverse across the face using tiny but positive handholds for balance, a better hold and a precarious stride gains the arête. Continue up the slab with some tricky moves at first, but then easing to gain the lower-off above. [I Lloyd-Jones, S Beesley 02.06.08]

Jon Ratcliffe and Andy Scott on **The Koala Brothers** F6b photo: Si Panton

The Botany Bay Level

The narrow level below the G'day Arete Level has several excellent routes reached by (carefully) descending the wobbly ladders.

▶ **12. Birthday Girl F7b/+** ∗ 12m
The narrow flake line up the wall right of descent ladders provides an intense route with a desperate crux which may be easier for the tall. Lower off. [J Ratcliffe 16.03.2010]

▶ **13. The Garret Slide F4** 12m
The obvious slabby feature 15m left (facing in) of the descent ladders. The crux arrives at half height when the line of helpful footholds fades away for a few metres. 7 bolts lead to a lower-off/belay. [I Lloyd-Jones 29.01.09]

▶ **14. Sylvanian Waters E2 5c** ∗∗ 20m
15m further left of *Snakes and Ladders* is an obvious wavy slab. Climb direct to the 1st bolt and make a hard move left to the 2nd bolt. Continue up the natural line passing a 3rd bolt on the way to the top. Belay well back.
[M Wells, C Davies 23.06.93]

▶ **15. Wave Rock F6c** ∗∗ 16m
30m further left of *Sylvanian Waters* is a prominent buttress. The attractive 'Wave' feature on the front gives a fine route. 7 bolts to a lower-off. [I Lloyd-Jones 21.02.09]

▶ **16. Impact Zone F7a** ∗∗ 16m
A technically interesting and sustained route on good rock. Follow *Wave Rock* to the 4th bolt before breaking left out of the groove; follow the line of bolts to a lower-off.
[I Lloyd-Jones, P Targett 06.03.09]

▶ **17. Road to Botany Bay F7a** ∗∗ 16m
Another hidden slate classic tackling the left arête of the buttress. 5 bolts to a lower-off.
[M Turner, C Goodey 24.8.87]

The Pen Garret hut on the G'Day Arete Level still has old boots and coats left behind from when the quarries were still worked. The 'Hogiau Pen Garret' inscription, which lists the names of a crew of local quarrymen, is slightly crowded out by more recent scratched name tags (see this chapter's opening spread graphic). Nonetheless the aura of times past remains in this remote Caban.
photo: Si Panton

The Botany Bay Level • **Australia East Braich** 95

13 — Access Ladders → ← Sylvanian Waters

12 — ← The Garret Slide

The East Wall

The big intimidating facet dropping down from the near end of the G'Day Arete Level is home to a couple of wild routes. 2 massive rock falls have rendered this section of the cliff much changed from its 80s form when *Daddy Rabbit* E4 5c was climbed. This was a stiff, dogleg crack pitch and apparently quite good. It is no more.

▶ **18. The Serpent Vein F8b** ★★★ 47m
A stunning pitch connecting 2 snaking dolerite veins on the leaning wall. Approach by a 5m abseil down to a belay below the cliff edge, then a further 30m abseil to a double bolt belay on a small ledge. It is also possible to reach the double bolt belay via a scary but technically straightforward pitch up a pillar (12m). Use the *Buffer in a Crackhouse* approach for this. The route overhangs gently all the way and has a desperate (i.e. V8/9/Font 7B/C) crux in the central section which leads into some easier, but still eminently 'fluffable' territory. It then finishes with a steadier (i.e. F7a+) groove leading to the top belay. [J McHaffie 04.07]

▶ **19. Buffer in a Crack House XS** 80m
An infamous Crook/Kay route that was once the only true chimney on Slate; it now presents the ultimate evidence of the fact that geological time is NOW! The chimney has opened up and is currently more of a canyon. On first acquaintance the route will have appeared to have fallen down, but this is not the case, it can still be climbed!
The approach is quite harrowing in itself, but here goes: skirt round the outside of *Where the Green Ants Dream*, and traverse across rightwards, treading as lightly as is possible.
P1 4b 40m Ascend the appalling looking cracked pillar and continue into the obvious cleft. Belay at the back of the gully, with a kevlar umbrella (essential to protect the poor belayer).
P2 5b 40m Bridge up the void to stacked blocks above (with a strong feeling of impending doom); undercut through the blocks with much trepidation to eventually make the final mantel onto steep scree. Scurry up this quicker than it scurries down (on to your belayer!) and belay on the toilet block above.
[M Crook, R Kay 09.98]

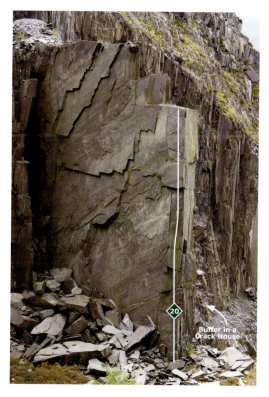

Vilcabamba
The bottom level has a single lonely route. It is best reached by descending and skirting down past the crevasse wall. The ladders are in a particularly dangerous state and should be avoided

▶ **20. Where the Green Ants Dream E5 6a** 15m
The obvious narrow prow provides a bold challenge. Climb the arete, easily at first, then boldly to a flat jug. Attain a standing position on the jug and continue up the arete to its top. Belaying is rather problematic and requires some lateral thinking. [E Stone 20.04.88]

G'Day Arete Level photo: Si Panton >

Dali's Hole Area

Style: Trad/sport
Aspect: Varied
Approach: 15 minutes
Altitude: 350m
OS grid ref: 595 605

100 Dali's Hole Area

Twm Dre (Monkey on a Stick)	E6
Cuts like a Knife	E5
Yuk Hunter	E4
The Chiselling	E4
Stretch Class	E4
Holy, Holy, Holy	E2
Dali Mirror	E2
Grandad's Rib	E2
Making Plans for Nigel	E1
Coy Mistress	E1
Mu Hat Mu Ganja	E1
Launching Pad	E1
At the Cost of a Rope	E1
John Verybiglongwords	E1
Le Cochon	HVS
Medicine Show	HVS
Zambesi	VS
Con Quista Dors	F7b
Mfecane	F7b
Return of the Visitor	[E5] F7a+
Escape from Coldbitz	F6c+
Minder	F6c+
Her Indoors	F6c
The Telescopic Stem Master	F6b+
Harvey's Brassed off Team	F6b
Tower of Laughter	F6b
Emerald Dyke	F4a

A fine selection of trad and sport climbs in an atmospheric location. In recent years the low grade sport routes on the Emerald Slab have become very popular, so much so that the landowners, First Hydro were prompted to erect a new security fence to discourage casual visitors accessing the area from the main path. There have been negotiations between the BMC and the landowner with a view to establishing a management agreement for the site – however as we go to press this has not been concluded. Please consult the BMC regional Access Database for an update on the situation before your visit.

The name, Dali's Hole, was inspired by the surreal dead tree quarry pool around which the walls and slabs of this crag are spread. The drainage into the pool was diverted a few years back; the net result being that the tide is out a lot more often these days.

Conditions: The open aspect ensures that the routes are generally quick drying. Access to routes in the hole itself are obviously affected by the water level which varies according to how much rain there has been.

Approach: From the turning circle by Bus Stop Quarry, walk into the quarries along the main track and pass a huge cutting shed on the left. Go left through the gate, heading towards the massive quarried cwm of Australia. The path turns right and drops down to a dip from which Dali's Hole is visible on the left. Since the second security fence was erected the recommended access lies back up at the apex of the bend in the path. On the other side of the 5 bar gate a path leads diagonally rightwards above the Holy, Holy, Holy Wall/Emerald Slab then up a slate staircase to Dali's Wall. From here it is possible to contour around and down past the California access tunnel to reach the other sections of the crag.

Dali's Hole Area 101

Dali's Hole Area • Dali's Wall

Dali's Wall
Not as popular as the other parts of Dali's Hole; nonetheless there are some good routes here. The first part of the wall is disappointing, but it soon increases in height and quality.

1. First and Last E1 6a 6m
The 1st (and perhaps least) route climbs a hanging flake up the short wall. Climb the short wall past a bolt to a lower-off. The top is quite shattered. [1992]

2. Hemulin E2 5c 11m
The attractive little open groove to the right is climb direct past a bolt to the top. [26.01.91]

3. Rock Video E2 6a 13m
The next groove along, 2m left of *Grandad's Rib*. There is a peg on the crux near the top.
[B Wayman, F Crook 11.10.86]

4. Grandad's Rib E2 5b * 15m
Ascend the obvious green rib passing a bolt low down. There are some nice moves on the upper section. [F Crook, B Wayman 11.10.86]

5. Coy Mistress E1 5c 15m
The wall just right of *Grandad's Rib* is very unstable at present. Climb onto a ledge and clip the bolt on *Grandad's Rib*. The V-slot above has recently got larger and threatens to get even larger. [B Wayman, F Crook 11.10.86]

6. The Dude in the Orange Hat XS 15m
An extremely unstable route tackling the V groove created by a rockfall (2006/7). Not recommended. [N Bradford 03.07]

7. Salvador 16m E5 6a
The groove to the right of the rockfall V groove may also be unstable. Climb the groove with protection on the right. There was a peg in the upper wall but this is now missing.
[B Wayman, F Crook 12.10.86]

8. Moth to the Flame E3 6b 16m
Start a little to the right of *Salvador*. Boulder up to a ledge, then follow the finger crack to the top. [A Woodward 06.11.87]

9. Dali Mirror E2 5c * 18m
The obvious system of open grooves in the arete 4m right of *Salvador*. Ascend the grooves past a bolt, with some interesting moves by the bolt, to gain another groove and then ledges.
[B Wayman, F Crook 12.10.86]

Dali's Wall • **Dali's Hole Area 103**

▶ **10. Dali Express E3 6a** 18m
The suspended groove right of *Dali Mirror*. Ascend the crack to a peg. Move left then back right to a ledge. Make a blind move to enter the groove, which eases towards the top.
[B Wayman, F Crook 12.10.86]

▶ **11. Dali's Dihedral E5 6b** * 18m
A serious and strenuous route up the deep groove/pod situated at the right side of the scree cone. Hard to start, then steadier on the middle section, and finally – as it should be – desperate to finish. [M Crook, J Tombs 28.03.87]

▶ **12. Return of the Visitor E5 6b** * 15m
The curving overlap/arch on the compact wall right of scree cone gives a good, intense route. Difficult moves past a bolt give access to the groove; move onto the wall on the right and ascend this past 2 bolts.
[P Hawkins, G Smith 22.02.87]

▶ **13. Cuts like a Knife E5 6a** * 14m
Climb the obvious finger crack right of *Return of the Visitor*, passing a peg on the way.
[B Wayman, J de Montjoye 12.10.86]

▶ **14. Making Plans for Nigel E1 5c** * 13m
A tough but reasonably protected route up the right hand crack. Ignore the bolt in the wall right of the *Cuts like a Knife* and instead gain the crack from the right. Hard moves up the crack lead to a shot hole thread. Scramble or abseil off.
[M Crook, J Tombs, M Boniface 21.03.87]

▶ **15. Con Quista Dors F7b** ** 23m
Quite a unique route for the quarries; well worth seeking out. It climbs the pillar of green dolerite up to the right of Dali's Wall. The wonderful world of friction is revisited! Follow the wandering line of bolts, via tenuous and technical moves up and out left to the arête. A steep and juggy finish leads to a lower-off.
[B Wayman, J De Montjoye 3.12.87]

▶ **16. Stretch Class E4 6a** * 23m
The hamstring-stretching groove to the right of *Con Quista Dors* is rather testing, especially for the inflexible. Climb the groove past 2 bolts and a peg to a lower-off.
[G Landless, B Wayman, M Rudolph, D Kirton 03.10.87]

104 Dali's Hole Area • Dali's Wall • Dali's Hole

Follow the level round, passing through a boulder strewn section, until a slippery path leads down to a lower level. The path (which leads to the access tunnel for California) rises up slightly and a small bolted slab is reached:

▶ **17. Slip Not F6a+** 7m
Take the left hand side of the slab. 3 bolts to a lower-off. [I Lloyd-Jones 16.11.07]

▶ **18. Why Knot? F6a+**
Start as for *Slip Not* to the 1st bolt; a further 2 bolts lead up the right hand side of the slab to a lower-off. [I Lloyd-Jones 16.11.07]

Contour across on the broken path, ignoring the tunnel entrance to California on the left and dropping down in front of a prominent arête, which is home to a pair of unstable looking routes which are best avoided in case they fall down.

▶ **19. Jex's Fumble Clipping Arete HVS 5a** 12m
The obvious arête with a couple of old bolts and a lower-off. [I Lloyd-Jones, C Jex, P Targett 19.05.91]

▶ **20. Dali's Lemming Ducklings E3 6b** 12m
Just to the right of *Jex's…* is a short hard crack. The route went up this to a good hold and then moved left onto the arête to finish up *Jex's…*
[I Lloyd-Jones 07.06.91]

Dali's Hole
When empty, the contorted trees at the base of the pool are reminiscent of Dali's famous surreal images. In dry periods the routes can be accessed by walking down a little gully close to the base of *Jex's…* If it is the monsoon season, some of the routes can be accessed by abseil; you can even indulge in a spot of deep water soloing if the right water depth occurs, just beware of submerged trees!

The 1st route starts below the roof to the right (facing in) of the descent.

▶ **21. A Good Slate Roof/Tribulation of Bob Marley and Peter Tosh E3 6a** * 15m
Climb the roof crack to a good hold on the left. Surmount the bulge and follow the crack up the wall to a ledge; move 3m right and follow a 2nd crack to the top. [R Newcombe, H Walmsley 06.89/M Boniface, A Shaw 03.09.88]

▶ **22. Mu Hat Mu Ganja E1 5b** * 12m
The corner/groove to the left of *Twm Dre* has 2 bolts. [M Boniface 04.89]

Dali's Hole • **Dali's Hole Area 105**

▶ **23. Twm Dre
(Monkey on a Stick) E6 6b** ∗ 12m
The rising groove line in the centre of the flat wall gives a hard route. [M Barnicott, W Wayman 10.86/ S Ohly, S Warren 2000]

The corner at the right of the flat wall yields a nameless and allegedly poor VS.

▶ **24. Le Cochon HVS 5b** ∗ 18m
This route tackles the obvious pinnacle, the top of which sits opposite the *Holy, Holy, Holy* wall. Move up past a bolt belay and continue up and rightwards to a ledge. The crack above has a hard move at its top. From the summit of the pinnacle drop down the far side and set up a belay on the *Holy, Holy, Holy* wall.
[A Maddison, J Martin 27.09.87]

▶ **25. Simion Street E2 5c** 15m
3m left of the prominent fin of *John Verybiglongwords* is a corner with a bolt belay to its left. Move up to the bolt then traverse right into the corner and climb it past another bolt with improving holds leading the way to the top.
[A Maddison, J Martin 27.09.87]

▶ **26. John Verybiglongwords E1 5a** ∗∗ 15m
The arete of the prominent rock razor protruding from the left wall of Dali's Hole is a 'must' for the aspiring stegophilist (*someone whose pastime is climbing the outside of buildings*); harder for the homunculus. Abseil to its foot, or approach across the quarry floor, water level permitting. Leave the ground and conciliate height, using a sequence of rugosities upon the very crest of the arete proper. At 12m, one is at a position to cogitate the internecine consequence of a plummet from the crux; this would induce a dire attack of schizophrenia, the reason for this being obvious during an ascent. The arete above facilitates an easy passage - a pretentious little pitch. (NB. This is the original Paul Williams description, kept alive as a tribute to the great man.) [P William, S Howe 06.10.86]

▶ **27. Velvet Walk VS 4c** 13m
Climb the twin cracks just to the right of *John Verybiglongwords*. Previously described as being "quite reasonable and with good climbing" – it is now mossy and neglected.
[A Maddison, J Martin 27.9.87]

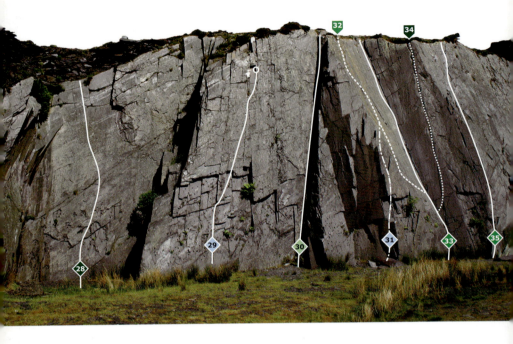

Holy, Holy, Holy Wall

The short walls and slabs situated just above and left of the hole have a high concentration of easier routes and are therefore an ideal introductory venue or for a quick hit. In recent years the addition of several low grade clip ups have proved to be extremely popular.
The base of the left side of the wall is peppered with drill holes which provide a curious musical instrument – try patting them with your open palm. Different holes give different notes, indeed they were used for John Redhead's 'soundscape' to his book *Soft Explosive, Hard Embrace*.

▶ **28. Andrei Chertov
(aka: Lob Scouse) E6 6b** 12m
This scary route is currently defunct because of the new security fence. It may, or may not be possible in the future, depending on what happens to the fence. Ascend to the drill rod, and then clip the bolt above. A long stretch leads to a hold; sprint to the top and whatever you do, don't fall off!
[A Woodward, C Stephenson D Dutton 10.89]

▶ **29. Escape from Coldbitz F6c+** ** 15m
The shot hole peppered wall left of *Zambesi* yields a fine route. Hard moves past the initial overlap lead into a harder side pull sequence on the upper wall. Lower off. [L Cottle, J Kelly 10.09]

▶ **30. Zambesi VS 4c** * 15m
A pleasant route up the obvious leaning corner. Take some large gear and save some energy for the strenuous finish. [T Taylor 05.06.86]

▶ **31. Harvey's Brassed Off Team F6b** * 15m
A tough little route retro bolted by mistake in 2008. Tackle the steep groove directly then continue up the arete to a lower-off. (AKA: *General Public*) [A Cummings, M Adams 01.10.88]

▶ **32. Launching Pad E1 5b** ** 15m
A good and popular route. Climb the left hand side of the slab left of *Holy, Holy, Holy*, with an awkward move to reach the 1st bolt and good climbing above.
[M Boniface 1988]

▶ **33. Holy, Holy, Holy E2 5c** *** 14m
A fine and sustained climb. The clean cut V groove might look about the same grade as *Zambezi*, but don't be fooled; this is a completely different proposition.
[C Phillips 28.05.84]

▶ **34. The Chiselling E4 6a** * 15m
Another intense route. Start up *Holy, Holy, Holy*, before making a hard move into the strenuous crack. Continue up the crack which eventually eases. [N Harms, M Anthoine 27.02.87]

Liam Desroy on the classic **Holy, Holy, Holy** E2 5c >
photo: Jethro Kiernan

When our coaches aren't working at the crag you will find them at the crag.

Our climbing coaches live and breathe climbing. They climb all day at work and when they finish work - they go climbing. They just love to climb. That's why they work at the National Mountain Centre and that's why they are so good at what they do.

But what makes them truly unique is their drive to share this love for their sport. They want others to discover and enjoy climbing and to develop their skills. They've spent their lives not only developing their climbing skills but improving their coaching skills too. So they know exactly how to help climbers climb better.

They understand how to enhance learning, how to build confidence, how to develop balance and body awareness and how to make sure the process is always enjoyable.

So when you choose a coach to help improve your climbing, make sure you select someone who is committed, experienced and passionate, not only about climbing but about coaching too.

For a free colour brochure e-mail brochure@pyb.co.uk or call 01690 720214 now.

PLAS Y BRENIN
Canolfan Fynydd Genedlaethol • The National Mountain Centre

www.pyb.co.uk

Plas y Brenin Capel Curig Conwy LL24 0ET Tel: 01690 720214 www.pyb.co.uk Email: info@pyb.co.uk

110 Dali's Hole Area • Emerald Slab

Emerald Slab
The green streaked slab is home to a collection of basic, albeit very popular, low grade sport routes.

▶ **35. At the Cost of a Rope E1 5b** * 15m
The arete/crack 2m to the right of *The Chiselling* gives a pleasant enough route. Step right at the top. [M Boniface 1988]

▶ **36. Le Gendre F6a+** * 14m
The 1st bolted line right of *At the Cost Of a Rope* is a cruxy affair. 5 bolts to a lower-off.
[R Spencer, C Goodey, K Goodey 01.06.07]

▶ **37. Mon Amie F5b** 14m
The 2nd bolted line is nice enough. 5 bolts to a lower-off. [C Goodey, C Wigley 05.06.07]

▶ **38. Tolerance F5b** 14m
The 3rd bolted line gives another pleasant route. 5 bolts to a lower-off.
[C Goodey, C Wigley 06.06.07]

▶ **39. Le Grandpere F5c** 14m
The 4th bolted line continues the theme of 'okayness'. 4 bolts to a lower-off.
[C Goodey, S Goodey 31.05.07]

▶ **40. Pour Tout le Monde F6a** 14m
The bolted line left of *Aliens...* gives a good technical climb. 5 bolts to a lower-off.
[M Simpkins, C Simpkins 12.06.07]

▶ **41. Aliens Stole My Bolt Kit/ Departure Lounge F3c** 12m
The blocky, diagonal ramp. 4 bolts to a lower-off. [Julia Widjaya, J Kelly, C Goodey 16.03.09]

▶ **42. Kinder Sport F4a** 10m
Climb up past the obvious ledge to a lower-off shared with *Emerald Dyke*.
[C Goodey 23.05.07]

▶ **43. Emerald Dyke F4a** 10m
Climb the green dolerite dyke on good holds. 2 bolts to a lower-off. [M Dicken 10.06]

▶ **44. La Grandmere F5b** 10m
Bolted line right of *Emerald Dyke*. 3 bolts to a lower-off. [S Goodey, C Goodey 23.05.07]

▶ **45. La Famille F4c** 9m
A very thin start leads past 2 bolts to easier climbing and a lower-off. [C Goodey, S Goodey 12.03.09]

▶ **46. Binky Bonk Central F4b** 9m
The main difficulty comes with a hard move low down. 2 bolts lead to a lower-off.
[J Widjaya, J Kelly 02.06.08]

▶ **47. My Wife's an Alien F5b** 9m
Climb the clean groove direct, passing 3 bolts to reach a lower-off. [J Widjaya, J Kelly 15.06.08]

▶ **48. Captain Slog F4c** 9m
The well cleaned groove just left of *Petit Pois*, moving left at the top to the same lower-off as *My Wife's an Alien*. [J Widjaya, J Kelly 23.06.08]

Emerald Slab • **Dali's Hole Area 111**

▶ **49. Le Petit Pois F6a/6a+** 10m
The black slab has a thin and technical start. 2 bolts lead to a lower-off.
[P Targett, I Lloyd-Jones 08.10.07]

▶ **50. Slate Arrivals F4c** 10m
Follow the slabby groove left of *Telescopic Stem Master*. 2 bolts lead to a lower-off. There is a harder (F5a) left hand variant clipping the same bolts. [J Widjaya, J Kelly 16.07.08]

▶ **51. The Telescopic Stem Master F6b/6c ∗∗** 6m
A tough little test piece and an essential tick for would-be slateheads. Climb the groove with difficulty to reach a lower-off. About V3/Font 6A+ in new money. There are actually 2 possible lines of attack. The true line keeps right of the bolts and accepts the challenge of the groove, whilst an easier version tackles the left arête.
[N Harms 28.02.87]

▶ **52. Aardman Productions F5c/6a** 10m
The wall just right of the tunnel grid has a hard start. 4 bolts lead to a lower-off.
[P Targett, T Hughes, S. McGuiness 24.10.07]

▶ **53. Tower of Laughter F6b ∗ 13m**
Another neat and cruxy route tackling the dolerite tower right of the tunnel mouth at the right side of the level. Climb the tower with a thin (i.e. British 6a) rockover by the 2nd bolt. Lower off. [I Lloyd-Jones, C Jex 19.07.91]

The Hidden Wall
Although in some respects this is an extension of the Emerald Slab area it is accessed from Dali's Wall area up above. Drop down the scree slope beneath the wall.

▶ **54. Immac Groove E2 6a** 8m
This route lies at the bottom of Hidden Wall on the edge of the lower pool level. Climb the obvious clean groove left of the groove/roof of *Mfecane* to arrive on the Emerald Slab level.
[C Davies, P Targett, C Stephenson 14.10.89]

▶ **55. Mfecane F7b** ∗∗ 22m
A rare and wonderful thing: a slate route with a roof crux, requiring a short burst of power. Ascend the technical corner to a breather below the roof. A difficult move around the lip leads to an absorbing wall. Lower off.
[D Dutton 09.09.93]

▶ **56. Her Indoors F6c** ∗∗ 15m
Up and right of *Mfecane* is a ledge beneath a compact slab. Move up the crack feature to the 1st bolt then trend up right to a 2nd bolt. Continue up directly passing a ledge, a 3rd bolt and a short wall to reach the lower-off.
[M Hardwick, M Barnicott, W Wayman 15.10.89]

▶ **57. Yuk Hunter E4 6a** ∗ 15m
The smooth corner to the right of *Her Indoors* is good but a bit reachy. A rude move from the pedestal guards the start.
[M Barnicott, T Taylor 20.11.86]

▶ **58. Minder F6c+** ∗∗ 17m
The arete right of *Yuk Hunter* is superb. Gain the 1st bolt to the left of the arête then swing round the arete to reach another bolt. Continue up past a 3rd bolt, stepping left onto the arête and finishing direct to the lower-off.
[W Wayman, M Barnicott, M Hardwick 10.86]

▶ **59. Arthur Dali E3 6b** 20m
A neglected route that once gave a problematic sequence up the central corner. Move up and right to a peg. Gain the good ledge above (peg). Climb the corner and right wall until a peg on the left can be reached. The route originally finished at an in situ sling – this has long since vanished. [M Barnicott, W Wayman 10.86]

▶ **60. Come off it Arfer VS 4c** 18m
Climb the prominent arete on the right-hand side of the wall, finishing slightly right at the top. [G Barnicott, M Barnicott 03.11.86]

Dali's Slab • The Hidden Wall • **Dali's Hole Area** 113

▶ **61. Rycott E3 5c** 15m
Another neglected, broken climb, which is somewhat loose. Start on the right hand side of the wall. Climb the obvious corner/groove capped by a tree. The original peg has disappeared. [M Barnicott, G Barnicott 03.11.86]

Dali's Slab
The small compact slab facing the California access tunnel has a few neat routes. It is best reached from Dali's Wall level by scrambling down the scree slope to its base. There is a double bolt belay on top of the fin.

▶ **62. Schmitt Hammer S** 13m
A poor, loose route. Start just right of the foot of the slab. Follow the vague crack all the way to the top of the fin. [19.04.87]

▶ **63. Medicine Show HVS 5b** ✶ 13m
A pleasant jaunt up the centre of the slab. Climb up past a bolt and continue up taking care with some friable rock high up.
[A Newton, K Griffiths, I MacMillan 19.04.88]

▶ **64. When the Wind Blows E3 6b [F7a]** 12m
A suitably intense affair. Climb directly up to the right hand bolt before heading up and right towards the 2nd bolt, making an obvious mantelshelf to clip it. Finish with difficult moves up the groove to the right, clipping another bolt on the way. [P Hawkins, A George 29.01.87]

▶ **65. Toad in Toad Hall E3 6b [hard F7a]** 10m
A direct version of *When the Wind Blows* has a thin and desperate crux. Climb directly up to the 2nd bolt on *When the Wind Blows* and continue as for the mother route. Side clip the 1st bolt if you want a safer outing.
[P Targett, C Stephenson 20.11.90]

⤴ Liam Desroy on the lower slab of **Her Indoors** F6c
photo: Jethro Kiernan

California

Style: Trad/sport
Aspect: Varied
Approach: 20 minutes
Altitude: 150m
OS Grid ref: 596 605

Route	Grade
Fruit of the Gloom	XS
Stairway to Silence	E7
The Big Sur	E6
Sombre Music	E6
Spider Pants	E6

Route	Grade
Wedlock Holiday	E5
The Hobbit	E5
Simply Peach	E5
Central Sadness	E5
Unpaid Bills	E5
Waves Of Inspiration	E5
Dwarf Shortage	E4
Esprit de Corpse	E4
Sad Old Red	E4
Shtimuli	E4
Primal Ice Cream	E3

Route	Grade
A Pair of Six	E2
Aultimers Groove	E2
Californian Arête	E1

Route	Grade
Tambourine Man	F8a

Route	Grade
Slabs 'R' Us	F7b+

Route	Grade
We No Speak Americano!	F6a

The magnificent walls of California have a distinctly secluded and atmospheric feel, bolstered in no small part by the fact that they are hidden from view and guarded by a double tunnel approach. Here lies some of the most impressive lines in the quarries. Indeed the magnificent California Wall routes are a must for any aspirant slatehead. There are also a number of hardcore aid routes which have seen little or no traffic since a minor aid climbing boom in the 90s. And last but not least, there is Tambourine Man F8a and Fruit of the Gloom XS; the former a desperate slabby groove, the latter, an alarmingly serious undertaking!

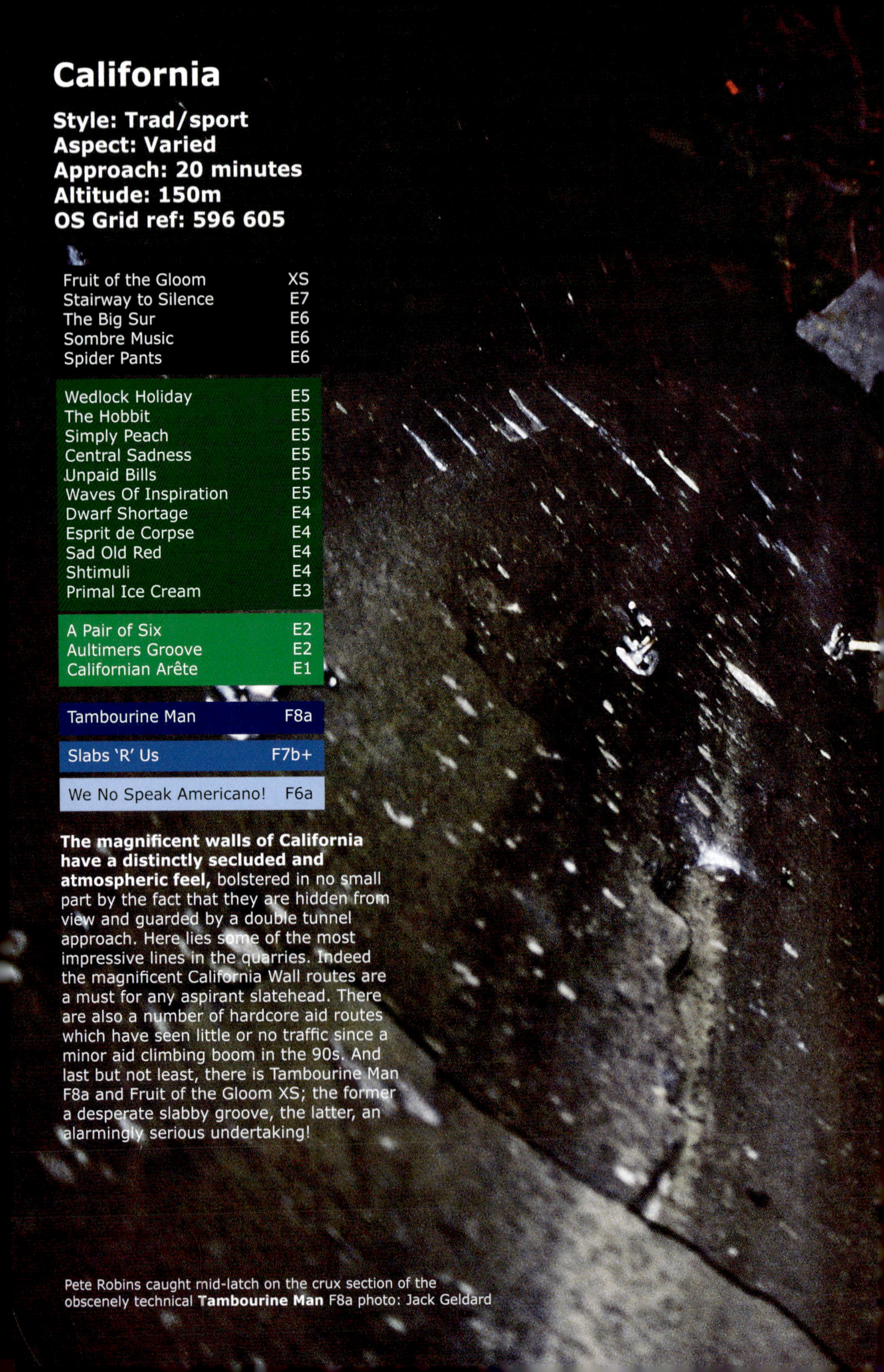

Pete Robins caught mid-latch on the crux section of the obscenely technical **Tambourine Man** F8a photo: Jack Geldard

116 California • Introduction

Conditions: The California Wall receives plenty of sun and dries quickly. The rest of the quarry is much more shady and consequently prone to dampness after rain.

Approach: From the turning circle by Bus Stop Quarry, walk into the quarries along the main track passing a large stripped out cutting shed on the left. Go left through the gate, viewing the massive quarried cwm of Australia above. 50m from the gate the track turns right and dips down hill; a gate is seen immediately on the left. Beyond this it is possible to walk diagonally right above the main Dali's Hole slab and round beneath Dali's Wall. Continue around to the right on the same level all the way to the opposite side of the Dali's Hole area. Here a quick drop down a skiddy path leads to a tunnel. Walk through the tunnel and exit carefully past a large chunk of slate partially blocking the exposed path. (NB. This is the infamous 'guillotine block' which used to sit above the tunnel mouth. In recent times it had been dropping down at a rate of about half an inch per annum! In late 2009 it finally parted company with the crag and dropped out!) You are now stood on a narrow path beneath the dank and green walls of an amphitheatre. A stream flows down into a dark cave below - this is the Entrance to Hades. The first few routes can be found in this bay. (For the main area of California, make your way through the next tunnel.)

The Hobbit Wall • California

▶ **1. New Rays from an Ancient Sun A4** 20m
A serious proposition, which is probably best soloed (i.e. only one person will die if the suspect shield of rock in the top groove pops off!!!). Move up from the mouth of the 1st tunnel and continue straight up the hairline crack and the groove above, passing the aforementioned shield of doom. Abseil off and go and have a long hard think about what you're doing with your life! [J Howel 1993]

▶ **2. Old Farts A3/4** 30m
Start on the level below the mouth of the the 1st tunnel on the right edge of the *Entrance to Hades* (which can be gained by walking through the 2nd tunnel and around to the left past *California Arete*). Gain and climb the thin crack line leading up to a dangerous top out onto grassy ledges on the right.
[D Williams, M Ryan 1998]

On the wall above the path linking the 2 tunnels a couple of futuristic looking lines catch the eye. At the left side of the wall is the 1st free route:

▶ **3. Ya Twisting Ma Melon Man E3 6a** 26m
Climb the large corner clipping 3 bolts and utilizing various natural placements (including a cam #1 and 3). At 20m step left and up into the loose and run out finishing groove of *The Sneaking*. Abseil off. [M Boniface, A Shaw 05.90]

▶ **4. The Sneaking E4 6a** 26m
Start right of *The Hobbit* flake crack at the base of a small pillar. Climb up the left side of the pillar to reach a bolt. Continue up and left past another bolt to reach a small overlap and a weaving groove just to the right. Enter the groove and climb up to a foot ledge. The final section to the top is quite run out and loose. Abseil off.
[J Barton, B Gregory 19.05.90]

▶ **5. The Hobbit E5 6b** ∗∗ 26m
A brilliant bolt protected line, taking the striking flake crack. Hard moves and a high step crux guard access to the flake crack. Once there, undercut and layaway with gusto to a double bolt belay. Abseil off.
[B Gregory, J Barton 20.05.90]

▶ **6. Happy Hooking A?** 26m
Follow the line of 5 bolts just left of *The Hobbit* flake crack to a lower off. All moves done on bat hooks; lots of fun and fall potential apparently.
[D Williams, M Ryan, M Hanford 1998]

▶ **7. NYQUIST A?** 26m
Follow *Happy Hooking* to the 4th bolt, then branch out left past a final bolt to reach a lower-off.
[D Williams, J Williams, G Middlehurst 1998]

∧ James Howel repeating (!) his own route, **New Rays from an Ancient Sun** A4 photo: Al Leary

The 2nd wet tunnel leads through into California proper.

▶ **8. Tambourine Man F8a** ∗∗ 22m
The slabby corner gives a brilliant technical test piece. Attack the lower corner, cranking through a succession of radical contortions, before following the line of weakness out right and up to a straightforward but glory-infused romp to the lower-off. [P Robins 16.04.07]

▶ **8a. We No Speak Americano! F6a** ∗ 30m
A pleasant route with an entertaining crux. Climb the blocky groove which leads up to the grassy ledge (possible belay, F5 to this point). Make a tricky move to leave the ledge before continuing up the imposing line of weakness. Surmounting an awkward bulge provides the rather unique crux. Lower-off. [C Lloyd-Jones (aged 8) lead P1, T Lloyd-Jones (aged 11) lead P2 27.08.10]

▶ **8b. A Pair of Six E2 5b** ∗ 35m
The obvious crack feature 8m right of *Tambourine Man* is a strong line; the climbing is not bad either. Head up past a bolt to the right hand side of the halfway ledge and a further bolt. Continue up the crack passing 2 more bolts and some wire placements. There is a tree belay and descent is via an abseil off the *California Arete* chain.
[C Davies, M Williams, I Lloyd-Jones 05.06.10]

▶ **9a. Slabs 'R' Us F7b+** ∗∗ 26m
The bolted line left of *Shtimuli* yields (surprise, surprise!) a thin and technical slab climb. Attack it using a combination of intricate holds which lead with much difficulty to the 3rd clip. Further enjoyable climbing leads to the 5th bolt where a bore hole provides a useful foothold aiding progress up and left to easier ground and the lower-off. Could well be harder than the given grade. [I Lloyd-Jones, S McGuinness 11.06.10]

▶ **9. Shtimuli E4 6a** ∗ 40m
The sharp arête is an alluring line, said to be easier for the tall (aren't they all?). Climb the arête on its left side passing 4 bolts and a #1.5 cam between the 1st and 2nd bolts.
[C Dale, A Dale, P Colquohoun 05.89]

▶ **10. Aultimers Groove E2 5c** ∗ 39m
The large, undulating groove just right of *Shtimuli* gives an absorbing route. Enter the groove steeply and continue via the slabby right wall to a rest ledge and bolt. Make hard moves above past a peg and bolt to reach a large ledge. Finish rightwards into *Californian Arete*.
[K Goodey, C Goodey 11.89]

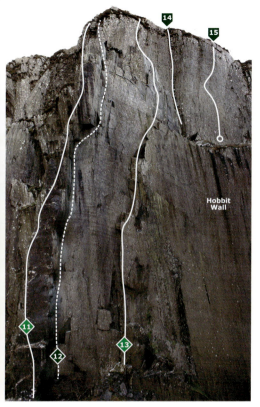

▶ **11. Californian Arête E1 4c ✶✶✶** 42m
The eye catching pillar with a blast shelter running through its base gives one of the most famous routes in the quarries. A classic frightener with fairly straightforward climbing but an alarming lack of protection. Ascend the left side of the pillar; at 15m height pull back round onto the front of the pillar. Continue to the top more easily, albeit with an ever present sense of isolation. From the bolt belay either make an abseil retreat or perform a careful scramble off left across heathery ledges. Pass a bad step (some stay roped for this) and continue around beneath the blunt rib of *The Whale's Tail* HVS 4c [C Muskett, S Ridgeway, E Wyn 19.05.10] to a hidden tunnel from which leads out to the upper part of the Serengeti area.
[C Phillips 16.06.84]

▶ **12. Wedlock Holiday E5 6b/c ✶✶✶** 40m
The extraordinarily smooth groove marking the right edge of the *California Arete* pillar gives a stunning but somewhat testing pitch. The start is reached via the blast shelter/tunnel which runs through the base of the pillar. Climb the groove passing the 1st bolt with a hard move and continuing up to the small roof with much effort. It is possible to step left onto the arête here for a rest. Once recovered head up rightwards past a bolt and make a desperate move to a ledge. Continue more easily past a final bolt to the top. [G McMahon, C Dale 17.07.89]

▶ **13. Classy Situations E2 5a** 39m
A thrilling but rather serious route tackling the groove line 5m right of *Californian Arete*. A few easy moves, then a technical move gain a better situation. Stay in the groove line, which gives good climbing, and then finish via some well-spaced and airy ledges up the pinnacles at the top. [C Phillips 16.06.84]

▶ **14. Pitch Two E4 6b** 18m
As the name suggests, the shallow groove in the upper tier can be linked with an ascent of any one of a number of routes; failing that, just abseil in from the double bolt belay at the top. The groove is predictably desperate; 3 bolts and a peg protect. [C Parkin, G Smith 21.03.87]

▶ **15. Midnight Flier E5 6b** 18m
Another neglected line, this time with no in situ gear save the bolt belay at the start. Ascend the flake line right of *Pitch Two* with care; thin slings and small wires might save your neck should the unthinkable happen.
[B Wayman, G Landless 12.08.87]

California Wall

A stunning sheet of rock home to a number of definitive slate classics. A 50m abseil descent is possible from the chains at the top of *Esprit de Corpse*. There are also 2 double bolt belays, the first being at the top of *Waves of Inspiration*, about 2m back from the edge near a little gully. The 2nd is on top of *Central Sadness* at the slate shed; there is one bolt inside and one outside.

▶ 16. The Wooley (or won't he) Jumper E3 6a 30m
A loose approach pitch leads to a difficult crack line.
P1 4c 10m Ascend the chossy groove system until is possible to move right onto the wall. Step up to a ledge and a poor belay on suspect spikes and large cams.
P2 6a 20m Climb the crack line with difficulty until a hand traverse right allows a heathery exit.
[J Webb, M Boniface 1991]

▶ 17. Unpaid Bills E5 6b ** 42m
The magnificent greenstone pillar yields a great route with a pumpy finish.
P1 6a 18m Start on the left hand side of the dolerite pillar below a thin crack. Climb the thin crack, with a hard move at the bottom to a groove, climb the groove and thin cracks above past a bolt to a double bolt belay on a ledge. (E3 6a)
P2 6b 24m Climb the steep wall above, trending slightly right to climb the left hand side of the arete at first past 2 bolts, climb back left into the centre of the wall at its steepest point past a bolt, via some quartz pockets to a large, often damp pocket, leave the pocket with difficulty (crux) to an easy finish. (F7a)
[*Big Greenie*: J Silvester, C Dale 09.04.86/ J Barton, B Sheen 11.06.94]

▶ 18. Primal Ice Cream E3 5b * 45m
The large right facing corner gives a bold climb with some run out 5a territory in its upper section and a memorable mantel out right onto a jug near the top.
[C Dale, J Silvester 10.04.86]

The following 5 routes start from the ledge system gained by climbing the chain (about HVS!) which hangs from the tunnel.

▶ **19. Esprit de Corpse E4 6b** ✶✶ 30m
A superb finger crack is gained from the tunnel. Exit the tunnel by its left edge to join the crack which provides a sustained tussle.
[J Silvester, C Dale 12.04.86]

▶ **20. Simply Peach E5 6b** ✶✶ 28m
A sustained and strenuous route tackling the wall right of *Esprit de Corpse*. Start on a ledge just right of the tunnel. Follow a thin crack past a bolt then move up right to a bolt (shared with *Sad Old Red*). Climb up and left to another bolt. Hard moves past this lead to better holds and the top.
[G Smith, C Parkin, D O'Dowd 21.09.86]

▶ **21. Sad Old Red E4 6a** ✶ 24m
The wall 'twixt *Simply Peach* and the corner of *The Mad Cap*, starting 5m left of the latter. Climb up to a bolt and then a flake before moving up past a 2nd bolt (shared with *Simply Peach*). Swerve right into a flake line at a small spike, and then finish left to the chains.
[C Parkin, G Smith 21.09.86]

▶ **22. The Mad Cap Laughs E3 6a** 45m
A loose start leads to interesting climbing above. Climb carefully up the lower open corner and enter the upper corner/groove which provides a sustained and technical finale. Take plenty of small wires. [C Dale, J Silvester 11.04.86]

▶ **23. Spider Pants E6 6b** ✶✶✶ 87m
A spectacular and sustained girdle of *California Wall*. Start just left of *Central Sadness* at the base of a thin groove.
P1 6b 30m Ascend the groove, passing 4 bolts on the way, until a flat ledge and a 5th bolt is reached. Traverse right to the belay on *Central Sadness*.
P2 5c 12m Follow *Central Sadness* to the perched block.
P3 6b 45m Traverse right to the bolt runner on *Sombre Music* and go up for 3m to gain more protection. Drop back down then head rightwards past a bolt into *The Big Sur*. Move up to clip a bolt and have a quick rest before dropping back again and traversing across right underneath a small roof to gain jugs and a bolt on *Waves of Inspiration*. Follow *Waves...* right for 3m, then up until 6m below the top when it is possible to finish rightwards on large ledges.
[G Smith, D O'Dowd 20.05.87]

▶ **24. Central Sadness E5 6a** ✶✶✶ 66m
One of the best E5s in the quarries, with a rather bold initial pitch and a stunning 2nd which follows an immaculate crack system.
P1 6a 30m Start at the obvious crack left of the bolted line of *Dwarf Shortage*. Climb the crack with some difficulty and continue up on insecure ground to a wobbly spike runner. Climb the bold wall above to the ledge and bolt belay.

P2 6a 36m Step left and trend up and right to join the long, sustained crack. Follow this to an easier hand crack on the right to finish.
[J Silvester, C Dale 05.05.86]

▶ **25. Sombre Music E6 6b** ✶✶ 39m
Another awesome lead from the Big G. Climb the thin crack left of *Waves of Inspiration* passing a cam 0.5 placement and a bolt before heading leftwards to a juggy break which leads left to another crack and good wires. Follow the crack past 2 more bolts to reach the bay. Scramble out the back to top out.
[G Smith, P Hawkins 12.04.87]

▶ **26. The Big Sur E6 6c** ✶✶✶ 45m
A dazzling pitch running the full height of the wall. A long reach is said to be useful. Start up *Waves of Inspiration*; at 6m move left to pass a bolt, and then make fierce moves to gain a key finger hold. Continue up with more difficulty to another bolt; step up and then move left to a good crack and a bolt. Climb the crack for 5m, clipping a bolt on the left, before committing to another series of hard moves out left to reach a large flat hold. Finish direct past a final bolt.
[G Smith, C Parkin 21.02.87]

▶ **27. Waves of Inspiration E5 6a** ✶✶✶ 45m
An old school slate classic and for once not too run out. It is still a big lead though, despite the 'reasonable' reputation. Start by scrambling up to a bolt belay on ledges up and right of *Central Sadness*. From 3m left of the belay, climb the diagonal crack then trend right up a curving crack to the crack proper passing 2 bolts. Traverse left and climb a flake to good holds and clip the next bolt. Traverse back right for 3m and head up passing another bolt en route. Follow a line of good flat holds and a thin crack to the top, clipping a peg on the left.
[C Parkin, P Hawkins, G Smith 04.08.86]

▶ **28. Stairway to Silence E7 6b** ✶✶✶ 42m
A stunning route of the highest calibre, perhaps best done in one epic pitch. Once again the long reach issue must be flagged up – this time though, the short may find it to be impossible (Now, there's a challenge!). Start by scrambling up ledges to a bolt and peg belay 15m right of *Waves of Inspiration*.
P1 6b 10m Move out left from the belay (sky-hook on right) and continue up leftwards to a large hole, then easier ground. Move up right to a bolt and cam #1.5 belay.
P2 6b 32m ascend to a jug (wire thread), rock over, then make a hard layaway move to a good hold and bolt. Climb up to the next break (sky-hook on the right and RP/IMP #1 on the left). Move up again to good holds which lead past another skyhook placement to reach ledges at the top. [G Smith, C Parkin 03.08.86]

122 California • Fruit of the Gloom

Slateheads • John Silvester and Chris Dale

Right of clean sweep of California Wall the crag hangs a right and changes in character. This back wall of the quarry has a blocky and unstable appearance. Thus far it has escaped the attention of the new routers, save for one daring breach up on the right side. Here there is a hidden chimney reached via an alarming scramble up some extremely rickety terrain to a belay ledge on the right.

Another prolific slate partnership, who were the first to venture onto the huge and imposing California Wall, their best addition being the ultra-classic **Central Sadness** E5 6a taking the striking finger crack in the middle of the wall. John originally discovered the Rainbow Slab and staked a claim on the incredible 'rainbow' feature. Mark Lynden nipped in and climbed the first few routes, while Redhead and Towse grabbed **Poetry Pink**. The next day John made a bold lead of **The Rainbow of Recalcitrance** E6 6b with Mark Lynden. Aesthetically, this route is unrivalled anywhere in the quarries.

Together Chris and John found another amazing line, **Prometheus Unbound** E6 6c; a wild and exposed arête hidden away in Mordor. Chris went on to produce a number of bold solos on the Rainbow Walls and in Vivian, including the terminal **Love Minus Zero** E6 6a. Amongst other impressive exploits, **The Bone People** E4 6a in Gideon is an esoteric classic well worth seeking out.

John subsequently abandoned his climbing exploits in favour of cutting edge paragliding; Chris worked for many years as a British Mountain Guide based in the Lakes, but sadly died of cancer early 2011.

▶ **29. Fruit of the Gloom XS ★★**
A compelling but ultimately crazy proposition. From the belay ledge traverse left across a series of loose ledges to reach the base of the evil fissure. Shuffle up this until terra firma is reached and with it an overwhelming sense of relief. After you've calmed down a bit, spare a thought for your poor second, who's true horrors are just about to begin. [W Perrin, D Rudkin 2000]

▶ **30. The California Express F3+** 10m
An easy route linking California with Serengeti, which is also useful in reverse as an approach into California. After exiting the 2nd tunnel ascend the scree path upwards, and then head back right along a vegetated level between 2 trees (one of which was planted as a memorial for Will Perrin). From the top of the slate steps climb the arete following 4 bolts to a mantel finish and twin bolt chained belay on the shelf above. The tunnel to the left leads onto the Serengeti Level. [H Gilbert, S Ratcliffe 10.06.08]

Big Jim Jewell making an early repeat of **Central Sadness** E5 6a photo: Paul Williams
John Silvester cleaning **Central Sadness** prior to the first ascent photo: Nicky Thomas
< Chris Dale sporting war paint for John Redhead's 'Shaft of the Dead Man' film project at North Stack, Gogarth photo: Martin Crook

Serengeti

Style: Trad/sport
Aspect: Varied
Approach: 20 minutes
Altitude: 200m
OS Grid ref: 565 608

Leo Houlding making the first onsight ascent of **My Halo** E7 6b in 1999 photo: Ray Wood

126 Serengeti • Introduction • Approach

My Halo	E7
Windows of Perception	E6
The Book of Brilliant Things	E5
Out of Africa	E5
Tentative Decisions	E4
Slug Club Special	E4
Balance of Power	E4
Remain in Light	E4
Short Staircase to the Stars	E3
The Great Curve	E2
Slippery People	E2
The Stick Up	E2
Seams the Same	E1
Neat Arête	VS
Seamstress	VS
The Medium	F8a
Nick the Chisel	F7b
Heading the Shot	F7a+
Y Gwaedlyd	F7a
Sans Chisel variation	F6b
Peter Pan	F6a+

One of the most popular areas in the quarries and understandably so given the numerous excellent routes. The Seamstress Slab is home to several classic test pieces and, in the shape of its namesake, one of the best VSs on slate. Elsewhere on the level there is a diverse selection of absorbing routes, in fact something to suit most tastes and abilities.

Conditions: Both the Seamstress Slab and Yellow Wall catch lots of sun and dry quickly. The *Nick the Chisel* wall is shady and a bit lichenous, but on account of its aspect does afford some shelter in light showers. The only routes that suffer significantly from seepage are *Laund Arete* and those on the *Y Gwaedlyd* wall.

Approach: From the turning circle by Bus Stop Quarry, walk into the quarries along the main track passing a large disused factory unit on the left. Go left through the gate, and follow the track as it turns right and dips down hill to Dali's Hole (which is seen on the left). Continue along the track as it rises up hill; 100m after it flattens out a large circular air vent building can be seen just left of the track. A path on the left leads up the scree and out onto the Serengeti Level at the back edge of the Seamstress Slab butte. The 1st routes are situated on the right side of the level above the Never Never Land slab.

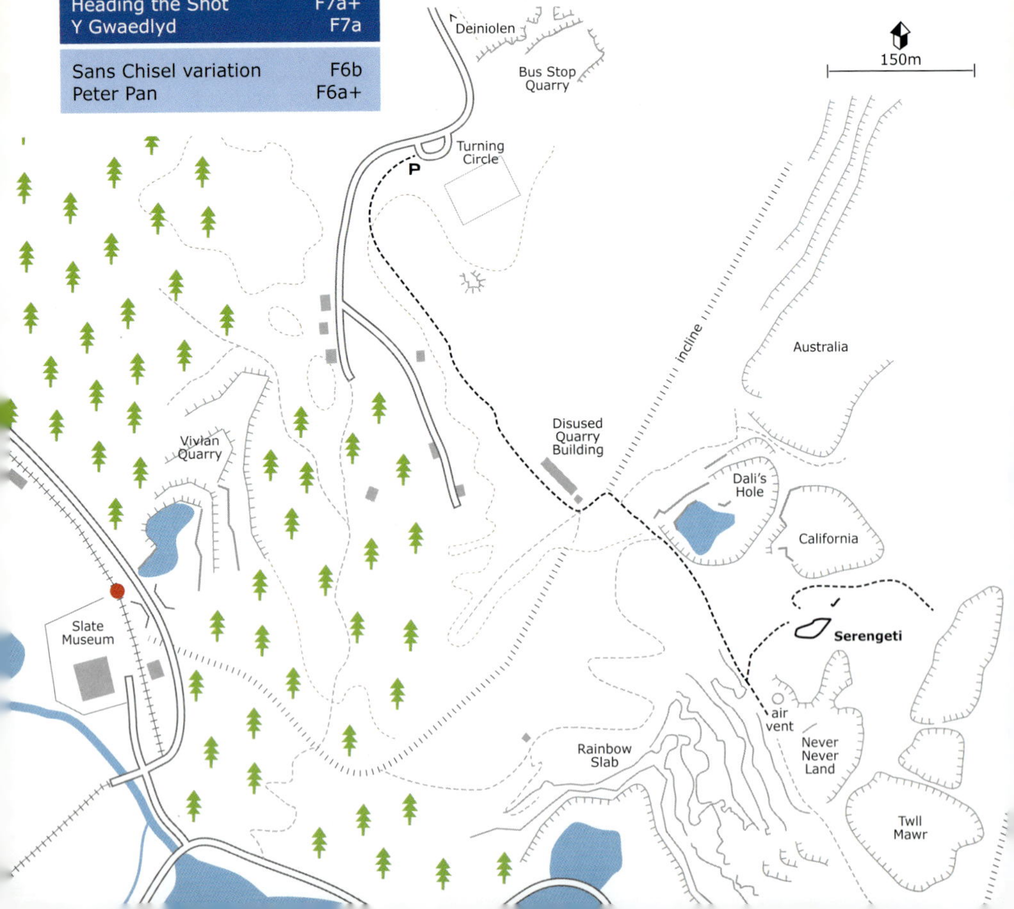

Peter Pan Wall

This wall abuts the right edge of the upper third of the main Never Never Land slab. The 1st route tackles the arete just right of Watch Me Wallaby Wank, Frank.

▶ **1. Unsexual E2 5a** 18m
A serious challenge - vintage Cliff Phillips in fact. Start at the foot of the arete and climb this bold and airy feature direct to the top.
[C Phillips 23.05.84]

▶ **2. Peter Pan F6a+ ✶✶** 18m
An excellent route with a baffling crux right where it should be, i.e. the top. Ascend the diagonal line of flakes that mark the edge of the smooth wall. If you don't find the hidden hold on the headwall take a F6b grade, but if you do then F6a+ seems more appropriate. It is possible to take an easier diversion out to the left arete and sneak up and round to the lower-off from the last bolt.
[M Crook, C Phillips 20.05.84]

▶ **3. Nick the Chisel F7b ✶** 18m
The blank wall right of Peter Pan gives a superb, bouldery test piece. Gain the porthole (hard for the short) and then make crux moves up to gain good holds - there are 2 distinct methods favouring the short or the tall climber. Continue more easily up the right edge of the smooth wall to the lower off, taking care not to fluff the final moves. Once given E5 6c, and now a sport grade, but perhaps most accurately described as a V6/Font 7A boulder problem with a F6b finish. Lower off. [T Hodgson 20.05.87]

▶ **4. Sans Chisel variation F6b ✶** 18m
An alternative start breaking out left from Hole in One allows the upper section of Nick the Chisel to be enjoyed. A good pitch with a crux at the top. [P Robins 09.06]

▶ **5. Hole in One VS 4c** 16m
A rather dirty route. Climb the rippled wall trending right up to a large step up a rib and into the V groove which leads to the top. The start is bold. [C Phillips 23.05.84]

Towards the right end of the wall are 3 short pitches.

▶ **6. Walking Pneumonia VS 5a** 11m
Climb the groove immediately left of Stick's Groove; it degenerates into broken ground after 7m. [C Phillips 08.06.84]

▶ **7. Stick's Groove VS 4b** 11m
Ascend the obvious clean-cut groove 12m right of Hole in One; the crack has recently been cleaned and will take a couple of nut placements. Sling and small cam belay. [N Walton 20.05.84]

▶ **8. Stuck up Fruhstuck E1 5c** 12m
Start at the groove just right of Stick's Groove. Enter the groove via some tricky moves from the rib on the right. [C Phillips 08.06.84]

SLATEHEADS CLIMBING

Guided climbing, coaching & new routing with local slate activist

Ian Lloyd-Jones
Cert Ed. APIOL SPA.
Masterclass Coach (Neil Gresham)

slateheads1@aol.com

Matt Rawlinson on the desperate crux of **Nick the Chisel** F7b photo: Si Panton

Seamstress Slab

The prominent butte is fronted by an attractive slab where several quarry classics can be found. The first routes tackle the steeper side wall round to the left.

▶ **9. Karabiner Cruise V4/Font6B** 6m
A neglected boulder problem marked by 2 decayed bolts. [P Targett 07.91]

▶ **10. Diagonal Dilemma F7b** 18m
Start up the wall left of the *No Problem* groove then swerve right and cross that route, heading diagonally rightwards along the thin, technical crack line into the finish of *Y Gwaedlyd*. (NB. Originally given E5 6c.)
[I Lloyd-Jones 07.91]

▶ **11. No Problem E4 6b** 12m
The steep diagonal groove yields a fierce little test piece. Climb up left passing 2 bolts to an easing at the top.
[I Lloyd-Jones 06.07.91]

▶ **12. Y Gwaedlyd F7a** ∗ 15m
A fine sustained route running right up to the highest point of the wall. Climb out of the small alcove and trend up left through the overlap, before veering rightwards up the head wall to the lower-off. [I Lloyd-Jones, E Jones 20.05.91]

▶ **13. Silent Homecoming E2 5c** 15m
An intense lower wall leads into a choice of lines connecting with the finish of *Neat Arete*. Climb boldly up to the 1st bolt; the most obvious line then continues up and slightly right to a juggy diagonal rail. Step back left to clip the 2nd bolt before traversing out to reach easier ground on the arête. It is also possible, and slightly harder, to move up directly past the 2nd bolt before traversing right to the arête.
[P Targett, I Lloyd-Jones 21.05.91]

▶ **14. Neat Arête VS 5b** ∗ 15m
A good route with a tough bouldery start up the undercut arête. A difficult move at 3m leads to a good hold; continue more easily to the top. The belay just over the lip is poor, but there is a block 10m back that can be slinged.
[C Philips 08.06.84]

▶ **15. Broken Memories E5 6a?** 15m
The bulge to the right of *Neat Arete* once sported a bolted line. The bolts and part of the cliff appear to have fallen down. [1989]

▶ **15a. Yorkshire VD VS 4a** 17m
A serious line up the blocky wall 4m left of *Balance of Power*. Scramble up to a shothole then continue up trending slightly left and staying away from loose rock on the right. [H Goodall 02.05.10]

The next route starts from just left hand arete of the Seamstress Slab proper.

▶ **16. Balance of Power E4 6a** * 18m
Better than it looks. Climb up to the 1st bolt and swing up to the arete. Continue up the arete clipping the bolt on *Out of Africa* on the way.
[C Davies, B Davies 29.12.89]

▶ **17. Out of Africa E5 6b** ** 18m
A fine but serious route. Climb up the slab right of the arete, moving inelegantly rightwards along the break before continuing up boldly to the bolt. Finish up the delicate groove.
[L Dutton, C Stephenson, S Winstanley 04.88]

▶ **18. The Book of Brilliant Things E5 6b** ** 45m
A majestic left-to-right sweep of the slab which gives much entertainment and not a little difficulty and boldness, especially if the spike on *Stack of Nude Books* is not lassoed before setting off. Start as for *Out of Africa* but keep going on the rising traverse line, passing the cracks of *Seamstress* and *Seams the Same* to clip the peg on *Windows*... Continue rightwards with an anxious moment or two before gratefully clipping bolt/s on *Heading the Shot*. Step out right again and finish up the arete of *The Stick Up*.
[G Hughes, I A Jones, M Roberts 5.4.86]

▶ **19. Slug Club Special E4 6a** ** 20m
A superb pitch which improves *Stack of Nude-books* with a direct finish. Start with a steady but nerve wracking solo up polished holds to reach the obvious metal spike. Some choose to lassoo this from below. Step left and continue up past a bolt with difficulty and then more steadily past a peg. [P Hawkins, R Caves 08.08.85]

▶ **20. Stack of Nude Books
Meets the Stick Man E4 6a** 20m
The original line is somewhat overshadowed by its direct finish. Follow *Slug Club Special* to the spike then escape right into *Seamstress*. [N Walton, M Crook 04.84]

▶ **21. Seamstress VS 4c** *** 20m
Your 1st slate lead? The left hand of the twin central cracks is nicely sustained with gear placements shaped to the exact profile of your rack. Popular and polished, but still good. [S Haston 06.83]

▶ **22. Seams the Same E1 5b** *** 20m
Another excellent and very popular line. The right hand crack is harder and more sustained than the left; the placements are obvious, but not as frequent. [S Haston 06.83]

An eliminate 'blinkers-on' line, **Seam Stress E5/6 5c/6a** [I Lloyd-Jones, S McGuiness 20.09.10] tackles the strip of rock between the 2 cracks.

Seamstress Slab • **Serengeti** 133

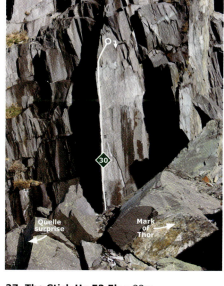

▶ **23. My Halo E7 6b ∗∗** 21m
The shallow groove to the right of *Seams the Same* makes for a very bold lead. Climb up into the groove and pass a poor micro wire placement as you pick your way carefully upwards. Finish rightwards into the top of *Windows...* (tricam useful in the shot hole). [N Dixon 05.87]

▶ **24. Windows of Perception E6 7a ∗∗** 23m
Bold, but comparatively speaking, easy (i.e. 6a) moves lead leftwards to a ledge and bolt. The next manouevre is the rockover to end all rockovers. You know a move is tough when you hear climbers talk about doing it in overlapping halves. The best training method is to sleep with your left leg over your shoulder. Once the peg is gained, carry on up the easier (6b) wall above (tricam useful in the shot hole). Worth F7c+ for the move alone but not really a sport route with only 1 bolt in 23m! [J Dawes 24.10.85]

▶ **25. The Medium F8a ∗∗∗** 23m
A fantastic technical exercise, sporting a sustained and excruciating crux. It follows a faint groove, with each move thinner than the last, culminating in a desperate step up for a 'jug' (i.e. a 9mm edge), followed by easier climbing to the top. [J Dawes 24.07.86]

▶ **26. Heading the Shot F7a+ ∗∗∗** 23m
A classic slate test piece. Thin and sustained climbing with the hardest section above the 2nd bolt. After the 3rd is clipped traverse left to a 4th bolt and finish direct to a lower-off. Given the spacing of the bolts, some might prefer an E5 tick. [S Haston, N Walton 08.84]

▶ **27. The Stick Up E2 5b ∗** 22m
The right arête of the Seamstress slab is a bold lead. Such is the dearth of obvious protection that before the first ascent Nick cut a slot in the arete with a hacksaw to take a sling! [N Walton 23.05.84]

The next routes are situated around the back of the butte.

▶ **28. Proliferation Bang On E3 6a** 16m
20m right of *The Stick Up* is a neglected and serious route. Start 2m right of the arete at a left facing layaway. Climb up on flat holds then move left to the arete. Follow the arete then move right across an apparently loose horizontal flake (keyed in?) and pull over to finish up the crack at the back. [C Phillips 08.06.84]

▶ **29. Proless Cliff's Arête E2 5b** 10m
Climb the prominent sharp arete, with some difficulty, but unsurprisingly – given the name – no protection. [C Phillips 23.05.84]

30m right of the Seamstress butte is a broken wall with a clean slabby ramp:

▶ **30a. Quelle Surprise F4c/5a ∗** 18m
The ramp gives a pleasant route guarded by a tricky start. Lower off. [C Goodey, S Goodey 16.08.10]

▶ **30. Laund Arête E4 6b** 12m
20m to the right is a short sharp arete with 2 bolts and a lower-off. [N Harms 02.04.87]

< Colin Goodey making the first ascent of **Quelle Surprise** F4c/5a photo: Si Panton

134 Serengeti • Mark of Thor • Yellow Wall

30m right of *Laund Arete*, directly opposite the Seamstress Slab there is:

▶ **31. Mark of Thor E3 6a** 15m
The prominent crack leading to a big ledge on the right. Another neglected and somewhat dirty line. The original lower-off/belay is long past its sell by date.
[N Walton, S Jones 20.12.91]

Further right on an airy ledge overlooking Never Never Land slab is a slabby greenstone pillar sporting 2 well positioned, low grade, clip ups.

▶ **32. Exploding Goats F4b/4c** 17m
From a bolt belay follow 4 bolts up to a double ring lower-off.
[M Dicken 1998]

▶ **33. All for One F4c/5a** 17m
Start 5m right of *Exploding Goats* and climb the clean green slabs with a tricky move past the 2nd bolt. Head out to the right on good holds to gain the crest of the arête which leads up on huge holds past a further 2 bolts and a peg to a lower-off.
[M Goodsmith, C Goodey, D Goodey 05.05.08]

Yellow Wall
An attractive wall which sits up and right of the Seamstress Slab is home to a good collection of routes. It is reached via a small hanging valley of scree situated behind the the Seamstress butte.

▶ **34. Short Staircase to the Stars E3 6a** * 18m
The direct start to the *Slippery People* has some creaky holds but is good nonetheless. Climb the left hand arete of the Yellow Wall on its right hand side to a bolt at 5m. Move up directly to clip the 2nd bolt of *Slippery People* and continue up this or the arete to the top. [L Dutton 10.89]

▶ **35. Slippery People E2 5c** ** 18m
An interesting and well protected route. The obvious groove on the left of the wall features a move that definitely punishes the shorter climbers. Lower off.
[P Hawkins, D Cuthbertson, J Silvester 11.04.86]

▶ **36. Tentative Decisions E4 6a** ** 18m
A well named route requiring commitment both above and below its lone bolt. The climbing is involved and rewarding, but never too desperate. Start just to the right of *Slippery People*, and climb up to a bolt then continue up the wall, trending slightly rightwards towards the top.
[C Davies, P Targett 23.12.89]

▶ **37. Loved by a Sneer E4 5c** 18m
Once upon a time an exceptionally bold proposition. It has since been vandalised into a more amenable state. Start 5m right of *Slippery People*. Climb up to a flake, then move up and right to go back left at 15m, easing towards the top.
[R Drury 24.04.86]

▶ **38. The Spirit Level E7 6b** 22m
An extremely bold proposition which offers succour for those still mourning the loss of *Loved by a Sneer's* original E7 status. Start to the right of *Loved by a Sneer* below a white streak. Climb directly towards an in-situ RURP?! at about half height. Move past this with difficulty; your next runner is a small IMP/RP at 19m.
[M Katz 1998]

▶ **39. The Great Curve E2 5b** * 23m
A good and slightly bold line. Start in the centre of the wall below a curving flake. Climb up and right to reach a good ledge and bolt at 5m. Step up to gain the curving flake and follow this up rightwards past a bolt to join *Long Distance Runner*, bolt. Step up, then back left to finish up a crack to a lower-off on the right.
[R Brookes, R Austin 20.02.87]

▶ **40. Remain in Light E4 6a** ** 22m
A fine route with a pushy upper section. Start below a ledge 2m right of *The Great Curve*. Gain the ledge at its left hand end, bolt, and follow *The Great Curve* flake to the next bolt. Forge a direct line up the wall passing a couple more bolts on the way. Lower off.
[R Austin, R Brookes 16.02.87]

▶ **41. Long Distance Runner E3 5c** 22m
Start about 5m left of the right hand corner of the wall. Ascend rightwards to ledges at 5m. Difficult moves gain a ledge, gear on the right; Continue up the wall past a bolt on *The Great Curve*, then head right past a bolt and up to the lower-off. [M Murray, R Austin 11.02.87]

photo: Ray Wood >

136 Diary of a Slatehead

Seige Tactics

"The industrial future of Snowdonia is undoubtedly a promising one, with its vast mineral and hydro electrical resources, its excellent railway system, its extensive anterial road developments, its Marconi wireless station. The land of Eryri appears to be entering a new era of prosperity"

R D Richards In the Mountains of Snowdonia ?
HRC and George A Lister 1925

By the early 1980s the above prediction had not in preceding years born fruition and despite having a hydro electric scheme that pumped water between Marchlyn and Llyn Peris providing input to the National Grid. Snowdonia, along with North Wales in general could hardly be described as a prosperous place to live either for heads engaged in rock climbing activity nor the general populace.

In 1951 Snowdonia became a National Park roughly, though not strictly encompassing coasts and crags from Snowdon to Cadair Idris whose outcrops, cliffs and cwms already contained much climbing history documented in climber's guidebooks beginning in 1909 with Archer Thompson's 'The Climbs of Lliwedd' after much encouragement from Geoffrey Winthrop Young.

Such hieroglyphics were interpreted by succeeding generations of climbers who, in time, began developing and extending climbing's orbit throughout the area. From the late 19th century until shortly after the Second World War this development continued at a leisurely pace and largely, though not exclusively, remained the preserve of middle class protagonists under the auspices of the Climbers' Club.

Until, as mentioned previously, an increase in availability and affordability of mechanised transport heralded working class inclusion. Yet it might be noted by students of climbing history that by the time slate came into vogue after the Rock and Ice, the Alpha males, the puzzle-me-quicks and rock athletes no longer held exploratory high moral ground that those in the vanguard far from, their even earlier antecedants lofty social stature as pontiffs, professionals and pedagogs was according to local disdain now championed by punks, puffs, piss artists and petty thieves.

Martin Crook and Nick Thomas perusing the 'stack of nudebooks' at the base of the Seamstress slab photo: Nick Walton

Killermangiro

In the Pad: "What's green and gets you drunk?" he would say, answer: a giro.

Yet to answer correctly could mean your round, since the initial question couched as it was in joke form also contained what lawyers call a leading question whose punchline remained best left delivered by original askers, lessening their opportunity to overwhelm hoodwinked aswererers with pleas to the bar. Thus in this context a simple 'dunno' would in fact suffice and this was especially so throughout Thursday evenings when the good, the bad and the lovely embraced on windfall nights.

Earlier that same morning they had eagerly anticipated the postal delivery, becoming at times pavlovianly expectant at the sound of approaching vehicles until calmed by the arrival of one bearing red and yellow insignia belonging to the mail service and known for obvious reasons as 'the Golden Hind'.
Such were our respective fates a few days or so before engaging a stint in Serengeti. The team comprised myself, the captain, Nick Thomas and Nick Walton and our first task involved retrieving my climbing rope from a premises in Clwt y Bont known as the house of Big T. It came to be there under circumstances far removed from any climbing action yet was borrowed in a social context that if graded on a rock climbing scale seemed to warrant at least E6 and had it seemed placed opposing factions in extreme difficulties.

Twenty four hours earlier JR and I had visited Big T on account of a proposed black market roofing job with which we required some assistance only to learn that for two nights previously his house had been under siege so that the terrace had taken on the form of a beleaguered enclave after dark.
The besiegers, an outfit known as the Hair Bear Bunch and including a character known as the Weirdhead, and the Space Invader had to all intents and purposes imposed a curfew under their own bizarre rules of engagement which if not directly analogous with medieval siege warfare (they did not, for example, catapult the corpses of decapitated victims over the wall) gave at least something of its flavour.
The dispute began in Deiniolen high street when the bunch, seeking a scapegoat for an apparently missing wallet containing cash and a small amount of marijuana entered into a fray after confronting Big T on the grounds that he'd been last to leave an impromptu weekend party hosted by one of their number, and after which the gear went missing.
Big T seemed an unlikely culprit, now approaching middle age with a young family, who in his youth claimed to have burgled famous actor David Niven as well as occasionally 'going over the pavement' (underworld argot for armed robbery). Yet such shenanigans were however well behind him and whatever the nuances, embellishments or otherwise of his former criminal career, he had clearly fried bigger fish, so that on the initial allegations, insulted by the pettiness inherent in the charge he had driven off after telling the accusers to get 'facking tooled up'. Whilst they in turn threatened to 'coum round later', further claiming that he had tried to run them over.

This, it would transpire they had done, yet their arsenal was not so powerful as Big T's who kept a squeezy liquid bottle containing hydrochloric acid on an easily accessible shelf above his front door whilst a broom handle (used as a kung fu staff) was also easily to hand. The borrowed climbing rope now formed a kind of cat's cradle behind the front window, which had been penetrated on the first night of the siege by a half brick.

Diary of a Slatehead

Killermangiro (cont'd...)

Their technique, he explained, was to launch an attack or attacks aimed at intimidation somewhere between the hours of ten at night and one o'clock in the morning by launching missiles at the front of the house, which being positioned a few feet from the road and well served by numerous escape routes, either on foot or by motorised transport leant itself vulnerable. Coming after dark such attacks also gave something of a covert nature to the altercation, which although enveloping the minds of the combatants, largely remained conducted without much neighbourly knowledge and therefore police intervention. Compounding the issue, the same evening had also seen an attack by an unknown assailant on an associate of Big T's known as Iron Horse who lived in a caravan a mile or so beyond Clwt y Bont located in a lonely farm setting. He (Iron Horse) had been roused by noises outside, gone to investigate, then caught a glimpse of a balaclavered, bullied up figure swinging at him with a baseball bat. The cudgel missed its mark as Horse shrieked in terror causing the the would be assassin to flee in the nocturnal confusion.

Bespectacled and bearded, Horse, who bore a striking resemblance to beat poet Allen Ginsberg, gained his local moniker from riding an old motorcycle, pillioned on occasion by the brave, the foolhardy or the insane. Horse however could not be certain that his punishment beating stemmed from his friendship with Big T or was the result of his involvement in a local love triangle, though nevertheless billeted at Big T's throughout the siege both to lend moral support and possibly avoid further ambush.

After an escalation in hostilities including episodes involving the firing of a crossbow and at least one of the bunch being anointed with dulux gloss in a manner akin to a disgruntled sleeper lobbing buckets of water over howling cats, the siege was broken by the intervention of the police, with both parties eventually succumbing to fines, but despite the smashing to pieces of a motorcycle (not Iron Horse's) with a sledgehammer, no custodial sentences. Only then was it possible to retrieve my climbing rope which after all had gone to a worthy or unworthy cause depending on individual perspective and for a short period did allow a remarkable pretext for borrowing a replacement so that instead of it being cut through by slate shards, jammed on abseil, stolen or simply lost, it was I could candidly appeal, 'being used in a siege' of the type more normally associated with armed insurgency rather than hanging in situ from top runners on some wind blown crag.

Leaving those engaged in localised soap operatics to their own devices, we finally headed for Dinorwig's dubious sanctuary only to enter into further dramatic events, this time of our own making.

> An ascent had been made up a unanimously striking feature forming a corner style crack, ominous in appearance, which could be accessed by crossing slate moraine rimming a sort of pipe filled crater opposite an as yet unclimbed slab (Never Never Land). Haston had done it with Mike (the Yob) Howard, who in breach of contract had described it, like its author as 'weirdly desperate'. They had protected it with chube chocks, but these had proved barely sufficient, rattling down the meat slicing fissure at regular intervals so that they could not be retrieved by the extremis laden leader who in a tour de force display eventually escaped incessant parallel sided torment at a cost estimated later as little more than a grazed knee. Nevertheless the grade reckoned at E6 swiftly heralded a reputation and provided slate with its first route at that standard, which if you could climb in the early 1980s meant you were pretty much lapping the pack; Fear of Rejection it was called.

Diary of a Slatehead

Sadly any pretensions to grandeur we may have had before attempting a possible second ascent soon gained prominence in future fairy tales when on close inspection the undertaking looked decidedly horrendous, even discounting technical difficulties so that a severe couched in similar aspect may have accounted the same disgruntled looks.

Fortunately fate smiled upon us leading to a road not taken yet no fear of rejection by sanctioning as if by demand a lightning soaked thunderstorm though even without its imposition democratic all in favour say 'I's decreed it time to retire to the nearest blast shelter where silhouetted against a magic camping gaz blue flame we made alternative plans. A tier above lay an excellent looking slab with two obvious thin crack lines, the right hand of which presented itself as obviously the most difficult though clearly not in the same vogue as 'Fear' which by now all hands had conveniently forgotten about, little assuming that in any case it was destined to fall down some time later, thereby exorcising it from route thought completely, except in a forlorn lament for what might have been.

Contented below the right hander and amazed at slate's fast drying properties, I lead off after realizing someone had already cleaned it (in fact Stevie Haston had made the first ascent a week previously: Seams the Same). I promptly came to a halt at a kind of overlap which seemed to exude technical difficulties which when tackled determinedly proved at first glance over-exaggerated by the mind's eye, yet in no sense could be described as easy.

> Nick Walton was already atop the left hand line (Seamstress) having despatched the second ascent with relative ease, pausing momentarily here and there whilst testing laminated flakes, some of which have stood the test of time.
> As I approached his belay leaden skies opened up again causing a panic stricken exit on my part thus avoiding any blemish in ascent caused by being trapped three metres from terra firma ending in inevitable top rope trauma. Seamstress now formed a natural gutter channelling water, aided with inclusion throughout its length by a now in situ 9mm, whilst Seams the Same faired little better.

Abandoning the enterprise once again about this time with crag besieged we stooped anarak hooded back through cutting shed portals as if in Crimewatch reconstruction yet our sole purpose was easily identified as nothing more than seeking shelter. To onlookers, if chancing upon the scene, it might appear that grappling hooks had been thrown aloft before fixing in crevices festooned with heather atop a steep smooth bastion twenty or so metres high, though why marauders were not yet swarming up ropes attached to them might remain a mystery, or at least a source for discussion.

In reality we had left fixed lines to give each second opportunity at climbing and cleaning both routes when next presented with a weather window, whilst for the next hour we ourselves remained under siege as if framed in advert for various types of cagoule. Clearly this form of embargo differed considerably from that embracing the house of Big T's, nor could it be compared with climbing reference to other tactics employed by those deliberately setting out to siege routes into submission with premeditated mandate for each climber to take over from the other's highpoint until the route succumbed.

> Thus with a realisation that the day had been played out under a procession trumpeted by sieges, seconds tied on with countenances expectant of bombardment from heavy rain before topping out triumphant in a final salute.

Martin Crook

Never Never Land

Style: Trad/sport
Aspect: Varied
Approach: 20 minutes
Altitude: 1-200m
OS Grid ref: 565 608

A **justifiably popular area** with numerous excellent routes. The main event of course is the huge glinting shield of the *Never Never Land* slab. The Monkey Bar Area, situated on the other side and down below the main quarry path, is also particularly worthwhile investigating, if only to experience the marvel that is *Patellaectomy*. There are also a number of superb modern additions here and a new dry tooling wall.

Conditions: The main slab catches lots of sun and dries very quickly. The harder routes in the Nuremburg area are prone to seepage, but the easier ones tend to be okay. Further right *The Carbon Stage* and *Gargoyle* do start to weep after rain, and downstairs in the shady Monkey Bar area there can be much seepage on *Shock the Monkey* and the dry tooling wall. The main wall here does not suffer from seepage, but can become green in the winter months.

The Machine in the Ghost	E5
Short Stories	E4
Scheherezade	[F7a+] E4
Igam-Ogam	E4
Watch Me Wallaby Wank, Frank	E4
Khubla Khan	E3/4

Dyke Rider	E2
Patellaectomy	E1
Squashing the Acropods	E1

Beyond the Pail	F7a
State of the Heart	F6c+
Pail Rider	F6c+
The Carbon Stage	F6c+
Steps of Escher	F6c
Penblwydd Hapus (i Fi)	F6c
A Little Pail	F6b+
Yossarian	F6b+
Home Run	F6a+
Tomb Raider	F6a+
Fresh Air	F6a
Hawkeye	F5c
362	F5c
Bambi	D9+
Ibex	D7+

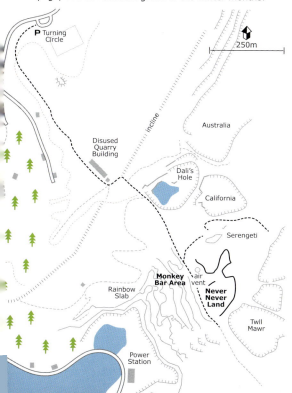

Approach: From the turning circle by Bus Stop Quarry, walk into the quarries along the main track passing a large disused factory unit on the left. Go left through the gate, and follow the track as it turns right and dips down hill to Dali's Hole (which is seen on the left). Continue along the track as it rises up hill; 100m after it flattens out a large circular air vent building can be seen just left of the track. The crag behind it is Nuremburg. 50m further on the impressive slab of *Never Never Land* swings into view.

< Rachael Barlow wrapped up warm for a mid winter ascent of **362** F5c photo: Pete Robins

Nuremburg

The Nuremburg area is so named because of the presence of an old concrete platform and scaffold pole frame situated by the side of the path leading up to the Serengeti Level. The passing resemblance of this structure to one of Hitler's podiums inspired the name. Another podium can be found at the top of the Dyke Rider wall in the Monkey Bar Area.

The 1st route is found at the far left of the level, 40m left of the ventilation tower and just below the path leading up to the Seamstress Slab level:

▶ **1. Hawkeye F5c** ∗ 20m
An enjoyable saunter on excellent rock. After a reachy crux on the lower section the difficulties ease, before a series of delightful, slopey scoops leads to a lower-off.
[I Lloyd-Jones, C Goodey 18.06.07]

15m to the right is the Nuremburg Slab, a narrow right facing facet with a trio of routes:

▶ **2. Fresh Air F6a** ∗ 20m
A pleasant sustained route taking a direct line 2m right of the arête to a lower off. The original route (*Breaking Wind* [J Tombs 26.02.86]) followed a similar line but finished up the left arête; the keen eyed will spot a rusty old bolt sleeve at half height. [C Goodey, K Goodey 19.07.07]

▶ **3. Hot Air Crack HVS 5b** 21m
The slab is split by a shattered crack and flake. Start as for *Fresh Air*, but traverse up and right into the crack and continue up via a scoop and thin semi-layback to finish.
[J Tombs, B Jones, N Jones 22.02.86]

▶ **3a. Swiss Air F6c** 20m
A thin technical crux leads to a blocky groove. Climb the slab via 2 bore holes and some thin crimps, and then continue up to gain the blocky groove which gives some interesting moves on the way to the lower-off.
[T Mueller, I Lloyd-Jones 06.03.11]

To the right of the Nuremburg Slab is an old project that attempted to climb the overhanging half pipe, the hangers are no longer there, but bolt heads and threads mark the proposed line of attack!

Nuremburg • **Never Never Land** 143

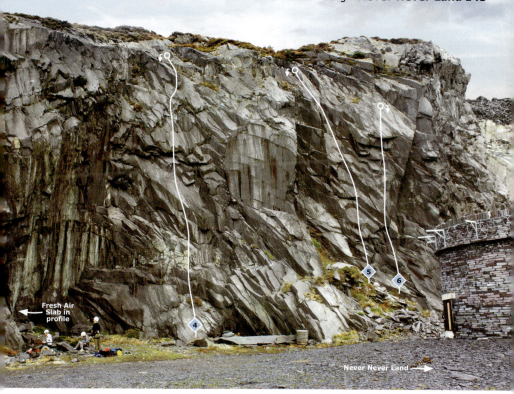

▶ **4. State of the Heart F6c+** ✶✶ 20m
An excellent pitch. The wall to the right of the project is featured with a series of interlocking mini slabs and overlaps; follow the bolts up with reachy crux moves through the main bulge/overlap. The run out to the last bolt can be reduced with a #1.5 cam. Use long quick draws and move right above last bolt to reach the lower-off. Shorter climbers may think F7a+.
[M Raine, M Dicken 22.03.08]

▶ **5. Yossarian F6b+** 18m
Be warned: there is a bold mantel at the top. In the next recess to the right: climb the overlapping slab between the 2 obvious arêtes, moving right to pass the 3rd bolt on layaways. Lower off.
[P Targett, I Lloyd-Jones 29.05.08]

▶ **6. Steps of Escher F6c** ✶✶ 16m
The hanging arete to the right of *Yossarian*. Pad up the black slab to the foot of the V groove. Swing up and left and follow the line of bolts to a lower off. Steep climbing on big holds which run out for the crux rockover through the top roof.
[P Targett, I Lloyd-Jones 14.06.08]

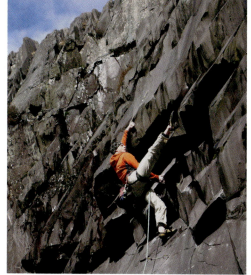

Mike Raine on the first ascent of **State of the Heart** F6c+   photo: Raine collection

144 Never Never Land • Never Never Land Slab

Never Never Land Slab

Further right, beyond a large complex section of rock, the impressive sweep of the main slab swings into view. The 1st routes start in the complex section at a short concrete coated slab:

▶ **7. Back in the Saddle F6b+** 18m
A tricky number with a hard crux. Start up the initial slab of *Tomb Raider*, but continue direct with difficulty, veering left into the hanging scoop. The easiest line of resistance moves out right to the large ledge before moving up to the belay. It is possible to force a line up the left side of the small roof, but thereafter the holds lead you back to the same place. Good climbing, just a shame the line wasn't more independent. It is probably best to use a single screwgate on the 3rd bolt to avoid the possibility of the rope cutting on a sharp edge. [C Davies, I Lloyd-Jones 28.05.09]

▶ **8. Tomb Raider F6a/6a+** * 40m
An entertaining and novel multi-pitch line.
P1 F5c 18m Climb the difficult slab just to the right of the decaying concrete veneer and continue up rightwards along the ledgey ramp to reach a ledge with bolt belays.
P2 F3a 10m Traverse right along Dandelion ledge to gain another airy perch on the far arête where there are bolt belays.
P3 F6a/6a+ 12m Climb directly up the corner to below the roof (2 bolts). Either climb directly over the roof (F6a+), or easier, move out left and up (bolt) to rejoin the corner. Continue up the delightful corner crack (3 bolts) to a good stance and bolt belays.
[C Goodey, S Goodey, B Williams 19.10.07]

▶ **9. Road to Nowhere VD** 45m
A pleasant but serious ramble on the stepped rib and corner, left of *Scheherezade*, finishing left of the tree. [J Tombs 26.2.86]

▶ **10. Rodent to Nowhere E1 5a** 42m
Climb the corner immediately left of the main slab (poor protection). Follow the ramp rightwards to the top bolt on *Igam Ogam*, then go back left and up the corner to the top. [05.04.92]

▶ **11. 362 F5c** * 25m
A great 2 pitch sport route. The name is a respectful reference to the number of quarrymen who died while working the Dinorwig Quarry.
P1 F5b 18m Start on the left hand side of the main slab on the arête. A tricky start leads to easier climbing following the line of bolts up the arête to a sloping ledge with a lower-off.
P2 F5c 7m Step up the steep wall behind the belay to a good ledge, rest and then make a powerful move up to gain better holds on the small arête. Finish by mantelling onto the belay ledge as for *Tomb Raider* P2. Make an abseil retreat, or finish as for *Tomb Raider*.
[B Williams, C Goodey 29.10.07]

Never Never Land Slab • **Never Never Land 145**

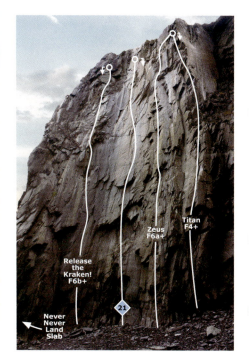

▶ **12. Piper at the Gates of Dawn E5 6b** 45m
An illogical girdle which wanders up and down as well as across the slab. It does provide plenty of pendulum (and perhaps deck out) potential. Follow *Scheherezade* to the 3rd bolt, move down and make some difficult moves to clip the 3rd bolt on *Machine in the Ghost*. Go back down and traverse easily to a good foothold, before moving up to lasso the spike on *Never Never Land*. Descend once more and traverse right to a groove and then a bolt. Continue rightwards for 10m to a large ledge and move up the manky groove to the belay ledge. [T Forster 03.08.89]

▶ **13. Scheherezade E4 6b [F7a/+]** ✶✶ 18m
A difficult and fingery lower section leads to slightly run out but easier finish. Lower off.
[N Harms, C Stephenson 11.88]

▶ **14. The Machine in the Ghost E5 6b** ✶✶ 18m
More thin and technical slab climbing; this time with a more spicy feel, despite having the same number of bolts as its neighbour with which it shares a lower-off. [A Woodward 10.8.86]

▶ **15. Never Never Land E5 6a** ✶✶✶ 42m
A splendid but bold route. An iron spike protects the crux, but only if you can put the repercussions of slipping onto it out of your mind. Start below the staggered overlaps in the centre of the wall and battle up and round them to gain the spike. The crux section above leads via a sustained finger flake to a rest and a wire. Continue up trending slightly left to an easing near the arete. A bold finish on large sloping holds and ledges awaits, so keep it steady. The belay is way back; reachable with 60m ropes.
[M Crook, N Walton, A Newton 02.84]

▶ **16. Khubla Khan E3/4 6b** ✶✶ 26m
A desperate, well protected crux and a runout, albeit steady, groove above combine to give an interesting, varied route. Climb the slab between the overlaps of *Never Never Land* and the bolts of *Short Stories*. The move above the bolt is hard, but can be circumnavigated on the left (slightly easier) and the upper reaches of the groove above can be protected by lassoing the spike. Finish on the ledge on the right (double bolt belay). [M Crook, A Newton 3.85]

▶ **17. Dark and Scary Stories E5 6b** is a good direct variant of *Kubla Khan*, low in the grade. Climb *Kubla Khan* up to the bolt, sprint up the slab via some bold climbing to reach the 3rd bolt of *Short Stories*, finish as for that route.
[C Muskett, T Pearson 09.09]

▶ **18. Short Stories E4 6a** ✶✶✶ 26m
An excellent, sustained route marked by the line of spaced bolts starting on the right of the slab before curving leftwards and upwards to the obvious ledge on the right. The very last bit is reachy. Bolt belay on the ledge.
[S Howe, S Harland 02.04.87]

▶ **19. Ghengis E6 6a** 26m
A once good but now very dangerous route since a crucial peg and flake departed. Follow *Short Stories* to its 1st bolt then head up right to where the flake and peg used to be. Continue up the slab with a ground fall possible from the crux. It is possible to still do the route without the threat of a deck out by clipping the 2nd bolt on *SS* and traversing in at the same height - this would rate E5/6. [A Holmes, M Thomas 13.05.86]

▶ **20. Andy Pandy E1 5a** 25m
A poor route. Start on the righthand side of the slab. Gain a faint crack from the groove on the right, then follow it to the Serengeti Level.
[M Roberts, M Crook 23.05.84]
(**The Ascent of the Vikings 6a** is the direct start [A Winterbottom, B Cralis 24.05.84]).

In the narrow alcove to the right are a series of clip ups; see the Addendum on page 320 for full details of the undescribed lines.

▶ **21. The Carbon Stage F6c+** ✶ 20m
The central line on the wall is slightly spoilt by a possible escape to ledges on the right and some suspect rock. Otherwise it is a good climb, albeit one with a reachy finish (a jump for shorties). Lower off. [M Jones 19.08.94]

146 Never Never Land • Lower Tier • Upper Tier

Upper Tier

This is best reached from the Seamstress Slab Level (Serengeti) where an exposed ledge leads around the arête of *Unsexual* to the base of the routes.

▶ **22. Watch Me Wallaby Wank, Frank E4 6a** ** 15m
A tricky route with good climbing in a lofty position. Climb the slab just left of the arête passing 2 bolts then stepping right to a good foothold on the arête before continuing up to a ledge. Finish, either up left of the final bolt, or up the arête (easier). Bolt belay on top.
[N Harms, G Alderson 03.08.86]

▶ **23. Kookaburra Waltz E4 6a** 15m
A barely independent, squeezed-in line. Start left of *Watch Me Wallaby*. Climb up to the 1st bolt out to the right, which is difficult to clip. Continue up a groove and slabby wall, to make an awkward mantel (crux) to clip the 2nd bolt. A wire is required for the top bolt.
[D Dutton, C Stephenson 10.89]

▶ **24. Squashing the Acropods E1 5b** * 18m
A worthwhile pitch with an airy feel. Climb the rib passing a bolt on the way.
[C Davies, I Lloyd-Jones 07.10.90]

▶ **25. Igam-Ogam E4 6a** * 18m
Another exposed pitch at the top of the slab. From the left hand end of the ledge zigzag past 3 bolts to the top. There is a belay bolt at the top.
[I Lloyd-Jones, C Davies 07.10.90]

Lower Tier

Below the main slab is a small slab on the near-side of the large hole. There are 4 minor routes on the slab:

▶ **26. Snap E1 5a** 10m
Ascend the left hand weakness past a bore hole high in the slab. Step left and finish direct
[M Roberts 02.04.84]

▶ **27. Alpen E1 5b** 9m
A barely worthwhile eliminate. Start 2m right of *Snap* and climb directly to a ledge at 6m. Trend left to finish. [13.07.88]

▶ **28. Crackle VS 4c** 9m
A poor, loose route devoid of protection. The shallow weakness leads to a choice of cracks and a loose top out. [M Roberts 02.08.84]

Lower Tier • **Never Never Land** 147

▶ **29. Pop HVS 5b** 9m
Climb the weakness just left of the crack on the right hand side of the slab. [M Roberts 02.04.84]

Directly opposite the main Never Never Land slab a broken wall runs rightwards from the arête marking the edge of *The Carbon Stage* alcove. 20m right of the arête is:

▶ **30. The Gargoyle F6a+** 18m
Climb up the narrow slab which runs into the steep arête. Difficult balance moves allow the gargoyle above to be surmounted; more awkward moves lead past 2 bolts to easier ground and a lower-off.
[K Goodey, C Goodey, D Smith 14.08.08]

▶ **31. Obsession F6a+** 29m
An excellent quality route unfortunately blighted by its location in the firing line of a recent rockfall. Approach with caution; several of the bolts are now unsafe. Wander up through the debris to view the hidden groove line approximately 30m right of *Gargoyle*. Gain the hanging groove with difficulty and continue up it with less trouble to a good ledge with bolt belays. (NB. The route can be split here with a 12m F5c top pitch to follow.) Continue up the corner for a few metres before striding out left to gain the arete. Climb this in fine position to an impressive mantelshelf finish which leads to a double bolt belay/lower off. Numerous bolts and a peg protect. A 60m sport rope will get you back to the ground in a single lower.
[C Goodey, M Helliwell 06.06.08]

During the aforementioned rockfall a recently climbed route, **The Finger Slicer E3 6a,** which was situated to the left of *Obsession*, fell down.

Further to the right (and directly opposite the main Never Never Land slab) is a mess of blocks and scree leading up to a light coloured band of rock, which runs right across to Watford Gap. At the top left side of the wall, at the junction with the steep return wall, there was, once upon a time, an old Stevie Haston route: **Fear of Rejection** This fearsome crack line has long since fallen down. It was given E4 5c, 5c at the time (1983) even though it was noted that a leader fall on the main crack pitch would have meant certain death for both members of the team.

Diary of a Slatehead

The Fissure Haston

In June 1983 Nick Walton, the Captain and I went up to Dinorwig made second ascents of Seamstress and Seems the Same then spent some time hanging out in a dank blast shelter having been caught out in a downpour, which had begun whilst descending the butte atop which both routes finish.

Early in slate exploration it became obvious that although fast drying it was not a medium suited to wet conditions coming, under those circumstances, a debatable second in slipperiness to seaweed encrusted block boulders commonly found below sea cliffs. Despite this knowledge and a few days or so being rained off the butte Stevie Haston, suffering a bout of cabin fever in Pete's, clung to the idea that a certain short chimney crack he'd noticed in a wall near Serengeti might somehow have been spared the mind numbing drizzle that had, apart from engulfing central Snowdonia in a sort of depressing leaden skied cask, reduced slate goers to Space Invaders experts or, and participants impromptu back room pull up competitions. Reflecting on the scene with pessimistic aplomb, whilst glancing sideways through partially steamed up specs at no one in particular JR remarked: "No house, no job, no girlfriend, no car, might as well be dead man." Which as an invitation to philosophical discussion may have been well served though one suspects that even if he'd satisfied the four provisos in his statement, a sort of Schoppenheimer acceptance that "human existence must be a void of mistake" had already set in so after declining to comment, Haston and I set off on a kind of Nietschean trek in which we struggled, not exactly optimistically against saturating downpours that seemed to pursue us with unrelenting zeal on our way to Dinorwig.

Arriving below the crack after front pointing up unstable slate scree cones behind Watford Gap brought us face to face with an alarming truth, the crack was drying the same way as open fronted bus shelters which dependant on wind direction always guaranteed a soaking, or at best a chilling windswept wait in generally grim surroundings. Neither was our appointment heartened by the ? form since at no point did it look possible to shuffle inside. No, not then a chimney crack, just a crack, an evil froth coated affair which in nature displayed all the attributes of being formed by an earthquake's aftershock.

Thus whilst debates no doubt still continued in Pete's seven pillared worthy house Steve set about his work leaving me to contemplate previous wrestling matches similar in character to what inevitably lay above. Gaining experience through gritstone cracks, mostly in company with Paul Williams on one of his G.A.S, or Gritstone Appreciation Society trips it became prudent to accept that what might barely pass for HVS on grit, might in Wales be E2 and that egos previously puffed up by success in the mountains invariably received a severe pummelling lest the contenders already possessed a certain open handed apprenticeship which in any case did not always guarantee success. For my own part I remained conscious of barely passing through Grond, whose initial ascencionists, rudimentary equipped as they were, had probably done in better style, climbs that thirty or so years later I found desperately difficult, sometimes impassable and often astonishing as I'd grappled with their drop dead gorgeous, green eyed monstrous hues.

No surprise then when Haston, already a crack aficionado on all types of terrain leant over cagoule hooded, after belaying to what from below looked to be little more than a disintegrating pile of slate blocks shouted own, "It's only HVS." I immediately prepared for an ungradeable struggle which when pushed would afterwards be defined as E2.

In truth he'd swarmed up it rather like I imagined an anaconda might pull a man under water, that is with powerful intent yet the game was not won easily, since at half height a couple of iron bars that in dry conditions might have proved adequate levers kept expelling the tyro slowly downwards with wrist cutting intent. Nor was the constriction protectable with friends since we did not have

any and the two runners so far placed, six inch sawn off scaffold bars with
slings attached (better known as Tube chocks) rotated uncomfortably in their
parallel sided universe as the leader's rope snaked out.

Seconding soon revealed that although the fissure's unreachable innards appeared
dry its offwidth outer edges were coated with a film of algae which under
constant rain had produced a lather of bubbles making them as difficult to grasp
as a bar of soap. Here there was no such thing as faith in friction, only a
two moves up and slide down kind of motion, requiring patience, tenacity and an
'anything will do' technique.

Seconding Haston meant just that and one could not expect any aid from the rope
above, in fact any calls to 'take in' would guarantee loops of slack though if
really in trouble rather than simply not trying or out for an easy ride, he
could be completely relied upon to get you up in one piece, provided of course
you had not untied and gone home.

At half height (twenty feet) came the crunch, a small overlap mitred as if
specially for garment ripping ensured that even after moving up one became aware
of being held from below so that a reverse motion, unnatural though it was,
proved the only way to free the snag lest one ignored it and became degloved or
at worst caught in situ whilst moving on up. Engaging in a final filibuster gave
chance to escape and by means of an epilogue unconvincing in delivery won out
over easier ground on handfuls of slate.

                                                        Martin Crook

Dinorwic Quarries

(35) 3RD ASCENT Nick.
BOSS ROUTE

Seamstress. HVS 5a 70' left hand crack SHIT GEAR.
Seems the same. E2 5c 70' 15' to the right s/thn about
E3 5b   S Haston solo '83.

In the pit before 'the Big hole' which contains Final
rejection   is   a   short crack 60' E1 5b
      Bar of Soap S Haston & M. Crook '83

In the Hot Air Gulch!

NEVER NEVER LAND 165ft E5 6A *
Follow the obvious line up the centre of
the slab to the stepped roofs. Move left and
go up to an insitu spike runner in a
borehole. Move up to thin flakes and three
poor peg runners. Move left on the obvious
line to the arete. finish up this move easily
in one position. 50m ropes needed.
      M. Crook. N. Newton. Anewton. March 24
NB. On the first attempt a lot of loose flakes
snapped off. the route is relatively clean now
but an ab inspection is advisable..

▶ **32. Stairlift to Heaven E1 5a** 60m
Gaining the attractive hanging slab feature on the left side of the face provides an adventurous outing.
P1 4c 30m Start at the base of the leftward leading blocky ramp. Follow this up left than switch back right traversing the block ledge system to reach a belay stance by a big flake.
P2 5a 30m Pad carefully up the scoop on the left edge of the hanging slab to reach the 1st runner in the large triangular niche. Top out in the corner then pick your way up the scree to a drystone wall belay. [M Dicken, C Neale 11.05.03]

▶ **32a. Stannah to Hell XS 5c** 95m
The obvious line of loose ramps linking *Shame and Embarrassment* and *Stairlift to Heaven*.
P1 5c 10m Follow *Shame and Embarrassment* to its 1st bolt.
P2 4c 55m Pick your way along the ramps to the cluster of rubble just before the *Stairlift to Heaven*. belay.
P3 5a 30m Join and finish up P2 of *Stairlift to Heaven*. [C Muskett, M Dicken 10.04.10]

Further right a conspicuous triangular scar marks the high point of an aid project attempted by Dave Anderson in the mid 90s. The whole flake peeled and took Dave with it; amazingly he escaped with fairly low key injuries.

Further right again, in the centre of the light coloured wall, a major rock fall has occurred. This appears to have just missed the following route:

▶ **33. Shame and Embarrassment E5 6b** ∗ 30m
An impressive pitch tackling the narrow curving flake on the highest point of the wall. Start just right of the large flake embedded at the base of the wall. Climb up left for 6m to a slabby ledge and a bolt. Move up and right, then back left past a 2nd bolt runner. Gain the base of the thin diagonal flake and follow it into the thin crack line leading to the top.
[J Dawes, T Hodgson 14.09.86]

< A bloodied, but glad-to-be-alive Dave Anderson after his ill-fated attempt on the Aid Project photo: Al Leary

Slatehead • Martin Crook

Martin has maintained a mischievous presence in the Llanberis climbing scene since the seventies; if there was ever something interesting going on, he was usually involved. Along with a cast of glorious misfits (Nick Thomas, Nick Walton, Cliff Phillips, Andy Newton, Stevie Haston, John Redhead and Dave Towse, to name a few) he became a major player in the 80s slate boom. Although an experienced alpinist, Martin was just as happy to go bouldering or pick off plum lines in the absurd landscape of the slate quarries. Many of his routes have now attained classic status, but in later years he also turned his attention to the less travelled sections of the quarries and in the process produced some seriously adventurous rubble horror shows.

The following selection illustrates an admirable eye for quality, plus Martin's distinctive penchant for memorable route names:
Nostromo E4 6a, *Never Never Land* E5 6a, *Bela Lugosi Is Dead* E1 5b, *German School Girl* E2 5c, *Brewing up with Morley Wood* E1 5b, *The Reclining Bloon* E4 6a, *Buffer in a Crack House* XS, *Big Thursday* XS ABO and *Conquistadors of the Useless* ABO.

He is still active today, whether it be searching out boulders in the Beddgelert Forest or putting up new routes, such as *Clippopotamus* F6b in Mancer Quarry.

An unknown climber making an early repeat of **Never Never Land** E5 6a photo: Paul Williams
Martin Crook on **Telescopic Stem Master** F6b+, Dali's Hole, back in the early 90s photo: Crook collection
Martin doing his best Gollum impersonation in more recent times photo: Ray Wood

152 Never Never Land • Lower Tier • Monkey Bar Area

▶ **34. Bar of Soap E1 5b** ∗ 13m
A pitch for the crack connoisseur: the wide crack in the corner provides a meaty struggle; take some big cams. [S Haston, M Crook 06.83]

▶ **34a. Hollow Heart E2 5c** 25m
The obvious flake line left of *Bar of Soap*.
[R Brookes 13.05.87]

▶ **35. Suspension of Disbelief [F7a] E4 6a** 18m
An unstable looking line that is probably best left alone. The route climbs the left side of the obvious arête which hangs over the Watford Gap. 5 decayed (and obviously dangerous) bolts mark the way to the lower-off.
[I Lloyd-Jones 01.06.93]

On the opposite side of the track is a prominent greenstone pillar:

▶ **36. Name Unknown E3 6a** 15m
Another good looking route marred by suspect rock. Originally there were 3 bolts and 2 in situ wires. Although inspected for re-equipping, it was considered to be rather unstable.

Monkey Bar Area

The following routes are situated in a hidden amphitheatre on a lower level below the main track and opposite the circular air vent. To reach it go over the gate opposite the entrance to Dali's Hole and follow a footpath along the narrow level that leads leftwards below the main track.

▶ **37. Shock the Monkey F6a+** 25m
The slabby ramp on the left side of the bay provides a worthwhile route. The bottom 6m has been affected by a recent rockfall, consequently, reaching the second bolt is tricky and a bit scary. Above the climbing is good, but there are still a few suspect holds. Lower off.
[I Lloyd-Jones, N Manning 06.04.93]

The steep (and often wet) back wall with a tunnel at its base has 2 radical dry tooling lines:

▶ **38. Bambi D9+** ∗∗ 22m
The obvious steep line left of *Ibex* gives powerful and reachy climbing utilizing the shallow flake system above the tunnel entrance, with

Monkey Bar Area • Lower Tier • **Never Never Land** 153

a couple of exciting 'designer danger' run outs. Figure-four the right hand shot hole to start, and straight away move into a series of very tenuous and powerful locks up the flake system until an all-out launch leftwards leaves you pondering the drop. Another powerful lock up leads to a move back right, the last bolt, and a lonely final section to the chains. [R Gibson 24.11.10]

▶ **39. Ibex D7+** ∗∗ 22m
A good sustained route with fun moves and a crux near the top, though maybe not the easy warm-up route its builders intended it to be. Start 4m right of the tunnel next to the boulder - there may be a Quarryman's clip-stick in place for the first bolt. Monopoints and jug-handle tools pretty much mandatory, or take the D10 tick for an old school 'Vertiges with homemade leashes and dual-point crampons' ascent. Lower off. A free ascent, with good old fashioned fingers and rock shoes might just be possible...one day! [P Harrison 19.02.09]

▶ **40. Rest in Pete's Eats E1 5a** 27m
Start at the back of the bay, at a short crack to the right of the tunnel and *Ibex*. Climb the crack and the wall on the left to some large loose flakes. Go up on the left of those to a broken corner (protection), then traverse leftwards on the steep ramp, being careful with hand holds.
[R Liddle, L Dow 23.04.93]

▶ **41. Home Run F6a+** ∗ 21m
Start 3m to the left of *Patellaectomy* at the overhang; go right at the 1st bolt and climb up on small but positive holds. Make a difficult move right to a side pull before continuing up to easier ground and a juggy finish. There is a bolt belay on the level above. [J Bowman, A Bowman 06.07.93]

▶ **42. Monkey See Monkey Do E2 5b** 21m
Start 2m left of *Patellaectomy*. Climb direct through the overhang (small wires) to arrive at a horizontal break, traverse this rightwards and go up a small crack system. A tougher section at the top leads to an easy finish.
[S Beal, A Scott, N Harford 23.06.08]

154 Never Never Land • Lower Tier • Monkey Bar Area

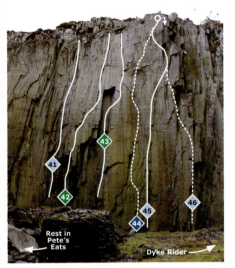

▶ **43. Patellaectomy E1 5c** ✱✱✱ 23m
An entertaining route switching from a tricksome chimney to some monkey bar action. Gain the hanging chimney (bolt) and shuffle up it until it is possible to exit onto the iron bars. Swing upwards and make an awkward mantel onto the shorter bar and continue past a bolt to the top.
[C Parkin, M Robinson 23.04.92]

▶ **44. Beyond the Pail F7a** ✱✱ 24m
An enjoyable and airy pitch sharing bolts and some ground with *Pail Rider*. Start as for *Pail Rider* at the 4 shot holes at the base of the wall. Use these (Don't delve too deep as they're full of water at the back!) to gain the large flake on the left and follow this to a small ledge and the 3rd bolt. Step precariously left to the 1st shot hole under the bars. Keep going up the wall to the good edge on *Patellaectomy* and rock over to grab the right hand bar, (a short sling handy for protection) mantel this and head diagonally right to another bolt. Thin moves lead out to the last bolt near the arete, joining *Pail Rider* for its final moves and lower-off. [A Scott, J Ratcliffe 25.06.08]

▶ **45. Pail Rider F6c+** ✱✱ 23m
A splendid and continually interesting route. Start at the 4 shot holes at the base of the wall and follow the flakes directly up past 3 bolts. Thin side pulls, tasty footwork and a long stride out right gain the flake out near the arete with a small ledge and bolt. Climb up the short crack to an awkward mantel onto the ledge below the final arete. Reach out left to clip the last bolt and move onto the wall and arete with a fierce little pull for the lower-off. [A Scott, J Ratcliffe 24.06.08]

▶ **46. A Little Pail F6b+** ✱ 23m
A good route with great climbing. Starts a couple of metres right of *Pail Rider*. Climb the pleasantly delicate shallow groove to a niche, pull into and up this to the base of a short crack on the left and a junction with the previous route. Continue following *Pail Rider* to its lower-off, the final move being the crux of this route.
[J Ratcliffe, A Scott 25.06.08]

▶ **47. Donkey Rider E1 5a** 18m
The wall and crack system left of *Dyke Rider*. Climb boldly up the lower wall to reach a collection of spikes (sling) and good wire slot above. Step left to a good crack and climb to the top with one hand in the crack and the other on the edge of broken ground to the right. At the top sling a good block then traverse right to the *Dyke Rider* lower-off. [G Desroy, S Panton 28.04.10]

▶ **48. Dyke Rider E2 5c** ✱ 16m
20m right of *A Little Pail* a narrow dyke feature, just left of a tunnel, catches the eye. Climb up pleasantly past 2 bolts to a point where an obvious tricky section looms; press on through to big holds and a lower-off. [S Beal, A Scott, J Ratcliffe 25.06.08]

▶ **49. Penblwydd Hapus (i Fi) F6c** ✱ 17m
An intense, technical route with a steady but airy run out at the top. Climb up from the lip of the tunnel into the hanging groove. Intricate moves lead up to good holds; once stood on these step left into the bold finish of *Dyke Rider* and lower-off. [S Panton, A Scott, G Desroy 01.05.10]

▶ **50. Offa's F6b** 15m
Tackle the middle of the steep wall 10m right of *Penblwydd Hapus*; 5 bolts to a chain lower-off. Nice climbing. [C Davies, M Williams 08.05.10]

Jon Ratcliffe making the second ascent of **Pail Rider**, F6c+ (a proper lower-off subsequently replaced the ad hoc set up)
photo: Si Beal

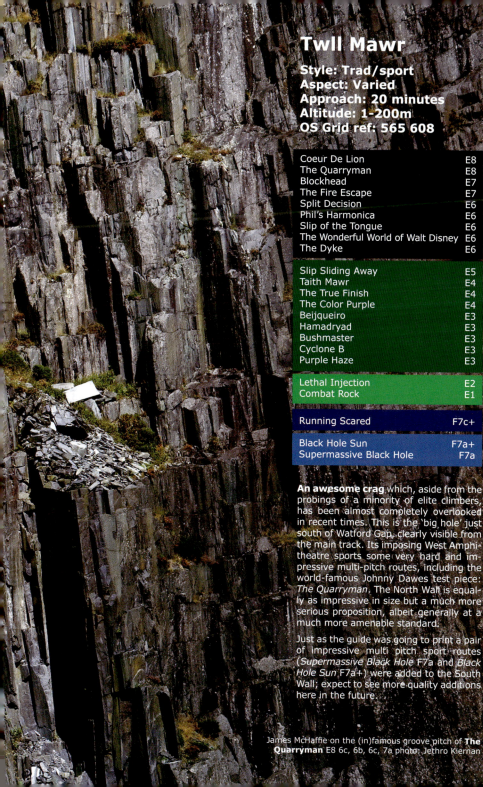

Twll Mawr

Style: Trad/sport
Aspect: Varied
Approach: 20 minutes
Altitude: 1-200m
OS Grid ref: 565 608

Coeur De Lion	E8
The Quarryman	E8
Blockhead	E7
The Fire Escape	E7
Split Decision	E6
Phil's Harmonica	E6
Slip of the Tongue	E6
The Wonderful World of Walt Disney	E6
The Dyke	E6
Slip Sliding Away	E5
Taith Mawr	E4
The True Finish	E4
The Color Purple	E4
Beijqueiro	E3
Hamadryad	E3
Bushmaster	E3
Cyclone B	E3
Purple Haze	E3
Lethal Injection	E2
Combat Rock	E1
Running Scared	F7c+
Black Hole Sun	F7a+
Supermassive Black Hole	F7a

An awesome crag which, aside from the probings of a minority of elite climbers, has been almost completely overlooked in recent times. This is the 'big hole' just south of Watford Gap, clearly visible from the main track. Its imposing West Amphitheatre sports some very hard and impressive multi-pitch routes, including the world-famous Johnny Dawes test piece: *The Quarryman*. The North Wall is equally as impressive in size but a much more serious proposition, albeit generally at a much more amenable standard.

Just as the guide was going to print a pair of impressive multi pitch sport routes (*Supermassive Black Hole* F7a and *Black Hole Sun* F7a+) were added to the South Wall; expect to see more quality additions here in the future.

James McHaffie on the (in)famous groove pitch of **The Quarryman** E8 6c, 6b, 6c, 7a photo: Jethro Kiernan

158 Twll Mawr • Introduction

Conditions: The Watford Gap, Golgotha and main Quarryman Wall all get sun during the morning, while the North Wall remains sunny throughout the day. The South Wall stays in the shade at all times. As for drainage, *Razors Edge* takes a long time to dry; other than that there are no significant seepage issues.

For more specific conditions advice for the North Wall see the introduction to that section.

Approach: From the turning circle by Bus Stop Quarry, walk into the quarries along the main track passing a large disused factory unit on the left. Go left through the gate, and follow the track as it turns right and dips down hill to Dali's Hole (which is seen on the left). Continue along the track as it rises up hill and after a few hundred metres reaches the Watford Gap and just beyond a massive quarried hole on the left.

Alternatively it is possible to follow the zig-zagging track up from the Nant Peris end of Llyn Peris. The North Wall, Golgotha and the Lower South Wall are best approached by walking around underneath the Peregrine Walls from Dali's Hole. For the full details see the introduction to the North Wall section.

Access Restrictions: There are some specific access restrictions relating to North Wall

Watford Gap

The routes here are fairly neglected and are mainly passed by on the way to better things. The rock harbours much vegetation, is often in the shade, and the belays are on the cavalier side of adventurous. The slab routes have been climbed and claimed numerous times over the years, the examples here being the most recent, and more importantly, most fully described.

▶ **1. In Between Red and Green E1 5a** 18m
Tackle the left hand crack of the trio in the slab and continue up the cracked headwall. Rubble thread belay. [B Lillington, J Teed 26.03.03]

▶ **2. Snoring Exploring E1 5b** 20m
Ascend the wider right hand crack on the slab, before attacking the corner and headwall above. Rubble thread belay. [B Lillington 26.03.03]

▶ **3. Watford Gap West VS 4b** 21m
Start on the Twll Mawr side of the pillar in the right wall of the Gap. Swarm up the corner to a tricky slump over a block at its termination. Pick your way up the wall above to gain a heathery groove, which awkwardly leads to the top. The rubble thread belay is quite a walk away.
[C Philips 19.05.84]

Combat Rock Area

These routes lie on the shore of Twll Mawr, right up to (and over) the very edge of the beckoning abyss. The rock is somewhat flakey and suspect, demanding a certain coolness and a workmanlike attitude to gear placement. All routes are equipped with bolted belay stations, however due to the length of some routes attempts to lower off rather than abseil may result in your ropes coming up short. Double ropes are strongly recommended.

▶ **4. Combat Rock E1 5a** * 27m
Climb the crack line emerging from the left hand side of the cave, passing some ironmongery on the way. Good, if somewhat creaky climbing.
[P Trower, A Howard 20.04.84]

▶ **5. Rhyfelwr E2 5b** 27m
The right hand crack line exiting the cave is a bolder proposition. Although there are plenty of gear placements, their holding power is largely suspect. Lace it and hope for the best.
[I Lloyd-Jones, S Salter 24.09.89]

▶ **6. Teenage Kicks E4 6a** 27m
This line weaves around a thin seam, and starts from the pinnacle of rock on the edge of the abyss at the abseil station to the Birdman area. Climb up to join the *Combat Rock* belay. RPs essential. [D Lee, J Warburton 08.05.05]

▶ **7. Purple Haze E3 5b** ** 33m
This classic line starts from a rock spike out on a ledge over the abyss, which can be backed up by the abseil station. The obvious flake line is gained via a committing pull off the top of the very pointy looking spike. Continued fretting gains the termination spike of these hollow monoliths, where a mantel right gains the lonely ledge system leading up to the abseil station. Those feeling excessively fretful at this point may lean over to clip the 1st bolt of *The Color Purple* before committing to the unprotected upper section. [P Trower, I Wilson 04.04.86]

8. The Color Purple E4 6b ** 33m
The groove above the *Purple Haze* flake system has an intense crux followed by a bold and exposed upper wall. Follow either *Purple Haze* or *Cyclone B* to the ledges on the arête. Move left to reach the first of 2 bolts in the groove. Hard moves past the 2nd bolt lead to an easier upper wall and an abseil station. An airy route.
[C Parkin, J Smallwood 29/4/92]

9. Cyclone B E3 6a * 18m
The exposure continues with this spooky groove. Belay as for *Purple Haze*. Step up and right along a ledge system to enter a groove. From here a flake and a couple of bolts leads on to the podium and a double bolt belay. Those who want more may like to step out left and join The Color Purple. [F Ball, C Parkin 26.04.91]

The Alcove
The rock here feels more solid, although it is often hollow. Perched high above the quarry floor, there is a sense of isolation that seems incongruous with its proximity to the tourist path. Manoeuvring around the Alcove itself makes you feel like a penny shuffling away to oblivion in some dusty old victorian arcade, ha'penny cascade. Needless to say, care should be exercised.

Approach: Step down from the *Purple Haze* belay and shuffle across to the dry stone base of the Alcove and ascend with extreme vigilance. Roping up is recommended and bolt stations are available for back roping partners.

10. Lethal Injection E2 5c * 32m
This starts at the belay at the base of the podium, and weaves its way up the left arête of the Alcove. A line of bolts leads the way up the podium, clip the belay of *Cyclone B*, and quest out right to a crack (gear), from above which the slim groove of *Legal Murders* can be gained (bolt). This is followed to a 2nd bolt which marks this route's traverse to the arête. Climb easily to the *Purple Haze* abseil station.
[C Parkin, J Smallwood 29.04.92]

11. Legal Murders E3 6a 25m
This starts further up the left side of the alcove at the base of a wide flake crack that tapers away at about 7m. Climb the crack until it kicks out right. Here, a delicate rising traverse past a bolt gains an uber-slim groove. This is followed past 2 bolts and up a flake, where this route rejoins the arête and ascends to the *Purple Haze* abseil station. [C Parkin, F Ball 26.04.92]

12. Top Gear E1 5b 22m
Past *Legal Murders* is a wide right facing corner crack rising to a monolith at the top of the wall. This is ascended to arrive at the left side of the monolith and a bolt belay.
[C Parkin, K Robertson 06.06.97]

13. Drunken Laughs E2 5b 25m
This route ambles up the back of the alcove to provide a route of 3 distinct parts. Firstly a boulder problem onto the shelf, then a crack climb, and a bold slab (bolt low down) to finish. The lower off of this route can also be used as an abseil point back into the alcove for routes on the quarryman wall. [M Pugh, M Dicken 14.02.07]

Slatehead • Johnny Dawes

Perhaps the ultimate slatehead, Johnny shone brightly in the slate quarries, just as he did in the mountains and on the gritstone. The 15 routes to his name were all masterpieces of hard climbing, starting off with the immaculate hanging slab of **Dawes of Perception** E7 6c; a subtle mix of serious and desperate climbing, ever pushing the ethics of the day. He went on to almost single-handedly develop the imposing West Wall of Twll Mawr including the best and most famous route of all: **The Quarryman** E8 7a. He continued to establish routes which have gained national status including **Coeur De Lion** E8 7a, **Windows of Perception** E6 7a, **The Medium** F8a, **Bobby's Groove** F8a, **The Untouchables** F8a and of course, his last creation, the unbelievably thin: **The Very Big and the Very Small** – at F8b+ still the hardest climb on Welsh slate 20 years after it was first ascended.

^ A youthful Johnny relaxing after a hard day's bolting with the Bosch drill of justice!
photo: Martin Crook

> Johnny Dawes and Trev Hodgson in colourful mid 80s garb on **The Quarryman** groove pitch
photo: Paul Williams

↑ Drew Coleman on the easy access **Combat Rock** E1 5a photo: Gareth Hutton

The Quarryman Wall

To the right of the scree filled Alcove, the main West Wall emerges from the depths of Twll Mawr. This is the dark horse of the quarries, but truly gob-smacking; every route presents a formidable challenge and some are the hardest and longest routes on slate.

The routes on this wall are a tribute to the genius of Johnny Dawes, who almost single handedly created a tour-de-force of cutting edge adventures. Many of the cruxes are only just climbable and remain friable. Any slight change may ruin everything so it is imperative to be 'light' on your feet and caring with your hands.

Approach: Around the right arête of the Alcove is an abseil station (again, access with extreme caution) which takes you to the starting ledge of the routes. Abseil down a few metres to some bolts on the main face and then abseil down from here (this will avoid knocking scree down) for 20m to the base of the main face, some 30m above the true bottom of the hole. Alternatively, do the 1st pitch of *Opening Gambit*.

▶ **14. Beijqueiro E3 6b** * 39m
(Beh-Ka-Whero) This is a corruption of Beijoqueiro, meaning 'the Kisser', a certain Brazilian eccentric notorious for snogging unsuspecting celebrities. All this bears no relation to this exposed and unnerving route, both bold and strenuous in parts. Begin at the abseil point belay, the route starts near the arête proper.
P1 5c 18m Step off the scree onto a notch in the arête proper. Ascend the arete to a sloping ledge and a peg. Follow a groove out left to another peg, then move right up to a cracked ledge (peg) below a twin grooved arête. Climb initially up the right groove to a bolt. From here either continue upwards (hard but safer) or move into the left groove, via an undercut, for an easier but bolder route to the Rome belay.
P2 6b 21m Step nervously round the sharp arête to clip a bolt. Ignore the consequences of this action and utilise the solitary hold (an undercut) to transport you down and round the next arête to a rest in the corner. Ascend the corner to gain the easier finishing crack. Continue up the scree above and belay well back with imagination.
[J Dawes 25.04.88]

▶ **15. Coeur De Lion E8 7a** *** 76m
The 1st pitch is perhaps the hardest to date on this wall. It features a mixture of bold and desperate climbing, with an air of tension maintained throughout. Start as for *The Quarryman*, by a low bolt in the centre of the wall.
P1 7a 25m Clip the low bolt then immediately trend leftwards along the slight lip to a rest. Facing a deck out, step up delicately to easier ground and a 2nd bolt beneath an overlap. Pass this on the left and trend rightwards to some spikes and a bolt. Several of the thinnest moves imaginable up the smooth shield gain a slim flake which again is barely climbable and (in case you hadn't noticed) a long way out from the bolt. Once a jug is reached, head for the next bolt above an overlap, followed by more difficult moves up and right to gain the last hard move of *The Quarryman* leading to the London belay.
P2 6c 30m From the left hand end of the ledge, continue straight up past a peg and a bolt to gain twin cracks. Just above this, move left into the base of a groove on the left of the pillar to a bolt. Contorted climbing leads up the groove to a jug and a peg, then scary moves lead up to a ledge and the Rome belay.
P3 6b 21m Swing right past a bolt runner then teeter up for 7m to reach jugs. Finish up the pillar past a bolt, initially on the left, then on the right. [J Dawes, J Tombs 28.03.87]

▶ **16. Blockhead E7 6c [F7c+]** *** 50m
A brilliant climb tackling the obvious twin cracked continuation to P1 of *The Quarryman*, which runs the full height of the crag. The meat of the route battles with some vertical cracks, which require some decidedly sketchy smearing. Start from the London belay, gained from *The Quarryman* P1.
P1 6c [F7c+] 30m From the left end of the ledge climb up the twin cracks passing 3 bolts to reach easier ground. Belay up and right on ledges.
P2 6a [F7a] 20m Climb the wall above the belay, passing a couple of bolts, and moving through 2 overlaps. [A Wainwright, M Thomas 1992]

▶ **16a. King of the Mezz E7 6c** * 18m
A hard and bold addition with a perplexing crux. From the New York belay (at the top of *The Quarryman* groove) clip the bolts on the initial section of *The Firé Escape* then drop down and follow the obvious line of overhangs until it is possible to climb up to the *Blockhead* belay. The hardest section is reasonably close to the bolts (which is a good thing as it's desperate!) but beyond that there is a heart chilling run out.
[J Dawes, N Dyer, O Anderson 05.11]

< Johnny Dawes and Trev Hodgson making the second ascent of **The Firé Escape** E7 6c.
The route was described by Johnny as *"the ultimate in designer climbs"*; the epic runout to reach the crag top is certainly 'well designed', assuming you don't mind facing the potential for a whopping 50m fall into the void!
photo: Paul Williams

▶ **17. The Quarryman E8 7a ★★★★** 78m
Unquestionably the best route on slate, deviously linking 4 amazing pitches of unrelenting difficulty up this impressive and exposed face. Each pitch has its own unique charm and the groove pitch is like no other on Earth, it will blow your mind, and probably spit out your body! Start in the centre of the main wall, by a low bolt to the left of some obvious twin seams running up to the London belay.
P1 6c 25m A blistering pitch in its own right, crammed with crux after crux and healthy run-outs in between, though everything feels in moderation. From a low bolt, climb up and right to make a scary move to clip a 2nd bolt. Carry on more easily past a couple of wire placements and make a committing step left to a bolt. Suitably 'in-bulk', gain a jug in the groove on the left with difficulty. Continue more easily for a while to an overlap beneath an immaculate wall split by twin seams. More hard and bold moves lead up here past 2 bolts to arrive at the London belay.
P2 6b 10m A short link pitch traversing right along the break, past a bolt and a peg, to the Paris belay.
P3 6c [F8a] 18m This is the line of the quarries; an ever widening mirror–smooth groove in the middle of the huge face. It requires good old fashioned determination and hard work to succeed; not enough force and you'll slide down quicker than you move up, too much force and you'll be spat out. After about 10m, some holds appear and the climbing becomes marginally more conventional, though hard moves keep on coming right to the very end. Belay, with a huge grin, amongst the skyscraper blocks of the perfectly formed New York belay.
P4 7a 25m The top pitch contains the crux move, but is an easier proposition than the groove for most. Scramble up ledges and traverse right and up to a bolt on the upper slab, just out of reach. Work leftwards to the arête, bolt, and swing left to climb the awkward groove and arête to another bolt. Move up the slab to a bolt below an ultra thin section. Standing comfortably on friable edges, carefully mould your hands around tiny edges in the hope of gaining a distant crimp followed by a jug and a bolt. That's it, you're in! Big holds and big smiles lead to victory at the Dinorwig belay and only 20 minutes from the café. (NB. If you thought the crux was 'tricky', remember that it used to be even harder!)
[J Dawes, R Drury 10/11.09.86]

▶ **18. The Meltdown (project)**
An old project of Johnny's; rumoured to be F8c.

▶ **19. The Firé Escape E7 6c ★★★** 30m
An alternative top pitch to *The Quarryman*, though it couldn't be described as a soft option. Rumoured to have the longest run out in Wales, and now even longer since the peg above the lip has gone. From the New York belay, move up and traverse out left to 2 twin bolts. Go up to the roof and pass this leftwards with difficulty. Continue for a long way to the top...gulp!
[J Dawes 22.09.86]

▶ **20. Phil's Harmonica E6 6c ★★** 36m
Another alternative top pitch to *The Quarryman*, going straight up from the New York belay. Step into a sentry box below a flake, then follow it to a peg. Move up to a bolt and pass it leftwards into a friction groove. Climb the groove to a pinch grip, bolt, then climb the groove to the right of *The Firé Escape*, exiting right. [J Dawes 26.04.88]

▶ **21. The Wonderful World of Walt Disney E6 6b ★★★** 90m
A great adventure, taking in the full experience of the West Wall, but at a more amenable standard than its neighbours, and it gives you a good peek at *The Quarryman* groove. Low in the grade but sustained. If you're generally the smooth and static type, then be aware of the dynamic P3 'leap'. Start at the right end of the wall by 2 bolts, beneath a green, widening groove.
P1 6a 33m A tough pitch which has some interesting bolt positions. Scramble up the corner/groove and make a committing move to clip the 1st bolt on the left wall. Weird climbing leads up the left hand groove to arrive at the Paris belay.
P2 6b 20m Climb up right past a bolt, crux, to continue up an arête (past a further bolt) to reach a resting ledge. Head diagonally leftwards up the wall, past a bolt which is difficult to clip, to arrive at the New York belay. An easier method of clipping the last bolt is to go up right to make the clip, before stepping back down and climbing past it.
P3 6b 17m Scramble up ledges and traverse out right to a bolt. Get established on the wall and pick your spot over on the arête of the groove on the right. 1,2,3....jump! Scramble up to the recessed headwall and belay.
P4 6a 20m A lovely finish up the obvious shallow groove, passing some bolts and pegs to a bolt belay before the scree.
[J Dawes, R Drury, M Thomas, A Popp 1989]

▶ **22. The Dyke E6 6a ★★** 18m
From the top belay on *The Wonderful World...* traverse out left and follow the dyke leftwards to meet the top section of *The Quarryman*, past its crux (you'll be glad to hear). Clip the 1st bolt on the top pitch of *The Wonderful World...*
[J Dawes, M Raine 11.04.88]

▶ **23. The Gay Blade E6 6a** was once a variation arête start to *The Dyke*, but it appears to have partly fallen down. There is something still there but it is of the consistency of MDF. The obvious approach pitch is the original line of *Opening Gambit* (prior to the rockfall) and goes at about E1. [J Dawes, R Drury 02.07.88]

North Wall

Joe Brown rates the North Wall as *"One of the 4 most adventurous walls in North Wales"* – (See if you can guess which the others are?). Almost 150m high, its foreboding flanks are home to some of the earliest and longest routes on Welsh slate. Clearly this is a committing place to climb; a decision to climb here should not be taken lightly. The rock is loosest at the point where the North Wall meets the Quarryman Wall, and also where the tide of rubble on its eastern edge has compressed and shattered the buttresses. In between is an expanse of ramparts and grooves, sloping ledges and soaring slabs. There is loose rock on most ledges and occasional shattered zones; however the rock is generally compact with little shattering (or gear) - guaranteed excitement really.

The great rockfalls of the 80s and 90s have affected the initial pitches of all routes, and some of the upper pitches. The continued advancement of the East Wall's immense boulder glacier may change things further, so take all descriptions with a pinch of salt. Useful additions to your slate rack include skyhooks, blade pegs (beware of their splitting capability), big cams and gaffa tape for sticking down slings and securing loose blocks.

Key landmarks which can aid route recognition are the rising faultline of *Hamadryad*, the grey slab of *The True Finish*, and the Balcony; a floral terrace at the top right of the wall as you view it – this latter feature is accessible via a tunnel from Middle Earth (see page 183 in the Lost World/Mordor chapter).

Conditions: Given its great size, it does seem to drain pretty well; with the exception of *The Razor's Edge*, a day's dry weather seems sufficient. The key factor is temperature; on a cloud shaded day it can be Baltic. Conversely, there is very little shelter from the sun if it gets roasting, providing the added burden of dragging plenty of water up with you. Finally, unless you don't mind abandoning lots of gear, don't get caught in the rain.

Approach and Access Restrictions: Access to the floor of Twll Mawr is through the mouth of the 'skull', whose eyes can be seen when driving from Llanberis to Nant Peris. This is located on the upper level of the Peregrine Walls. In the past these levels were subject to a voluntary climbing ban. This meant absolutely no climbing on either level of the Peregrine Walls and no foot access during the entire nesting season, which required an alternative 'death scree' scramble to access Twll Mawr. It has now been recognised that the nesting birds inhabiting these cliffs are not exclusive to these levels, but are found throughout the wilder areas of the quarry. Rather than concentrating our efforts (and restrictions) on these 2 levels, a more holistic and common sense plan has been adopted. Consequently there are no current access restrictions, on the grounds of conservation, for both the lower Peregrine Walls (see the Rainbow Walls Upper chapter on page 226) and on Golgotha, the clean buttress adjacent to the Twll Mawr tunnel entrance.

Nonetheless, it is important that all visiting climbers endeavour to avoid causing any disturbance to wildlife in the quarries. **On a specific level, this means not prospecting new routes close to bird nests, and moreover, during the sensitive period between April to June such sites that do exist should be passed by quietly and with the minimum of loitering.**

To access the majority of the routes, cross the gate opposite Dali's Hole and gain the terrace below the Monkey Bar level. This is followed with increasing effort to Golgotha (meaning 'the place of the skull') and the tunnel. The only exceptions to this approach being the *Birdman of Cae'r Berllan* zone and *Bonza Crack*, the details of which are found in the relevant descriptions.

Golgotha

This diminutive buttress, situated just before the tunnel, boasts a clean bolted slab and a dolerite prow. All routes are equipped with lower offs to avoid disturbing the wildlife on top.

▶ **24. The Daddy Club E1 5b** 27m
Climb the groove on the left hand side of the dolerite prow to a bolt. Continue up until forced our left to the arête (small friends and wires). Once out the groove, follow your nose to the lower-off (the right arête being prettiest).
[M Dicken, P Jenkinson, C Muskett 22.08.08]

▶ **24a. Green Slip F7a** 24m
A slightly snappy direct start to *The Daddy Club*.
[C Muskett 11.10]

▶ **25. Slip of the Tongue E6 6c ∗∗** 26m
A superb route protected by 3 bolts and some small wires. Climb direct to the 1st bolt and enter a slim groove which is departed at the 3rd bolt for a direct finish. [P Robins 11.10]

▶ **26. Slip Sliding Away E5 6b ∗** 26m
The obvious shiny groove right of *Golgotha Original*. Tackle this with much determination to gain its rightward trending continuation, which is easier but less solid. Lower off
[C Muskett, J Dawes 09.09]

▶ **26a. Split Decision E6 6c ∗∗** 24m
Another excellent addition. Follow the precarious crack line up to an enigmatic move for a sloping hold before joining and finishing as for *Slip Sliding Away*. [C Muskett 11.10]

The tunnel leading into Twll Mawr divides; the left hand path leads to an abseil point, the right hand path to a terrace, from which a straightforward scramble leads to the quarry floor.

The North Wall • Twll Mawr 167

The North Wall

▶ **27. Opening Gambit MXS** 168m
The original route of Twll Mawr crosses a band best described as 'geologically lively' and has significantly altered since Joe Brown's ascent in 1971. The description is currently on its 3rd rewrite, hence the upgrade from HVS to MXS. Potential ascentionists should be prepared for substantial looseness on all pitches varying from mild exfoliation to tottering of Jenga proportions. Start at the top of a scree cone in a corner, below *The Quarryman* ledge.
P1 45m Pick your way up the scree coated ledges to arrive at *The Quarryman* ledge, where the bolt belay of *The Wonderful World of Walt Disney* provides some safety.
P2 4c 25m Traverse gingerly rightwards to a deep groove and ascend this to a sloping ledge. This is followed to a 'bad step'; above is a large bay where a thread belay can be made amongst the boulders.
P3 5a 33m Pick your way across the bay to its right arête. This used to be barred by a huge detached pillar known as the Banana Flake; the tottering tower left by its demise should be treated with respect. Surmount the blocks to the left of the arête to gain some reliable gear in some hairline cracks. Monkey out onto the crystal ledge on the arête, and ignoring the 100m of air beneath your heels, mantel and gain the ledge above (a possible belay, but requires some inventiveness). Ascend the tower of blocks above the ledge to gain a bay of steeply sloping scree. Good belay at the back at a slanting crack.
P5, **P6** and possibly **P7** 4c 65m Layback up the crack and take the easiest line up the variety of ledges above, belaying where applicable, until a point where the faultline of *Hamadryad* terminates in a steep wall is reached. The ledge here provides the final belay. Exit left along the ledge, over a hut roof. Descent is either up towards Heavens Walls and over to Serengeti's Yellow Wall incline, or down towards Watford Gap, for the *Bar of Soap* scramble descent, or the abseil station of *Drunken Laughs*.
[J Brown, C Davies, J Smith 09.04.71, replacement P3 and P4 climbed by M Dicken, T Shaw 2002 and P3 partially re-climbed while journeying on *Taith Mawr*]

(P3 of *Opening Gambit* originally climbed up what is now the logical approach to *The Gay Blade*. It then traversed a ledge system rightwards back into the current line. This area of rock suffered considerable rock fall in the late 80s.)

▶ **28. Hamadryad E3 5c** ** 146m
A fine if serious feeling expedition, which follows the obvious fault line rising from a sloping terrace to the top left corner of the wall. Gear is sufficient on all but the initial pitch, and the crux jamming crack has cleaned up enough to give bomber cams, making the rusty aid bolts redundant. The route starts below a hanging triangular slab that lies below the sloping ledge a little to the left of the start of the fault line. This is currently marked by a large green boulder.
P1 5a 30m This is the least protected and most serious feeling pitch. A strenuous pull off the scree or a leap from the boulder gains a broken ledge system, which leads to the bottom edge of the slab. Pad boldly up its right edge until below the impending steep wall and traverse back left (cams in a borehole strike), here a sloping mantel gains a block belay on the ledge above.
P2 5c 39m Pick your way up leftwards to gain a rising rampline to the start of the crack (good cams and rusty bolts). Jam up this (crux) and continue to a tree belay.
P3 5a 45m Continue up the crack to a silver birch where it is necessary to pad out left to avoid the 'Bastard Bush of Twll Mawr'. Rejoin the crack above and continue to a stepped block ledge and belay.
P4 4b 45m Continue following the faultline until the exit belay of *Opening Gambit* is reached. If you judged the last belay correctly that is, otherwise pitch as appropriate. [J Brown, C Davies 10.04.71/ FFA: B Davidson, A Cope 29.10.88]

168 Twll Mawr • The North Wall

The North Wall • **Twll Mawr** 169

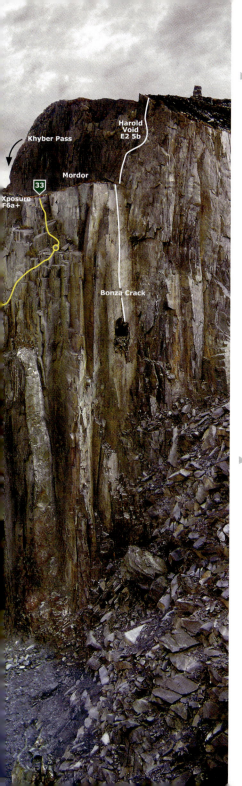

▶ **29. The Razors Edge E3/4 6a/6b** 174m
This is a very exposed climb, which forces a line up the compact centre of the wall. Here the smooth walls and sloping ledges make for very difficult route finding. The fiercely technical crux also suffers badly from seepage, and requires a good dry spell to keep you out of etriers, as does the approach to the Razor itself. Start by pulling up the chain situated at the far right end of the sloping terrace, to belay at its terminus.
P1 4c 15m Move left to a chimney. Climb this and exit right where a short traverse reaches the tree belay.
P2 6a/6b (5c with 1 pt) 40m Move left to enter the overhanging fault line, ascend this until the steepness gets worrying and a bolt on the right is attainable. Dynamic gymnastics gain the sloping ledge beyond. Continue by squirming past the 2nd bolt to exit the steepness onto a ledge system. Once on the ledge a faint groove, with some ironmongery wedged in its base, leads to the ledge above and a bolt belay.
P3 4c 36m Follow a rising traverse line right to arrive at a bay next to the buttress of *Bushmaster* below a steep wall. Belay.
P4 5b 36m A ramp line leads leftwards out of the bay and takes you up into some intimidating territory. After 10m, and just before it steepens alarmingly, fix a slate spike runner and drop left towards a notch in the arête. Cross the arête via a sloping ledge, pausing to ponder the route name, and continue shuffling left to gain a rising line of holds, bringing you to the safety of the belay ledge. Big cams (#4+) in dolerite pockets, and whatever else reassures you.
P5 4a 51m Climb left out of the bay and exit up to the col as for *The True Finish*.
[J Brown, C Davies 05.71/FFA: S Haston, T Carruthers 07.82]

▶ **30. The True Finish E4 6a/b** * 160/170m
This attempt to straighten out *The Razors Edge* provides a fine outing at the grade.
P1 4c 15m *The Razors Edge* P1.
P2 6a/6b (5c with 1 pt) 40m *The Razors Edge* P2.
P3 5a 15m Climb the corner on the right of the ledge to gain the terrace below a looming dolerite prow. Belay off assorted wires.
P4 5c 50m Above and left of the belay is a section of black rock squeezed between the dolerite pillar and a sharp grey arête. Ascend a bad step to gain the blackness (often wet - if so the original finish might be worth a look), and shuffle to where it abuts the grey slabby face of the arete. Ascend this margin until level with a reasonable ledge out on the grey slab; borehole runner up right. Gain the ledge and ease into the central seam (fairly insecure) and climb to better ledges and a blocky arête. Belay on the catwalk above.
P5 4a 20m After an awkward step trend out rightwards to the col. From here either exit left through the fence to gain the heather and scree (and descend as for *Hamadryad* adding 20m), or weave up the stacked gangways on the right to gain the Twll Mawr summit somewhat precariously, and rowan sapling belays (descend as for *Bushmaster* adding 30m of climbing with some 5a). [C Dale, G McMahon 07.89]

∧ Joe Brown on the first ascent of **Hamadryad**
photo: John Woodhead

∧ Pete Crew and Ian MacNaught Davis making the second ascent of **Opening Gambit** photo: Claude Davies

< Joe Brown stood beneath Dinas Cromlech on his 80th birthday photo: Ray Wood

It is rather fitting that the greatest climber of his generation played a key role in the early development of the Dinorwig quarries. In 1971, and only two years after work had ceased Joe was encouraged by Claude Davies to explore the possibilities of the huge North Wall of the appropriately named Twll Mawr (Big Hole). At first he was sceptical about the rock quality, but a binocular recce at Easter 1971 sealed Joe's interest in this fascinating cliff.

The first foray with Claude and Morty Smith yielded *Opening Gambit*, a fine excursion quickly repeated by Pete Crew and Ian MacNaught Davis. The original grade of VS has now been re-assessed at MXS following some serious rockfall.

Flushed with success Joe returned the very next day with Claude, Morty and John Woodhead (who came along to take pictures) and attempted the epic line of *Hamadryad*. This proved to be a time consuming exercise and much more challenging than *Opening Gambit*. In the end Morty and John retreated, leaving Joe and Claude to reach the summit seven hours after they had started. The route required a number of aid points and the placement of two bolts.

Next up was *Razor's Edge* – this took four separate visits before it succumbed; it also required a few aid points which were eventually freed in 1982 by Stevie Haston and Tim Carruthers.

With regard to the aid points it is worth remembering that Joe was forcing these lines in a strictly ground up style, hand placing bolts only as a last resort to bypass excessively loose or blank sections.

It's hard to imagine how wild the quarries must have felt in these early days, but a quote from Paul Williams' Slate of the Art article published in High magazine in 1985 gives some indication. Glyn Rhonwy had been used as an ammunition dump during the Second World War and prior to a clean up by the MOD in 1975 it was possible to stumble upon bombs and mortar shells in many of the quarries

"There is a story that Joe and Mo Anthoine were eyeing up a line in one of the quarries and smoking. Simultaneously they finished their cigarettes and stubbed them out on the floor, before discovering to their horror that they were standing on a box of gelignite."

Joe returned to Twll Mawr in the early 80s and made further attempts on a number of lines. Success came on *Scorpion* and *Bushmaster* (another route subsequently freed by Stevie Haston) but several unfinished projects remain for those brave enough to step out into this extremely adventurous territory. Would be suitors should bear in mind that on one of these lines Joe got higher than a subsequent attempt by master of looseness, Ray Kay.

172 Twll Mawr • The North Wall

▶ **31. Bushmaster E3 6a/b** ∗ 135m
The startling P2 struggles to atone for the looseness of the other 3. A double set of RPs/IMPs might help to settle your mind. Cross the scree to a deep groove, slightly above and opposite where you leave the security of the tunnel ledge.
P1 4c 30m Enter the pod on the left hand wall of the groove. There is still some looseness, so be aware. Cross onto the left arête where comfortable and follow this feature, which becomes a rib, to a flat, gorse strewn ledge below a steep slab.
P2 6a/b 45m Climb right off the ledge to the crozzly beginnings of a soaring, hairline crack, which carves up the slab above. Gain the base of the crack proper, which thins down to a fine seam. This in turn becomes a groove, the right wall of which rises and pushes you out left onto a ledge. A scary teeter regains the groove where many small wires and bewildering bridging may gain you its conclusion: a gorsey sloping ledge. Plants and scree defend the top out; a hand traverse right just below the Balcony will see you up and at the block belay.
P3 5a 45m Gain the vegetated ledge behind and to the left of the belay. Shuffle up ledges, trending slightly left, to gain an obvious left facing corner crack which terminates as a pinnacle. Follow the grooves behind to belay on a large ledge.
P4 4c 15m Continue up to the summit taking the line of least worry to gain the heathery summit. Descend right via the rust chain to Kyber Pass. Alternatively replace P3 and P4 with those of *Scorpion* for a full Twll Mawr experience.
[J Brown, C Davies 27.03.82]

▶ **32. Scorpion MXS** 133m
This route was probably always rubble, but lying as it does on the margins of solidity, pressure from the boulder glacier has given it a good jiggle. Essentially an early exploration of this section of the wall, it follows a line of least resistance, weaving round another fault line to gain the Balcony where it gains its sting: a deep rift rising to Twll Mawr's summit. This route starts about 5m right of *Bushmaster*, where a leftward rising rampline rises out of the scree.
P1 4c 32m Climb the least worrying stack of blocks up the ramp line into a groove of sorts. This is followed until below a wrinkled looking gnarly arête. Belay in a groove below this arête.
P2 5a 39m Climb the 2m groove to reach a bergschrund-like rising shelf below the wrinkled arête. Follow this shelf back left into the corner. Rising in the back of the corner is a blocky prow. This is ascended on its left hand side past a shrubby tree. Once on top, step right onto a gentle ramp, which then switches back onto the Balcony. Belay at the tunnel entrance to Middle Earth.
P3 5b 40m You didn't come all this way to escape out the tunnel did you? Scramble above the tunnel to the bottom of the big rift. Climb this with great effort and trembling to a sloping ledge ridden with dog rose. A rather exposed reach out to the left arête and big holds lead to the tunnel boulder belay.
P4 5a 22m Continue towards the summit up the final steep and juggy wall, gaining a hidden grassy col and rowan tree belay. Escape is down the rusty chain to Khyber Pass.
P3 and 4 make a rather enjoyable E2 5b (worth a star) in their own right, access is via the tunnel from Mordor. [J Brown, C Davies 17.04.81]

▶ **33. Taith Mawr E4 6a** ∗ 283m
The Epic Girdle; ED2 is more like it! To get it in a single push will definitely require a summer's day, prolonged dry weather and an early start. Begin by abseiling into *The Quarryman's* ledge and belay as for *The Wonderful World of Walt Disney*.
P1 4c 25m As for *Opening Gambit* P2.
P2 5a 18m As For *Opening Gambit* P3, to the "possible" belay on the arête; big cams and an array of slings, hooks, whatever...
P3 5b 25m Traverse right to the end of the ledge and drop down 1m onto a continuation ledge. This terminates in a ledge with a shot hole in it which will take a folded nut. Continue traversing right in a gingerly fashion, with hands on a rail of flakes (occasional sky hook placements). Eventually a vertical crack and some good gear is reached. Drop down a little and continue traversing to a hanging flake. Ascend this to belay in the groove of *Hamadryad*.
P4 5b 40m A poorly protected pitch. Follow *Hamadryad* until level with the Bastard Bush of Twll Mawr. Traverse underneath this to gain a big ledge on the right hand arête of the *Hamadryad* groove. Climb up a series of sloping ledges, keeping slightly right of the arete, until level with a sloping triangular ledge perched in a corner above some alarming steepness. This is your belay; the gorse may have returned so bring some secateurs.
P5 5a 40m The secateur pitch, clear at the time of writing, but the gorse keeps growing... Climb the groove behind the belay until it is possible to step right and up onto a sloping ledge. Slither right to a big flat hold and continue to a jug by a gorse stump which allows upward movement. More slopey slithering follows, heading rightward below a perched terminator block, around a rib and into the groove beyond. Clamber up onto the ledges on the right, gain the dolerite arete and mantel to the belay of *The True Finish*.
P6 4a 20m Walk along the ledge and down to *The Razor's Edge* belay below.
P7 6a 30m Now it gets serious; check the daylight and seepage as the next 2 pitches are fairly inescapable. Down climb *The Razor's Edge* a few metres to the 1st significant sloping ledge. To your right is a series of sloping holds terminating in a gap, above and beyond which there is a slate spike and another slightly higher foot ledge. Lasso the spike, and rock over up onto the ledge (poor

cam slot above next to a rounded jug). Bridge across towards the arête on huge foot holds and limbo under the impending holdless headwall to gain the jug on the arête proper (crux). Scamper round, remembering to protect your second, and belay in the corner below.
P8 5c 30m Climb above the belay until it is possible to pull out right onto a sloping ledge, shot hole protection. Insinuate right around the sharp arête and pop for the jug in the right wall. Campus to the ledge (pro), and continue right down a bad step to a vegetated ledge. Belay on the far right at a crack.
P9 4b 45m Drop down to the Balcony. Traverse above the belay of *Bushmaster*, above the tunnel entrance, and up towards the chimney of *Scorpion*, drop right and proceed to the huge perched block at the end of the terrace. Surmount this and belay on the ledge above.
P10 4a 10m Follow the ledge back left until it is possible to gain the Khyber Pass.
[M Dicken, J Byrne P1-P4 05.10.08, P5-P8 19.02.07, P9-P10 M Dicken 28.01.08]

▶ **34. The Punters Retreat E3 5b** 55m
This is a handy exit from the belay at the end of P4 of *Taith Mawr*, should things turn awry. Leave the bay heading left to gain a series of sloping ramps. This should lead you to a blocky tower with a V shaped cam slot on its right hand side. Climb this tower and head upwards to a steep bay with a stepped arête projecting from its middle. Ascend the arête, shuffle left and move up to a verdant, shelf-capped bay just below the top (possible belay). Climb onto the shelf on the right and bumble left around a sharp arête to an easier exit. [M Dicken, J Byrne 05.10.07]

The South Wall

The routes on the South Wall, which lies between the Tunnels of the Skull and the Quarryman Wall, are very different in character to those found on the lonesome expanse of the North Wall. Aside from being much shorter they are much more conventional and stable climbs. There was an E2, **Practically Esoteric** [N Dixon, A Popp 13.07.86] which ventured into the walls above the large terrace leading away from the tunnel, but it fell down. Happily, the surviving routes are on solid walls and are generally single pitch. This area does suffer from a lack of sun (excepting summer mornings) and more seriously, tourists and adolescents lobbing rocks on your head. Bring a helmet, or select a quiet day.

The Lower South Wall

Comprised of routes originating from the Quarry floor, and accessed through the tunnel from the Peregrine Walls. See the addendum on page 320 for details of recent additions: *Supermassive Black Hole* F7a, F6b+, F6c+, F6b and *Black Hole Sun* F7a+, F7a, F7a.

▶ **35. In the Line of Fire F?** 30m
The grade is unknown (Steve can't remember), but it does look good. Climb the corner (some gear is required to gain the 1st bolt), exiting left at the roof, then head for the hanging ladder. A bolt out left marks the departure from ladder; continue up the line of bolts to a ledge and a bolt belay. Abseil into the tunnel entrance below. [S Mayers 1993]

▶ **36. Running Scared F7c+** * 20m
The attractive, smooth slab between the bottom pitches of *Supermassive Black Hole* and *Black Hole Sun* gives a good, hard pitch. The lower half leads easily to a delicate step left and a rest before the crux section. Climb up until the holds blank out and then go right on tiny edges and up to some good holds leading to a crack and the right arête. Bolt belay. [S Mayers 1993]

The Upper South Wall

This ledge system is accessed via abseil from the bolt station at the start of the Alcove approach, to a bolt belay.

▶ **37. Wolfhound E4 6a** 15m
This is the hanging finger crack left of the belay, so called because it's a bloody big dog! Gain the crack, placing a skyhook if you get scared, and tussle to the top, wriggling in small wires wherever possible. Blocks and fence posts for belay. [P Hawkins, R Deane 10.05.86]

▶ **38. Birdman of Cae'r Berllan E2 5c** 15m
The wide crack right of the belay provides good wholesome fun with a bit of a struggle at the top. [R Deane, P Hawkins 10.05.86]

Lost World & Mordor

Style: Trad/sport
Aspect: Varied
Approach: 30 minutes
Altitude: 1-200m
OS Grid ref: 565 608

Prometheus Unbound	E6

The Long and Winding Road	E5
Lost Crack	E5
Lord of the Rings	E4
The Wall Without	E4
The Coolidge Effect	E4
Dinorwig Unconquerable	E3
Geographically Celibate	E3
Pain Killer	E3

Harold Void	E2
Bonza Crack	HVS

Sauron	F8b
The Wall Within	F7c+

Full Metal Jack Off	F7a+
Saruman	F7a
Dragon Slayer	[E4 6b] F7a

The Porphyry Chair	F6c+
Journey to the Centre of the Earth	F6a+

An atmospheric and secluded section of the quarries with many esoteric wonders and a good mix of traditional adventures and modern sport lines, including two of the most impressive clip ups in the quarries: *Sauron* F8b and the brilliant *Wall Within* F7c+.

Conditions: These are deep, steep holes, so the general rule is that the north east facing walls are shady and slow drying (eg. *Journey to the Centre of the Earth*), while the other side of the quarry will dry quicker and get sun (Khyber Pass, Lost Level, *Prometheus* etc). The deeper the routes are, the slower the dry time. Seepage is only really a problem on *Barrel of Laughs* and some of the Middle Earth routes, but *Wall Within* can get a bit grubby.

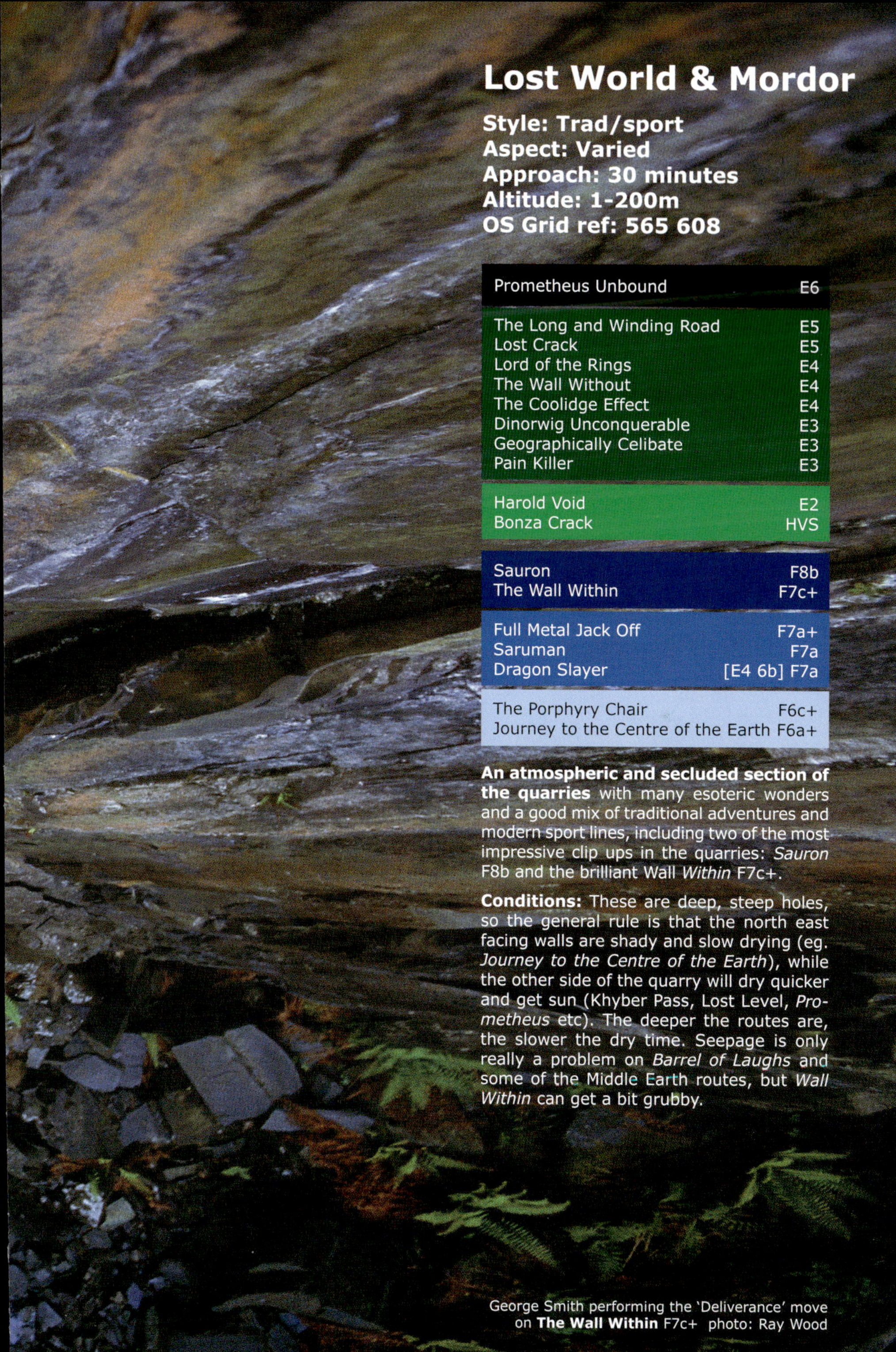

George Smith performing the 'Deliverance' move on **The Wall Within** F7c+ photo: Ray Wood

176 Lost World & Mordor • Introduction

Approach: The recent landslides into the back of Twll Mawr have rendered access to this area of the quarries a bit more awkward. The original approach involved crossing a level to reach the ladders leading down into these little visited holes. This level has now collapsed and in the process left a rather comical looking railtrack suspended above a terrifying scree shute. Future slumps seem likely in this vicinity so take care and be prepared to revise your plans accordingly.

For now the best method is to follow the main quarry track from the side of Twll Mawr towards Nant Peris for a few hundred metres until it is possible to access the Matilda incline. Walk up the incline, noting the collapsed level with the hanging rail track on the left, but continuing up to the next level. Walk left and follow the metal pipe down the scree by a winching tower to reach the far side of the collapsed level. A double ladder leads down to a col known as the Khyber Pass, the site of the initial batch of routes. A further set of ladders drops down into Mordor and thereafter a tunnel leads through to the aptly named Lost World.

An alternative access route (and one which avoids the land collapse area) is via abseil to Heaven Walls, which can be reached from Serengeti or the East Braich of Australia.

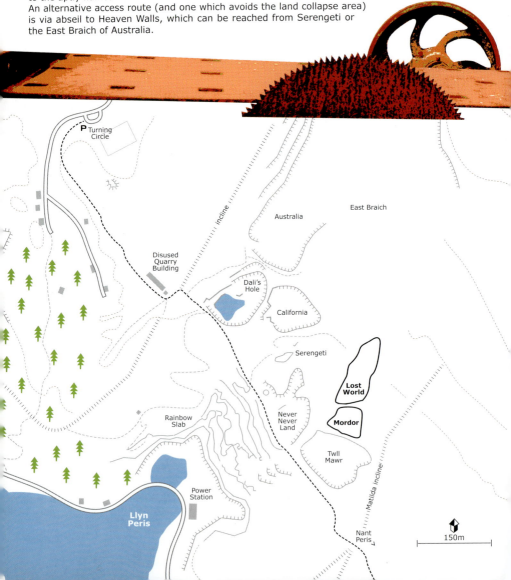

The Khyber Pass • **Lost World & Mordor 177**

The Khyber Pass

The 1st routes start from the col at the bottom of the 1st set of ladders.

▶ **1. Two Steps to Heaven,
Three Steps to Hell E4 5c** 20m
A bold chop route. Start as for *The Wall Without*, then move rightwards around the arete and climb up a series of stepped ledges and continue directly up the scary wall to the top. The hut provides the belay. [M Reeves, I Roberts 01.05.00]

▶ **2. The Wall Without E4 5c** ✶ 18m
A quality pitch tackling the obvious greenstone arete close to the ladders. Climb up past a thread at 5m. gain better holds and continue, before moving slightly left at the top. The hut provides the belay. [R Kay, M Crook, J Tombs, N Craine 09.98]

▶ **3a. Harold Void E2 5b** ✶ 18m
The incredibly exposed arete opposite *XXXposure* provides more than a little excitement! Gain the groove, turn the roof and revel in over 100m of air between your toes. Lots of rope required to gain the hut thread. See the Twll Mawr topo on page 168. [Mark Dicken, Calum Muskett 10.04.10]

▶ **3. XXXposure F6a+** 8m
An exposed and photogenic little route high above the North Wall of Twll Mawr. Climb the short arete on the edge of the void; 3 bolts to a lower-off. See the Twll Mawr topo on page 168.
[I Lloyd-Jones, P Targett 06.07.07]

▶ **4. Dragon Slayer F7a [E4 6b]** ✶✶ 18m
An excellent route that would be a sport route were it not for the alarming 2nd clip. Tackle the obvious, exposed arete close to the top of the ladders dropping into Mordor; 5 bolts lead to a lower-off. See the topo on page 182.
[D Taylor, P Robertson, M Davies 06.96]

The next route starts from the tunnels that lead through to Lost World.

▶ **5. Prometheus Unbound E6 6c** ✶✶ 60m
An impressive route with some long reaches and difficult clips. Start from the roof of the shed situated at the entrance to the tunnel which leads through to overlook Lost World.
P1 6c 35m Climb up the obvious groove with a crack in its left wall. At 6m pull round left and move up to a 2nd bolt, then go up past another 3 bolts then pull out left to gain a 6th. Move up again for 6m, keeping to the arete on the right, to reach a double bolt belay.
P2 6b 25m Climb the arete above, or if lacking in stature try the wall left of the bolts. At the 2nd bolt move left for a couple of metres and head directly to the top.
[C Dale, A Grey, J Silvester 05.87]

Prometheus Unbound is a play by Shelley, named after a lost play by Aeschylus. Prometheus stole the secret of fire from the gods.

Mordor

As is befitting of its Tolkien based name, this 130m deep hole has a profoundly adventurous atmosphere. Aside from the sport climbs located at the bottom of the quarry, all of the routes demand a significant level of commitment.

Approach: Descend the shakey ladder taking care where the rungs are missing. At this point a level runs almost all the way around the top of the Middle Earth level. *Bonza Crack* is actually in Twll Mawr but is now only accessible via the tunnel by the ladder.

▶ **6. Bonza Crack HVS 5b** ∗ 28m
The original approach, across right hand side of Twll Mawr, is now not possible. the good news is that the climb is still possible, and the new, and rather convoluted, access route adds a bit of adventure and mystery to the outing. Nonetheless it should be noted that the entire pillar containing the route is now alarmingly detached! See the Twll Mawr topo on page 168.
P1 5b 18m Step out of the tunnel and climb the hand crack in the wall on the right (facing out) in a sensational position to reach a belay on a ledge just below the Khyber Pass.
P2 10m Carry on more easily to reach block belays on the Khyber Pass.
[N Lowry, T Woodhead 25.08.96]

Back in Mordor at the level at the bottom of the wobbly ladder are the other routes that are found around this amphitheatre. Just before the huge rock fall is a wall of stacked blocks leading up to a massive, steep groove that goes nearly the full height of the quarry.

▶ **7. Tick's Groove Project**
The Tick being Paul Williams. The initial loose pitch was climbed in the late 90s by Martin Crook and Ray Kay, but the main pitch remains unclimbed. A word to would be suitors: please respect the onsight, bolt free ethic on this line. (see the topo on page 179).

As you continue round the level over large debris from yet another large rock fall, there are 2 tunnels leading through to the Lost World.

▶ **8. Geronimo's Cadillac HVS** 90m
A serious slate adventure; it is probably advisable to be climbing well within your grade! Start to the right of the tunnel leading through to Lost World.
P1 4c 35m Amble up avoiding any real difficulties to just below the col, then move left of the tree to belay at a tunnel entrance.
P2 5a 18m Climb the rubble filled chimney (easier than it looks) to belay on the loose spikes as for *Young Man Afraid of Horses*.
P3 27m Walk leftwards to reach a further chimney and follow this to the top.
[R Kay, S Haston 04.87]

▶ **9. Wild Horses E3 5c** 68m
An adventurous route finishing in a spectacular position up the arete above the col. Said to be excellent, but the state, or even existence, of the peg on the top pitch is unknown so the E3 grade may not apply. Start in a small bay left of the Lost World tunnel.
P1 5c 38m Move up past an iron spike, then go up right and past a mantelshelf before moving right again to enter a groove, peg. Continue up grooves moving right at their top before gaining a block belay below the final arete.
P2 5c 30m Go up to a peg runner before gaining the arete (crux), which is followed on large flat jugs to the top. Iron stake belay.
(NB. On the 1st ascent a belay was taken in the tunnel entrance as per *Geronimo's Cadillac*.)
[R Kay, M Crook, D Holmes 18.09.98]

Sep'arete HVS 4c, 4c [P Richardson, P Jenkinson] followed P1 of *Geronimo's Cadillac* to a belay on the col. It then took a groove at the base of the left arete and followed the arete direct to the top. The relationship between this and the top pitch of Wild *Horses* is unknown?

▶ **10. Young Man Afraid of Horses E5 6a** 82m
A serious undertaking with deckout potential on the poorly protected last pitch. Start at the foot of the buttress at a thin crack left of the bay of *Wild Horses*.
P1 5a 27m Climb the crack, then go up via ledges and a groove to a flat ledge; belay in a crack behind the gorse bush.
P2 5a 37m Trend up rightwards on ledges to a slabby orange area and a thin crack. Climb this, exposed, on good holds then finish up large ledges to gain loose spike belays.
P3 6a 18m Go up slightly left of the belay and up a shallow groove past some hard moves on loose holds. Finish up jugs to reach the summit of the spur. A dangerous pitch.
[S Haston, R Kay 04.87]

Further up left is a small wall with a bay (ie. The Alcove) above.

▶ **11. Lord of the Pies E1 5c** 10m
An insignificant route tackling a small corner. Lower off. [M Payne, M Reeves 1999]

Mordor • **Lost World & Mordor 179**

The Alcove • **Lost World & Mordor 181**

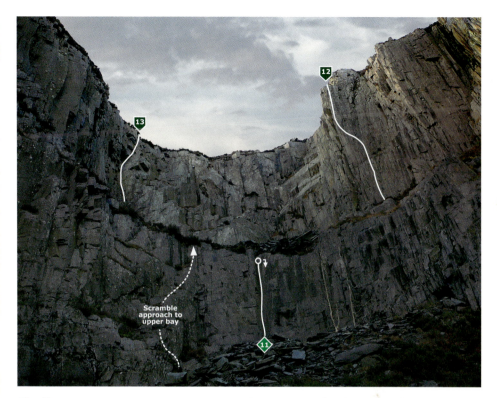

The Alcove
It is possible to scramble up to the left of *Lord of the Pies* to reach the hanging bay above. The next route is situated up to the right.

▶ **12. Lord of the Rings E4 5c** ✶✶ 38m
A reasonably protected crack up the slab precedes a bold section leading to the stunning knife edge arete above. Climb the crack up the centre of the slab on the right hand side of the bay to a ledge. Make a move to clip the 1st bolt and move up and left passing a difficult move to reach the 2nd bolt on the arete. Continue easily up the arete passing another couple of bolts to belay well back. [M Reeves, T Luddington 1999]

▶ **13. Fellowship of the Ring E3 5c** 38m
Yet another adventurous undertaking. On the left hand side of the bay is a tree; left of this is a left to right trending system of grooves. Climb up to a block to enter the wide groove, and follow this with much excitement to the top.
[T Luddington, M Reeves, M Payne 1999]

Carrying on around the level leads to the last set of routes; these start from a point beyond the triple ladders to Middle Earth.

▶ **14. Rosen the Chosen E2 5b** 57m
Start adjacent to the ladder which descends into the hole, by a rusty peg.
P1 5a 45m Move up into the middle of the wall via ledges and cracks to the top of a large block via a mantelshelf. Move up and go diagonally up right via a flake and ramp line to a poor belay on the arete.
P2 5b 12m Straight up the arete via long reaches and steep climbing to a final loose crack. Bold!
[R Kay, M Crook 26.09.98]

▶ **15. Josy Puss E5 6a** 47m
More serious terrain; The obvious groove left of *Rosen the Chosen* leads to a crack in the headwall.
P1 6a 40m Climb the steep pillar to a good ledge, and then take the groove to reach the fine crack. Go up this, over a small roof and into more cracks. Climb the cleft moving left into a groove which leads to a ledge and a spike belay.
P2 5a 7m Foot traverse rightwards and make a long step to the arete. Move up and finish up a shallow corner with care. Stake belay.
Descend via the rusty chain to the Khyber Pass.
[R Kay, J Tombs 09.89]

< Ian 'Wraith' Wilson high up on the classic **Dinorwig Unconquerable** E3 5c, Lost World   photo: Ian Parnell

182 Lost World & Mordor • Middle Earth Level

Middle Earth Level • **Lost World & Mordor** 183

▶ **16. Maupin Rey Route E3 5c** 54m
Alledgedly an "excellent outing with a stunning final pitch" up the obvious hanging corner crack. Start at the end of the level by a tunnel.
P1 5a 25m Climb the groove and fin to a ledge. Move left into a corner and crack and follow the obvious groove on the right to the top. Traverse left to belay on ledges.
P2 5b 13m Climb the serrated edge on the left to a bird's beak. Interesting moves round this lead to a rightwards traverse into a grassy bay. Go up left to belay.
P3 5b 6m Climb the bulge on small holds to gain better ones, then traverse right to belay at the base of the corner crack.
P4 5c 10m Climb the corner crack above with difficulty in a fine position. 2/2.5" gear useful. Descent: as for *Josy Puss*.
[R Kay, N Peplow (AL), M Crook 10.98]

Mordor • Middle Earth Level

From the base of *Rosen the Chosen* there are 3 suspect looking ladders dropping down to the very bottom of the quarry. Descend these carefully. Or if you don't fancy that it is possible to reach the lower-off bolts at the top of *The Porphyry Chair* from the base of *Maupin Rey Route*.

▶ **17. Whitemate V 5** ✶
The icefall adjacent to the ladders occasionally forms in hard winters. [S Haston 1980s]

Further left are 3 bolted lines.

▶ **18. The Porphyry Chair F6c+** ✶✶ 30m
The long corner 10m to the right of *Journey...* past 7 bolts to a bolt lower-off (assuming you have a 60m rope). An odd sitting move by the 6th bolt provides an inspection point for those with ambitions to lead the Catholic church.
[P Pritchard, A Wainwright, T Leppert 19.07.96]

▶ **19. Journey to the Centre of the Earth F6a+** ✶✶✶ 32m
Originally pitched as "one of the only ace E1s in the quarries" - Paul even left a metal 'E1' layed out on the floor after his ascent to emphasize the point. Climb the central groove/rib. 7 bolts to an abseil station.
[P Pritchard, D Kendal, A Wainwright 30.07.96]

▶ **20. Full Metal Jack Off F7a+** ✶✶ 30m
Another esoteric bombshell. To the left of *Journey...* is a massive corner with a mirror smooth right wall. 7 bolts protect; move left at the last one. Lower-off (assuming you have a 60m rope). [P Pritchard, G Westrupp 26.06.96]

Slatehead • Ray Kay

A man who deserves more than just a passing mention and one who famously risked everything, often with unsuspecting partners, on the huge unstable walls of Mordor and Australia.
Ray's slate routes are legendary and include such horror shows as *Hong Jagged Route of Death* E3 5b in Vivian and several deeply adventurous lines in Lost World (*A Small Rusty Nail on a Large Mantelpiece* E5 6a) and in Mordor (*Josy Puss* E5 6a and *Maupin Rey Route* E3 5c). All of these routes were done in impeccable ground up style – a remarkable achievement given the unpredictable nature of the rock.
Although Ray was generally a mild mannered chap, he was also more than capable of going toe-to-toe with anybody who wound him up sufficiently. He once had a colourful altercation with his old pal Stevie Haston, a man not known for his shyness in the 'dobbing' department. This spilled out onto the Llanberis High Street from an adjacent house. Stevie had a set of ice axes, yet Ray was said to have been armed with a machete (allegedly)! Remarkably no serious harm was done to either party.

Ray Kay and Nick Peplow on the first ascent of **Maupin Rey Route** E3 5c photo: Martin Crook
Ray Kay photo: Martin Crook

Lost World

This little visited, secluded hole has a peculiar atmosphere and a number of intriguing routes. The verdant foliage and red streaked walls add to the sense of stepping into a mysterious place, a place where the imagination can run riot.

Assuming you have entered via the Mordor tunnel you will be presented with a striking red wall on the right. The 1st line of bolts is:

▶ **21. The Wall Within F7c+ *** 30m**
A brilliant clip up that may yield to the talented or the patient. A crux section leads up to a memorable undercutting scenario. Thereafter a very pushy layback sequence gains a good hold; steadier, but still eminently fluffable ground leads to the top. [G Smith 06.96]

There is a partially bolted project to the left.

▶ **22. North West Face of the Druid E6 6a 97m**
The original line to breach the full height of the quarry snakes up the huge pillar feature to reach a quality crack finish on the headwall. Adventure guaranteed!
P1 3c 15m Scramble up the left hand side of the pillar, to belay in a tunnel mouth.
P2 6a 26m Move right and onto the slab and climb it for a few metres before making a traverse rightwards to a ledge and a poor peg. This peg was removed and replaced by hand on the first ascent of *The Colridge Effect*! Enter a small niche above before exiting from it and traversing right to a crack line. Follow the crackline until it is possible to move right to the arete and a peg belay. On the first ascent P1 and P2 were linked together.
P3 5c 30m Step out right from the belay and climb the arete to a large loose flake. Move up right and then diagonally back left to a large ledge and spike runner. Move up right to another large spike and keep right to finish on a larger ledge.
P4 5b 26m Climb the obvious crack/flakeline to finish out rightwards from the top groove.
[T Hodgson, S Chesslett 01.05.87]

(NB. For many years there was confusion over the top pitch of the *North West Face of the Druid*. It was known erroneously as *The Lost Crack*, an E2 claimed by Steve Sinfield and Mark Katz in 1998.)

▶ **23. Towse's Project E?**
This is reached by following the tunnels from above the Khyber Pass to the final window that overlooks the Lost World at a large block (i.e. just beyond the window with bolts at the top of *The Wall Within*). It is from this window that you can gain access to Towse's serious onsight project, and the upper pitches of *The Coolidge Effect* and *Small Rusty Nail*...
The groove above the blocks, at the end of the tunnel, marks the line. There is an old peg 6m up.

▶ **24. The Coolidge Effect E4 6a * 91m**
Something of a rambling adventure, although it does have merit; the groove of P3 for example, is one of the strongest lines on slate. Start at the toe of the pillar 50m left of *The Wall Within*. The 1st 2 pitches share ground with *North West Face of the Druid*.
P1 3c 15m P1 of *North West Face of the Druid*.
P2 5c 20m Climb the arete on the left side of the tunnel (looking out) arrange gear in the roof of the tunnel, before stepping out right and climbing the slab to the next tunnel mouth.
P3 6a 28m At the end of the tunnel is a block; above is a deep and intimidating groove. Climb rock up and left into the groove, to establish yourself on the left below a short wall capped with scree. Climb up with a compulsory pull on the scree, to arrive at another ledge. Above is the main corner, climb the crack on the right to reach another ledge with some stacked blocks. Move left into the corner proper and carry on until some jammed blocks are reached. Now move out right into 2 discontinuous crack systems to arrive on the Lost Level.
P4 5b 28m P4 of *North West Face of the Druid*.
[M Reeves, L Morris, D Hollingham 1999]

(NB. P3 of the *Coolidge Effect* was first climbed on the 2nd October 1987 by Paul Jenkinson and Mike Thomas. The lads took the final chimney section direct with some "manic squirming". It was named *The Tampon Trip* and hailed as "the loosest pitch on slate".)

▶ **25. Small Rusty Nail on a Large Mantelpiece E5 6a 86m**
Start at the end of the tunnel at a large block belay as per *Towse's Project*. Or, alternatively, approach via *The Coolidge Effect*.
P1 4a 20m Traverse across ledges to belay in a corner at some situ stakes.
P2 5c 18m Climb the right arete past an in situ hammer (blade peg removed).
P3 5c 18m Head diagonally left in an off-hands corner crack. Belay at large tombstone-like flakes.
P4 6a 10m Traverse across the left wall, in situ wire, then follow the crack to large ledges.
P5 5c 20m Wander up slopey ledges and cracks to the top.
[R Kay, T Hodgson, D Towse 08.08.98]

Lost World • **Lost World & Mordor 185**

Contrary to popular belief, 'Big G' doesn't live amongst the seals in the deep dark zawns of Gogarth. He actually has a house in Fachwen and has regularly strolled into the quarries over the past 25 years to bag classic first ascents. George usually resorts to two knee-bars per pitch on his routes; an ethic based on Joe Brown's two pegs per pitch and later Redhead's two bolts per pitch. However, this controversial stance is largely unattainable on slate and he has resorted to conventional 'grab and pull' techniques. Amongst many fine creations, his best is undoubtedly *The Wall Within*, an essential yet brutally exhausting tick. Together with Chris Parkin, another important slate activist who is still keen today, they finished off the development of California Wall, producing several big leads including the magnificent *Waves of Inspiration* and the lonely *Stairway to Silence*.

George was actually responsible (along with Perry Hawkins) for the first slate guidebook. Dinorwic Slate Quarries came out in 1986, and provided a template for the classic Paul Williams/Climbers' Club Llanberis guide which was released the following year.

∧ Big G and his gaffa tape repaired watch photo: Si Panton

The Lost Level

This is an isolated ledge high on the walls of Lost World. The least frightening access is to approach as from the level above the access ladders to Khyber Pass. Follow the grassy hillside over a hidden level to just above the col between Lost World and Mordor (the site of some hairy slack lining and a BASE jump once upon a time). A tentative gander over the edge hereabouts will locate a deathly scramble, or more sanely an awkward-to-rig abseil (stakes might be useful).

▶ **26. Lost Crack E5 6b** * 18m
This plumb line gently looms overhead. Once lashed to its base, get stuck in and enjoy the struggle. [G Smith 1998]

On the opposite side of the quarry and down left of the Heaven Walls is the following:

▶ **27. Geographically Celibate E3 6a** * 18m
An attractive looking line. Start beyond the hut below an arete at the right hand end of the wall, beneath a line of bolts. Climb up to the base of the arete from the right, until it is possible to ascend ledges up the right side of the arete. From the top of these ledges swing left onto the arete and carry on past another bolt and some small wires to belay on the ledge above.
[M Reeves, M Payne 2001]

Heaven Walls

These intriguing walls lie high up on the back left side of Lost World. They can be reached by a series of ladders running up from the base of the quarry, but the more usual approach is from the Serengeti area: walk up the scree path behind the Seamstress butte and up the incline that rises up across the top of Yellow Wall. Continue up, following a vague path through heather until it is possible to drop past a hut into a wide cutting. Walk rightwards through the cutting until it terminates above the void.

The 1st route is found in the cutting:

▶ **28. The Barrel of Laughs E1** 18m
The rounded rib on the left wall of the cutting provides a minor diversion with a trio of amusing variations:
The Mere Giggle 5b steps up and right from the 2nd bolt.
The Sniggering Smear 5c steps left from the 2nd bolt to finish diagonally left past the 3rd bolt.
The Biggest Joke 6a is the directissima!
[M Raine, S Howe 15.10.86]

All the other routes lie below in Lost World itself. There is an in situ abseil station (2 bolts) on a short wall just below the edge. It is possible to scramble the line of the abseil, but it is much safer to rope up.

The Lost Level • **Lost World & Mordor** 187

▶ **29. Dinorwig Unconquerable E3 5c** ✱✱✱ 41m
The clean cut corner left (facing in) of the abseil is cleaved by an immaculate, parallel sided crack; depending on your upbringing you will either love or hate this outstanding route.
P1 5b 26m Climb the crack with a combination of jamming and laybacking manoeuvres, passing a small roof shortly before a ledge and bolt belay is reached. Take plenty of mid sized cams (especially #2 and #2.5) if you want to stay safe; remember, cam placements can be a bit 'skiddy' in smooth slate cracks!
P2 4c 15m Step up rightwards and wobble up tottering scree to gain a belay well back.
[M Raine, J Gladstone 6.4.86]

▶ **30. The Long and
Winding Road E5 6b** ✱✱ 49m
A stunning and exposed pitch. Start down and left of *Dinorwig Unconquerable*, at the base of the next corner. The route climbs the right wall of the corner following a line of pegs and bolts; there is also scope for the odd small wire placement too.
P1 6b 26m Climb up onto the pedestal and lasso the poor peg above (there is also a bolt to back this up). 'Powerglide' up rightwards for a distant side pull (this enigmatic crux has defeated a few strong teams) then ascend the wall in a fine position past 2 bolts to reach a bolt and peg belay.

P2 5c 15m Pull up onto the top of the crag. Shake right to the arete, and then wobble up over tottering scree as per *Dinorwig Unconquerable*. Or alternatively just abseil off and save yourself the horror. [M Raine, J Silvester 07.5.86]

▶ **31. Pain Killer E3 6a** ✱ 27m
The corner left of *The Long and Winding Road* provides a sustained route with good protection. Lower-off. [M Raine, S Howe 15.10.86]

▶ **32. Sauron F8b** ✱✱ 25m
The awesome, searing crackline on the big blank wall left of *The Dinorwig Unconquerable* area yields a desperate test piece. Tenuous bridging leads quickly into the crux section which involves some eye-popping 'elevator door' moves and a lunge to a finger jam. The upper half of the route eases in standard to around F7c+ and features a series of technical problems interspersed with better holds. [J McHaffie 03.03.08]

▶ **32a. Saruman F7a** ✱ 30m
An atmospheric sport pitch with a technical and precarious crux on the upper section. Lower off.
[I Lloyd-Jones, S McGuiness 05.05.11]

▶ **33. Gay Lightweights and
Hetro Stumpies E5 6a** 33m
To the right of the abseil (facing in) there is a line of flakes. These are climbed into a steep crack.
[E Stone, P Johnstone 10.87]

THE LOST WORLD

Diary of a Slatehead

The Lost World photo: Paul Williams

If Sir Arthur Conan Doyle imagined a lost world high above sea level where prehistoric beasts roamed at will he may have been interested to learn that a century or so later slatehead explorers revamped his oft copied theme in attempting to describe remote and largely subterranean quarry pits defining Upper Dinorwig's Chwarel Fawr.

Thus by descending two or three hundred feet clinging in alarm down rain rusted iron ladders into Mordor's gimletted abyss, ignoring leftwards a further depth charged black cauldron, waterfalled and yokker streaked near its crippled ferrata, slimed slippy in chain hung doom, it was possible, after a few hundred razor block yards, straight ahead, to enter, via a short tunnel, slate's Lost World. Here it seemed a silvanian epoch existing in undisturbed state had given rise to a species of giant ferns stalking vermillion beyond a glycerine pool circumferenced no more than four feet and fringed by certain lurid almost fluorescent mosses which did not seem to grow anywhere else in the quarry and if in whose waters velociraptor had swooped down to drink it might have given only slight surprise. Above us towers of slate, portalled in places, vertical and rising out crayoned and coloured these walls within. Sky open like a spartan cathedral for the unemployed in a lost world of work.

Whilst Mordor would later become the scene for several extreme slate climbs including Paul Pritchard's remarkable Journey to the Centre of the Earth and Ray Kay's Jossypuss it was Stevie Haston's leap from a rusting steel cable which at one time spanned its activity that drew attention both to the relatively remote hole and to the bizarre sport of cable jumping, a sort of ultra bungee experience using fifty metre climbing ropes attached only to slings usually around ancient rusting winding cables when and if such edifices could be found.

The Lost World itself, although close by and again the setting for subsequent high standard slate forays like Trevor 'Carlos' Hodgson's eerie North West Face of the Druid and George Smith's Deliverance moved Wall Within.

Diary of a Slatehead

The spring of 1986 saw it slumbering in peace yet containing one of the best slate lines as yet unaccounted for and visited only occasionally by whirling choughs. It had been a big night at the monastery, the Tombs had been arrested on unfounded suspicions: namely car theft, and toking interrupted by the arrival of the police. Earlier a commando knife had ensured a trip to the pub since it had enabled us to gut a skip bound settee before extracting lost tariffs from sundry visitors whose change, long since piggy banked beyond their grasp lay for many months undisturbed and sealed as if in a giant terylene envelope, sublime in its grimness, waiting to be opened.

A further five pounds discovered whilst shaking out a sleeping bag known as the Turin Shroud gave rise to a certain euphoria expressed by father Abbott throwing a couple of doubles whilst juggling with a wood axe. I, seated in an armchair being rocked back and forth by the performers free hand, caught occasional glimpses of the blade in its downward arc. Next morning leant into afternoon by which time the Tombs and I having failed to enlist anyone else with enterprise set off for Dinorwig in fine weather. Because the line lay aback the Lost World, but above some evil looking terraces we approached via switchbacks and slate ginnels above Serengeti, eventually reaching the Daddy Axel cutting. There embedded at one end in brilliant green moss lay the iron monster, its shaft extending and glove wheeled in rust symbolising former glory. Beyond it and higher a kind of short canyon lead out plateau like to overlook the Lost World where it became obvious that any attempt on the proposed line was bound to be compromised by a knuckle stretching scramble which we knew from experience were seldom easier in reverse.

Against better judgement we voted for such action figuring to take the route on sight, an unusually optimistic decision premised more on laziness than sporting pride with added allure provided by the promise of a Friend eating corner crack. Logically then cleaning on rappel seemed hardly necessary, yet we would never discover the true nature surrounding this theory in practice since moments after beginning the unpleasantness a sort of slate portcullis partially concealed in peat swung open in an ankle jarring motion and after tipping me off balance, closed back to resume its original unobtrusive position.

This event coupled with an unexpected down pour saw us easily rebuffed without making even initial moves and in turn lead towards a fickle bias anticlockwise which now favoured an abseil approach. This too was later abandoned after a half hearted attempt at procuring safe rappel stations yet it was done so in good style with a full retinue of excuses which in more inspirational mood on a different day may have been easily overcome.

Thus vowing a return it was a gentleman's retreat from the col of unconquest that somehow left us if not jubilant, at least satisfied with self imposed adjournment. Exiting this spook cloudland in time for a second appointment above Dali's Hole constituted Plan B, a strategy defined more by circumstance than careful premeditation that in the end served up further confrontation this time based on sheer technicality in a further disturbing setting.

> Dali's, so named because the master painter might have conjured such a convincingly surreal landscape has dual aspects. When flooded the hole appears no more unusual than other quarry pools surrounded by slate yet when partially or fully drained, during periods of fine weather it is home to an extraordinary petrified forest preserved in concrete, their roots submerged under a shotcrete floor carpeted in ashen grey slate blocks which help to disguise a still roofed building. The shores of this hadean pit prove a lost resting place for fetid and contorted black rubber hoses, some sparsely decorating various walls, whilst others lay languid and listless, phantom octopusses immersed in time, creatures from a black lagoon.

Diary of a Slatehead cont'd...

A tunnel entrance behind and above this defrocked aquarium gives access to California, which despite containing harder climbs hosts the magnificent arete bearing its name. A three runner Very Severe, being the Captain's seal and considered in greasy conditions a more difficult lead than the Dervish.
Only ten feet from Dali's however is the magic talking wall were tunes can be played by anyone with or without a musical bent by slapping a vertical slate facet so honeycombed with boreholes that it can be played like an instrument yet is best left as a flute for the wind.

The Captain had also been active here roped soloing the obvious V groove, Holy, Holy, Holy at 6a during a fruitful flurry of activity in 1984. "Slate man, that's where it's at" he had said. A few years later Nick Harms would add perhaps the most bizarre route in this area, The Telescopic Stem Master, twenty foot long, a slick narrow groove slabbed steep on its left wall whose 6b crux is bolt protected, and whose initial moves used to require climbers negotiating a low wall of mummified sand bags running parallel to a two foot wide stream whose unknown source emanates spring like from a dark tunnel some ten feet beyond its starting point.

The focus for Plan B however lay on the gallery above, a lone Zukator sheened smooth as if polished like a Hard Rock classic without ever having received an ascent which John Tombs and I had dubbed Dali's Diehedral.
After an easy approach I began bouldering out the first few moves unroped, whilst John conversed with 'the pigeon' who had miraculously appeared in speoleogical attire from a hidden tunnel whose entrance was concealed behind slate bergschrund a few feet to our left.

Unfettered by rope and runners I had via some unconvincing acrobatics been able to make a few moves upwards yet once tied on and attempting to place an RP1 matters became more complicated necessitating several downward exits with the proposed protection held between the teeth. An hour or so went by before the rope clipped in signifying an all important island of retreat.
Despite levying a gamut in techniques nothing much seemed to bring any progress, facing out, facing in, half bridging with a drop knee or simply trying to go for it squaddie style gave the same result and non championed the other in failure. Eventually we resigned ourselves to a second rebuttal having lost all aspiration with the ebb of day, yet as climbers do and have done since time immemorial vowed once again to return.

Thus two proposed route attempts drowned failures during one day, yet failing or retreat at worst lost in tragedy, under various circumstances are no strangers to climbing experience especially when involved in exploratory probes or pushing personal limits.

We then - the ships tied and sailing on time's heroin masts - would return, but for now, pensive in mood, walked away, away down familiar quarry paths, through slate graveyards, skiffled over fences tattooed with warning signs before crossing open ground as if accompanied by a displaced Von Trapp family singing 'Auf Wiedersein' which echoed round the slag heaps and hillsides, where you were not always welcome, in piss taking mockery. Who could blame them?

Postscript

The first route attempted was climbed in April 1986 by Mike Raine: Dinorwig Unconquerable E3 5c.
The second route finally succumbed to myself and John Tombs in 1987: Dali's Diehedral E5 6b

Martin Crook

James McHaffie on the first ascent of the desperate **Sauron** F8b photo: Ray Wood

Colossus Area

Style: Trad/sport
Aspect: South/South-East
Approach: 30 minutes
Altitude: 100m
OS grid ref: 593 602

Light and Darkness	E5
Big Wall Party	E5
Shazalzabon	E5
Major Headstress	E5
Wall of Flame	E5
Great Balls of Fire	E4
Jack of Shadows	E4
Ride the Wild Surf	E4
Colossus	E3
Catrin	E2
Bella Lugosi is Dead	E1
Horse Latitudes	F6a+/b
Alive and Kicking	F6a+

The main feature of this area is the imposing Colossus Wall, a 50m high sheer face, striped with a range of magnificent wall climbs. The routes here are big, pumpy and often quite thuggy.
By way of a contrast, the adjacent Bella Lugosi Slab offers more typical slate challenges at an accessible standard.

Conditions: The Colossus Wall faces south, so catches all available sunshine, however it does suffer from prolonged seepage after rain. The Bella Lugosi Slab dries quickly after rain, but loses the sun mid/late afternoon.

Approach: Park in the Dolbadarn Castle car park, situated on the left as you approach the power station from Llanberis. Walk along the road towards the Power Station. Just beyond the left turn leading to the Slate Museum and the Gilfach Ddu car park (and Vivian Quarry) an obvious and initially walled footpath cuts up leftwards, thereafter zigzagging up and through the trees to a longer walled zig-zag section. This leads to a small bridge at an old winding house. (NB. This point can be reached by walking up the incline from the entrance to Vivian Quarry in the Gilfach Ddu car park.) Turn right on the far side of the bridge and follow the main path until it bends left and heads up hill; cross the fence (next to the warning sign) carrying on at the same level until you reach the old quarry buildings on the left. Drop down to some broken down buildings and follow a vague path down rightwards on the right of the stream until it is possible to cross it. Continue down rightwards following a more distinctive path until you can cut back left on the Rainbow Slab level. Contour round left to reach the Bella Lugosi Slab, and just to the right, Colossus Wall: both overlooking the Power Station. The Rainbow Slab is situated further along the level, just out of sight.

Descent: From the top of the Colossus Wall head across above the Bella Lugosi Slab and follow an obvious drainage line/stream that runs back down through the woods connecting with the approach route.

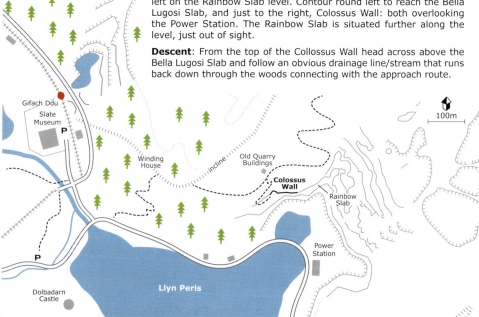

Colossus Wall Area 193

Nick Bullock burning rubber on **Great Balls of Fire** E4 6a photo: Ray Wood

Bella Lugosi Slab

The 1st routes are located on the superb steep slab to the left of the Colossus Wall.

▶ **1. Nearly but not Quite E1 5c** 25m
The open corner just left of the slab, starting on the right. A left hand start is possible.

▶ **2. Horse Latitudes F6a+/b ✶✶** 28m
The dolerite dyke inlaid into the left arête of the slab yields a great but quite pushy climb. Originally, an escape left was made from the ledge at 18m, but *The Horsin' Around Finish* makes for a better pitch, climbing the short arête on the right to a double bolt lower-off over the top.
[M Crook, I A Jones, R Drury, D Jones 15.06.85/The Horsin' Around Finish: A Holmes and S Long 20.05.86]

▶ **3. Bella Lugosi is Dead E1 5b ✶✶** 25m
An excellent route up the prominent crack in the slab to the left of Colossus Wall. The climbing is well protected with wires and cams. Sustained difficulties lead to a slight impasse, just where the crack widens near the top. Make crux moves right and up to gain the finishing ledge.
[M Crook, N Walton 28.05.84]

▶ **4. Alive and Kicking F6a+ (E1/2) ✶✶** 20m
Almost a sport route, were it not for the amusing/alarming bolt positions. Climb boldly up left from the diagonal flake to a high 1st bolt (possible micro wire below). Stand up in the niche and make crux moves past a cruelly located 2nd bolt before continuing up easier but run out ground to the lower-off shared with *Catrin*. A superb route.
[G Hughes, I A Jones 06.04.86]

▶ **5. Catrin E2 5c ✶** 20m
A feisty pitch. Start up the diagonal flake then step back left to an intense section up the shallow groove past 2 bolts. Continue up on gradually easing, but increasingly bold ground. Clip the bolt on *Alive and Kicking* and climb direct to the shared lower-off. [L Morris, M Reeves 10.03.07]

▶ **6. Frogs HS 4a** 30m
The corner is often wet. In extreme winter conditions, it gives rise to *Combined Colours* [IV].
[A Williams, A Popp 06.04.86]

▶ **7. Nifty Wild Ribo E1 5a** 43m
An uninspiring line up the back of the scrappy recess. [C Philips, S Andrews 26.02.87]

▶ **8. Shazalzabon E5 6b ✶✶✶** 40m
The striking groove line left of *Jack of Shadows* gives a memorable trip.
P1 6b 22m Climb the groove past a small overlap (Rock #3) to a bolt. Move out left onto the wall and go past a precarious spike (bolt) to good holds on the lip of the bulge, and then move back right. Rock over onto the good holds, and then execute a scary mantel to gain a ledge (cam #3 above). More difficult moves lead past a further bolt to the belay.

Jack of Shadows • Colossus Wall • **Colossus Wall Area**

P2 6b 18m From the end of the belay ledge, climb past 2 bolts, and then move left and go up to another bolt. Step right to gain an obvious undercut before making a desperate move leftwards over a bulge to eventually gain good holds. Follow these to the top.
[B Gregory, I Barton, D Gregory 16.07.89/P2 22.07.89]

▶ **9. Jack of Shadows E4 [F6c+]** ✱✱✱ 40m
Spaced bolts but just about a sport route. It is possible to lower-off after the 1st pitch. Start below a groove, left of the main face.
P1 6a 25m Gain a horizontal borehole then move up into the left-hand groove. Shuffle blindly right into the groove proper and climb up casually until forced right on flakes to a steep finish up to the ledge and double bolt belay/lower-off.
P2 5c 15m Climb the slabby groove to the top.
[O Jones, R Whitwell (AL) 22.06.86]

▶ **10. Light and Darkness E5 6a** ✱✱✱ 43m
A steep climb up the narrow front face of the pillar between *Jack of Shadows* and *Big Wall Party*.
P1 6b 25m Make a steep pull up onto the overhanging face of the pillar and go up to clip a bolt on the left. Move left on underclings past a 2nd bolt, to climb a bomb-bay chimney. Exit left at its top onto a ledge. Move right past a 3rd bolt and ascend a groove exiting right onto *Big Wall Party* at the jugs. Move left under the overhang via a finger jug on the lip (cam 1 just to the left) then awkwardly climb the slim groove on its left side to the 2 bolt belay on *Jack of Shadows*.
P2 5c 18m Move precariously right onto the front face and make a very long reach for the ledge above. Climb up the strenuous overhanging corner crack to the top. [C Dale, N Dixon 17.07.86]

Colossus Wall

▶ **11. Big Wall Party E5 6b** ✱✱✱ 47m
A very fine technical route up the left arête of the Colossus Wall.
P1 6b 30m Start just right of the slate wall at the left edge of the front face. Follow a crackline and sloping holds up to a large jug at 8m. Move left and go up to a bolt. Continue with difficulty past another 2 bolts, trending left to a good wire on the arête. Step back right and climb to a bolt (reachy); before making a long span diagonally left to reach large holds on the arête, and so gain the *Jack of Shadows* and *Big Wall Party* belay ledge, 2 bolts. Move delicately right onto the front face and make a very long reach for the ledge above, (as for *Light and Darkness*). Belay here at the foot of the steep corner crack.
P2 6b 17m Lean out and make a few desperate (but well-protected) moves right, to get established in the smooth clean crack splitting the front face. Climb this in a fine position to reach the haven of a good ledge just below the top. [J Allen, P Williams 05.07.86]

Slatehead • Paul Williams

Ironically, Paul Williams initially snubbed the quarries, dismissing them as a pile of crap, but later became the media spearhead driving the slate 'boom', enthusiastically touring the UK with a brilliant slide show called 'Slate of the Art'. He was the original Simon Panton, who also declared the quarries were rubbish a few years back, and then subsequently became a fan! So all you cynics out there; don't knock it till you've tried it! Paul left a legacy of classic extreme routes all around North Wales including those on the Colossus Wall which he made his own with a string of big steep leads, and the biggest chipped hold ever, the literally colossal 'Chipadeedodah' hold at the bottom of *Ride The Wild Surf*.
His classic 1987 Llanberis guidebook included an exciting 60 page slate section, which introduced a host of humorous slate-specific climbing terms ('hypens', 'turbo glides', 'flying hours' etc.) to the climber's lexicon and really put the quarries on the map.

^ Paul Williams and John Redhead in the mid 80s
photo: Williams collection

Chipadeedodah. photo Paul Williams

▶ **12. Major Headstress E5 6a** ✱✱✱ 45m
Another classic pitch, with bold and reachy climbing; initially independent, then swerving right to a common finish with *Ride the Wild Surf*. Steady for E5, but a little friable. Climb the crack, just in from the left arete, to a sloping niche. Clip the bolt above and climb the left arete of the V-groove to a long reach by the 2nd clip. More sustained climbing gains the sanctuary of the 3rd bolt. Pass this on layaways, then move right to good holds by the next bolt. Continue right to join *Ride the Wild Surf* and do battle with its crux groove and headwall.
[P Williams, C Gilchrist 05.06.86]

▶ **13. Ride the Wild Surf E4 6a** ✱✱✱ 45m
A tremendous direct line up the left hand groove in the centre of the wall. The route often seeps around the 2/3rds height and is best avoided if this is the case. The start passes the infamous 'Chipadeedodah' hold, right of the groove. Gain the 1st bolt then move right to clip the bolt on *Great Balls of Fire*. Move precariously back left with your feet in the chipped hole and layback the flake to a ledge. Continue up the corner, passing a number of bolts to reach a small roof. Bold climbing for 6m leads to a junction with *Major Headstress*. Swing right (junction with *Wall of Flame*) and move up into a hanging groove which provides the crux of the route. Above the ledge the final headwall is thankfully easier, but not by much!
[P Williams, D Jones 26.04.86]

▶ **14. Wall of Flame E5 6a** ✱✱ 50m
An interesting but rarely climbed eliminate which links the start of *Great Balls of Fire* with the groove of *Ride the Wild Surf* before traversing across to finish up the left arête. Follow the right hand groove, moving right into the obvious niche on *Colossus* at 23m. Step out left and climb boldly up to a bolt 6m above; hard moves left into the top of the groove just below its capping roof (bolt on left). Pull over the roof in a very exposed position with a long reach for good holds. Traverse strenuously left to the foot of the short problematic groove on *Ride the Wild Surf*. Climb this to a ledge at its top, then make an airy traverse left, bolt, into a peapod shaped groove. Struggle up this, escaping left at the top on huge holds. Stroll left to the arête and finish with ease. It is also possible to finish up *Ride the Wild Surf*. [P Williams, D Lawson 01.05.86]

▶ **15. Great Balls of Fire E4 6a** ✱✱✱ 50m
A big pitch with big holds and spaced bolts; though the climbing is never desperate. The route starts to the left of *Colossus* before crossing it and finishing in the immaculate grooves up on the right of the wall. Start below the right hand groove in the centre of the wall. Climb past a bolt to 2 bolts at 11m. A short and difficult section allows a further bolt to be reached and a groove leading to the niche on *Colossus*. From the foot of the V groove on *Colossus*, traverse right to the base of a short smooth groove. Awkward and bold climbing leads up a series of grooves and ledges to the top.
[P Williams, J Allen 12.04.86]

▶ **16. Colossus E3 5c** ✱✱✱ 51m
A fantastic route and the easiest way up this colossal wall, making it a popular outing. Although bolted, a small rack is needed to complement the fixed gear, as is a large number of quickdraws. The crux is high up and often seeps, making it very hard indeed. Start by a boulder at the bottom of the wall and make hard moves up to a ledge. From here a line of weakness snakes its way up and right to another ledge at 12m. Step left and move up to improving holds and a crack leading to the top of a pinnacle. Move up and left into a large niche, before going back right to a V groove. The top of this is capped by a roof, step up and left into a crack and climb this, crux, to eventually make an easy but airy mantel onto a ledge out left. Ledge shuffle upwards past a final awkward move to belay on bolts at the top of the crag. 60m ropes make reaching the belay easier.
[P Williams, A Holmes 27.03.86]

▶ **17. Colostomy E4** (1pt Aid) 52m
A girdle of the Colossus Wall, taking in some interesting ground. Start as for *Jack of Shadows*.
P1 6a 22m *Jack of Shadows* P1.
P2 6a 30m From the belay ledge, move onto the front face and climb up to the ledge above to arrange protection. Come back down and pendulum across to a good hold on *Major Headstress*, bolt. Climb up and right to join *Ride the Wild Surf* at a groove, and then reverse *Wall of Flame* rightwards before moving into *Colossus* at the slanting V groove. Step right into *Great Balls of Fire* and follow this to the top.
[G Farquhar, G Ettle 09.88]

There is an attractive project line right of *Colossus* and *Great Balls of Fire*, however to the right of the Colossus Wall the cliff face deteriorates, losing height and becoming more broken.

▶ **18. OM 69 Runner Bean VS** 40m
This route has a small section of good climbing, but little else to recommend it. It climbs the vague rib 30m left of the edge of the Rainbow Slab. The name comes from painted label on the white cylinder protruding from the ground beneath the rib. Ascend the rib to reach a large block. Continue up the crack above on good jams to a ledge. Climb the slabby rib to finish.
[C Philips 26.10.84]

Colossus Wall • **Colossus Wall Area 197**

Jack of Shadows

Bella Lugosi
10m

OM 69 Runner Bean and
Rainbow Slab

Diary of a Slatehead

Bella Lugosi's Dead

"The bats have left the bell towers, the victims have been bled, bled, bled, coz Bella Lugosi's dead, yeah."
Bauhaus 1984

The slate climbing experience was in most cases heightened by bizarre surroundings together with a constant threat of being guillotined by razor sharp blocks falling from above. Even after routes had undergone pre 'cleaning' (in many instances, though not all, little more than perfunctory inspections to scrape or prize off any loose flakes or dagger littered ledges rather like one might sweep a mantelpiece clear from unwanted ornaments, think lets go climbing) prior to first ascents this possibility remained the same since all top outs could not be cleaned thoroughly owing to varying amounts of debris present on individual levels, nor could it be guaranteed that local youths would not appear, oblivious of the climbers below, for a trundling session, raining down infeasibly large slate blocks which shattered on impact sending ? volleys towards unseen victims.

Bearing these points in mind, Nick Thomas and I set off for a look at what he described as a 'boss looking line somewhere near Rainbow'. Like many slateheads Nick had ranged all over the quarries, yet his specialist climbing interest often lay beyond their perimeters and rested on seemingly effortless ascents of desperate boulder problems, in which pursuit by 1984 he was well ahead of his time.

To reach the proposed route entailed an ascent of the zig zags as far as the iron bridge, before levelling off right past the temple of the mantels (several massive slate cantilevers overhanging the path) continuing via the icon of the black Madonna until rounding a bend ransacked buildings cast in 1938's pre war gloom and acting as a windswept pergola for self exiled sheep demarcated a cut off point where horizontal terrain is exchanged for steeply inclined scree leading eventually into a watershed amphitheatre whose vertically featured charcoal streaked walls provided the subject of our interest.

Once there our climbing prospect was not enhanced by a general stiffness in limbs brought about by the attendance the previous evening at a party which we did not leave until, as it were, this morning, and at which a great deal of bull in various forms had taken place. Thus against a mountain backdrop of gurgling brooks drowned out by a stereo summer heartbeat that pulsed so loud it seemed as though it would last forever, we talked climbing, whilst people danced in silhouettes that sometimes gave their sex away and the air hung heavy with drifting perfumes that seemingly came from the night boats of Xanadu, though those less romantically inclined knew that such odours bore all the hallmarks of cheap Bethesda deals.

The reality check imposed by launching onto a rock face (particularly a slate one) drew out stark contrast against previous reverie and about 6m up I began to have doubts about my ability to carry on. Arthur Birtwhistle had discussed this very problem in his seminal essay 'On leading on difficult rock' and since had lead Diagonal on Dinas Mot in 1938 with barely a runner in sight

Here it was possible, looking down double nine millys arcing in red and blue fleck snaking through karabiners attached to a blade peg, some RPs and a few Rocks, to note my lifeline's termination at Nick's sticht plate, though the device remained partially hidden from view being obscured by Nick's long hooded smock top which also served at least some protection from an ever increasing swarm of midges which now tormented him.

Bella Lugosi's Dead Diary of a Slatehead

Suddenly a Lurcher dog loped into view followed shortly afterwards by three climbers headed for the Rainbow Slab, they wore apparel that was colourful even for the style of the time and one individual in particular seemed to resemble a human Lovehearts wrapper, whilst another presented himself in the form of a moving Wine Gum packet. Thankfully these dedicated followers of fashion soon moved on so that their prismatic presence no longer distracted proceedings on the crack above, which although splendid in line, seemed only protectable by largish sized Friends, in which we had failed to invest.

Now my reasons for continuing largely rested on a premise that unless an invisible assailant chopped my arms off I would simply not let go, unless satisfied that each jam provided absolute security for the previous one to be released, a course of thinking that theoretically ensured three point contact at all times, yet took no account of failures in this system which might arise due to becoming out paced by the pump phase of the doomed, where even with superhuman will to power, strength saps away as if on an ebb tide, before inevitable ejection relegates leaders, 'if unhurt', to the cast list of also rans.

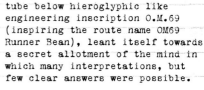

The dog came back to drink from a sort of argile river of lorna which perpetually flowed from a six inch circumference aperture with a cast iron lip some six feet right of our starting moves. This feature imbued an already bizarre physiography with further wonder which when coupled with Cliff Phillip's amazing nearby discovery of a single steel bolley emerging from the ground and seemingly protected by a cylindrical hard plastic tube below hieroglyphic like engineering inscription O.M.69 (inspiring the route name OM69 Runner Bean), leant itself towards a secret allotment of the mind in which many interpretations, but few clear answers were possible.

Returning to action curiosity lead me on so that what John Stuart Mill called the internal culture of the individual gave rise to a challenge on the parallel sided authority persisting above. What followed was hardly a revolution in technique, yet in those seemingly hour long minutes described by 'seconds' as 'ages' I had attained a standing position, after several shouts of 'watch us' atop gravestone wide slate ledges which lead with no real difficulty other than that of not severing the rope, towards cement bag belays on the edge of the exit culvert.

Martin Crook

Martin Crook, a ropeless acolyte scaling the gothic rampart of Horse Latitudes
photo: Crook collection

Rainbow Slab

Style: Trad/sport
Aspect: South-East
Approach: 30 minutes
Altitude: 100m
OS grid Ref: 594 602

The Rainbow Slab is an impressive sight to behold. A vast sweep of perfect purple slate, littered with minute edges and cast with a fan of rippled rainbow features arcing off rightwards into a sea of blankness. It is quite simply one of the finest and most majestic sheets of rock, not just in this corner of Wales, but also in the whole of the UK. The slab plays host to a number of the fabled 'designer danger' routes. In general, bolt protection comes only when it really matters, and then only to the brave or, in the case of the trio of hard sport routes, the very talented. This is not a place for the timid or uncertain, even the few easier lines require a steady head and a notable degree of commitment.

Conditions: The slab gets the sun until early/mid afternoon and main part of it dries quickly. However, the right hand side, specifically in the DOA/Drury Lane/Jai'a'n area, is plagued by a persistent drainage problem.

The Cure for a Sick Mind	E7
Raped by Affection	E7
Naked Before the Beast	E6
Prick up Urea's	E6
DOA	E6
Released from Treatment	E6
Drury Lane	E6
Stiff Syd's Cap	E6
The Rainbow of Recalcitrance	E6
Jai'a'n	E6
Ringin' in Urea's	E6

Cystitis by Proxy	E5
Chewing the Cwd	E5
Splitstream	E5
Poetry Pink	E5
Over The Rainbow	E5
Memorable Stains	E4
The Richard of York Finish	E3

Pull My Daisy	E2
Cabbage Man meets the Flying Death Leg	E2
Eros	E2
Red and Yellow and Pink and Green, Orange and Purple and Blue	E1

The Very Big and the Very Small	F8b+
Bungle's Arête	F8b
Cwms the Dogfish	F8a

∧ Jon Garside on **Splitstream** E5 6b photo: Alex Messenger
< Paul Pritchard stepping out on **The Rainbow of Recalcitrance** E6 6b photo: Paul Williams

Approach: Park in the Dolbadarn Castle car park, situated on the left as you approach the power station from Llanberis. Walk along the road towards the Power Station. Just beyond the left turn leading to the Slate Museum and the Gilfach Ddu car park (and Vivian Quarry) an obvious, and initially walled footpath cuts up leftwards, thereafter zigzagging up and through the trees to a longer walled zig-zag section. This leads to a small bridge at an old winding house. (NB. It is possible to reach this point by walking up the incline from the Gilfach Ddu car park.) Turn right here and follow the main path until it bends left and heads up hill; cross the fence (next to the warning sign) carrying on at the same level until you reach the old quarry buildings on the left. Drop down to some broken down buildings and follow a vague path down rightwards on the right of the stream until it is possible to cross it. Continue down rightwards following a more distinctive path until you can cut back left on the Rainbow Slab level. The hulking Colossus Wall should be very obvious at this point, with the Bella Lugosi area just before it. The Rainbow Slab is situated further along the level, just out of sight.

Descent: It is possible to abseil from 2 ring bolts at the top of Cystitis by Proxy. Alternatively head across above the Colossus/Bella Lugosi area and follow an obvious drainage line/stream that runs back down through the woods connecting with the approach route.

202 Rainbow Slab • Approach

Rainbow Slab

▶ **1. Freak Yer Beanbag E5 6b** 18m
The first route sits round to the left of the main slab on a steep orange coloured wall. Start above the threatening jut of rock. Ascend the groove and thin crack above with some hard layback moves. Thereafter a leftwards hand shuffle (spike runner) leads to the finish up a groove. [P Pritchard, P Dowthwaite, S Edmonson 19.07.86]

▶ **2. Cabbage Man meets the Flying Death Leg E2 5c** * 25m
A serious pitch, which traverses leftwards along the lip of the slab. Start 6m left of *Red and Yellow...* and climb a corner until a step left and up gains a scoop. Continue leftwards to the top of *Freak Yer Beanbag*. [P Pritchard, G Hughes 03.11.86]

▶ **3. Red and Yellow and Pink and Green, Orange and Purple and Blue E1 5a** ** 40m
The absence of any workable gear throughout its length ensures that this route is commonly soloed. Route finding can be tricky. Start just in from the left arête and link a line of marvellous positive edges and ledges up and right to awkwardly gain a good ledge. Move up and trend back left on positive holds to a broken area, with poor runners. From the left end of the ledge move up for a good hold and finish directly on more positive holds. Arrive at the top and savour the feeling of relief. All together now: *"Red and Yellow and ..."* [M Lynden 06.84]

▶ **4. The Richard of York Finish E3 5b** ** 40m
From the right-hand end of the broken area on the previous route, carefully climb up a thin crack to the top. [M Lynden, W Lockley 07.84]

▶ **5. Eros E2 5b** * 40m
A bold but technically straightforward route that links the 2 (more logical) adjacent routes. Follow *Red and Yellow...* until it moves back left then climb up until level with the pipe. Traverse boldly over to it (your first runner) and follow *Pull My Daisy* to the top.
[M Lynden, S Long, J Silvester, D Towse 07.84]

▶ **6. Pull My Daisy E2 5c** *** 38m
A classic and extremely popular route despite its run out finish. The first half of the route is well protected by a thin crack running up to a protruding pipe half way up the cliff. Take a deep breath and climb up until it is possible to finish out left. Thankfully the climbing eases considerably as you run it out.
[M Lynden, J Silvester 07.84]

▶ **7. Chewing the Cwd E5 6b** *** 45m
A poor mans *Rainbow of Recalcitrance*, though still excellent. Follow *Pull My Daisy* to the metal pipe then step right and up to more runners before trending delicately rightwards along a miniature ripple until easier moves lead up to the top. [P Pritchard, T Jones, M Thomas 14.02.87]

▶ **8. Released from Treatment E6 6b** *** 67m
A hard man's *Rainbow of Recalcitrance*. In reality there is only potential for 'small' pendulums, but the super thin traversing certainly accentuates the feeling of being 'miles out' from your gear.
P1 6b 37m Follow *Pull My Daisy* to the metal pipe and the runners in the crack above and right. Hard moves lead right into the crack of *Naked before the Beast* (small runners) then continue shuffling right past even harder moves to gain a solitary bolt and eventually the ledges on *Poetry Pink*. Move up to the bolt belay at the base of the prow.
P2 6b 30m Look right and make sure the coast is clear then traverse right to the bolt on *Raped by Affection*, then right again to the bolt on *Splitstream*. Continue confidently past the jug on *Cystitis by Proxy* and all the way to the right of the slab.
[D Towse, J M Redhead (AL), A Newton 25/26.04.86]

▶ **9. Naked Before the Beast E6 6b/c** *** 45m
A fierce proposition based on the hairline crack just left of the start of the rising ripple of rock (*The Rainbow..*) that runs the full height of the cliff. Climb the crack for 13m then step right onto the ripple, as for *The Rainbow...*. Step back left into the crack (it is possible and harder to climb direct up the crack) and continue with much hard work and commitment, to reach the finish of *Chewing the Cwd*. Don't be fooled by the crack; good protection is sparse. Originally, the route took a belay on the prow, though the climbing is straightforward from here.
[D Towse, J M Redhead 07.84 Direct version: J Dawes 1985]

▶ **10. The Rainbow of Recalcitrance E6 6b** *** 60m
The line of the quarries, taking the majestic ripple feature trending up and right across the slab. The hard climbing is not too far out from the protection in the crack, but big sweeping falls are possible/likely from further out.
P1 6b 30m Climb the crack just left of the Rainbow ripple for 13m to a jug, and then make an awkward step right to a rest on the ripple proper. Make a tricky move up the ripple and keep going in a tenuous fashion until *Poetry Pink* is reached (place some gear here). Continue by 'walking' confidently along the ripple, clipping the bolt on *Raped by Affection*, to arrive at the belay on *Cystitis by Proxy* (slings and high bolt).
P2 6a 30m Very bold and often very wet. Continue traversing rightwards in the same line without protection. A small ledge is reached after 12m. Finish easily up the lower of 2 black grooves. [J Silvester, M Lynden 07.84]

204 Rainbow Slab

▶ **11. The Cure for a Sick Mind E7 7a ✲✲ 28m**
A desperate line up the blank slab left of *Poetry Pink*. Start just right of *The Rainbow*... and climb directly to a bolt. Step left, then go back right to a 2nd bolt. Move left here and join *The Rainbow*... to climb its crux. Continue up to a make a scary clip of a 3rd bolt. Sustained difficulties lead up the slab into *Released from Treatment*. Carry on up and step right to the double bolt belay at the base of the prow. [P Pritchard 27.11.87]

▶ **12. Memorable Stains E4 6a ✲✲ 15m**
The left edge of the prow provides a well-positioned and exciting route. From the double bolt belay at the base of the prow, climb the arête (easiest on the left side) past 3 bolts.
[P Pritchard 14.12.87]

▶ **13. Bungle's Arête F8b ✲✲✲ 15m**
An absolutely brilliant route, proudly situated on the striking prow, high on the Rainbow slab. Although only about 12 moves long, the climbing is powerful, intense and insecure; an unexpected slip is possible at any point. There is a wall for each arm, with either hand setting the other up for an aggressive snatch to the next side pull. The feet do their bit, but are rendered clumsy by the lack of purchase, skating around like Bambi on ice, ever correcting in a desperate search for friction. Good luck, you'll need it.
[Sean Myles 12.90]

▶ **14. Poetry Pink E5 6b ✲✲✲ 43m**
The easiest and most popular of the hard routes on the slab. The argument about grade will run on, however for E5 it is a relatively steady tick.
P1 6b 30m Start beneath the prow below a bolt at 8m. Climb up to the break and make a committing mantel to clip the bolt. Make some hard moves up on shallow pockets, then run it out on easier ground to the 2nd bolt. A good rest here allows you to regain your composure before stepping left and up to the ripple. Teeter along rightwards and climb up to large edges, where gear can be arranged, before entering the awkward groove above and arriving at a double bolt belay at the base of the prow.
P2 5b 13m Either abseil off (not 5b), or climb the groove on the right of the prow.
[J Redhead, D Towse 07.84]

▶ **15. The Very Big and the Very Small F8b+ ✲✲✲ 35m**
In classic style Johnny placed a firm lid on the '80s slate frenzy with the hardest slab in the quarries. The numbers are very big, the holds very small. In fact, they are tiny: excruciatingly painful for the fingers and almost devoid of feeling for the feet. 3 bolts mark the line up the smoothest part of the slab, proving that anything is possible! Continue up *Poetry Pink* to the bolt belay on the prow.
[J Dawes 03.07.90]

▶ **16. Raped by Affection E7 6c ✲✲✲ 45m**
An astounding route; although it has been onsighted it is perhaps the boldest lead in the quarries. Inspired by Joe Brown's "2 pegs per pitch" rule, this climb has 2 bolts, the 1st being at a 22m height! Start 7m left of the foot of the abseil above the worst landing and below some blank starting moves. Thin ground (avoidable if you come in from the right) leads up to a break at 6m. Continue up the slight depression to the Rainbow (RP 2), trying not to stop and think too much. Clip the bolt above and take a moment to gather yourself; the crux is still to come. Continue to a traverse line. Either span/jump left to a crimp or continue direct and climb to a good hold and the 2nd bolt. Move right then finish direct. [J Redhead, D Towse 07.84]

▶ **17. Ringin' in Urea's E6 6b ✲✲ 45m**
A great addition to the slab which acts as a direct start to *Splitstream*. Low in the grade and never desperate, but the climbing is very sustained. Start as for *Cystitis*... and trend up and left straight away to a boss-feature from where the 1st bolt can be clipped. Thin moves lead up and right past a 2nd bolt to meet *Cystitis*... on easy ground. Climb a bold, direct line up the slab to meet and follow *Splitstream* at the end of its traverse. [N Harms 11.10.87]

▶ **18. Cystitis by Proxy E5 6b ✲✲✲ 45m**
A tremendous climb that requires a steady approach. Initially intricate and bold, then desperately thin. (NB. many people think it is a serious E6 as the gear placements have deteriorated in recent years.) Start by the small blocky ledges below a vague rib and shattered crack. Gain the crack, which offers poor micro wires, and then step boldly left and up to reach good holds at the end of the Rainbow. Move back right to some small ledges and flakes and a welcome respite. Recompose yourself and then tackle the desperately thin slab above past 2 bolts to get established on a jug. The final section is run out but tame in comparison to your lower tracks.
[D Towse, J M Redhead (AL) 29.06.84]

▶ **19. Splitstream E5 6b ✲✲✲ 48m**
Another awesome pitch, which deviously snakes its way up the slab, creating a sustained and airy piece of climbing; the hardest sections, however, are never too far from gear. Start above the small step at the base of the slab, 10m right of *Cystitis*.... Gain a thin horizontal break at 6m and continue up and left (small wire placements) to the 1st bolt. Hard moves above this allow the relative let-up on *Cystitis*... to be enjoyed. Go up to the 1st bolt on *Cystitis*... then traverse 4m left until a line of small holds leads up to the bolt shared with *Released from Treatment*. Carry on up and left to victory.
[P1: D Towse, J Redhead 05.04.86/P2: D Towse, A Newton 26.04.86]

206 Rainbow Slab

▶ **20. Stiff Syd's Cap E6 6b ✶✶✶ 52m**
The obvious crack that runs halfway up the slab is another immaculate pitch, best climbed in a one-er, but originally split with a belay on the flakes of *Cystitis by Proxy*. Start beneath the crack and 2 bolts, right of *Splitstream*. Climb up to a good slot and continue over a slight bulge to a break and the base of the crack. Climb the crack past a few spaced runners and 2 bolts to a tricky move reaching the traverse line. Head for the 2 bolts on *Cystitis by Proxy* and continue up that route. [J Redhead, D Towse 05.04.86]

▶ **21. Prick up Urea's E6 6c ✶✶✶ 45m**
Essentially a direct finish to *Stiff Syd's Cap*, launching out left from its 2nd (and last) bolt to a mantelshelf, and then continuing to another bolt, which is difficult to clip and desperate to pass. Upon reaching *Released from Treatment*, finish direct to the top of *Cystitis by Proxy*.
[N Harms, P Barbier 01.12.87]

The following 3 routes climb discontinuous cracks on the right side of the slab. Unfortunately, they are often affected by water drainage and even when dry, the rock may be coated in a scummy surface layer.

▶ **22. DOA E6 6c ✶✶ 20m**
Climb the left hand crack, passing a solitary bolt, to reach the bulge and double bolt lower-off, shared with the next route.
[R Drury, J Allen 04.07.86]

▶ **23. Drury Lane E6 6b ✶✶ 20m**
The central thin crack has a hard start followed by poorly protected climbing all the way to the bulge and a double bolt lower-off above, shared with the previous route. [R Drury, J Allen 04.07.86]

▶ **24. Jai'a'n E6 6b ✶✶ 28m**
The right most line is marked by 5 old bolts which are just too far apart for the route to be considered sport climbing. The difficulty steadily increases until very thin moves gain the recess and a respite. Continue up the short headwall on hidden holds to a single bolt lower-off.
[N Harms, J Anthoine 06.04.88]

The green stone pillar at the right hand end of the slab and the bay beyond gives rise to the following routes.

▶ **25. Over the Rainbow E5 6a ✶✶ 30m**
A brilliant and exposed top pitch up the blunt left arête of the green pillar. Steady for E5, but still quite 'out there' nonetheless.
P1 5b 15m Start at the foot of the dog-leg crack. Gain the crack and follow it diagonally rightwards, then up, to a scree covered ledge. Double bolt belay.
P2 6a 15m Go up and right onto the arete, follow this past 2 bolts until it is easier to step right, small ledge. Now follow a shallow groove back up to the arete. Just below the top, by the

4th bolt, an exciting step left around the arete leads to a fine, exposed climax.
[M Raine, M Campbell 14.04.87]

▶ **26. Cwms the Dogfish F8a ✶✶✶ 15m**
The obvious steep slab just right of the green pillar of *Over the Rainbow* provides one of the best routes in the quarries. A very sequencey pitch which will fully test an on-sight leader. The spaced clean blotches are linked in a devious fashion; continuously hard, it culminates in a perplexing capped groove. [N Harms 03.08.88]

▶ **27. The Race Against Time E3 5b 43m**
The flake crack to the right of *Cwms the Dogfish*, and pillar above, lead to a ledge and the top. A serious pitch. [S Britain, P Gilliver 25.05.86]

The next 2 routes lie in the bay to the right.

▶ **28. How Hot is Your Chilli? E2 6a 18m**
A steep start leads to the left arête of the hanging green slab on the right side of the bay. Trend right up cracks to the top. [S Lumley 21.06.87]

▶ **29. F Hot E2 5c 22m**
Climb straight up through the steepness to the slab, and finish as for *How Hot is Your Chilli?*.
[K Hawker 20.06.87]

Opposite the end of the Rainbow Slab is a slab and prominent arête.

▶ **30. Hooded Cobra E1 5b 22m**
The easiest looking broken line up the slab.
[L Hardy, C Parkin 08.07.86]

▶ **31. Little Urn E3 5b 22m**
The obvious curving right arête of the slab has a steep and loose start. [M Barnicott 27.05.86]

Slateheads • John Redhead and Dave Towse

The quarries would not be the same without the contributions of John Redhead and Dave Towse; a formidable partnership. Together they pioneered the main developments on the centrepiece Rainbow Slab and in doing so set a tough 'balls-out' ethic for the slab and the quarries in general. They allowed themselves a maximum of two bolts per pitch; homage to Joe Brown's (mostly) two pegs per pitch rule. This resulted in some massive run-outs, the biggest of which is on the infamous *Raped by Affection* E7 6c. They went on to produce more hard and bold lines in Vivian including two desperate sports routes from John: *Manic Strain* F8a and *Menopausal Discharge* F8a+ - controversially bolted, chipped, climbed and named but totally awesome and fully embraced today for the classics that they are.

⋏ Dave Towse photo: Andy Newton
⋏ JR hand drilling bolts on **Menopausal Discharge** F8a+, Vivian Quarry
photo: Andy Newton
∧ Dave bouldering on the Top College Walls, Bangor University in the early 80s
photo: Towse collection
> JR going for it on the first ascent of **Released from Treatment** E6 6b, Rainbow Slab with Dave and Andy Newton on the belay
photo: Paul Williams

Diary of a Slatehead

Somewhere over the Rainbow

The precise number of charges used to blast the great swage of smooth slate that came to be known among climbers as the Rainbow Slab, into being will probably remain a mystery except to those with fecund interest in long dust covered quarry log books. Geologists may also be furnished with a wider knowledge allowing an exploration through time as to just how and why such plans were formed whilst metaphysicians, poets and dreamers might imagine the earth's surface being cleft asunder by a ferocious axe blow from some mythical celtic giant.

What remained however would prove greatest in significance for a relatively small grouping of rock climbers who by 1984 had come be known as 'The Slateheads' and whose primary concern focussed little on the quandaries surrounding the making of the slab, but rather on attempts to climb it via various and almost invariably tenuous lines. When viewed as a whole the grey gouges, terraces, scree cones and caverns that extend almost from Elidir Fawr's summit towards bleak shorelines denting Llyn Peris and Llyn Padarn may represent a mile or so of tortured intrusion that otherwise surrounds onlookers in a landscape exemplifying natural beauty. Yet it is within this derelict sanctum the Rainbow is found dwarfed by total quarry mass, poised between the two terraces which it connects like a giant roofing slate almost one hundred and fifty feet high by two hundred feet across whilst its inclination is never less than eighty percent.

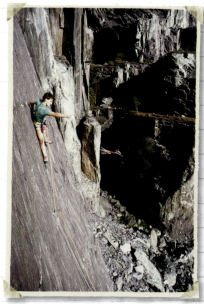

A very casual Johnny Dawes catching extra runners on Cystitus by Proxy E5 6b
photo: Paul Williams

Paul Pritchard balancing along the Rainbow during a mid 80s repeat of The Rainbow of Recalcitrance E6 6b
photo: Paul Williams

Diary of a Slatehead

Consequently few natural crags in North Wales match the unbroken grandeur displayed by the Rainbow except perhaps the legendary Master's Wall area on Clogwyn D'ur Arddu's East Buttress where those taking up gauntlets thrown down through generations in climbing history find themselves involved in at least comparable situations to those found on the Rainbow since both arenas although composed from different rock types and markedly different in aesthetic surroundings confront climbers with an inhospitable canvass necessitating a kind of slightly off vertical balance climbing usually incorporating poor protection with few escape alternatives other than long, potentially bone crunching, if not fatal, falls.

However by 1984, Clogwyn D'ur Arddu had a respectable hundred year recorded climbing history, whilst slate in general depended on relatively recent developments which started as we have seen with an isolated incident in July 1964.

In the new Rainbow drama initial attempts at climbing the slab began under a cloak of secrecy, however clandestine activity soon proved expendable when it became clear that those wishing to bag the main lines would be forced into climbing at least E3 on rock which typically gave extremely spaced protection often involving long run outs between psychologically calming islands provided by RP clusters backed up on occasion by tentative sky hook placements. These Clochetons de Ciel were rarely seen in Wales 'til the advent of slate slab climbing and even then sparingly used as a calming influence since even in the minds of the most talented leaders an exit strategy still played a part. Bolts too would become acceptable fixtures in developing 'Das Rainbow' yet again sparsely used, two in a hundred feet of climbing being normal providing climbs that without them would be virtual solos. Another tactic widely used throughout quarry operations was abseil inspection coupled with cleaning, which despite Pete Livesey's adoption of such methods whilst prospecting his historical Right Wall ascent in 1975 was still largely unorthodox on most natural crags.

Moose Thomas cranking his way up Cystitus by Proxy E5 6b photo: Paul Williams

There were many fine climbers who generally rejected slate in favour of more traditional climbing grounds, entering the quarries only occasionally for a certain route or other so that they did not really lend themselves to a roll call of 'heads' in first ascent terms. On the other hand some heads became so engrossed in slate exploration that they rarely ventured anywhere else preferring environmentally bungled surroundings to those of the picture postcard impressions associated with more aesthetically pleasing locations beyond the perimeter fence.

For my own part, concluding that they could never become an internationally renowned climbing area like Yosemite or the Chamonix Aguilles brought about a certain satisfaction which when coupled with a realization that we might, for a while at least, be left alone to do our own thing gave rise to plans for further participation in this theatre of the absurd.

Martin Crook

Rainbow Walls Lower

Style: Trad/sport
Aspect: Varied
Approach: 15-30 minutes
Altitude: 200m
OS grid ref: 594 601

The Homicidal Hamster from Hell	E5+
The Listening and Dancing	E5
Jaded Passion	E4
Jugs Mawr	E3
Unchain My Heart	E3

Pork Torque	E2
Midnight Drives	E2
The Colour Purple	E1
Tongue in Situ	E1
Come Inside	5.9
Saved by the Whole	HVS
Pigs in Space	HVS
Greedy Girls	HVS

Emerald Eyes	VS

The New Slatesman	F8b
The Untouchables	F8a
Concorde Dawn	F8a
The Mu Mu	F7c+
Chitra	F7c+
Rowan	F7c
Doggy-Style	F7c

Satisfying Frank Bruno	F7b+
Vermin on the Ridiculous	F7b
Song of the Minerals	F7b
Cig-Arête	F7b
Where are my Sensible Shoes?	F7b
Coming up for Air	F7a+
Pocketeering	F7a+
Gerbil Abuse	F7a
The Take Over by Dept. C	F7a

The Spleenal Flick	F6c+
Sleight of Hand	F6c
Drowning Man	F6b
Gwion's Groove	F6a+
Overtaken by Department C	F6a

An excellent selection of characteristically intense slate routes. The short levels to the right of the Rainbow Slab and behind the Power Station offer a friendly environment in which to climb. Vegetation has begun to reclaim the flat lands, partially masking the harsh reality of the industrial past. The climbing is typically 80s style, encompassing an intricate balance between trad and sport. There are no ultra-macho snuff routes here though; if the going gets tough, a bolt soon comes to hand! In fact some of the clip ups hereabouts are the best in the quarries.

The recent ascent of *The New Slatesman* F8b by slate ace, Pete Robins has brought the area back into the limelight. This striking arete line is one of the toughest routes around, with a crux sequence consisting of 2 consecutive 7a moves, one of which may be the hardest move in the quarries!

Conditions: The walls generally face south and are sheltered on both flanks from the wind making them a suntrap and ideal winter venue. The small bays and changing aspects also provide some welcome shade in the summer months.

The Take Over by Dept. C F7a >
photo: Alex Messenger

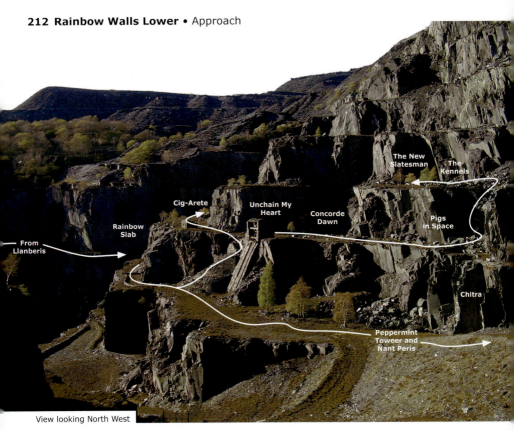

View looking North West

Approach From Llanberis: Park in the Dolbadarn Castle car park on the left as you approach the power station from Llanberis. Walk along the road towards the Power Station. Just beyond the left turn leading to the Slate Museum and the Gilfach Ddu car park (and Vivian Quarry) an obvious, and initially walled footpath cuts up leftwards, thereafter zigzagging up and through the trees to a longer walled zig-zag section. This leads to a small bridge at an old winding house. Turn right here and follow the main path until it bends left; cross the fence (next to the warning sign) carrying on at the same level until you reach the old quarry buildings on the left. Drop down to some broken down buildings and follow a vague path down rightwards on the right of the stream until it is possible to cross it. Continue down rightwards following a more distinctive path until you can cut back left on the Rainbow Slab level. The hulking Colossus Wall should be very obvious at this point, with the Bella Lugosi area just before it. The is situated further along the level, just out of sight. Walk around past the base of Rainbow Slab to reach the first area (25 minutes).

Approach From Nant Peris: It is also possible to reach this part of the quarries from the Nant Peris end of Llyn Peris. There is a parking spot on the right (if coming from Llanberis); from here walk towards Nant Peris for 100m then take the track/path turning left off the main road. Follow the tarmac track for 150m to a property entrance, then turn left and walk up the gently rising track leading up into the quarries. At the first sharp right turn hop over the gate on the left and walk across the plateau; the Peppermint Tower is soon reached on the right (20 minutes).

Start of the Zig Zag path on the Llanberis approach >
photo: Si Panton

Approach • **Rainbow Walls Lower 213**

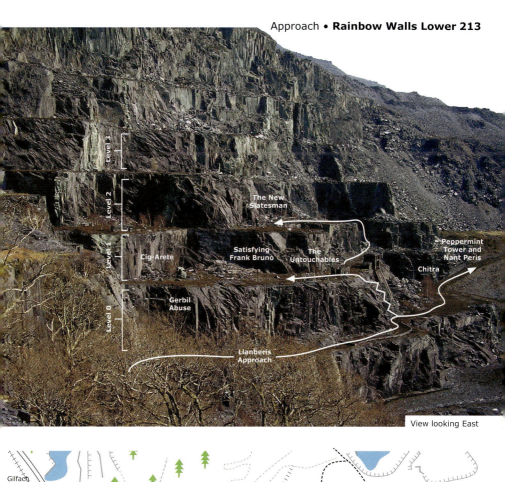

View looking East

214 Rainbow Walls Lower • Gerbil Abuse (Level 0)

Gerbil Abuse Level
These short walls are at the same level and to the right of The Rainbow Slab. Approach as for The Rainbow Slab and continue round to the walls on the right.

▶ **1. Gerbil Abuse F7a ∗∗ 18m**
The steep wall to the left of the obvious arête only succumbs to a determined and imaginative approach. Start to the right of the arête and climb onto a sloping ledge. Move up the groove, and then gain the sloping ramp round to the left of the arete. Traverse diagonally leftwards up this to the base of a slim, steep groove; climb this with sustained difficulties leading up to the lower off. It is possible, and slightly easier to make a cheeky span left half way up the groove to better holds. Lower-off.
[M Thomas, M McGowan 02.04.86]

Pete Robins on the super thin **Chitra** F7c+ photo: Si Panton >

▶ **2. Vermin on the Ridiculous F7b ∗∗∗ 18m**
A hard and tenuous route, with a few flamboyant moves thrown in for good measure. Follow *Gerbil Abuse* round the arête and along the ramp to the base of the steep groove. Desperate crimpy moves lead rightwards to flakes on the arête; continue up with another testing section to reach a monster razor-jug and the lower-off.
[G Smith 16.08.86]

▶ **3. The Homicidal Hamster from Hell E5 6c ∗∗ 22m**
The obvious corner high on the face with a thin crack on its left wall. Desperately awkward and frustrating for most, a true weak-man's, hard 80s climb. Start as for the previous 2 routes, but carry on up the ledges on the right side of the arête to the base of the corner. Give it your best shot! [P Pritchard 23.10.87]

▶ **4. The Spleenal Flick F6c+ ∗∗ 22m**
A right pain in the bum! The leftwards slanting groove, a few metres right of the arête has a very hard crux. Some gear or a long neck is required for the initial, friable start. Lower off.
[N Harms 27.09.87]

▶ **5. Dangling by the Diddies E2/3 5b 25m**
About 50m further right, between 5 vertical bore holes (running the height of the face) and an iron pipe, is a small overhanging arête with a small tree at half height. Climb the groove then step down and left before climbing up to the tree. Move diagonally right to a hanging flake and make a dangling mantel into a niche. Move over the next bulge, step right and finish direct.
[C Phillips, N Thomas 15.10.86]

Further along the same level, through a large black fence, before the level rises towards the Trango and Peppermint Towers there is a small bay on the left. This is home to the magnificent *Chitra*:

▶ **6. Chitra F7c+ ∗∗∗ 22m**
A truly great wall climb with a dynamic climax. The monotonous drag of relentless rockovers is not felt here; instead, technical and intricate shuffling and snatching leads to a minefield of inadequate crimps below the top. This last section will rarely feel solid as your feet are constantly sliding from beneath you, making your fingers grip the tiny edges even harder. There is a bolt above for access to the lower off – this can be reached by walking carefully round the boulder strewn level from the right. Also, when hanging out at the bottom, be aware of the tottering flakes and blocks on the opposite wall, which keep filling in the hole.
The latest (2008) rock fall has deposited a pair of railway sleepers at the base of the route and mangled one of the bolts. The route is still possible, although in its shortened form may only be worth F7c? [N Harms 27.03.89]

Gerbil Abuse (Level 0) • **Rainbow Walls Lower 215**

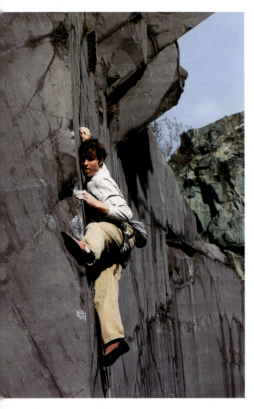

Cig-Arete Level

The next level up is either gained via a scramble up the back of the *Cwms the Dogfish* bay (i.e. right of the Rainbow Slab) or by a collapsing set of steps, 100m right of *Gerbil Abuse* and just before the big black fence.

Descent: if not from a lower-off, then there is a tree above *Drowning Man* – abseil from this. There is also a double ring abseil at the base of *L'Allumette* (by the bad step on The Mau Mau Level). Or scramble very carefully down the back of the bay to the left of *The Mu Mu*.

In the steep right wall of the left most bay, left of *Taken Over by Department 'C'* is:

▶ **7. The Mu Mu F7c+ ∗∗** 12m
A hard start, coming in from the left, gains a rising line of side pulls leading to some jugs. A desperate move involving a ridiculously small one finger pinch, and a high rock over, gains the ledge above. Alternatively, attempt a huge dyno. Continue up the easier arête to finish. Lower off. [A Hocking 2005]

▶ **8a. Overtaken By Department C F6a** ∗ 18m
The thin dolerite vein yields a pleasant route. Follow the vein of green rock up onto the hanging slab, continuing up the hairline crack to the lower-off. [I Lloyd-Jones, J Roberts, P White 15.06.08]

▶ **8. The Take Over by Dept. C F7a ∗∗** 15m
A technical offering which weaves up the wall which was once taken over by Department C; a quarryman's instruction painted on the rock. Start right of the graffiti 'Vernon and Alun' and climb the wall to a ledge and a still tricky finale. May be easier for Albatrosses? Lower off.
[N Harms, G Hughes 08.09.86]

▶ **9. Jaded Passion E4 6a ∗∗** 15m
The thin seam just right of *The Take Over by Dept. C*. Hanging in to place micro wires in the very thin and parallel crack dictates the character of the route, though the climbing is very good. Hard for the grade. [M Thomas, S Jones 08.09.86]

↖ Pete Robins on the intense and technical **Cig-Arete** F7b
photo: Jethro Kiernan

Cig-Arete (Level 1) • **Rainbow Walls Lower 217**

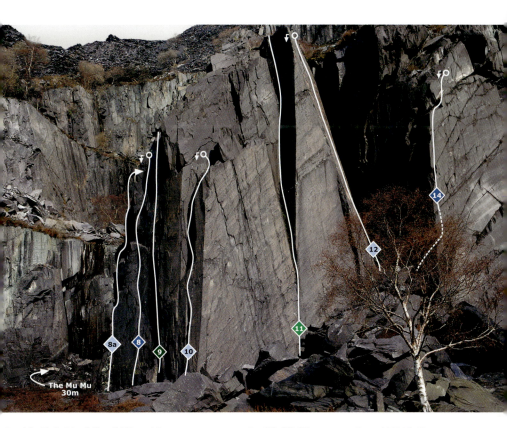

▶ **10. Sleight of Hand F6c** ∗ 10m
A funky little route. Right again and left of the arête is a niche/groove above half height. Tricky moves gain the niche. The exit onto the sloping ledge above is very awkward if taken direct; so nip up the right arête in a more civilised fashion. Lower off. [M Thomas 08.09.86]

▶ **11. The Colour Purple E1 5c** ∗ 12m
Originally a desperate layaway problem, slapping to a jug at the base of the attractive tapered V slot. The jug then came away leaving an even better move slapping for a flared hand jam. Both methods warranted E3 6c. Unfortunately, a rock fall in recent years has affected the start and the hard climbing can be avoided. The groove is pleasant enough anyhow. Finish up past the small tree to a single bolt belay. [M Crook, J Dawes 08.09.86]

Despite shortening both *The Colour Purple* and *Cig-Arête*, the aforementioned rock fall did provide 2 new routes:

▶ **12. Nik-Arête F6b+** 9m
The slab and arête on the left side of the slabby V-groove. Lower off.
[P Robins, M Reeves, A Wainwright 25.03.07]

▶ **13. Waiting on an Angel E1 5b** 9m
The obvious slabby V-groove emerged from the rock fall, with a bolt low down.
[M Dicken 07.12.02]

▶ **14. Cig-Arête F7b** ∗∗ 10m
The excellent left arête of the main face is very technical and precarious. Step onto the arête from the rock fall on the left and climb its right side past 3 bolts before swinging onto the left side near the top. Lower off.
[J Dawes, C Dale 08.06.86]

▶ **15. The Listening and Dancing E5 6b** ∗∗ 15m
Good energetic face climbing that fits together a lot better than it looks. Climb up the wall, a few metres right of the arête and place some cams on the left and on the right. Move boldly up to a slanting borehole and a runner at its top (it is possible to clip the bolt on *Cig-Arête* here). Move up to a good small wire slot and break out right on small positive slots and crimps until better holds are reached near the top.
[T Hodgson, M Thomas 15.09.86]

Cig-Arete (Level 1) • **Rainbow Walls Lower** 219

▶ **16. Where are my Sensible Shoes? F7b** ✶✶ 18m
Wonderfully hard climbing, weaving up the attractive wall. Climb up for a few metres then use a collection of unhelpful dinks, crimps and slopers to gain the weakness over on the right. Sustained and strenuous climbing leads to a break just below the top. Shuffle right and reach over. A direct last move, past a shallow borehole is a little harder. 5 bolt lower-off!
[M Thomas 17.09.86]

▶ **17. Gwion's Groove F6a+** ✶✶ 24m
A superb and sustained excursion, with a slightly bold section as *Drowning Man* is reached. Clip the 1st bolt on *Where are my Sensible Shoes?*, and then follow the obvious slanting flake/ramp rightwards to the finish of *Drowning Man*.
[M Dicken, S Dicken 20.03.07]

▶ **18. Drowning Man F6b** ✶✶ 22m
The slim corner 6m right of the previous route has continuously absorbing and strenuous moves until the sanctuary of the rightward trending ramp is reached. Finish up the short corner to a lower-off on the left.
[R Deane, P Hawkins 15.12.87]

▶ **19. Coming up for Air F7a+** ✶ 18m
A taxing and acutely technical route. Climb up past a metal spike into a scoop. Head rightwards to a spike, then up to a prominent horn, before latching a good hold up left and making a challenging move to gain the niche. Finish up rightwards, to reach a lower-off. [23.02.86]

▶ **20. Tongue in Situ E1 5c** ✶ 25m
Start 3m left of the overhanging chossy arête-thing. Go up and make a tricky move right into an alcove. Gain a fin on the left then use the tongue (no kissing) to swing right onto a ledge. Easier moves up and left on block steps lead to a tree belay. [C Phillips 30.09.86]

▶ **21. Saved by the Whole HVS 5a** ✶ 25m
A wandering line, but in a good, fun way. Start just right of the overhanging chossy arête-thing. Go up ledges a few metres then walk right along a ledge for 4m - harder for the chubby, but isn't everything (except eating)! Climb the first groove then move left into the larger groove. Awkwardly ascend this, taking note of the route name, and finish up ledges past a spike. [C Phillips 29.09.86]

< Neil Dyer soloing **The Untouchables** F8a photo: Pete Robins

50m over to the right, past a snappy wall, is a small, steep drill-sculpted wall. The blunt left arête is an optimistic and abandoned project.

▶ **22. Satisfying Frank Bruno F7b+** ** 11m
Powerful Buoux-style moves that can only be linked with the correct sequence. Make sure you lead with the right (or is it left?) hand. 2 bolts to a bolt belay. [P Pritchard 07.88]

▶ **23. Pocketeering F7a+ [V5/Font 6C]** * 6m
A series of hard cranks continuing direct from the Satisfying... start. [P Pritchard 07.88]

▶ **24. The Untouchables F8a** *** 7m
A fiercely technical and powerful problem up the short leaning arête left of a rusty pipe and behind the shelter house. The start is worth V8/Font 7B, followed by a scary 6b move. 2 bolts to a bolt belay, though it has been soloed. The micro-dink on the arête, used by Dynamo-Dawes, was pulled off on a subsequent attempt by Moose, leaving a jug and ruining the problem. He glued it back on to leave the present small edge. It must have been desperate!
[J Dawes 24.07.88]

Further right is a winding house, just to the left of which is a little buttress with a green dolerite dyke forming its right-hand end. The best descent from the traditional routes in this area is to be found over by L'Allumette and Drowning Man. See the intro section to this level for details.

▶ **25. Unchain My Heart E3 5c** * 22m
Inconveniently bolted to provide 'designer-danger'. Easy, but bold climbing leads up the centre of the buttress right of the crack, to reach a flake on the left arête. Traverse right to a ledge and make a committing move to reach the slim hanging groove and a bolt, and then the top. Belay well back on a tree.
[R Deane, P Johnstone, I A Jones 07.02.88]

▶ **26. Emerald Eyes VS 4b** * 22m
A nice steady route up the dolerite dyke on the right arête. Belay well back on a tree. At a similar grade, **Envy** [R Deane, I A Jones 12.02.88], trends boldly right from the previous route to reach the right-hand arête, about 8m below the top. [R Deane 12.02.88]

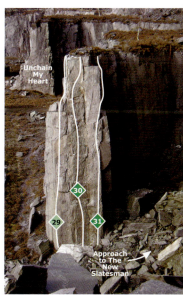

▶ **27. Pork Torque E2 5c ∗** 22m
Just around the right arête is an undercut corner. Boulder out the start with some flexible exertions, and then continue more easily up a series of smaller undercut corners to the top. Belay well back on a tree.
[R Deane, P Hawkins, S Howe 07.02.88]

▶ **28. Concorde Dawn F8a ∗∗** 20m
The bolted line on the steep black wall in the back of the bay. A relentless series of technical and fingery moves with poor footholds lead to a hard crux near the top. There is a bolt on a flat rock about 8m above the top to access the route from above. [R Mirfin 27.08.06]

The next 3 climbs are located on the south side of the obvious prow at the right end of the tier, 50m right of the winding house:

▶ **29. Snuffler VS 4c** 15m
The left arête of the buttress. Tree belay 12m back. [R Liddle, L Dow, K Turner 26.04.93]

▶ **30. Pigs in Space HVS 4c ∗** 18m
Ascend the green dolerite line up the centre of the slab past quartz ledges to reach a tree belay 12m back. Poor protection.
[L Hardy, Chief Superintendent J Peck, Detective Constable G Briggs 03.06.86]

▶ **31. Is Marilyn Monroe Dead? HVS 5b** 15m
The right arête of the buttress. Tree belay 12m back. [R Liddle, L Dow, K Turner 26.04.93]

The Kennels
The slightly unnerving scree slope to the right of the *Pigs in Space* routes leads to the next level on the left (*The Mau Mau* Level really, but not accessible from there). Immediately above the scree is an insignificant slab facing Nant Peris. **Nothing...** [L Dow, R Liddle 26.04.93] climbs the left arête and **Buxton the Blue Cat** [L Dow, R Liddle, K Turner 26.04.93] climbs the vague crack up its centre, both VS and 12m. The following routes are over on the left, directly above the aforementioned winding house.

▶ **32a. Doggy-Style F7c ∗** 12m.
An intense modern route up the steep wall 20m right of *The New Slatesman*. An immaculate, holdless corner leads to a bivy ledge; the headwall above provides a bouldery finale.
[P Robins 06.06.07]

▶ **32. The New Slatesman F8b ∗∗** 15m
The striking arete provides a brilliant technical test piece. [P Robins 25.02.08]

▶ **33. Rowan F7c ∗∗** 15m
The obvious rightwards-facing groove, left of *The New Slatesman*. A careful approach is needed at the start, but once on the route proper, the rock and climbing are excellent. The groove leads with increasing difficulty to the overlap. The remainder of the route is a continuous hands off rest but is also the crux. Be sure to mantel the lip to finish. Single bolt lower-off with back up bolt above. [P Robins, B Bransby 18.04.07]

Pete Robins entering the holdless upper groove on Rowan F7c photo: Si Panton

Slateheads • Mike Thomas and Gwion Hughes

Although it is common nowadays to meet indigenous Welsh climbers, back in the 80s the scene was dominated by incomers. Bucking that trend were local lads, Mike 'Moose' Thomas and Gwion Hughes. Both were key activists in the Slate scene, with Gwion sharing the infamous 'party' house with Trev Hodgson and Paul Pritchard on Goodman Street in Llanberis.

Gwion's best contributions in terms of new routes were **Teliffant** E4 6a in Vivian Quarry and **The Book of Brilliant Things** E5 6b on the Seamstress Slab.

Moose still lives in Llanberis, working at the DMM factory by day and occasionally engaging in epic fell runs with Noel Craine. During the 80s he was the young hot shot known for his incredible finger strength and propensity for taking massive falls, including some notable deck outs. In 1984 he soloed the 2nd ascent of **For Whom the Bell Tolls** E6 6b on the Dervish slab, the following year he took 2 ground falls attempting the first ascent of **The Spark that Set the Flame** E5 6b, also in Vivian Quarry. In 1986 he spearheaded development of the Rainbow Walls area, creating such classics as **Gerbil Abuse** F7a and **Where are my Sensible Shoes** F7b. On the repeat front Moose was prolific, ticking most slate test pieces including **Manic Strain** F8a, and getting close to repeating **The Very Big and the Very Small** F8b+ despite suffering from soft skin brought on by his day job: dipping Walnuts in industrial solution.

⋀ Paul Pritchard, Trev Hodgson, Gwion Hughes
photo: Paul Williams

⋀ L-R Moose, Richie Brooks, Paul Williams, Basher Atkinson
photo: Martin Crook

Moose on **The Untouchables** F8a photo: Glen Robbins

224 Rainbow Walls Lower • The Kennels • Peppermint Tower Area (level 2)

Peppermint Tower Area

Directly behind the Hydroelectric Power Station soars the impressive Trango Tower (Y Ceiliog). There have been a few poor routes recorded on here but climbing is now prohibited. To climb here could well threaten access to the entire quarries, so don't! Behind this lies a huge plateau, which has been a set in more than one film, but most famously in the final battle scene in *Willow*. For years afterwards, fake skulls littered the quarry floor. On the other side of the plateau is a smaller, green dolerite tower; the Peppermint Tower, and some surrounding walls.

The Peppermint Tower can be approached either from Llanberis, or from the main Nant Peris – Dinorwig track. From the Llanberis approach, walk beyond the foot of the Rainbow Slab and Gerbil Abuse Level, through a large black fence, (*Chitra* is in a small bay on the left) and up the rise towards the Plateau (30 minutes). Follow the main Nant Peris – Dinorwig track from the head of Llyn Peris up until level with the plateau on the left (the track takes its first sharp right turn at this point). Hop over the gate and walk across the plateau; the Peppermint Tower is soon reached on the right (20 minutes).

The first 2 routes tackle the south side of the tower, whilst the remaining routes are found on the walls behind.

< Paul Barker on his own creation **Song of the Minerals** F7b
photo: Gill Lovick

Peppermint Tower Area (level 2) • **Rainbow Walls Lower**

Peppermint Tower

▶ **34. Circles are Sound E5 6b** 37m
Start at the base of the left arête of the big corner that faces the Rainbow Slab, left of *Greedy Girls*. Climb boldly up the smoother, right-hand side of the arête for 8m, and then step left around the arête. Continue across the slab, under an overlap and into a corner system in the arête. Finish up this and scramble off down the other side. [C Dale 08.06.86]

▶ **35. Greedy Girls HVS 4c** * 37m
The scrappy green (peppermint) arête, which is undercut at its base; and only worth a star because towers are cool. Start on the left and traverse onto the arête, above the overhang. Wander up the arête taking care with loose rock. Scramble off to the right.
[C Dale 16.04.86]

▶ **36. Jugs Mawr E3 5c** ** 23m
A fine but unusual route, with big moves between ample holds. Start at the foot of a wide dolerite dyke, behind the tower. Ascend the initial steep wall on big holds to gain a thin crack and a peg. Continue past pockets and breaks to another bulge and a final rusty peg. There is a rusty, single bolt belay/lower-off below the top. Alternatively, top out past loose rock and belay well back on blocks then walk off to the left.
[G Turner, A Wells, J Wilson 18.06.88]

▶ **37.** A bolted line of unknown provenence.

▶ **38. Midnight Drives E2 5b** * 22m
A clean groove in the walls right of the Peppermint Tower. Start at the foot of a slab between 2 arêtes, 30m right of *Jugs Mawr*. Climb the centre of the slab to a small ledge at its top. Step left into the corner and follow this as it turns into a narrow chimney near the top. Walk off to the left. [J Beasant 16.09.88]

▶ **39. Song of the Minerals F7b** ** 22m
The appealing blunt arête of the tower facing the plateau. Climb onto the sloping ledge on the left side of the arête and clip 2 bolts. Leave the ledge on inadequate crimps, aiming for better holds above, and hoping not to return with a bang. Swing right onto the smooth golden face and make a desperate rock up and right to gain the slim groove leading to the top. [P Barker 1999]

▶ **40. Come Inside 5.9** ** 22m ®
To the right of *Song of the Minerals* is a deep fissure which provides a fun outing, reminiscent of a beefed up *Monolith Crack*. Slings do protect it fairly well, but you might like some comedy big gear. Worth avoiding in high winds (when it becomes a bit like Kerplunk) and between Feb and July as Choughs nest just inside. A tricky and precarious scamper past 2 chockstones gains entrance, then stiff swimming leads deeper and deeper inside, until a break for the surface gains a ledge and single bolt. This could be used to abseil off, rather than face the obvious scrambles up or down. [T Badcock, S Sinfield 1999]

Rainbow Walls Upper

Style: Trad/sport
Aspect: Varied
Approach: 30 minutes
Altitude: 200m
OS grid ref: 594 602

Route	Grade
Fruity Pear in a Veg Shop Romp	E6
Green Ernie	E5
Manatese	E4
Y Rybelwr	E4
Celestial Inferno	E4
The Coming of Age	E4
Silver Shadow	E4
The Mau Mau	E4
Ari Hol Hi	E4
Octopussy's Garden	E4
German School Girl	E2
Chariots of Fire	E2
Captain Black and the Mysterons	E2
Angel on Fire	E2
Brain Death	E2
Surfin' USA	E1
The Grey Slab	E1
Vertigo	VS
The Dark Half	F8a
The Master Craftsman (Il Miglior Fabbro)	F7c+
The Dark Destroyer	F7c+
Spong (is good for you)	F7c
Heatseeker	F7c
True Clip	F7b+
The Rock Dancer's Daughter	F7a+
Fruity Pear Gets Just Deserts	F7a
L'Allumette	F7a
Paradise Lost	F6c
Monster Hamburger Eats the Alien Baby	F6c

An essential part of the quarries hosting a range of classic routes, which are typically steep (relatively speaking) and often featuring some weird and wonderful moves. The ambience and climbing style is similar to that found below on the lower Rainbow Walls. Despite the slightly awkward access, these walls have always drawn climbers in, the lure of the elegant *German Schoolgirls* or the mighty *Mau Mau* proving too much to resist. Aside from these celebrated trad routes there are also a number of superb clip ups, *The Dark Half* being a shining example of the slate sport genre.

Mark Katz on his very own **The Master Craftsman** F7c+   photo: Ray Wood

228 Rainbow Walls Upper • Approach

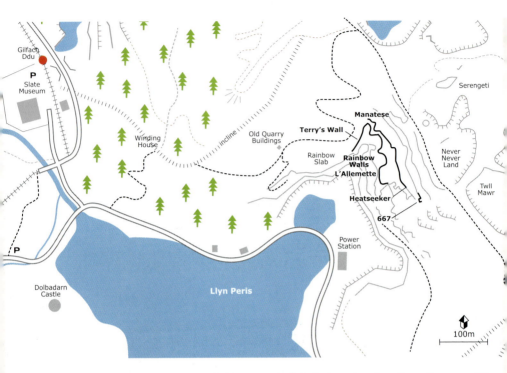

Conditions: The walls of these interlocking bays and promontories provide a range of aspects, although the predominant one is sunny and south facing. That said, some shade and/or shelter can be found depending on what best suits the prevailing weather. There are no major seepage problems, and most routes dry quickly after rain.

Approach: There are 2 main routes into the area, a lower approach from Llanberis, and an upper approach from Dinorwig; both take a similar amount of time. The lower option runs as follows: Park in the Dolbadarn Castle car park on the left as you approach the power station from Llanberis. Walk along the road towards the Power Station. Just beyond the left turn leading to the Slate Museum and the Gilfach Ddu car park (and Vivian Quarry) an obvious, and initially walled footpath cuts up leftwards, thereafter zigzagging up and through the trees to a longer walled zig-zag section. This leads to a small bridge at an old winding house. (NB. This point can be reached by walking up the incline from the entrance to Vivian Quarry in the Gilfach Ddu car park.) Turn right on the far side of the bridge and follow the main path until it bends left; cross the fence (next to the warning sign) carrying on at the same level until as it bears leftwards to reach some old quarry buildings on the left. At the point where the path runs up hill cross the fence on the right and continue round onto the Manatese level. The Mau Mau Level lies below and is reached by abseil; contour round from the fence to where the level opens out and walk over to a promontory with some stakes and a bolt on a boulder. The Mau Mau Level is also accessible by scrambling up the back of The Mu Mu Bay on the Cig-Arête Level (Rainbow Walls Lower). Terry's Wall is the left most slabby wall of the Mau Mau level and is best accessed via abseil down a rusty pipe on its left side. The pipe is reached from the track above, just past the top of the Colossus Wall, and before it starts to rise and bend round to the Manatese Level.

The upper approach to the area is as follows: from the turning circle by Bus Stop Quarry, walk into the quarries along the main track and pass a huge disused factory unit on the left. Go left through the gate, heading towards the massive quarried cwm of Australia. The path quickly turns right and goes down a small hill to a col. Dali's Hole is visible on the left of the track at the base of a dip. Go through the gate on the right and follow the path down hill until it levels out by some old quarry buildings on the right. From here you can cross the fence on the left and continue round onto the Manatese level.

The Mau Mau Level (Level 2) • Terry's Wall
This is the left most slabby wall of the level

▶ **1. Skinning the Ladder HVS 5a** 22m
The iron spikes that used to support a ladder now provide protection for this pointless route. You're not supposed to pull on the spikes, but no one's really bothered.
[M Boniface, A Shaw 17.03.87]

▶ **2. Big Bendy Buddha VS 4c** 25m
Start 12m right of the spikes and 5m left of a prominent sharp corner at the top of the wall. Ascend faint cracks for 12m then traverse right to the base of the corner.
[A Whittall and party 17.08.86]

▶ **3. Lesser Mortals HVS 5a** 22m
Boldly climb directly up the wall to reach the finishing corner of the last route.
[S Siddiqui, I Jones, P Stone 17.08.86]

▶ **4. Vertigo VS 4c** * 23m
The left side of the obvious dolerite pillar is the best route hereabouts. A serious lead, but the difficulties are short lived and low down.
[T Taylor 26.04.86]

▶ **5. Run for Fun VS 4c** 23m
The right side of the obvious dolerite pillar is a more serious lead than its neighbour. This time the crux is at the top.
[T Taylor 23.05.86]

The following routes to the right have all fallen down - no great loss:

Torrents of Spring [26.04.86], **Cornucopia** [27.04.86], **Sprint for Print** [27.04.86], **Senile Delinquent** [27.04.86] and **Bring out the Gimp** [1995]. **Sunk Without Trace** [03.07.86] climbed up the leaning wall on the right of the next bay. It has sunk without trace, and the rest of the wall will go any time soon.

The Mau Mau Area
A number of stunning routes are located on the conspicuous promontory.

▶ **6. The Dark Destroyer F7c+** ** 22m
Packs a mean punch! The steep bolted wall to the left of *The Mau Mau* on the dark side of the promontory. Lower off.
NB. In 2011 a hold broke on the lower section of the route rendering it considerably more difficult - perhaps F8a+?
[M Pretty 13.04.91]

▶ **7. The Mau Mau E4 6a** *** 22m
The splitter crack on the dark side of the promontory is steep and strenuous. Climb the crack to reach a ledge on the right. The crack above requires a certain sense of urgency, and just when you're reaching for the panic button, 'thank god' holds appear on the left...or was it the right!? [P Williams 20.05.86]

The Mau Mau Level • **Rainbow Walls Upper** 231

▶ **8. Ari Hol Hi E4 6a** ✶ 22m
Worthwhile but somewhat serious. Start about 5m left of the *Silver Shadow* arête, on the front of the pillar. Climb up to a huge ledge and follow a crack to a big block on the left. Step right onto another ledge, a triangular one this time. Then gain yet another ledge – this one slopes – on the left, crux. Walk off left to finish.
[C Waddy, D Crilley 06.87]

▶ **9. The Rock Dancer's Daughter F7a+** ✶✶ 22m
The steep wall and groove left of the arête is harder than it looks: getting established on the slopey ledge being particularly awkward. Climb the wall and groove to a junction with *Silver Shadow* and a common finish.
[M Delafield, C Goodey, D Goodey 21.06.91]

▶ **10. Silver Shadow E4 6a** ✶✶✶ 20m
Great climbing up the open left arête of the corner. Sustained and potentially very serious due to some precariously keyed in blocks high up. From the right, step left onto the arête and move awkwardly up to gain a small ledge and a bolt on the left side. Move up to the next ledge beneath the blocks, thankful for the opportunity to clip the bolts on *The Rock Dancer's Daughter*. Reluctantly commit all your weight to the blocks and gain a bolt on the right. Continue with a final move to the top.
[R Brookes, M Murray 03.03.87]

▶ **11. True Clip F7b+** ✶✶✶ 20m
The steep bolted slab on the left wall of the corner is very problematic and difficult to on-sight. The holds seem invisible from below and the moves between them unlikely. Persist and everything will be revealed...hopefully! Lower off
[N Harms 19.09.88]

▶ **12. German School Girl E2 5c** ✶✶✶ 20m
The obvious and immaculate right-angled corner has a hurried and intense start, followed by further intricate climbing right to its end. Well protected.
[M E Crook, N Walton 18.08.84]

▶ **13. Spong (is good for you) F7c** ✶✶✶ 20m
The character of *Spong* is completely dependent on how you get between the 2 sets of chipped jugs in the middle of the wall; either use a dirty crimp and an incredibly high step or go all out for a huge dyno. (See the pic of Pete Robins 'in flight' in the acknowledgements section at the back of the guide.) The climbing up to and beyond the crux is delightful, and thankfully, easier. Lower off.
[N Dixon 04.89]

232 Rainbow Walls Upper • The Mau Mau Level

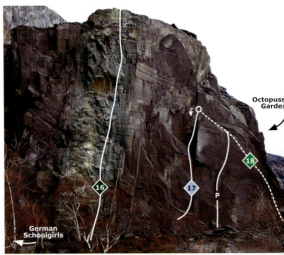

▶ **14. Werp HVS 5a** 25m
A poor, albeit clean and solid, route, which can be used as a useful escape onto the Manatese Level. Go up the slabs to the right of *German School Girl* and step left onto the smaller ledge. The final short wall is awkward. [12.05.85]

▶ **15. Monster Hamburger Eats the Alien Baby F6c** ∗ 12m
A fine little route on clean solid rock. Follow *Werp* along the sloping ledges to a bolt belay beneath the short steep face. Climb up on good holds until funky moves gain the final groove and a lower-off.
[Nick Harms, P Barbier 09.88]

100m right of the promontory, the level floor narrows and is only just passable via a scary section. The following 2 routes start to the left of here and right of a green dolerite section.

▶ **16. The Coming of Age E4 6a** ∗ 22m
Climb the thin crack in the right-hand side of the dolerite band, behind the tree.
[P Jenkinson, N Harms 20.10.88]

▶ **17. L'Allumette F7a** ∗∗∗ 12m
A great line and a typical slate experience with weird, enigmatic climbing. From a bolt belay at the base of the obvious left facing groove, enter the groove and attempt to exit onto a ledge and gain a lower-off.
[J Dawes, P Pritchard 07.01.87]

The next line of bolts is the Clock Face project which once saw attention from Johnny Dawes.

▶ **18. Brain Death E2 5a** ∗ 15m
The alluring ramp rising leftwards over the Clock-face. Bold but easy climbing with a factor-2 fall potential. Still interested? Belay from blocks where the level floor opens out again and scamper up the ramp to a metal spike and a lower-off, on *L'Allumette*. [25.02.87]

▶ **19. Octopussy's Garden E4 5c** ∗ 10m
As the level opens out again, there is a small slab of good quality slate, facing Llyn Peris. This route tackles the slim groove in the left side of the slab. Start off a sharp leaning block amongst a hideous landing zone. Brilliant, technical and (best of all) unprotected climbing leads to a niche on the left and poor small wires. Surmount the mini-headwall to a lower-off on the right. [C Dale 11.06.86]

▶ **20. Surfin' USA E1 5b** ∗ 10m
The central line on the slab is a little gem with good rock and excellent climbing: if only it was 10,000m higher. Climb into the shallow groove and all too soon, exit over the bulge via a flamboyant layback move. Lower off. [C Dale 11.06.86]

▶ **21. Brian Damage E1 5a** 10m
The hanging groovelet on the right side of the slab looks good but is altogether disappointing. But don't take my word for it. Climb the easy but loose corner until one can step down and left into the groove just before it comes to an end. Lower-off on the left. [G Hughes 1986]

▶ **21a. Walrus Wipeout E2 5b** is a poor variation starting a bit further right and finishing up the curving corner until a traverse can be made to the same lower-off. [I A Jones, R Deane 13.02.88]

The Mau Mau Level • **Rainbow Walls Upper** 233

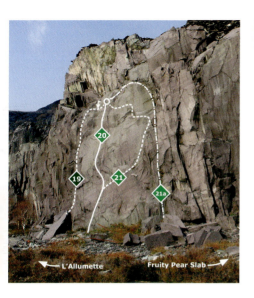

Slatehead • Nick Harms

From April to August 1986, a staggering 150 slate routes were put up in the most frenzied new route activity ever seen in Britain. Virtually all the plumb trad lines and bold slabs were swallowed up and the levels started to look worked out.

Nick Harms arrived in Llanberis in the autumn of 1986, immediately striking up a climbing partnership with Paul Pritchard and diving head first into the raucous climbing scene. Nick brought with him a fresh set of eyes and ethics. He stuck two fingers up to the brave but restrictive traditions and didn't hold back with the bolts. A whole new arena was opened up as steep blank walls were suddenly climbable, albeit with the odd chipped hold. What resulted was a string of utterly brilliant and impressively hard routes, and with it a completely new and inventive climbing style. *Cwms the Dogfish* F8a, *Chitra* F7c+ and *The Dark Half* F8a are his big three additions, routes that rank amongst the very best slate test pieces. Nick's vision extended to the blankest and most impressive pieces of rock around: he famously equipped and attempted the line of what subsequently became *The Very Big and the Very Small*, before passing the baton to slate slab master, Johnny Dawes.

In 1990 Nick produced the classic Llanberis Slate guide, which interestingly included sport grade assessments for all routes in the tick list. The following year his status as slate icon was cemented with his appearance in the striking front cover image of Dave Atchison-Jones' influential The Power of Climbing book - strung out in a dynamic crucifix position on the desperate *Bobby's Groove* F8a, he had become the recognisable face of hard slate climbing. Nearly twenty years later a new generation of Llanberis climbers were to follow in his footsteps producing a range of technical sport routes throughout the grade spectrum.

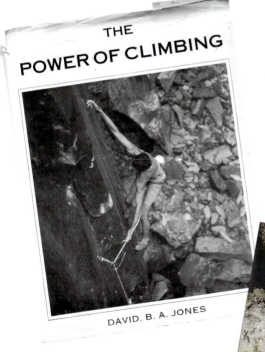

The Power of Climbing, Llanberis Slate and Nick Harms
Photos: David Atchison-Jones and R Pierce

Rainbow Walls Upper • The Manatese Level

15m around to the right lies the following route:

▶ **22. Scratching the Beagle E1 5b** 15m
A pleasant climb up the thin slab, starting by a thin crack and passing 2 bolts higher up.
[R Deane, P Hawkins 30.09.87]

Right again is a larger slab facing Nant Peris. The routes have lower-offs below some horrendously loose terrain. Top out at your peril!

▶ **23. A Mere Trifle E6 6b** 15m
The left hand line on the slab. Start as for the next route but boldly step straight up, aiming for a ledge just left of the peg. There is an RP 0 slot en-route and the tall may reach the shothole from the decent edge and hence avoid the crux; still doesn't make it easy though. Easier climbing leads up past a good RP 3 slot to cracks and a bolt lower-off.
[N Harms, J Anthoine 18.09.88]

▶ **24. Fruity Pear in a Veg Shop Romp E6 6b** ∗ 15m
The central and best line, but very bold and committing right from the word go. Climb frantically up and traverse right into the base of the shallow groove. The peg on the left is difficult to clip (hint: try lassoing it). The peg is also old, shallow and wedged in with wood! More hard (5c-6a) climbing leads up the groove above with no more gear to a lower-off. [N Dixon, M E Crook 14.07.88]

▶ **25. Fruity Pear Gets Just Deserts F7a/+** ∗ 15m
The right line on the slab is an altogether more friendly experience. The climb steadily increases in difficulty to an all-out rock-over for the lower-off. Hard E4 6b in old money.
[N Harms, J Anthoine 18.09.88]

Manatese Level (Level 3)
Most importantly, this level is home to one of the classic slate sport climbs: *The Dark Half*. A must for anyone who possesses the necessary prerequisites: strength and flexibility. The splitter crack of *Manatese* is also a must.

▶ **26. Walls come Tumbling Down E1 5b** 12m
At the start of the level is a short slab. This is the left hand line on the slab, past 2 bolts to a bolt lower-off. The left arête can be climbed at HVS 5a. The right hand line on the slab, past 2 bolts to the same lower-off, is of a similar standard; yawn, yawn, yawn.
[C Jex, I Lloyd-Jones 11.05.91]

▶ **27. Manatese E4 5c** ∗∗∗ 25m
The striking flake crack in the larger wall to the right, kinking right at half height. Originally there was a resting ledge on the left level with the kink in the crack. This has disappeared in a rockfall, making the route a much pumpier proposition. The crack becomes more of a flake higher up and keeps on coming right to its end on a small ledge. Pull steeply up the wall above past a bolt to a lower-off.
[R Lyon, A Wells, M Cluer 16.05.86]

▶ **28. The Master Craftsman (Il Miglior Fabbro) F7c+** ∗ 12m
A short and intense sequence up the neat little rib, past 2 bolts to a lower-off.
[M Katz 19.01.00]

▶ **29. Womaninstress E2 6b** (V4) 20m
A few metres right again, a discontinuous thin crack leads to a ledge at 4m. This could be treated as a boulder problem, or alternatively scramble up choss to the top. [06.02.87]

Ed Brown heading for the finishing line on **Manatese** E4 5c photo: Ray Wood

236 Rainbow Walls Upper • The Manatese Level

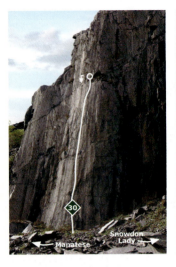

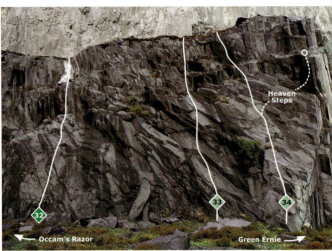

▶ **30. God Betweens Money E4 6a** 15m
On the opposite side of the pillar to *Manatese*, a nice short wall leads to a ledge at 15m and a lower-off. [A Williams 14.07.86]

▶ **31. Occam's Razor E1 5b** 30m
Start on the opposite side of the bay to *Gods...*, by a shattered boulder and short slate wall. Climb the shattered, rounded arête to a niche. Continue up the vague arête past a bolt to a bold but slabby finish. [31.01.86]

▶ **32. Pit and the Pendulum HVS 5a** 30m
Ascend easy slabs 6m right of *Occam's Razor*, aiming for a short white groove above a hidden pit. [I A Jones, T Mitchell 04.88]

▶ **33. Snowdon Lady HS 3c** 30m
The easy angled slabs to the left of the small oak tree at 3m are climbed on good solid rock. The name is derived from the side-portrait view of a lady looking north which is said to appear on the foothills of Snowdon across the other side of the valley (above a solitary tree by the wall running mid-height across the slope)...do you see it? [I A Jones 07.02.86]

▶ **34. Lone Pine HS 3c** 28m
A similar experience to the previous route, but this time right of the oak. *Heaven Steps* VS 5a [19.05.91] makes a slight deviation right from this route to climb the very short fist-crack near the arête to reach a bolt belay before the final headwall. [I A Jones 07.02.86]

▶ **35. Green Ernie E5 6a** * 20m
Round the corner from the slabs is an open left-facing corner formed in a green dolerite dyke. Climb the corner all the way and belay to a house. [M Barnicott 27.05.86]

▶ **36. Paradise Lost F6c** * 18m
The wall and arête right of *Green Ernie* takes in some good perplexing moves, at least once the hollow start has been dealt with. An easier and more solid start can be made from *Green Ernie*, past a bolt. The direct start, past a bolt, is worth F6c+. Lower off. [N Harms, S Young 11.89]

▶ **37. The Dark Half F8a** *** 28m
Thought by some top dogs of the day to be overly chipped, nevertheless it remains an absolute slate classic. The route climbs the dark half of a slightly concave smooth wall, starting up a flake/ slim groove, which yields some very precarious climbing. The crux sequence can be climbed 2 ways, depending on your stature, both equally baffling at first. The upper wall is easier, though could still deny the uninitiated or those carrying tired arms. Lower off. F7c+ for the tall? [N Harms 01.12.90]

▶ **38. Angel on Fire E2 5c** ** 28m
A great climb up the left-most of a collection of slim grooves in the right arête of the *Dark Half* face. Belay to the house. [P Williams, J Dawes 05.06.86]

▶ **39. Celestial Inferno E4 6a** ** 28m
The next groove immediately right with a small roof at half-height. Climb directly to a ledge and surmount the roof. Getting established in the smooth corner above proves very problematic. Continue up on good jams to an easier finish and a belay to the house. [P Williams, M Barnicott 06.06.86]

▶ **40. Chariots of Fire E2 5c** ** 28m
The third groove just left of the large capped corner. Climb up and move right over a detached block into a chimney. Continue up a steep crack (cams #2 and #2.5) to beneath the final overhang and a loose block. Step left and up to finish. Belay to the house. [J Brown, D H Jones 25.06.89]

667 Level • The Manatese Level • **Rainbow Walls Upper**

▶ **41. The Grey Slab E1 5b** ✱ 30m
50m right of *Angel on Fire* is a slanting, hanging ramp running right to left in the upper half of the wall. Start directly beneath the top of the ramp. Climb rightwards past 2 bolts to reach the right end of the ramp. Follow it leftwards to the top and huge boulder belay.
[A Grey, C Dale 05.87]

▶ **42. Captain Black
and the Mysterons E2 5b** ✱ 30m
A direct on *The Grey Slab*, climbing more or less straight up past a bolt to reach a common finish. Belay on huge boulders.
[I A Jones, S Howe 1988]

▶ **43. Heatseeker F7c** ✱✱✱ 20m
The obvious arête 50m right of *The Grey Slab*. From the ledge on the left side of the arête, switch round to the right side and embark on a shockingly technical journey to reach a ledge. After a tricky mantel onto the ledge, move up and pull round into a groove on the left side of the arête for a final steep and tenuous finish. Lower off.
[P Hawkins 13.04.88]

▶ **44. Y Rybelwr E4 6a** ✱✱ 22m
Ascend a slanting groove, and then move left across ledges to the main groove. Follow this past 4 bolts to the top.
[I Lloyd-Jones 11.05.91]

▶ **45. 667 Neighbour of the Beast E3 5c** 15m
A few hundred metres to the right and up half a level, an attractive bow shaped offwidth can be seen. Scramble up to the base of the inviting crack and make a belay, preferably not directly below the crack due to 'fall-out'. Climb the crack on loose blocks with large cams to where it is possible to escape out right to the arête near the top. [W Perrin, M Reeves 06.06.00]

< Pete Robins throwing shapes on the classic **Heatseeker** F7c photo: Alex Messenger

Vivian Quarry Lower

Style: Trad/sport
Aspect: South/various
Approach: 3-10 minutes
Altitude: 100m
OS grid ref: 587 606

Dawes of Perception	E7
I Ran the Bath	E7
Clap Please	E7
The Shark that Blocked the Drain	E6
The Dwarf in the Toilet	E6
Fat Lad Exam Failure	E6
Wishing Well	E6
Order of the Bath	E6

Watching the Sin Set	E5
Bathtime	E5
Heinous Creature	E5
Sanity Claws	E5
Dope on a Rope	E5
Moving Being	E4
Teliffant	E4
Stump Rogers	E4
Gideon's Way	E4
Soap on a Rope	E4
Four Wheel Drift	E4
Sup 2	E4
On Shite	E4
Wakey, Wakey, Hands off Snakey	E4
One Wheel on my Wagon	E4
Spread 'em	E4
Ladder Resist	E3
Sesame Street comes to Llanberis	E3
Sabre Dance	E3
Sanity Fair	E3

Too Bald to be Bold/The Turkey Chant	E2
Blades of Green Tara	E2
Psychotherapy	E2
The Blind Buddha	E2
Wendy Doll	E2
Sup1	E1
The Monster Kitten	E1
Aubergines, Aubergines	E1
Mental Lentils	HVS

Bobby's Groove	F8a
Sucked Away with the Scum	F7c
Le Voleur	F7c

Artichokes, Artichokes	F7b+
Two Bolts or Not to Be	F7b+
Time Bandit	F7b

The Weetabix Connection	F6c+

Vivian Quarry is the multi-tiered quarry rising above the large visitor car park (Gilfach Ddu) in Padarn Country Park. Such is its prominent position that it can be viewed easily from Llanberis on the other side of Llyn Padarn; a decent view of the Dervish slab can even be gained from within confines of Pete's Eats. It sits separate from the main Dinorwig complex, but offers an equally high concentration of excellent climbs, and only minutes from the car park. This section describes the lower levels surrounding the deep and eerie pool at the base of the quarry. This is an apparently fathomless abyss whose solemn and unsettling presence creates a foreboding ambience on all but the sunniest of days.

There are a number of interesting distractions from the climbing; the pool itself is very popular with the diving fraternity, and divers can often be seen bobbing about on the surface, or betraying their under water position by leaving trails of bubbling gas rising upwards whilst they explore the hidden depths. There is also the Slate Museum (which has a café), and the high ropes course, or various pleasant marked walks leading through the Padarn Country Park.

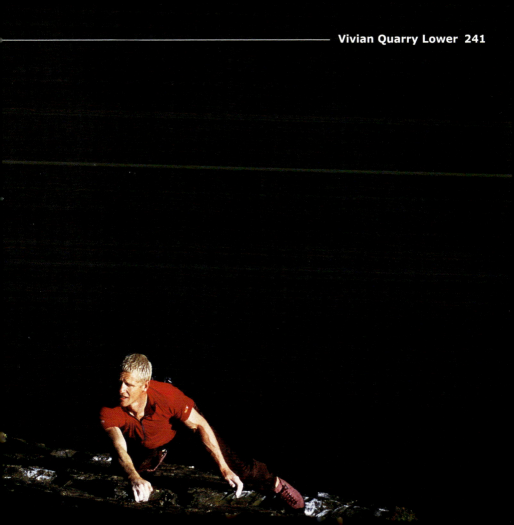

242 Vivian Quarry Lower • Approach

Conditions: Most routes dry very quickly, having a sunny open aspect. Shade can be found if needed on *Muscle Beach* or on the *Dark Side of the Prow*.

Access restrictions: The quarry is part of the Padarn Country Park, a designated conservation area of outstanding botanical interest, the management of which has been very sympathetic to climbers over the years. Please stay on the paths and avoid trampling on regenerating vegetation on the levels. It is vital to part of the access arrangement that no climbing or abseiling takes place on the walls above the viewing path on the Pool Level, i.e. to the right of *Moving Being*.
The quarry is also a popular diving venue: for obvious reasons please don't climb on the The Prow whilst the Diving Centre is open. To check the opening hours call 01286 870889 or go to **www.divevivian.com**.

Approach: From the Snowdon Mountain Railway on the A4086 in Llanberis, take the road opposite towards the power station. At the first junction turn left and follow the road into the Gilfach Ddu pay and display car park. The car park is normally open from 9.00 am, however the gate closing time is seasonal (be sure to check the time on the notice as you drive in). Alternative parking is available in the Dolbadarn Castle car park, which is passed on the road leading from Llanberis – a useful option if you are making an evening visit.
The Pool Level is reached via the archway next to the Diving Centre. A path runs along by the side of the fenced off pool to a viewing platform. The *Mental Lentils* wall lies just over the other side of the stile/gate; the other sections on this level can be reached by following (carefully) a path running around the side of the pool. Routes on the Prow are best reached by abseil from the wooded summit area. To reach this from the diving centre, go up the incline right of the archway to the first opening on the left. Go through this and turn left on to the road, After 100m, follow the steps on the right up a level, cross the fence and follow a small path out to the top of the Prow.
The Dwarf Level can be reached from the Pool Level by climbing various routes (e.g. *Mental Lentils – Monster Kitten*), or via abseil from the chains at the right end of the Conscience Slab (see Vivian Quarry Upper, p 261).

The Pool Level

From the viewing platform a quick panoramic scope round the level picks out the impressive hanging iron-shaped slab of *Dawes of Perception*, the small promontory containing *Bobby's Groove* on its right wall, the large vegetated *Blind Buddha Slab*, and the striking Prow jutting out into the pool. The routes are described from right to left.

Mental Lentils Wall

▶ **1. Moving Being E4 6b** ** 24m
A tough pitch. Start on the 1st slab on the right as you pass over the style. Climb a crack past a bolt to a triangular niche below the 2nd bolt. Clip this and make a series of hard moves left, the climax of which is a slap for the arête and good holds. Climb the arête in a fine position to a lower-off. [N Harms, J Barbier 23.08.86]

▶ **2. Mental Lentils HVS 5b** ** 18m
The well-worn slab rising from the silver birch trees is a fine and popular route. Starting near the arête, climb onto a ledge and teeter left along this (small wires) before pulling onto the hanging slab and gaining a bolt. The crack above (medium to large wires) leads to a ledge and a 2nd bolt. Hard moves up the slab above gain the top and a lower-off. Alternatively, go up to the ledge and over right to the base of *The Monster Kitten* for a good link up. [J Barbier 28.10.86]

▶ **3. Time Bandit F7b** * 18m
The slab to the left of *Mental Lentils* has a desperate finale. Follow *Mental Lentils* until after the 1st bolt, then head leftwards up a series of dinks and dishes before making some excruciatingly thin moves past 2 bolts. Continue up to a lower-off. [02.89]

The next 2 routes start on the sloping rubble strewn ledge up and right of *Mental Lentils*, which provides the best approach.

▶ **4. The Monster Kitten E1 5c** * 12m
A classic slate test piece following the thin diagonal crack until an alarming rightwards stride can be made to ledges at the top of *Ladder Resist*. The lower-off is just above. Some folk opt for the balancey foot traverse method, some go for the full pumpy hand traverse, but most choose a mixture of both. Take your pick! [S Andrews, S Britain 27.05.86]

Mental Lentils Area • The Pool Level • **Vivian Quarry Lower** 245

▶ **5. Ladder Resist E3 6a** * 12m
A low crux at ankle breaking height deters most; the brave are (briefly) rewarded with a bolt and pleasant climbing up the 'juggy' pillar to a lower-off. [N Harms, J Anthoine 22.05.88]

▶ **6. Dawes of Perception E7 6c** *** 25m
The hanging iron-like slab stands proud at the base of the quarry. The distant glistening of a solitary bolt, high on the slab in the middle of nowhere acts as a marker; committing to gain and desperate to leave. Start behind the long razor flake and gain the arête and a peg. Climb past 2 sabre teeth to a discontinuous crack and make sure you arrange a decent assortment of crucial and varied runners. Press on to the bolt, which is hard to clip, and work left to 2 slanting cracks (runners). Belay well back via a horrendous top out over loose slate scree. [J Dawes 23.10.85]

▶ **7. Split the Dog E3 5c** 25m
A route based on the broken rock between the 2 impressive slabs. Start at the right side of the *Clap Please* slab. Move up then left into a shallow groove. From the top of the groove, move right onto a big ledge and up the smooth groove above with a vertical shot hole on the right wall. Continue up ledges and cracks to a tree belay. [S Haston, G Hughes, M Raine 04.87]

▶ **8. Glurp (a.k.a. Dirt) E4 6a** * 25m
Start at the right side of the *Clap Please* slab and follow the line of eco-bolts running up leftwards to a lower-off. The old bolt/peg on *Clap Please* was used but is now missing. Take some wires. [M Jones, L Kathenes, H Owen 2001]

▶ **9. Clap Please E7 6c** ** 25m
A wandering line up the large black recessed slab with spaced protection. Start just right of the centre of the wall and climb diagonally right to a mangled old bolt/peg that offers little security. Make a hard traverse left to reach a crack and continue up to a bolt (NB. Ignore the rusty old bolt on the left in 'no-mans land'). Traverse left for 2m and make yet more hard moves up to a crack and gain a good hold and double bolt lower-off below the top. Originally, a further move and the loose top out were encountered; the lower-off was added during the Foot and Mouth crisis in 2001. [B Drury, A McSherry 13.10.86]

The scarred groove to the left marks the line of a recent rock collapse. It is unclimbed at present, and probably should remain so.

246 Vivian Quarry Lower • The Pool Level • Mental Lentils Area

▶ **10. Fat Lad Exam Failure E6 6b ** 22m**
Like a giant arcade penny-pushing machine with slate 'coins' perched on the edge of the shelf just waiting to fall. Somehow seems more fun! Follow a thin seam up the centre of the thin slab to a flattened but still clippable bolt. Hard moves above this gain the triangular pockets and a rest. Step right to the base of a flake/rib and follow this to a sobering scramble over loose scree to a bolt on the back wall. [N Harms 28.04.87]

▶ **11. Sanity Claws E5 6a * 22m**
The right-hand groove is harder than the left-hand groove but at least has some protection. Lower off a bolt. [C Dale 01.05.86]

▶ **12. Sanity Fair E3 5b * 22m**
Climb the bold arete between the 2 grooves to a hard finish. A good 'warm up' for the 2 adjacent grooves if you're into this sort of thing. Move right at the top to lower off the bolt on *Sanity Claws*. [C Dale 01.05.86]

▶ **13. Heinous Creature E5 6a * 22m**
The left-hand groove has no worthwhile protection. [C Dale 04.05.87]

Beyond the grooves is an alcove;

▶ **14. The Hong Jagged Route of Death E3 5b** 44m
Aptly named. Make sure your mate belaying is tucked away at the bottom when you rain down debris. A serious outing that is best avoided by all except devotees of loose horror shows. Start below the sabre-toothed ridge on the right side of the alcove. Follow the discontinuous rib past tottering death to The Dervish Level in one pitch. Care with the ropes is needed so as not to dislodge loose blocks. [C J Phillips, G Hughes, N Rice 12.04.88]

▶ **15. The Golden Shower E3 6a** 12m
This route may have been affected by rockfall. It used to start from behind the gendarme of rock on the right side of the alcove (just right of *The Weetabix Connection*) but now climbs on top of the gendarme. The short groove leads with much difficulty to an easier leftwards slanting ramp and a lower-off. [N Harms 03.11.87]

▶ **16. The Weetabix Connection F6c+ ** 12m**
The obvious steep crackline just right of *Bobby's Groove* is superb but has some unnerving/reachy clips. Hard moves all the way lead to a lower-off. It is possible (and easier) to escape off right near the top to hidden holds around the corner. [C Jex, L Zabloski 26.02.91]

▶ **17. Bobby's Groove F8a *** 12m**
Unfortunately, it proved too hard for Bobby! Despite its attractive roadside location, this often-tried micro route is rarely ascended in good style. The sequence moving through the 3 crux undercuts is extremely involved, and has a habit of stopping even the most gifted technicians dead in their tracks. Also, the route has become a little harder since part of the middle undercut broke off. Once the sanctuary of a crimp on the lip is gained, either escape left onto the slab (cop out version) or tackle the remaining groove direct to a lower-off. [J Dawes 13.04.88]

▶ **18. Two Bolts or Not to Be F7b+ ** 12m**
Some good long moves up the wall past 2 bolts (surprisingly!) to the left of *Bobby's Groove*. Be careful with the glued sidepull below the lip. Lower off. [S Scully 09.05.89]

▶ **19. Wendy Doll E2 5b * 87m**
The first 'proper' route in Vivian, linking pitches on 3 levels. Start at the base of the pool-end of the buttress, just left of the cable.
P1 4c 22m Climb the right side of the buttress to a small ledge and sapling (left of a leaning pinnacle) and continue to a tree belay at the top.
P2 5b 25m Walk along to the next face and head up to the smooth groove capped by the iron railway (the bad step across to *The Dervish* Slab).
P3 5b 40m Walk right to the base of *Last Tango in Paris*. Follow this up the parallel cracks to the arête and onto the ledge above. Where *Last Tango* steps left onto the slab, go up to a wider hanging crack. This is loose and it is much better to just follow *Last Tango*.
[S Haston, N Parker, M Howard 06.81]

▶ **20. The Sponge that Walked Away E1 5a** 18m
A terrible experience based on the loose and blocky left side of the buttress, passing a coniferous tree low down. [C J Phillips, D I Jones 19.06.88]

The next route is located on the level above, left of the 2nd pitch of *Wendy Doll*. Approach via either of the last 2 routes, or by scrambling up the back of the bay to their left, or via abseil from above (see topo on page 243).

▶ **21. Spread 'em E4 5c * 25m**
The prominent left-facing V groove, starting above a sharp flake. A cam #4 is useful.
[C J Phillips 25.08.88]

The next 2 routes are on the same level as *Spread 'em*, but further round to the left on the Boilerplate Slab. A bat refuge has been constructed here within the obvious cage. Bats are endangered species and it is essential that no one disturbs them or tampers with the cage. **The Muff Affair** [02.05.94] started from the cage and should not be repeated.

▶ **22. Imperial Leather E4 6b** 15m
A friable route based on the leftwards-curving arch on the right side of the slab, passing 3 bolts to a lower-off. [P Pritchard, S Jones, T Kay 11.05.88]

▶ **23. Working up a Lather E4 6b** 15m
Another friable route climbing the left side of the slab past 4 bolts to the lower-off on *Imperial Leather*. [S Jones, P Pritchard, M Thomas, T Kay 14.05.88]

Geoff Turner moving quickly through the post crux section of **Psychotherapy** E2 5c photo: Si Panton

Clattering off the Dwarf

Dervish Slab dominates Vivian, providing its most striking feature. Yet there are, on various levels, many hewn and sculpted facets leftover from quarrymen's labour which proved no less attractive for technical climbing purpose.

Dwarf level is an example and its most obvious challenge was taken up by JR after placing two protection bolts, there being perilously little else to sustain a fall. Seconding, it occurred to me that I was in a fortunate position, since atop a faint groove some distance above the last bolt, a long blind reach leaves climbers groping around from a position where, if 'thank gods' cannot be found, time levies an exacting plummet, inevitable with its passing.

There are many climbers that after seconding a pitch make it a proposition for future leading. Never a sight lead, but a lead nevertheless. In my case on Dwarf however this seconding business seemed quite sufficient and happy with that at E5 6b (NB. the route was subsequently upgraded to E6 6b) we left in high spirits.

John Redhead making the first ascent of The Dwarf in the Toilet E6 6b, in 1986 photo: Mike Raine

Returning a week later it transpired that Dave Towse, whippet-like and as technically proficient on slate as anyone, wished to make the second ascent. He did so with ease until beyond bolt two where the dreaded blind hand groping left him inches short from finishing jugs and an easy posing handrail. Losing balance and unable to levitate he was spat off, falling through air until biners clattered under load and rope stretch slapped him into vertical slate below Dwarf's groove. When suspended he shook himself down for another go. A second attempt, followed by a third and then fourth, gave similar results, but a fifth, ending with a spectacular flyer sent him inverted and head-touching as he came in on a slight arc upside down above us. This time mild concussion caused retirement after a spirited innings, which on most other occasions might have won a match and did so on the same ground a few days later.

Thus falling off even bolted slate could give cause for concern and in general the medium proved as serious if not more so than most natural crags; lobs like Yorky's (Paul Craven) from Flashdance became legend - a sixty-foot scraper, gaining as much social kudos and attention as any ascent at the time.

A month later, and heavy in heart, Noel Craine and I returned to Dwarf Level; this time climbing a memorial route for Gideon Wilson. Gideon's Way, an aesthetically pleasing ramp line, easier than the original at E4 6a, marked the passing of a young friend tragically taken after a fall from Tremadog's Falcon. It was a reminder, if any were needed, that climbing, as well as exalting the spirit, can sometimes make us poorer taking away those we have known on crag and heights without warning so that we are lost, see them only now in dreams or through the mind's eye of remembrance in the haunts and faces we once knew.

Martin Crook

The remainder of the routes are back down on the Pool Level.

▶ **24. Cat Flaps of Perception E4 6a** 12m
The short slab starting from an elevated ledge directly beneath the lower off of *Psychotherapy*. An initial unprotected step left gains easier but still bold climbing up to the lower-off on *Psychotherapy*. [R Mirfin, I Davis 06.07.93]

▶ **25. Psychotherapy E2 5c [F6a+]** ** 25m
A popular route up a thin slab at the back of the level, with the hard climbing concentrated near the 1st bolt. Start below a crack just left of the 1st bolt. Climb up to the bolt and make a hard move right to an edge and then a crack. Continue up this past the 2nd bolt and along the diagonal line of weakness to a 3rd bolt. Either follow the original route rightwards or go directly up the wall to reach a lower-off. [A D Newton, P Pritchard 08.05.88]

The huge vegetated slab on the left side of the quarry is the **Blind Buddha Slab**.

▶ **26. Stump Rogers E4 6b** * 45m
There is some good climbing on the small shield of smooth purple slate just below half height on the right side of the slab. Start as for *The Blind Buddha*. Follow that route to the cleaned groove at 12m then continue straight up the slab to a bolt. Hard moves past this are rewarded with yet more easy choss. [R Drury, A Amos 09.09.86]

▶ **27. The Blind Buddha E2 5a** * 45m
A few loose ledges, the odd weed and not much gear, but apart from that, this route has a good feel about it and the climbing is straightforward. Start left of a fallen block at the lowest point of the slab. Climb the groove to a spike runner at 12m. Step down and traverse left to a good ledge. Step up and make some harder moves to a crumbly flake, before ledge shuffling your way directly to the top. [M Boater, J Clinton 06.84]

▶ **28. Wave Out on the Ocean E1 5a** 30m
A similar experience to *The Blind Buddha*, i.e. fine open climbing, but taking in some loose and dirty ground. Start 10m left of *The Blind Buddha*, halfway up the scree slope. Trend right to a ledge then wander upwards to the top. [A Evans, S Bennett 25.07.90]

▶ **29. Poetry in Motion E3 5c** 28m
A very bold offering up the left side of the slab. [P Jiggins, P Dunkley 03.11.86]

▶ **30. Blue Touch Paper E2 5c** 12m
The short clean arête to the left of *The Blind Buddha* Slab offers no protection and is tricky gaining the top. [P Targett 03.11.89]

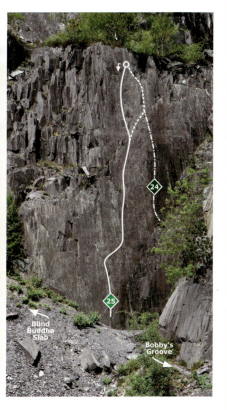

Slatehead • Paul Pritchard

"Slate's best when it's showery, it dries in minutes. It's where it's all been happening of late, why I came here. I saw a picture of a moustached, muscley guy [Trevor Hodgson] mantling these tiny edges, trying to put both feet next to his hands, grinding his nose into the purple rock and not a runner in sight…The falls you could take off the hard slate routes were already legendary and I wanted to take one" - Paul Pritchard, Deep Play.

It is clear from reading Paul's colourful account of life around Llanberis in the '80's that he has deep-hearted memories of rainy slate days and sun-baked adventures on the Red Walls of Gogarth – quite a contrast but equally special. Paul hopped on the Dinorwig roller-coaster in late 1986, plucking off the remaining lines around the Rainbow Slab including the bold and ultra-thin *Cure for a Sick Mind* (E7 7a) and the uncelebrated yet totally baffling *Homicidal Hamster from Hell* (E5 6c). The Prow in Vivian was a great 'find' for Paul where he was given a free reign and came away with a virtual clean sweep of hard and bold leads, the best of which is *Sucked Away with the Scum* (F7c).

Paul on **Rainbow Slab** in full 80s garb: piss stained lycra and a christmas jumper photo: Paul Williams

Paul Pritchard photo: Dave Kendall

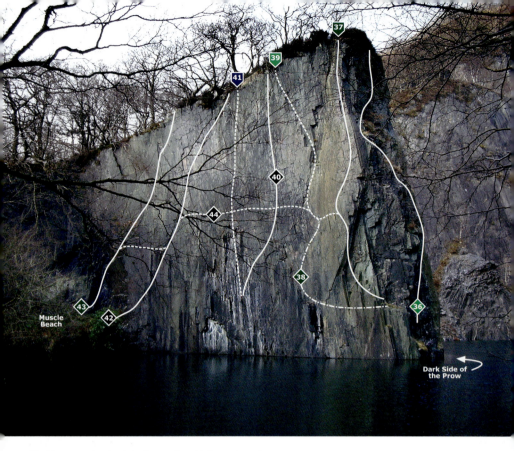

The Prow protrudes into the pool and is home to a selection of excellent sport climbs, trad climbs and deep water solos. The first routes are on the Dark Side of the Prow (north) and are best approached by abseil or by traversing round left from the main section of the Pool Level.

Access restriction: it is essential that no climbing takes place on The Prow when the diving centre is open. Please do not flout this rule, as to do so will threaten access to the whole of Vivian Quarry. To check the opening hours call **01286 870889** or go to **www.divevivian.com**.

▶ **31. Aubergines, Aubergines E1 5b** ∗ 12m
Start at the base of a crack in the bay right of the prominent groove of *Artichokes, Artichokes*. Climb the crack to an arête and continue into the trees. [M Boniface, I Wallis 05.88]

▶ **32. Sesame Street comes to Llanberis E3 5c** ∗ 18m
Abseil to the base of a groove, right of *Four Wheel Drift*. Climb the groove then move right, across and up a slab to ledges. Continue up past a bolt to good footholds and on to a bolt lower-off, or top out. [P Johnstone, P Pritchard 27.01.88]

▶ **33. Four Wheel Drift E4 6a** ∗ 25m
A route of 2 halves: safe and hard then bold and easy. Abseil down to a ledge at the foot of a crack on the left side of the north face of the prow. Climb the crack to a difficult move. Above this, go left along a line of jugs with no protection to the top. [S Haston, N Parker 08.80]

▶ **34. Artichokes, Artichokes F7b+** ∗∗ 28m
This route grapples with the prominent left-facing groove on the north wall, starting from the 'beach' on the right (best gained by abseil). Traverse left past a bolt and into the rib/groove. Continue past 4 more bolts to a long run-out to a ledge. Move left into a groove (peg) and on to a bolt lower-off, or top out. [P Pritchard 06.04.88]

▶ **35. Le Voleur F7c** ∗∗ 28m
A good and technical, yet infrequently climbed route, taking the bolted line left of the groove of *Artichokes, Artichokes*. Abseil to a bolt belay just above the water. Climb direct to sloping ledges then use a flake to gain a bigger ledge. Finish up the top corner (peg) of *Artichokes, Artichokes* to a bolt lower off, or top out. [S Mayers 23.03.92]

The Prow • The Pool Level • **Vivian Quarry Lower 253**

▶ **39. Bathtime E5 6a** ✱✱✱ 25m
A great and bold wall climb, which is often tackled as a deep-water solo. Abseil from a tree at the top of the prow to a bolt belay on a ledge above the water. Climb the groove right of the right arête of the wall for 5m. Swing left onto the wall proper and traverse out left to some flakes. Move left again to a crack, which is followed to a ledge (possible escape right into *Soap on a Rope*). A diagonal line leads leftwards to a mossy finish. [P Pritchard 04.06.87]

▶ **40. I Ran the Bath E7 6b** ✱ 25m
A bold and snappy lead with fine open climbing. Abseil down to the largest bolt hanger in the quarries. Climb up and right from a scoop into another scoop then go up a bulging wall to reach a line of jugs leading leftwards to a groove and the top. [P Pritchard 27.04.87]

▶ **41. Sucked Away with the Scum F7c** ✱ 25m
A hard climb up the blankest section of the wall. Abseil down to the huge bolt hanger, shared with the last route, but don't worry, chances are it will not be busy. Climb the wall direct passing 3 bolts to a crux finish. [P Pritchard 10.04.88]

▶ **42. Wishing Well E6 6b** ✱✱ 22m
The striking curved crack line on the left side of the wall, gained from dry land on Muscle Beach. Gain the crack and tussle up it to the top. The original peg and added bolt appear to be missing. [P Pritchard 23.04.88]

▶ **43. One Wheel on my Wagon E4 5c** ✱ 22m
A bold climb up the stepped ramp on the far left of the wall to a tree belay. [S Haston, M Raine 04.87]

▶ **44. Order of the Bath E6 6b** ✱ 30m
There has to be a girdle! Start from Muscle Beach. Climb *One Wheel...* for 6m then step right into the crack of *Wishing Well*. Move up and traverse right along a thin horizontal break, past a bolt, to reach spikes on *I Ran The Bath*. Continue right to a bolt and finish up *Soap on a Rope*. [P Pritchard, E Stone 30.04.88]

▶ **36. Blades of Green Tara E2 5b** ✱ 25m
Abseil down to a big grassy ledge just above the water level and 3m right of *Bathtime*, on the front of the prow. Climb diagonally right up the groove exiting onto a ledge on the left. Climb the wall to a sapling and flake runner. Move up 3m until a traverse leads out to the arête, and finish easily up this. Although there are runners, the route is a popular solo. [M Boater 06.84]

▶ **37. Soap on a Rope E4 6a** ✱✱✱ 22m
The easiest and most popular route on this wall, and most commonly soloed, although the 1st section up the groove isn't above the water. Abseil from a tree at the top of the prow to a bolt belay on a ledge above the water. Climb the groove above until it is possible to swing left onto a ledge. A hard move off this leads back to the arête and the 1st bolt. Climb up the arête to ledges and a final groove near the top.
[P Pritchard, P Johnstone 22.01.88]

▶ **38. Dope on a Rope E5 6a** ✱✱✱ 22m
An indirect start to *Soap...*, or a more logical start to *Bathtime*. From the bolt belay traverse left until it is possible to climb up to the spikes as for *Soap...* and *Bathtime*.
[T Kay, J Taylor 08.88]

254 Vivian Quarry Lower • The Dwarf Level

Muscle Beach

Immediately left of The Prow is an insignificant wall known as Muscle Beach. Don't all rush at once, this is not Miami. Approach by hopping carefully and discreetly over the fence on the left, just after the archway leading into the quarry from the diving centre.

▶ **45. Booby Building** HVS 5a 12m
The right-most line on the wall, left of *One Wheel on my Wagon*, and beneath an iron ring-spike. Climb past the ring and a bolt to the top.
[P Johnstone, P Pritchard 26.01.88]

▶ **46. Earwig Ho 87** E3 5c 12m
Climb straight up the middle of the wall, past a bolt, to the top. [M Raine, J Turner 05.04.87]

▶ **47. Silvester Still-born** E1 5c 8m
Start just left of another iron ring-spike low down. Hard moves past a bolt gain a niche and the top. [P Johnstone 01.88]

▶ **48. Boody Building** HVS 6a 6m
The right-hand line on the smaller wall to the left, passing a roof and a bolt. Tree lower-off.
[P Pritchard, P Johnstone 24.01.88]

▶ **49. Brinwell** HVS 6a 6m
The left-hand line on the smaller wall to the left, passing a roof and a bolt. Tree lower-off.
[P Pritchard, S Cheslett 06.04.88]

Further left, just right of the fence, are 3 neglected problems. From right to left, they are:
The Coleslaw that Time Forgot (V2/Font 5+),
Another Roadside Traction (V4/Font 6B) and
Pumping Iron (V3/Font 6A).

The Dwarf Level

On the right of the quarry, above the Pool Level, are some small slabs. The huge X in the slab on this level marks the routes of *Sup 1* and *Sup 2*. The routes are described from left to right.

▶ **50. Watching the Sin Set** E5 6b/c ✱✱ 15m
The slab left of the huge X has some brilliant and alarmingly thin moves in its upper section past 2 bolts to a lower-off.
[T Kay, S Jones, N Harms 07.88]

▶ **51. Sup 1** E1/2 5a ✱ 22m
The left-to-right leg of the huge X in the slab marks the way. Start at the base of the left leg and teeter rightwards along the ramp, past the right leg to a bold/terrifying pull onto the level above. [S Haston 08.82]

▶ **52. Teliffant** E4 6a ✱ 20m
A fine and open line to the left of *Sup 2*. Climb up on dishes to a solitary bolt, and then make thin, intense moves left to reach the ramp of *Sup 1*. Continue directly up the slab on small flakes and cracks to a lower-off.
[G Hughes, T Kay, C J Phillips, N Rice 12.04.88]

▶ **53. Sup 2** E4 6a ✱ 21m
The near vertical leg of the huge X is followed direct to where the legs cross. Make a hard move to reach the 1st bolt and a further desperate move for the ramp. Finish directly to the top.
[S Haston 08.82]

The Dwarf Level • **Vivian Quarry Lower** 255

▶ **54. The Shark that Blocked the Drain E6 6b** * 10m
An incredibly bold solo up the short slab to the right of *Sup 2*, behind a birch tree. Originally graded E5 but verging on E7; the problem with head-pointing! Climb the line of weakness with increasing difficulty until cracks lead off rightwards to the base of the next route.
[S Jones 05.11.87]

▶ **55. Wakey, Wakey, Hands off Snakey E4 6a** * 15m
Good climbing up the rightwards slanting crack in the slab right of the *Sup 1* slab. Start by scrambling up ledges to the base of a corner. Move out right onto the slab and reach a bolt. Hard moves rightwards along the crack lead to an easier finish. [P Barbier 22.08.86]

▶ **56. On Shite E4 5c** * 12m
A direct finish to *Wakey*, climbing straight up from the bolt on friable holds. [S Jones, T Kay 26.10.87]

▶ **57. Too Bald to be Bold/The Turkey Chant E2 5c** * 30m
A good combination linking 2 levels. Start 3m right of *Wakey*... and ascend the rightwards slanting crackline to reach a pedestal. Move slightly leftwards and up a slab past a bolt to broken ground. Traverse down and right to a triple bolt belay at the foot of a diamond-shaped hanging slab. Make some bold moves directly up above the belay, easier than it appears, then step left to the 1st bolt and continue up and left towards the 2nd bolt, a final hard move leads to a single bolt on the wall, and a 2nd bolt over the top of the route. [K Simpson, S Winstanley 15.04.89/ P Johnstone, P Pritchard 15.01.88]

▶ **58. The Dwarf in the Toilet E6 6b** ** 22m
A fantastic visual line, gaining the hanging slab and diagonal crack some 20m right of *Too Bald to be Bold*. Start beneath the hanging slab where a ramp leads off rightwards. Gain the ramp from the right and move boldly up to 2 bolts. Grapple with the steep shallow groove above and slap blindly round onto the slab. Follow the crack rightwards to a bolt belay.
[J M Redhead, M E Crook 16.05.86]

▶ **59. Gideon's Way E4 6a** * 22m
The rightwards-trending ramp in its entirety. Follow *Dwarf*... to the bolt on the right. Continue rightwards past a removable peg to finish on jugs leading left to the bolt belay on *Dwarf*....
[M E Crook, N Craine 14.06.86]

▶ **60. Sabre Dance E3 5b** * 30m
Bold climbing up the rightwards-trending ramp just right of *Gideon's Way*. Climb the ramp until a hidden shot hole allows a short open groove to be gained near the arête. Follow this to a ledge and finish up the corner above. [C Dale 10.05.86]

For those who like climbing trees, **Bungle in the Jungle** E1 5b [10.05.86], uses a cluster of 5 birch trees, some 25m further right, to bypass a steep blank wall and ramble up broken ground to the top.

Pete Robins approaching the bolt on **Teliffant** E4 6a ∧
photo: Jack Geldard

Diary of a Slatehead

The Vivian Diamond

Nothing much happened throughout September '86, but in October Johnny Dawes made a jaw dropping lead up a roughly hewn diamond shaped slab in Vivian Lower that although obvious seemed to be hewed so smoothly that most climbers simply regarded it as a kind of insitu sculpture and walked by content to marvel at its form. Johnny however had different ideas, revelling in holdless expanses such as the Vivian diamond. His only practice, a pocket-free hand traverse round the revamped Pad (Padarn Hotel) pool table, a feat also carried out without recourse to heelhooking (since rules concerning pool table traversing clearly stated that the use of such invalidated any attempts) under constant heckling from a liquor fuelled crowd.

John Redhead, Martin Crook and Dave Towse circa 1985 photo: Crook collection

Anyone wishing to speak with, or more usually listen to the Dawes on the 22nd October 1985, having called round to the flats above Y Bistro in Llanberis to find him not at home, could have done no better than to engage a messenger sending them post haste ('Emily loudhailer', not being at hand) in the direction of Vivian Quarry. Here he could be found duly engaged in tenuous moves which threatened ejection without warning toward serrated impalers in the form of two slate scimitars lurking below in a kind of "him the almighty power I hurled headlong" kind of way. This did not happen, rather a bolt was clipped at death stretch, which despite its fall permitting security otherwise offered no respite and signalled a crux sequence leading precariously left to ordinarily desperate rockovers, after which the Dawes, now free from his labours, barely had time to adjust his tiara before belaying well back. "Hey, hey, hey, ya."

The next day Johnny climbed the astounding difficult Windows of Perception, a fierce E6 7a on the Seamstress Slab. Although this contained Slate's hardest single move, everyone knew that Dawes of Perception at E7 6c was the big lead, elevating Johnny's status and challenging John Redhead's dominance in terms of hard climbing for the first time in years. As if cheered on by Hogiau Llanber' in beer glass salute: "Chwarae teg, Johnny, Chwarae teg."

Grasping the obvious gauntlet, JR, stuck geko-esque, sketched onto the half diamond with immaculate credentials to face death by a thousand smears, gone now all friction, with clip in sight. Which is to say, he fell off, ripped his gear out and ended up upside down more or less back where he started looking up at the bolt, down at the two rock fangs and out over the pool whilst suspended from one sling runner draped over a spike some way above. Dave Towse, belaying, perhaps in a forerunner of a future rope access career had somehow managed to create a counterbalance by leaping towards the adjacent pool, taking in enough slack to avoid his leader's deck out.

Diary of a Slatehead

Escaping major injury, JR nevertheless sustained a broken finger, yet it was the sheer effrontery of being spat off so close to success that hurt most. Lesser leaders may have left it at that, but soon after regaining finger mobility another attempt was planned and this time I went along as action watcher, first aid officer, and in the event of tragedy, relative informer.

JR meanwhile expressed a wish, should he fail again, but survive serious injury, to be "thrown in the pool naked youth" as a sort of Jesuit style punishment. Dave set about unfurling ropes, hoping this time for a conventional belay duty rather than unorthodox last minute adrenaline pumping turbo-gliding practice and watching his fate unfold in the mirror of the pool. JR's warm up consisted of sitting around sorting crucial gear, eliminating anything considered unnecessary or cumbersome from the rack, squeeking clean his boots and after some banter simply setting off.

Being for the moment superfluous to events I approached a route opposite and across the pool from Dawes, which now and again, depending on breaks in passing cloud gleamed, smooth and strange in the sunlight as if sheathed in grey glass or polythene. Having imagined a good camera position might be attained a few metres up Blind Buddha whence it should have been possible to shoot uninterrupted back towards the main action I found myself untrusting of footholds whilst trying to face out so continued halfway, stopping at a point where a large spike lent against the upper slab. Although technical difficulties were not great this Buddha proved unlacking in exposure or interest, forcing a technique informed by a certain lurking fear where constant hold testing before moving up kept at bay a descent into anarchy. Deeming that any photographic account might best be acquired in another position I continued by this method and exited the arena after successfully surmounting a barbed wire fence overlooking the quarry rim.

John had barely progressed opposite, so by a circuitous journey up and down huge slate steps, some tree climbing, hauling on hidden rust mantled chains and aiding on heather I arrived at a vantage point above him and peering gingerly over the edge found him moving up the slab with serious intent. There it was then, the rockover's rockover, whilst reaching fingers pianoing on flat edges somehow gained purchase, pulled spider like up, gained better rugosities, then kept it together and stylishly exited, before standing astonished like "albion arose" atop the slab.

It was as if as fanfare of trumpets would open up any moment and it would not have surprised me if they had. Instead John grinned aloud, whilst Dave, preparing himself below, shouted aloft.

                Martin Crook

Paul Pritchard on an early repeat of Dawes of Perception E7 6c
photo: Tony Kay

East Face of the Vivian • **Vivian Quarry**

A great multi pitch link up is possible by connecting routes on the different tiers of Vivian Quarry. A number of entertaining variations are possible.

▶ **The East Face of
the Vivian E2 5c/6a ✳✳✳**
The most accessible of the options. A 7 pitch link up that seeks out a devious and absorbing path with continuous interest. Quite a trip at the grade!
P1 *Mental Lentils* (HVS 5b) A gentle introduction that kicks in a little just below the top. Move up past the lower off to reach the belay at the base of *Monster Kitten*.
P2 *Monster Kitten* (E1 5c) A fierce pitch that ups the ante considerably. At the top continue up to the old chain belay on the Dwarf Level, where a 15m walk left leads to the base of *Too Bald to be Bold*.
P3 *Too Bald to be Bold* (E2 5c) Although no pushover this is a fairly steady pitch with the option to link into P3. At its top descend the ramp to the hanging triple bolt belay below Turkey Chant. Either split the pitch here or continue in a single run out.
P4 *Turkey Chant* (E2 5c) After a bold but reasonable start things turn decidedly tricky in the upper half. At the top lower off to the Conscience Level. Coil your ropes and walk/scramble across to the base of *Comes the Dervish* slab.
P5 *Last Tango in Paris* (E1 5c) A big pitch with hard moves off the deck, a pushy section leading up to the overlap and a testing step left before it is possible to pull through onto the upper slab. Once both climbers are on top, climb carefully over the blocky ledges and then down to the belay at the top of the *Dervish*.
P6 *The Missing Link* (E2 5c/6a) From the *Dervish* belay, walk left across the base of the slab and move very carefully up the loose scree ramp until stood below the 1st bolt (Having, of course first ensured that no-one is in the fall zone below!). Climb carefully up to the bolt (some friable rock), or perhaps more sensibly, lasso it first. Continue up with some very technical climbing, passing a 2nd bolt and a size # 1.5 cam placement, to make a final hard move to the twin bolt lower off. Traverse carefully onto the Ritter Sport level on the left.
P7 *The Madness* (E2 5c) And last but not least, an intricate line with lots of bolts. Once this is in the bag it will probably be beer o'clock – time to lower off and head to the pub for some post match analysis.

▶ **The East Face of the
Vivian Direct E3 5c/6a ✳✳✳**
A harder and slightly more classic variation taking in the iconic slate route, *Comes the Dervish*.
P1 *Mental Lentils* (HVS 5b) A good limber up.
P2 *Monster Kitten* (E1 5c) Feeling pretty warm now!
P3 *Too Bald to be Bold* (E2 5c) Getting warmer still...
P4 *Turkey Chant* (E2 5c) ...and properly cooking now!
P5 *Comes the Dervish* (E3 5c) Here it is, the big one! The splitter crack of the slab is one of the greatest lines in North Wales let alone on slate, and provides a fittingly classic centre piece to this epic journey
P6 *The Missing Link* (E2 5c/6a) Careful now!
P7 *Ritter Sport* (E3 5c) And lastly, a change in style for the pre-pub pitch.

▶ **The East Face Super Direct E5 6b ✳✳✳**
An even harder combination suitable for a strong team.
P1 *Moving Being* (E4 6b) Straight in at the deep end with the technical crux
P2 *Teliffant* (E4 6a) A superb, but little climbed pitch with a memorable crux.
P3 *Flashdance* (E5 6a) Perhaps your mate's big lead?
P4 *Missing Link* (E2 5c/6a) Keep it steady.
P5 *General Odours* (E4 6a) A final committing pitch!

▶ **The East Face Super Charged E7 6c ✳✳✳**
An entirely speculative outing for an elite team. Fancy a pop?
P1 *Dawes of Perception* (E7 6c) Ouch!
P2 *Dwarf in the Toilet* (E6 6b) Oooh!
P3 *Gin Palace* (F7b+) Aaaahhhh!!!
P4 *Tribal Blow* (E6 6b) Phew!
P5 *Private Smells* (E5 6b) It's not over yet!

Top tip: travel in style with a small rucsac packed with a spare top, some water and most importantly, some tasty picnic snacks. You can also carry trainers and have a comfortable walk down afterwards. Perfect!

Vivian Lake reflection   photo: Rob Wilson

Vivian Upper

Style: Trad/sport
Aspect: Varied
Approach: 10-30 minutes
Altitude: 100 – 200m
OS Grid ref: 587 606

Breakdance	E7
Menstrual Gossip	E6
For Whom the Bell Tolls	E6
Tribal Blow	E6
Love Minus Zero	E6

The Spark that Set the Flame	E5
Flashdance/Belldance	E5
Private Smells	E5
Flashdance	E5
Swinging By the Bell	E5
Nostromo	E4
Smokeless Zone [F7a]	E4
Sweetest Taboo Direct Start	E4
The Sweetest Taboo	E4
Menage a Trois	E4
General Odours	E4
Young and Easy Under the Apple Boughs	E4
Night of the Hot Knives	E3
Down to Zero	E3
Comes the Dervish	E3
Ritter Sport	E3

The East Face of the Vivian	E2
Two Tone [F6b+]	E2
One Step Beyond	E2
Is it a Crime?	E2
Never as Good as the First Time	E2
The Velociraptor	E2
The Madness [F6a+]	E2
Ride of the Valkyries	E2
Last Tango in Paris	E1
Silly on Slate	HVS

Menopausal Discharge	F8a+
Manic Strain	F8a

Gin Palace	F7b+
Pas de Chevre	F7b+
Colditz	F7b+
Child's Play	F7b

The Manimal	F6b+
Truffle Hunter's Roof	F6b+
Mister, Mister	F6b
The Full Monty	F6a

The Lost Tomb	F5b

James McHaffie keeping his cool on the bold **Flashdance** E5 6a
photo: David Simmonite

Vivian Upper • Introduction

The upper tiers of Vivian Quarry host some of the best slate routes in the area, including the iconic *Comes the Dervish* which was first climbed by Stevie Haston back in the early 1980s.

There is a surprising volume of routes hidden amongst the numerous levels stretching up to the top of the quarry. While the Dervish slab area is often busy, it is always possible to find a quiet corner elsewhere. Indeed, climbing in Upper Vivian can feel curiously peaceful; quite a contrast to the very public pool level routes situated below. The majority of the routes are in the slate trad style; the Dervish slab is bolt free, but elsewhere expect some bolts, albeit with the odd eye popping run out just to keep things 'interesting'. There is also a small, but very distinctive selection of sport routes on offer. The Nostromo Wall is home to some of the most celebrated clip ups on slate. The designer chipped lines of *Menopausal Discharge* F8a+ and *Manic Strain* F8a, and of course the exhausting and technically baffling *Gin Palace* F7c are must dos for people operating at this level.

Conditions: Some of the less popular bays suffer from drainage problems, but in general the better routes dry quickly. The aspect is mostly open and sunny, however it should be possible to shift in and out of the sun as desired.

Access restrictions: The quarry is part of the Padarn Country Park, a designated conservation area of outstanding botanical interest, the management of which has been very sympathetic to climbers over the years. Please stay on the paths and avoid trampling on regenerating vegetation on the levels.

Approach: All levels are accessed from a series of steps running up the left side of the quarry. From the Gilfach Ddu car park (see page 242 for more details), a path leads up to a road from behind the Railway Café and left of the Diving Centre. Cross the road and slog up the steps to a blast shelter on the right. Beyond the fence it is possible to contour round to the first bay of the Dervish Level. To reach the levels above continue up the steps.

The Dervish Level

The Dervish Level

The main event of the quarry, bursting with classic extremes and sport routes alike, and including the justifiably celebrated, Comes the Dervish. The 1st route lies 50m from the approach fence. It picks its way over a hanging slab, in a little wooded bay.

▶ **1. Lentil in a Stew HVS 5a** 25m
A nifty bit of exploration, if not a particularly amazing route. Start at the base of a flake which defines the slab's left edge. Follow this to its terminal spike where a bold scamper is required to breach the hanging slab. Once safely in the groove on the other side, all that is required is a bit of adventuring up the blocky, somewhat loose, bay behind. [P Barbier, R Leishman 13.07.86]

The next 3 routes are found on what was known as Lone Pine Slab. However, the loneliness must have got to it 'cos it jumped. This is the obvious large slab with the dead fir at the bottom.

▶ **2. Legs Together E2 5b** 25m
This provides a delicate pad up the left hand edge of the slab. The rock is friable in places and the gear rare and infrequent, saving the crux for the last few metres. [06.84]

▶ **3. Legs Akimbo E2 5b** 25m
An interesting route, but with some friable rock and little worthwhile gear. Start as for Legs Together. Climb up and rightwards, around the arête then make a horizontal traverse rightwards before ascending directly then either diagonally left using high side pulls to reach a good ledge, or by stepping across horizontally on small holds to gain larger ones. Finish up leftwards, scary, or move rightwards to finish up larger holds as for Feet Apart. [R Ebbs 01.04.78]

▶ **4. Feet Apart E3 5b** 26m
A poorly protected route taking a fairly direct line up the slab. Climb an obvious flake then surmount a small bulge, before finishing straight up.
[M Barnicott 22.05.86]

The large bay to the left of the Nostromo Wall often has a waterfall running down its back wall.

▶ **5. Love Minus Zero E6 6a** ✱✱ 30m
A lonely lead up the pillar just right of the left arête of the left wall of the bay. Start by an iron spike on the left of the pillar and traverse right at 6m to an obvious jug. Climb up on mainly good holds (bold) moving left near the top.
[C Dale 07.05.87]

▶ **6. Down to Zero E3 5b** ✱ 30m
A recommended 'warm up' before embarking on the previous route. Start by a tree below the centre of the left wall of the bay. Use the tree to get established on the wall then ascend to the left end of an obvious ledge. Continue more or less directly to the top.
[C Dale, N Thomas, J Tombs 06.05.86]

Pete Robins on the desperate **Menopausal Discharge** F8a+
photo: Jack Geldard

▶ **7. Yak Kak XS** 22m
The back right hand corner of the bay gives the substance of this esoteric horror.
[S Haston 04.05.86]

▶ **8. Age Concern HVS 5a** 22m
Start at an obvious corner on the right hand side of the bay. Climb the crack to a peg, continue up the corner/groove, protection in the crack; easing off towards the top. [C Goodey, S Goodey 08.05.88]

The next trio take on the dolerite buttress just left of the approach to the Dervish slab. The 1st offering commences just left of the toe of the buttress at a square cut groove.

▶ **9. Bong to Lunch HVS 4c** 20m
A bold and sparsely protected climb, which has been scoured to a fairly solid state by a previous rock fall. Ascend the groove until it peters out, trending out left via more flat edges, to crest the buttress near its left arête. Follow the scoop to a short crack on the left which gains the next level. [S Haston 1983]

▶ **10. Frustrated Lust HVS 5a** 20m
More of the same dolerite shuffling. Start to the right of the buttress, just right of a small steep face. Ascend fairly directly to gain the scoop on the top of the buttress. Pad up just left of the hanging slab to gain the next level. [S Haston 1983]

▶ **11. The Moon Head Egg Monster from Allsup E1 4c** 20m
Climb up broken ground as for *Frustrated Lust*, and then head rightwards before stepping left onto the slab. Climb this to finish via two large loose flakes, which may have fallen down, and if not, probably will soon! [N Smith, A Bond 08.88]

Nostromo Wall and Dervish Slab

From the first bay, negotiate a bad step to gain access to the corner of pleasure. The left, Nostromo Wall contains several amazing and desperate routes which are mainly bolted. The right, bolt-free slab has an overlap at 2/3 height and the striking central crackline of *Comes the Dervish*.

▶ **12. Nostromo E4 6a** ∗ 22m
The slanting crack on the left end of the wall starting just right of the bad step in the path. A hard/loose start leads to a ledge at 12m. Step awkwardly right and battle strenuously up the crack to the top. [M Crook, D Towse 02.10.83]

▶ **Variation: 13. Nostrodamus E4 6b** 10m
From the ledge at 12m, move left via a layaway to reach the left arête. Climb this until a crack leads rightwards to the top. This route also appears to have been affected by recent rockfall and is probably best avoided. [C. Jex 1992]

▶ **14. Menopausal Discharge F8a+** ∗∗ 18m
The name keeps changing (this time back to the original) but the grade stays the same; nails! Originally climbed with a tea break in the middle, this was subsequently eliminated by Andy Pollitt and eventually flashed by Ben Moon. WOW! Very thin and enigmatic moves deviously wander up the hacked wall without respite. The crux move is an extremely left challenging proposition indeed. With only one's left limbs in contact with the rock, throw your right foot onto a fashionable scratch and, with no feeling at all, attempt to rock over forever to snatch a distant side pull. [J Redhead 09.06.86]

▶ **15. Colditz F7b+** ∗ 18m
It's not all crimps on slate; the slim hanging groove to the right has a brilliant and dynamic crux involving slopers! Follow *Young and Easy*… until it is possible to launch out left and slap wildly past 4 bolts to a lower-off.
[S Myles, M Pretty 17.04.91]

▶ **16. Young and Easy Under the Apple Boughs E4 6a** ∗ 20m
The central shattered dog leg crack is awkward and a bit loose; nonetheless it yields a good route. [J Redhead, M Crook 02.05.86]

▶ **17. Manic Strain F8a** ∗∗ 20m
The Marmite of all routes; you either love it or you hate it. I like Marmite, especially with avocado and cheese. Although blatantly chipped, favouring the 6 footer, it is well chipped. Long, thrusting moves between harsh cracks and minute edges lead up the smooth golden wall to an 'all-or-nothing' rock over for the finishing crack. Lower off. [J Redhead 24.04.86]

▶ **18. Gin Palace F7b+** ∗∗∗ 18m
One of the finest lines on slate. Slippery and frustrating squirming up the hanging flake/chimney leads to an arm sapping finale up the crack in the headwall. Awesome. [C Smith 25.06.86]

The Dervish Level • **Vivian Upper 265**

▶ **19. Child's Play F7b ∗∗ 20m**
The wall to the right of the chimney is certainly not child's play. Follow the groove of *Hymen Snapper* until a line of bolts breaks out left onto the wall proper (or take a more direct line). A short 6c technical sequence is rewarded with an easier finish. [R Drury 02.06.86]

▶ **20. Hymen Snapper E5 5c** 25m
The slanting groove becomes loose and serious towards the top. [S Haston, L McGinley 08.82]

▶ **21. Reefer Madness E3 5c** 40m
The corner bordering the left side of the Dervish Slab. Technical climbing with some very hard to spot gear. The rock above the overlap is loose. Bolt belay on the right. [S Haston, P Trower 05.82]

▶ **22. For Whom the Bell Tolls E6 6b ∗∗** 40m
The hairline crack 3m right of the corner offers no reliable protection until above the overlap. The crux is low down but a few deep breaths may be needed to push on. Step right at the overlap and pull onto the easier upper slab. Bolt belay. [A Pollitt, M Crook, J Taylor 29.04.84]

▶ **23. Menstrual Gossip E6 6b ∗∗** 40m
The faint weakness left of *Comes the Dervish* is extremely bold with hard climbing to boot. Climb up to a crucial and precise wire placement at 10m. Continue, becoming ever more committed, to eventually gain a good wire slot way beyond the safety of the last runner. Continue up and over to join the final section of *For Whom...* [J Redhead 05.85]

▶ **24. Comes the Dervish E3 5c ∗∗∗** 40m
The splitter crack of the slab is one of the greatest lines in North Wales, let alone on slate. The crack was originally cleaned with a knife nicked from Pete's Eats, and justifiably graded E5. Over the years the route has cleaned up and the gear has improved to give a sustained, enjoyable and most likely soft touch E3. Start at the foot of the crack, and climb up past some micro wire placements to reach better gear at 8m. This section is extremely polished and not a little insecure. Above the climbing eases until a difficult swerve right is taken. Continue up to a comfortable foot ledge below the overlap before climbing over the step and moving up the bold but easing finish. Now turn round and take your bow, the whole of Llanberis could be watching you! Bolt belay. [S Haston 02.81]

▶ **25. Flashdance E5 6a ∗∗∗** 43m
A bold lead up the rising line of shallow scoops which meet *Comes the Dervish* about 3m below the overlap. Start up the twin diagonal cracks and break out leftwards onto the slab. Climb confidently past a few spaced runners (including a crucial, but iffy IMP/RP 4 or similar nut) to easier ground before the *Dervish* is reached and followed to the top. Bolt belay. [A Pollitt, T Freeman 08.83]

▶ **26. Flashdance/Belldance E5 6b ∗∗∗** 46m
This route originally started up *Comes the Dervish* but makes a much better pitch by starting up *Flashdance*. Follow all of *Flashdance* into the crack and a bomber runner. Step back right and make a series of very thin moves to gain the overlap. Move rightwards heading for a thin crack above the overlap and an easier saunter to the top. Bolt belay. [J Redhead, D Towse 19.03.84]

▶ **27. Breakdance E7 6b ∗∗** 45m
Extremely bold and committing climbing up the lonely slab between the adjacent routes. Follow *Flashdance* to its low runner just out from the twin cracks of *Last Tango in Paris* then confidently stride up the slab to a rest in a more featured spot in the middle of nowhere. Arrange a skyhook and make a difficult series of moves up to the overlap with no margin for error. Finish up *Last Tango In Paris* with relief. [A Wainwright 01.01.89]

▶ **28. Last Tango in Paris E1 5c ∗∗** 45m
A great route, especially in its upper half, once away from the blocky arête. Hard for the grade. Climb the twin diagonal cracks (hard at first) heading rightwards across the slab to where they join the arête. Go up the crack and arête above to gain a large blocky ledge. A thin crack then cuts back left across the slab and up to the overlap. Make a difficult move left at the niche in the overlap and pull quickly round onto the upper slab. Easier but occasionally loose ground leads to the top. [M Roberts, C Edwards 12.05.85]

P3 of **Wendy Doll E1 5b** follows *Last Tango...* up to the large blocky ledge on the arête. The remainder of the line up the arête is about to fall down and at least E2!

▶ **29. Swinging By the Bell E5 6a ∗** 47m
A bold right-to-left girdle of the Dervish Slab, a couple of metres below the overlap. From the right arête (on *Last Tango...*), traverse leftwards to where *Flashdance* meets *Comes the Dervish* at a jug and the first protection. Move down so hands are on the jug and step delicately left to a flat hold. Climb up and left, crux, to good holds below the overlap. Pull round this to finish as for *Menstrual Gossip*. Low in the grade, but terrifying to follow. [D Towse, M Roberts 20.03.84]

▶ **30. The Missing Link E2 5c/6a** 13m
A route that enables a continuous link from the Pool Level to the Ritter Sport Level; it has little merit in isolation. From the *Comes the Dervish* belay teeter left along the ledge, it is advisable to ensure that no-one is directly below on the *Dervish*, as some loose debris is likely to be dislodged from directly below the 1st bolt. Climb the crack past 2 bolts and a cam #1.5 slot to eventually step left onto the belay ledge, 2 bolts. Either lower off back to the *Dervish* belay or make a delicate traverse on to the Ritter Sport Level.

The Conscience Slab

The bad step approach from the Dervish Slab is protected by 3 bolts. The loose and scrappy gully, VS 4a [05.06.86], on the left of the slabs is best avoided. The next pair of routes are bolt protected but still have a run out, bold feel.

▶ **31. Mister, Mister F6b** * **30m**
The long thin slab just left of the Conscience Slab. A fine upper slab after a snappy lower half. Scramble up the short arête to the 1st bolt then follow the left line of bolts to a lower-off.
[M Raine, A Newton 23.12.06]

▶ **32. The Full Monty F6a** * **30m**
The right hand line shares the same lower half before breaking off on a rightwards leading line. Lower off. [M Raine, A Newton 23.12.06]

A couple of poor routes are encountered before the good lines can be described. **Slate's Slanting Crack E2 5b** [13.07.86], climbs the diagonal crack rightwards across the slab and **Foetal Attraction E4 5c** [01.03.88], is an even lower, poorer traverse!

▶ **33. Menage a Trois E4 6b** ** **25m**
A technical left hand finish to *The Sweetest Taboo*. Follow *The Sweetest Taboo* to where it moves right. Move left to a slanting flake crack and climb straight up past 3 bolts, trending right at the top, to a lower-off. [M Raine 24.07.87]

▶ **34. The Sweetest Taboo E4 6a** ** **25m**
A very good route in the middle of the slab, bold in parts. Start 3m left of the rising break on the right edge of the slab. Climb up past a difficult move left at 5m to good holds. Move right past a good wire to a bolt. Climb above this to a pleasant finish and lower-off.
[M Raine, J Dawes 01.05.86]

▶ **Variation: 35. Direct Start E4 6a** *
A bold variant starting up the slab directly, and then joining *Never as Good...* before finishing up *The Sweetest Taboo*. Lower off.
[N Gresham, I Lloyd Jones 28.08.88]

▶ **36. Never as Good as the
First Time E2 5c** ** **23m**
A good and popular route. Start at the foot of the rising break at the right edge of the slab. Climb boldly up the slab to a bolt. Traverse 2m left and ascend directly to a large flake on *The Sweetest Taboo*. Continue to the bolt then step right and follow the crackline diagonally rightwards to a double bolt lower off. A superb E3 6a links this route into the finish of route 34.
[M Raine, C Dale 10.05.86]

▶ **37. Is it a Crime? E2 5c** ** **23m**
Follow *Never as Good...* to the 1st bolt. Make a difficult move diagonally right then continue up to another bolt below a small overlap. Follow a thin crack above past a final bolt to a lower-off.
[M Raine, C Dale 10.05.86]

Slatehead • Mike Raine

Sean Villanueva on **The Sweetest Taboo** E4 6a
photo: Alex Messenger

▶ **38. That Obscure Object of Desire VS 4b** 18m
The unprotected rising break line is ascended to broken ground near the top. Move leftwards to the bolt belay of *Is it a Crime*? [M Raine 22.04.86]

▶ **39. The Spark that Set the Flame E5 6b** ∗∗ 15m
Small but unforgettable. A hairline crack leads up the slab to the right, pulling boldly through a mini overlap. [R Drury 1985]

▶ **40. Smokeless Zone E4 6b [F7a]** ∗ 15m
Another thin series of moves up the right side of the slab but this time there are bolts! Lower off.
[C Davies, M Wells, P Targett, C Stephenson 09.12.89]

▶ **41. You can Dance if You Want To HVS 5a** 15m
The right arête of the small slab is climbed to the lower-off on *Smokeless Zone*. [M Raine 23.05.86]

▶ **42. Vivander HVS 5a** 25m
Start in the bay to the right of the slabs. Go up over bulges and past a borehole. Move left into a loose couloir then go back right to a loose scree finish. Belay well back on an iron bar.
[C Philips, P Barbier 18.05.86]

Above the Conscience Slab, **Throttle with Bottle E2 5b** climbs a groove in the centre of a small slab.

The character of the delightful Conscience Slab is almost entirely down to Mike Raine. In 1986 placing bolts was still considered controversial in certain circles, so when Mike placed a bolt on **The Sweetest Taboo** the name reflected his mixed feelings at the time. Ironically the route is now usually climbed direct and is pretty bold! Ten days later he returned and placed yet more bolts to protect **Is it a Crime?** and **Never as Good as the First Time**. Further brooding on his actions prompted Mike to suggest the 'Conscience' Slab as a name for the area. Mike's final addition to the slab, **Menage a Trois**, however, may have an entirely different meaning!

Perhaps more noteworthy is his discovery of a trio of excellent but tough routes up on Heaven Walls: **The Dinorwig Unconquerable, The Long and Winding Road**, and **Pain Killer**. The former is a contender for the best E3 in the quarries, being an impeccable and perfect hand-sized splitter crack.

After a long spell in the south of England, Mike, like many other '80s Slateheads, was left unfulfilled with the outside world and returned to Llanberis with one mission: bolt more slate routes. He succeeded and a re-acquaintance with the Conscience Slab gave rise to **The Full Monty** and **Mister Mister**, which are amply bolted! To bring his development right up to date, the tricky little sport route **State of the Heart F6c+** in Nuremberg has spat off a few local hot-shots, which should please Mike no end.

Mike Raine, original slatehead and organiser of the ∧
recent Tremadog clean up festivals, manning the BMC
stall at Eric's Cafe photo: Si Panton

Diary of a Slatehead

Experienced Rock Cats

In some instances slateheads came under scrutiny from security guards responsible for general policing duties in and around quarry areas that allowed a more public view than the remote or secluded upper quarries. Vivian Quarry for example is located within five minutes walk beyond parking at popular tourist attractions (the Slate Museum and the Lake Railway in Gilfach Ddu), whilst Rainbow Slab is well seen from offices belonging to CEGB, which are in turn overlooked by obscure and seldom visited haphazard ziggurats of slate known by heads as The Trango and Peppermint Towers respectively.

Before slateheads began probing the quarries searching for routes it is possible to speculate that the security guard's lot centred around a set routine including duties involving dissuading adventurous tourists and local youths straying into areas off limits to them since without any form of climbing skills to rely on they might easily become accident victims.
When heads entered the equation the scene was set for a number of bizarre scenarios where previously unchallenged, and to most people, sensible authority, clashed with youthful anarchic elements from the climbing world who began to view the quarries not as dangerous post industrial sites, duly fenced off and out of bounds, but as serious new mediums for rock climbing exploration providing ready made forcing grounds for those willing to trespass.
As it turned out, gaining individual slate levels sometimes proved difficult in itself, so that once Stevie Haston completed his seminal slate masterpiece in Vivian Quarry, Comes the Dervish in August 1982 (Originally E5 6a, but now settled as a classic E3 since the gradual wearing away of small slate blocks from the crack thereby leaving larger finger locks.). Those contemplating repeating it would first have to negotiate not only the trifling matter of a barbed wire fence, but also thoughtful moments balancing across a few feet of old railtrack poised above a vertical slate groove that drops away towards razor sharp quartz spattered slate blocks 30m or so before terminating near gashed grey shores surrounding Vivian's green pool.

Yet such people usually already possessed climbing skills honed on natural crags, where experience had taught them that sometimes getting to and from certain cliffs could constitute major problems in themselves. Thus the railtrack 'bad step', as it would later be described in Paul William's now classic 1987 Llanberis guide, whilst treated with respect, was relatively standard fair for prospective Dervish teams. To the layman it was, and still is quite a different matter.

This point became clearly apparent one spring afternoon in 1983 when a few heads had gone over to the Dervish with 'Tom the hom' (Tommy Jones) who's recent good form had placed him as a candidate for an early repeat.

To sit facing the counter in Pete's Eats is not something customers might ordinarily dwell upon or imbue with any significance, unless of course they had their own secret reasons for doing so. Yet for slateheads in the early 1980s this position became a regular hang out since by turning the head diagonally right it is possible, by keeping to the line of gaze, to look out beyond the back yard of an establishment claiming to be a pub, known locally as 'The Prince', over Llyn Padarn's cold waters before open ground culminates in Vivian's prominent grey Dervish level framed on either side by an almost unbroken backdrop of apparently vertical deciduous woodland.

Diary of a Slatehead

Trev Hodgson making an early (check the EBs!) repeat of Comes the Dervish photo: Martin Crook

Thus on the same afternoon Tom began his Dervish ascent it was just possible for me, sitting in Pete's, to make him out as a speck starfished middle distance on the 40m high slate obelisk. Thirty or so minutes later I crossed the 'bad step' before exchanging a few words with Tom who by now had reached a resting place below the overlap which splits the entire slab like a horizontal eyebrow three quarters of the way up. It seemed he required nought and one RPs which having been overlooked were still packed within his rucsack and as it appeared unnecessarily precarious for a rope lowering manoeuvre it was decided I would attempt dropping them to him from a vantage point above the dervish level atop what would later become the Nostromo Wall. This I managed without much hassle and eventually Tom, armed with the RPs, steadily won out over easier, but less well protected ground which led to a belay where the angle eased. Unfortunately for the lone security guard who had now appeared, our individual positions made his initial attempts to reach us untenable. He could not, for instance cross the 'bad step', he didn't know how to reach the next level and Tom was clearly beyond his ken, attached to ropes suspended 40m up an apparently featureless rock wall.

Despite an outburst from the official in which a somewhat distant diatribe informed us that we were "trespassing", it was "a hell of a dangerous place", "the police would be called" and so on. The guard's authority was further undermined not only by taunting abuse but by Tom informing him that:

"It's okay, we're experienced rock cats, man." A comment that has since passed into climbing folklore.

As well as heralding a head shaking withdrawal by a somewhat frustrated law enforcer who having entered the fray with all the strutting authoritarian confidence his shiny black Doc martin shoes, black crimpoline kecks, silver buckled belt, light blue sky scraper shirt and macho 'tashe could muster, now faced a 'walk of shame' which in a few years became common to those who had either failed on the Dervish, or failed to throw heads out of the quarry.

Martin Crook

Gav Foster on the recent addition **Birdsong** F6a+ photo: Si Panton

The Hot Knives Level • **Vivian Upper** 273

The Hot Knives Level
Continue up the steps on the left of the quarry to the next level and hop over the fence on the right.

▶ **43. Birdsong F6a+** 10m
The arete on the left hand side of the level passing 4 bolts to a lower-off. Hard moves come at half height and with a mantel onto the ledge at the top. [P Targett I Lloyd-Jones 13.05.08]

▶ **44. Binman HVS 5a** 25m
Further round is a long, loose, slabby wall. Start a few metres right of the hut near the left end of the wall. Climb up, trending right then finish direct. Serious for its grade. [M Boater 06.84]

▶ **45. Abus Dangereux E2 5b** 25m
Another serious route up the thin cracks in the centre of the wall. [M Mariner, M Nuttal 17.07.91]

▶ **46. Fallout VS 4c** 25m
A line on the right-hand side of the wall. Climb the groove then step left and continue past a peg to the top. Abseil from an in situ sling or climb a tottering pile to the next level.
[J Tombs, P Barbier 10.05.86]

▶ **46a. The Quartz Scoop VS 4c** 10m
The short, sculpted dolerite rib in the middle of the slag heap between *The Manimal* and *Fallout*. A bold and delicate excursion. [C Muskett 27.02.10]

▶ **47. The Manimal F6b+** ∗∗15m
A nice little route up the small slab in the back of the bay, past 3 bolts to a lower-off. Some wires may be needed at the start.
[G Sewell, J Cleford 04.03.92]

▶ **48. Baby Nina Soils Her Pants VS 4b** 10m
Reminiscent of *Sup 1* but with ample gear. It unfortunately replicates its heather/scree mantel finish. Follow the rightwards slanting rib tucked behind a mass of slate blocks.

▶ **49. Night of the Hot Knives E3 5c** ∗ 18m
The slanting flake crack on the left of the main slab. The difficulty gradually increases to a tricky finish past a poor rock.
[M Crook, D Cuthbertson 03.01.86]

▶ **50. Tribal Blow E6 6b** ∗ 15m
The slanting crack right of *Hot Knives*. Committing and technical with poor protection. Climb the crack to some poor wires then boldly press on up to join *Hot Knives* just below the top.
[R Drury, S Britain 24.04.86]

▶ **51. Solvent Abuse E3 5b** 13m
The hardest of the *Sup 1* clones; this is another rightward slanting rib. The good news is that the top out is very straightforward. The bad news is that there's only 1 poor skyhook for gear.
[M Crook and a 'cast of thousands' 27.04.87]

▶ **52. Under the Glass HVS 5a** 11m
The right hand dolerite pillar provides a bold route, but one with some reasonable climbing. Climb direct up to a ledge below a bulge via a hairline crack and then ascend the arête/groove on the right to the final mantel. [C Philips 25.05.86]

▶ **53. The Velociraptor E2 5c** ∗ 13m
This route lies on a small slab right of the dolerite pillars. Climb the corner until a triangular pocket can be reached on the slab on the left. Continue up the slab past bolts to a lower-off.
[T McClean and party 19.01.92]

Vivian Upper 275

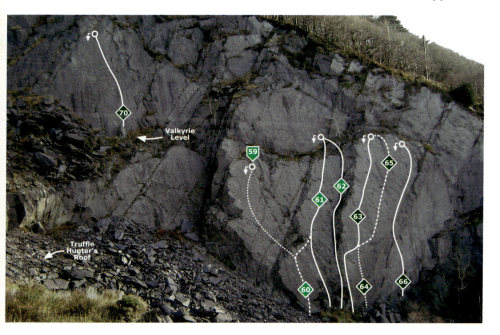

The Ritter Sport Level
The next level up, gained from the steps on the left and hopping over the fence on the right. The first route climbs through the obvious roof on the left wall of the level.

▶ **54. Truffle Hunter's Roof F6b+** ** 13m
A hidden gem (but no truffles) and totally different from the normal slabby experiences found hereabouts, being a roof climb. Follow the bolts up the surprisingly awkward lower wall to below the roof. Pull left through this to massive holds over the lip, dangle around for a while then attempt to get stood on the ledge above the roof. Carry on to a lower-off.
[P Johnstone, D Cuthbertson, K Read 11.12.87]

▶ **55. Satires of Circumstance E2 5b** 26m
A choss-tastic heap of a route with a couple of interesting moves and a lot of disposable grot. Ascend the shattered groove right of *Truffle Hunters* with trepidation to a switchback, where the following groove is less loose and a trifle trickier. At this point the lower off of *Truffle Hunters* can be clipped by those with more sense than pride. Pick your way up the slabby groove to the top. [P Jenkinson, M Boniface 20.04.88]

▶ **56. Jumping the Gun E1 5b** 30m
Start below the wall. Climb a short steep groove, then surmount the bulge leftwards to easier ground. Follow the obvious crack up left, then move back right to finish up another crack.
[M Campbell 27.05.86]

▶ **57. Puff Puff E2 5c** 32m
Start at the base of the groove, as for *Jumping the Gun*. Climb the groove, but at the bulge move right and continue up to below a crack and groove. Climb the crack to the top of the groove, hard, step right and finish up a crack.
[J Banks, L Naylor 29.05.86]

▶ **58. A Tourmegamite Experience VS 4b** 54m
A rambling route with little solid rock. Start at a green and white banded arête in the middle of the level.
P1 4b 18m Climb the arête with care.
P2 18m Climb up the green band for about 3 or 4m, then traverse left for 5m. Go up grooves and a slab to finish at a tree.
P3 18m Climb the arête right of the obvious deep grass-filled groove to the top of the quarry. Other alternative, but equally throw away finishes are possible. [C Philips 22.05.87]

The attractive slabs on the right side of the level provide the next routes.

▶ **59. One Step Beyond E2 6a** * 25m
Start as for *Two Tone* and continue up left past 3 more bolts to a lower-off.
[M Raine, M Reeves 05.08.07]

▶ **60. Two Tone E2 6a [F6b+]** ** 22m
A better start to *The Madness*, up the short slab to its left past 2 bolts. The line jumps straight in with a hard move to wake you up then continues up to the ledge. Traverse easily right to reach and finish up *The Madness*.
[A Newton, P Johnstone 05.05.88]

276 Vivian Upper • The Ritter Sport Level

▶ **61. The Madness E2 5c [F6a+]** ** 22m
A fine climb up the slab to the left of the shattered groove of *Silly on Slate*. Climb straight up the slab, following an intricate line of scooped dishes and passing five bolts to a lower-off on the ledge above.
[A Newton, K Griffiths, P Johnstone 20.04.88]

▶ **62. Silly on Slate HVS 4c** * 22m
The obvious rightwards slanting shattered groove is climbed boldly to the ledge and lower-off on *The Madness*. [N Clacher, T Hodgson 04.04.86]

▶ **63. Private Smells E5 6b** ** 25m
An aesthetic rising line, which sweeps right across the big smooth hanging slab. Thin moves and gripper-clip bolts provide a very memorable outing. The start is barely independent, so most people just go up *Silly on Slate* initially. Lower off.
[P Pritchard, N Harms 10.87]

▶ **64. Private Smells Direct Start E5 6b** 22m
A poor and desperate looking direct start to *Private Smells*, protected by a dodgy bolt.
[P Pritchard 31.12.87]

▶ **65. General Odours E4 6a** * 30m
This energizing lip trip breaks out right from *Private Smells*. Equal commitment is required from leader and second alike. Once safely across to the bolt at the traverse end, the top is sought with urgency and not a little rope drag. Lower off either at the top of *Private Smells* or *Ritter Sport*. [Piggy Johnstone, A Newton 1988]

▶ **66. Ritter Sport E3 5c** ** 25m
A well protected route of surprising quality. Start below the obvious steep flake with 2 bolts. Climb up to the spike just below the crack and arrange some runners, step down and attack the crack. Reaching the 1st bolt is the crux; after this, continue laybacking up the flake to the pinnacle. A committing reach off this leads to the mother of all holds. Continue along the rightwards rising ramp line, until a tiny spike runner is reached; follow the crack leading back up and left to the lower-off.
[J Redhead, A Newton 25.04.86]

The Top Level • The Valkyries Level • **Vivian Upper** 277

The Valkyries Level

A further slog up the steps leads you to a great little sport route and a worthwhile E2 slab.

▶ **67. Pas the Duchie... F6a+** 8m
The slab left of the steep arête is quite fierce, especially if you do the left hand start. Lower off.
[P Robins 01.02.07]

▶ **68. Pas de Chevre F7b+** ** 10m
A sustained, complex and quite brilliant collection of moves up the unassuming steep arête, just left of the fence. Lower off. [N Harms 18.05.88]

▶ **69. Ride of the Valkyries E2 5c** * 26m
A pleasant open slab near the top of the quarry, away from all the hustle and bustle below. Beyond the fence there is a slab containing 2 pegs higher up. Start in the centre; bold moves lead to a depression and then the 1st horizontal break, peg. Continue up past the next break, interest increasing with height.
[L Hardy, I Stevens, C Ayres 05.87]

▶ **70. Power Tool Resurrection E4 6a** 15m
On the far wall of the level, situated across a slightly worrying band of scree, is a neat triangular face reaching almost to the trees. This route arcs its way up the right side of the triangle to a bolt lower off. Some of the bolts look worse for wear. It is equally harrowing to approach from the Madness Level. [1992]

The Top Level

If you really want peace and quiet, you'll find it here, along with some poor loose routes.

▶ **71. Goodbye Natterjack Toad HVS 5a** 15m
The central open groove and rib on the left wall of the level, past 2 bolts to a single bolt lower-off. [T Taylor, A Hughes 1993]

The following 2 routes are located on a tottering pillar at the back of the level.

▶ **72. Faulty Towers E2 5c** 20m
The left-hand weakness (and I mean weakness!) up the tower, passing loose cracks, niches and ledges. Abseil off.
[T Dale, C Dale 20.04.87]

▶ **73. Caleduwlch E4 6a** 20m
Not a bad route; perhaps the best of the trad routes hereabouts. The slanting crack on the right of the tower leads to a small groove and loose arête to finish. Abseil off.
[P Littlejohn, P Judge 15.11.91]

▶ **74. The Lost Tomb
(aka: Dog Day Dogfish) F5b** * 20m
Originally a neglected VS, now a cleaned up and bolted sport route. The prominent V groove gives a delightful climb. Lower off.
[M Podd, L Lovatt 17.09.89/Re-cleaned and bolted up by M Helliwell, S Traynor 19.10.10]

Diary of a Slatehead

Vivian Stories - Encounters with Vivian

Living in Dinorwig in 1981, being unemployed and, at least in any legal sense, transportless meant on occasion walking to the Pad in Llanberis, the climber's pub as it then was, where lifts for the round trip, if not guaranteed, remained open to negotiation when Fay Ray battered out tunes from their one and only album, Contact You, fronted by a beautiful girl singer in a style of home grown cool.

At weekends in summer the place swayed and sweltered, noised by visiting climbers, some slowly limbering up before Harris parties, later to become far flung and heady, caught on strobes in the dance floor night. Silhouettes in stray cat struts against Clogwyn D'ur Arddu's great profile, backdropped and well hung, home of the brave. Whatever the nuances surrounding particular social scenes, descending or ascending a pied between Dinorwig cloud land and Llanberis usually entailed pilgrimming a slate stepped quarry mouth's path, 'the zig-zags'. Switchback supreme in its submergence, private and walled in places on each side like a single lane alley bisecting the hillside.

Dave Towse on the 2nd ascent of Belldance E5 6b photo: Martin Crook

Alternatively, a more meandering course, almost in its entirety overlooking Vivian, which by 1981 had remained unworked for twelve years, provided a less gruelling option. Vivian with its many tiered gantries encircling and rising above its pool sunk floor contained at each level much flora and fauna in regenerative bloom unfettered by interference or design between pillars, prows, slabs and walls of dark hung slate as if awaiting ascent.

The first encounter yielded Haston's Wendy Doll, a three pitch E2 premised largely on its 40m finale up cracks in the arete defining dervish slab, the big prize which would be unveiled the following year. For now though further tentative probing relied on an ascent taking in a prominent prow rising vertically from Vivian's black lagoon and finishing abruptly at about 30m where a horizontal platform, itself the scene for much to-ing and fro-ing by those contemplating the obvious air rush plunge, gave sudden respite when Haston, this time accompanied by an unfortunate London dentist serving belay penance, lead Four Wheel Drift, apparently Slate's first extreme single pitch crack climb on the prow's north face. Eclipsing these sojourns in spectacular fashion came the leap and whilst retaining no clear climbing value it remains a Vivian tour de force. First descended by local, Nicki Thomas when, amongst much macho posturing and procrastination, for obvious reasons, she simply trod across the last few feet of terra firma and leapt. Then poseidon moments after slap fractured surface into butterfly effect, triumphant, aloof as Joan de Arc she emerged into local folklore.

It is said that Oscar Eckenstein invented crampons, Geoffrey Winthrop Young the British Mountaineering Council, Peter Harding the hand jam, though the latter is more normally attributed to Joe Brown, Whillans his famous harness, Pierre Allain rock shoes and Ray Jardine, when not working for NASA, Friends.

Hardly conclusive these random examples punctuate climbing history as luminaries in the sport brought about change in one way or another, almost inevitably developing aspects lamented by each generation's old guard, whilst attempting to push standards higher than previously thought possible sometimes championed under new or extended wedge thin ethical codes.

Vivian Stories ——— My generation had Haston.

It is however rare that some climbers in a generation chance on an entirely new medium where routes of all standards are open for exploration once the terrain has permeated a climber's psyche in such a way becoming acceptable, even desirable, over time. Yet in the early 1980s after an encounter with Vivian culminating in a lead of The Dervish, I entered the slatehead fold along with various compadres, who rarely fastidious, promoted forth campaigns based on climbing almost anything slate coloured.
It did not take long before some heads began raising the stakes ? To what could be climbed and how such extraordinary features might turn out once engaged. Climbers they and young blooded in tradition, anarchic and new.
Whippet thin Andy Pollitt in pink lycra leggings was by 1983 a 'lean mean clinging machine' contributing along with his companions towards a rise in technical standards throughout Snowdonia.
Pollitt had made an early ascent of The Dervish, mindfully noting a line based on shallow scoops running ground up right to left and joining Dervish near its overlap. Hardly a secret, this line extended a guarded, friction poor, runner shy welcome reserved perhaps for those blithe spirits endowed with what Paul Williams called 'massive tessies'. Many of whom, having mulled over potential arcing fall factors failed to leave ground level with any serious intent.
In August 1983, almost a year after Dervish's cutlery cleaned first ascent, Andy breezed back to Vivian and, Capercaillie cocksure in Scarpa boots, led the line, apparently without blinking, belayed by Tim Freeman. It was thought 'necky' E5 or E6 6a, whilst further clues aimed at informing what subsequent ascencionists might encounter on Flashdance in grip factor terms were recorded in Pete's along side the route description which stated that:

"Bicycle clips count as one point."

Although harder slab routes were to follow, it was Flashdance that alerted slateheads to future possibilities since it proved that with a certain cool long stretches of slate initially conceived as unjustifiable allowed those possessed with mental fortitude and a little extra trust in RP placements tenuous rites of passage.
Keen to repeat this excursion undeterred by either run outs or RP capabilities was JR 'a warlock with a loping dog' as Jim Perrin had described him so that in due course with Dave Towse and myself in tow up the steps over the fences and past the 'do so at your own risk' sign we went.
Two encounters along the way, the first with a woman who, perhaps unkindly, I referred to as the Dinorwig Heda Gabler, and the second with two heads who after completing an ascent of Reefer Madness, a battle scarred corner groove left of the Dervish were keen to embrace the relative sanctuary provided by Pete's, gave pleasant interludes to our serious intent.
Sitting below Dervish slab, Dave and I barely had time to focus on ritual preparations before JR quickly performed a sort of Balinese temple dance as knee high wellies were exchanged for two sizes too small EB rock boots and with sticht plate still unloaded he set off cat like and inquisitive,
"No point puttin' us on 'til the 'arps' are in." he had said.
Musing on our surroundings it seemed that at any time the quarries could be subject to a myriad of future schemes or a stringently enforced climbing ban yet entering any particular area within their boundary gave rise to surreal sense of curatorship coupled with a real sense of irony.
Thus by trespass it was possible to reclaim a former work site which bore physical remainders dating back to laissez fair capitalism's heyday in the last century. They had not meant to leave anything, nor had they cleaned up, those owners of the means of production, yet inadvertently and with no environmental qualms their labour force had created an arena man made containing at least as many climbable surrogates as nature had provided in the Llanberis Pass. Elidir itself had simply belched the quarries a mere tick bird on the rhinos back for if mountains can be said to know anything it is that there is no end to the folly of men.

280 Diary of a Slatehead Vivian Stories (Cont'd...)

Above JR, a craftsmen about his work, now 10m up and looking down with a wry grin meant he was probably about to embark on a crux sequence some distance from his last RPs. After a few pensive moments for Dave and I the bearded commisor rocked leisurely, but not without care between chamfered dishes until attaining a standing position and leaning left after the top one he held something better, turned torso until out repeated the wry grin and said: "jug".

Hanging in the Capodimonte museum in Naples is a painting by Fransiscan monk Luca Pacioli Jacofi Barbari depicting fria Luca Paciolo di Borgs in close proximity to the duke of Urbanis whose involvement in a brutal slaying, the assassination of Guiliano de Medici in 1478 remains historically unresolved.
What can be said accurately about Fra Luca Paciolo di Borgs however is that in 1509 he authored 'divine proportion', which delves into pythagorus's 'Golden Mean' seeking to reveal how art and architecture often religiously inspired at the time achieves balance and harmony.

JR on For Whom the Bell Tolls E6 6b
photo: Martin Crook

Many centuries later after the industrial revolution, with its at times grand, grim wall of ugliness, as if left as a kind of secret apology arrived at by mistake quarry owners in North Wales hardly concerned with artistic sensibilities whilst blasting out slate's natural resource inadvertently created a topograhical legacy which in places conformed to some rock climber's minds as something like a 'Golden Mean' and best exemplified in this sense by Vivian's Comes the Dervish which even after a recent eclipse into polishdom remains a reigning toast in any climbing gallery, described since early 1987 by the archdeacon of the slate cult, Paul Williams as a 'solid gold pitch'.

What made it a Golden Mean to us, 120ft or so of calf pumping (madness...)

The climber as artist (H Drasdo)

JR on the FA of Manic Strain F8a
photo: Andy Newton

The Colourful Quarrymen

In October 1983 Dave Towse and I returned to Vivian for a go at the obvious thin searing crackline in the wall overlooking the Dervish Slab. Starting involved desperate moves on fingerlocks whilst kung fu kicking out to footholds above the left hip. Later Paul Williams would dispense with the introductory moves by building a stone cairn of which barring the edifice collapsing, it was possible to engage the climb.

After this boulder problem start further strenuous locks led to a hands off rest where I was able to remove the hinderence of a stupidly chosen neck scarf, which had conspired to strangle me as I moved up the route as it had somehow become entangled with the climbing rack which mostly hung from a bandolier worn around the shoulder and torso. To onlookers the sight might have looked bizarre, a youth stopping halfway up a slate face to remove a fashion item whilst swearing at no-one in particular. It would have also been noticed that the youth wore red and yellow boots (Hanwags, or handbags in head slang), some kind of orange harness (an old Whillans) and a striped bib and brace overall, his companion meanwhile stood silently underneath a grey trilby hat, his studded leather motorcycle jacket giving way to lurid electric blue lycra tights more commonly associated with ballet dancers.

A colourfully atired Martin Crook on the first ascent of Nostromo E4 6b photo: Crook collection

Yet I would later learn that quarrymen over one hundred years earlier provided colourful animation against a generally dark background in the course of their employ. It is worth remembering that because surviving photographs illustrating quarrying and quarrymen at work are invariably in black and white format it is easy to admonish colour from their labours either in surroundings or dress yet this view is misleading since from a series of letters written by an unknown special correspondent reporting for the Caernarfon and Denbigh Herald in 1873 a description concerning Dinorwig quarrymen demonstrates that in his opinion:

"The principal failing of the quarrymen in the district is, I should think, a little weakness in the way of dress, I am strongly inclined to think that the quarrymen nourish the inner man as well as they clothe the outer form. The average Englishman no doubt goes to the other extreme, and is inclined to be an epicure. This is not to be emulated, but, nevertheless is the vanity of the quarrymen. The beaux seems to be fascinated with velvet waistcoats, bright green ties, and perhaps a pair of violet coloured kid gloves (to match) many sizes too large for the wearer's hand."

By this token the quarrymen may not have considered us such a blot on the landscape as I first suspected. Despite an obvious incongruity in activity, we matched them for vanity and not inconsiderable "little weakness in the way of dress".

The Fachwen Quarries

These are a series of scrapes in the ground, scattered amongst the woods west of Vivian, along the shore of Llyn Padarn. The quarries themselves are, with the possible exception of Muriau Gwynion Bach, scrappy affairs, with looseness and vegetation galore. The routes themselves tend to be slight, but packed with character. They may, however, not be to everyone's taste.

Conditions: If it's warm you are going to get midged, and water seeps from the oddest places.

Approach: Although widely scattered, it's best to use the same parking place and general approach. Park as for Vivian in the Gilfach Ddu car park, and then follow the white marked posts towards the Quarry Hospital. Continue along this path until it drops down to the old mill ruins. From here, sneak down to the railway and back towards Vivian for Allt Wen Quarry, or continue up the white post-marked path for the rest. The next quarry encountered is Muriau Gwynion Bach. This is found shortly after passing the first house of Cae Mabon, a woodland communal project, which is on your left. After passing this and continuing through a 5 bar gate, it's above the track on the right. If you reach the slate promontory and communal car park, known as the helipad, you've gone too far. Muriau Gwynion Mawr is on the other side of the helipad, on the right of the track above the path. The final quarry in here is Chwarel Terfyn. This is situated behind Cei Llydan station. It is best reached by continuing along the track until the Padarn Café signs then descend through the Café grounds, into Cwm Derwyn, and down to the station itself.

Allt Wen Quarry • OS grid ref: 579 609

This is the cutting above the railway line seen from the other side of the lake. The slate itself is friable and occasionally loose, with a tendency for choss bergschrund, and gorse and earth seracs.

Conditions: The solitary route is found on a small open face that doesn't seem to suffer seepage.

▶ **Psychic Sidekick E2 6a** 10m
This route is on the left of the cutting, on the edge of the slab. Follow the clean groove to an earthy exit. [P Targett 20.11.90]

Muriau Gwynion Bach • OS grid ref: 579 615

This hidden cutting has a peaceful ambience, complete with wooded grove and a picnic meadow. It also contains the best routes of the Fachwen quarries.

Conditions: Can get midgey in warm damp conditions. Both routes suffer some seepage; Woodflower definitely needs time to dry.

▶ **The Woodflower E2 6b** 6m
The left hand wall (facing in) has an undercut, a bit of a layaway, and a bolt. Use a combination of these to get to the top, or if you're as tall as the 1st ascencionist, a running jump and a mantel will suffice. [G Smith, M Crook 06.87]

▶ **Brewing up with Morley Wood E1 5b *** 10m
The back of the quarry boasts a mighty fine flake crack, wide enough to swallow kettles, stones, ram's skulls, and anything else you would like to throw in as protection. [M Crook, G Smith 06.87]

Muriau Gwynion Mawr • OS grid ref: 577 616

The largest of the quarries hereabouts; much of its potential is spoilt by its apparent instability and the fact that it is essentially a bog. It is also very near someone's house, so discretion is required.

Conditions: Some of the midges are the size of your thumb. Best enjoyed on a sunny winter's day when the bog might be frozen.

The easiest scramble in is found on the corner nearest the helipad. Rock hopping round to the left will reach the only current route. Alternatively, locate it from above and abseil in.

▶ **If You Want HVS 5b** 10m
The miraculously clean slab has a bolt in the middle and a tree at the top.
[A Shaw, M Boniface 4.89]

Chwarel Terfyn • OS grid ref: 575 615

Skulking round the back of the station buildings and helpfully screened by barbed wire and bins, there is very little to recommend this quarry apart from its exclusivity. Very few people have been (bothered) to climb here. Whilst tradition requires an approach in black clothes and ski masks, the modern visitor may prefer a blank look and feigned ignorance. *"Is this Mental Lentils?"*

Conditions: There is some seepage and it is a dark little hole.

▶ **Steve Lineman E1 5c** 15m
Immediately after the fence on the right hand side are some yellow bolts. Follow these to the top. [M Boniface 11.89]

▶ **The Niche HVS 5b** 15m
The juggy line through the algal bloom ledge.

Nant Peris Quarry 283

Nant Peris Quarry • OS grid ref: 602 583

More properly known as Gallt y Llan (or indeed Chwarel yr Allt), this easily accessible quarry on the hillside above Nant Peris was always something of a back water, even in its working days, as the slate is of very poor quality. The rock is reminiscent of that found in the Culm in Devon, with thick layers laid down like an onion skin. Unlike most of the Culm, it's a lot steeper, with less friction to bond it together. Consequently, routes on the main wall are prone to collapse.

Conditions: It rarely gets the sun, other than a bit in the morning. However, the combination of quick drying slate, good drainage and the wind rattling down the Pass, means it is one of the quickest drying rock piles.

Approach: It's easiest to park in the layby by the side of the Llanberis - Nant Peris road opposite the end of Llyn Peris. From here it's a short walk through the kissing gate to the inclines, which lead up into the quarry.

Descent: To descend from the main wall routes, follow the edge of the quarry down the hill to the ramp marked on the topo.

Main Wall

▶ **1. The Hooligan E1 5a** 40m
Although this is one of the more solid routes, it's also one of the more overgrown. An obvious corner system leads to a slab out right. [P Williams, P Jewel 11.03.79]

▶ **2. Vandal E2 5b** 28m
This is another mostly solid route, with a rubble filled gully at the top being the only real cause for concern. Wide cracks rise up the corner to the roof. Here adequate gear leads to a technical groove, with a fine crack at its back giving occasional wire placements. As it finishes, the rubble starts...
[P Trower, C Hudson 11.78]

▶ **3. The Deceiver E3 5c** 28m
This route is somewhat laminated onto the wall, with strenuous crack climbing, giving finger tip to hand jams and few face holds for feet. Applying excessive outward force is not recommended.
[P Jewel, P Williams 24.04.79]

The top half of the following groove system has fallen off. The following 2 routes have therefore changed dramatically, with *The Poacher's* top crack now a groove, and *Butcher's* top groove now a crack.

▶ **4. The Poacher MXS** 28m
Climb the crack to the fanged ledge, follow the arête/corner system to the top. Yet to be ascended in its present condition. [P Jewel, P Williams, M Patterson 10.03.79]

▶ **5. Butcher MXS** 28m
Follow the shallow groove to the near the top of the fang, where a wide loose crack leads eventually to the top. Yet to be ascended in its present condition. [P Trower, C Hudson 01.79]

Opposite the main wall is the arête of *Nice Guy*.

▶ **6. Nice Guy E1 5c** 15m
The arête is climbed direct, without any worthwhile gear, but at least it's attached to the rest of the quarry. [A Evans 23.07.90]

The Quarries as a Film Set

The otherworldly landscape of the quarries has provided the backdrop for numerous film productions over the years, most recently in 2009 with Clash of the Titans which saw the main access path through the quarries shut down for a couple of months.

Nick Harms, author of the 1990 Llanberis Slate guide recalls the scene in the late 80s:

"Every now and again there'd be some film work either for S4C, or some movie company. The Gideon, aka Film Set Quarry had already doubled as a WW2 labour camp. Dinorwig was next and a mock castle was constructed for the battle scenes of Willow. The production used vast numbers of extras, no CGI back then, and everyone who could ride a horse in North Wales, or anyone who was willing to give it a go i.e. Paul Pritchard, got a job. There was a bit of off screen work too, Gwion [Hughes] and I did some of the catering, and Trevor [Hodgson] was the pig wrangler, spending night after night herding the Pigs of Recalcitrance in and out of the castle."

"As I recall I got two further TV and film jobs, the first with Paul as an extra playing a soldier in the Spanish Civil War, much of which we spent lying in a ditch on Anglesey in the pouring rain. The Vivian Quarry was the venue for my last movie job, stunt doubling Harrison Ford's brother (no, I didn't know he had one either) on a film so bad I didn't even think it made it to video, it was called The Runner for those connoisseurs of truly toe curlingly bad movies. Still, wandering round the quarry with a pukka Uzi was rather fun and scared the tourists no end."

High up on the East Braich of Australia photo: Paul Williams

The Quarries of Glyn Rhonwy

Style: Trad/sport
Aspect: Varied
Approach: 10-20 minutes
Altitude: 1-200m
OS Grid ref: 565 608

Senior Citizen Smith	E5/6
The Mosquito	E5/6
The Bridge Across Forever	E5
The Second Coming	E4
Liquid Armbar	E4
The Bone People	E4
The New Salesman	E4
Pandora Plays Sax direct start	E4
The Hand of Morlock [F6c+]	E4
Gender Bender	E3
Good Crack	E3
The Mancer Direct	E3
Ladybird Girl/Giddy One	E3

Cracking Up	E2
Giddy Variations on a Theme	E2
Near Dark (After Dark)	E2
The Wriggler	E1
Pandora Plays Sax	HVS
Gideon	HVS

Beating the Raine	F7b
Synthetic Life	F7a+

Autocrat	F6b+
Clippopotamus	F6b

Cabin Fever	F5+

Chain Wall	D8+

Mark Dicken on the spectacular arete of **Bring me the Head of Don Quixote** E2 5a photo: Ray Wood

Oft described as the Gideon quarries, these scattered holes pepper the hill side on the other side of the Llanberis valley, starting above the Gallt y Glyn Hotel and rising all the way to just below the summit of Cefn Du. While quarrying started much more recently than in the Dinorwig quarries, production ceased much sooner; in 1930, due to the smaller quantities of useful slate. This is reflected in the flavour of climbing; adventure is the name of the game, with areas (and occasionally an entire route) of loose to crumbly rock. Most routes are on the more solid sections, and apart from the man eating cracks, are often fairly bold, with any useful natural protection quite thin on the ground. The approaches are often challenging in themselves, be it herbaceous scrambles or thought provoking abseils. Aside from the gloriously convenient Gideon Terrace section there is very little here for the timid. Indeed some routes demand full immersion and no small amount of commitment.

Seasonal Conditions: These quarries have had 40 years longer to return to nature than their Dinorwig counterparts and subsequently are fairly shrubbed up. The smaller holes hold the damp and harbour midges in the summer.

288 Glyn Rhonwy • Introduction

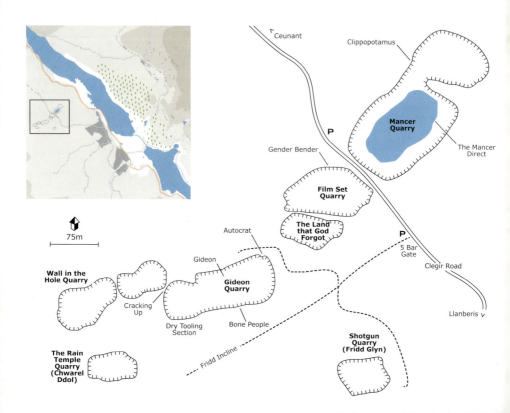

Getting there: Most of the quarries are best accessed from the Clegir Road which runs between Llanberis and Ceunant. This road is most easily reached from Llanberis via Goodman Street up the hill directly opposite the Pete's Eats cafe. Once you pass the last row of houses, you're on Clegir Road. Follow this road until it widens out and the high barbed wire fencing starts. There is limited parking here close to a wooden 5 bar gate on the uphill side – this gate is the main access point to the majority of the quarries above the road. Mancer Quarry, which lies below the road, is best accessed 100m further up the road from a square parking bay on the right. The Cefn Du Quarry is best reached From Waunfawr on the Donen Las Road.

Access restrictions: The quarries are owned by Gwynedd County Council, and climbing is not officially tolerated. Consequently it is essential that all visitors keep a low profile.
There are nesting Choughs and Peregrines in the Bone People area and dry tooling section of Gideon Quarry. Consequently a seasonal ban has been agreed with the RSPB. Please avoid this area from 1st March - June 30th.

Approach photo: Mark Dicken
Tony Hughes repeating his own creation, **The Hand of Morlock** E4 6a (F6c+), an easy access route on Gideon Terrace photo: Ray Wood

Mancer Quarry

Also known as 'The Beach' by the locals, this secluded hole has perhaps the most relaxed atmosphere of the Glyn Rhonwy quarries. The hidden lake from where this name arrives is a popular swim spot in the summer months, although the water is cold enough to warrant a wetsuit. The rock can be quite challenging, and switches from solid red to friable mush of the poorest quality across the quarry.

Conditions: Despite the lake, it's no more midge prone than the other holes. *Clippopotamus* and *Damocles* do suffer from seepage after rain, but elsewhere the routes are quick drying, indeed the main pitch of *The Mancer Direct* even seems to stay dry in the drizzle.

Approach: This can become a little jungle like, so follow carefully. Drive from Llanberis up the Clegir road until you pass the spires of Filmset Quarry seen on the left. Park in the square bay on the right immediately after this. Beyond the fence and ditch behind a faint path leads to the right edge of a slate waste promontory, follow this until a large dolerite boulder is seen poking out of the undergrowth. It is possible here to pick your way down the scree until alongside the boulder, where a bit of boulder scrambling gains a small oak. On the other side of this is a rocky ridge that leads away parallel to the quarry edge. As this starts to dive down into the undergrowth, break right through the hawthorn trees to arrive at the remains of the old fence, the other side of which is the top of *Clippopotomus*. It is now possible to either skirt round to the base of this route, or continue round to the main path into the quarry.

Access Restrictions: The tunnel high on the walls of the promontory is a frequent nest site of a kestrel. Please don't harass it in any way.

A zigzag path takes you to the base of a promontory that shields the lake from view. The first sign of climbing activity is a single bolt on a short wall; gaining access to the promontories mid terrace. Further round there is a black bay, its left wall has an old project (marked as 1a on the topo); a crackline to an old single bolt lower-off. The right wall has one old sport route:

▶ **1. Black Butte F?** 20m
A good looking line of unknown origin or grade. 4 old bolts up a solid wall next to a thin corner, to a single bolt/mailion lower-off.

To reach the top of the next 2 routes skirt around the top of the quarry following the fence until a small oak tree with a quarry sign nailed to it is seen below. Pick your down to a hidden wooded level below.

▶ **2. Liquid Armbar E4 6a/5.11** ** 25m
The striking off width crack provides a brilliant exercise in sustained thrutching. Size #6 cams essential. Abseil in to reach the ledge at base of the crack. Squirm forcefully up the unrelenting crack to collapse in a state of exhaustion at the half height ledge. Once recovered all that remains is a short section of 5.9 wide and some ledge shuffling to join the finish of *The Mancer Direct*.
[09.09 M Dicken]

▶ **3. The Mancer Direct E3 5b/5.10/HVM** ** 38m
The daddy crack is approached from above, via abseil off a large birch on the wooded ledge (drop over the fallen tree). This leads to a scrappy ledge below, 7m above the lake. Belay off a long leash on the iron spike. (Otherwise the crack can spit any rocks you dislodge at your belayer.)
P1 5b 18m Fight your way up the impressively fat flake crack to flop onto the belay above. The crack will take nothing below cam #4, ditto the belay unless you climb into P2.
P2 4c 20m Get behind the worrying but semi permanent pinnacle behind the belay and chimney to its summit. The cracks above lead to a wooded ledge, where behind a holly tree, a flake crack allows escape. [S Haston, L McGinley 09.82/08.81]

▶ **4. The Mancer Original Start E1 4c** 20m
Belay as for *The Mancer Direct*, but tackle the stepped arête and chimney above the belay. This leads to a ledge where a worrying pull gains a capped corner. From here, a swift hand traverse gains the belay. Follow *The Mancer Direct's* P2. This is a better option than swimming should the offwidth on the direct version prove to be too epic. [S Haston, L McGinley 08.81]

From the end of the promontory follow the right edge of the lake to the back of the quarry, as far round as you can go. On the walls up to the right is:

▶ **5. Good Crack E3 6a** * 15m
Tackle the thin, leftward slanting finger flake crack, to a ledge. Tree abseil point. Cracking!
[G Smith, C Parkin 06.88]

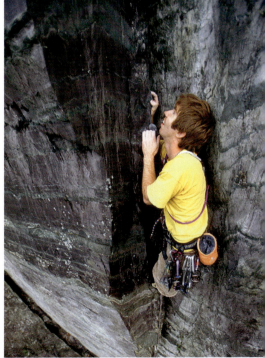

Mark Dicken fully engaged with the offwidth flake on **The Mancer Direct** P1 photo: Ray Wood

292 Glyn Rhonwy • Mancer Quarry

Opposite the end of the promontory high up on the quarry wall is a fairly compact white slab. The first 2 routes on this slab start at a large boulder below a rising overlap. This most comfortably reached by abseil, from either a birch or oak tree, found side by side in front of a large boulder. The rock is friable in places and frost shattered, and recently the slab shed a significant portion of its arch, therefore, please proceed with caution.

▶ **6. I Don't Wanna Pickle E4 6a** 30m
The same bold start as *Blah de Blah*... leads into a hard technical finish. Follow *Blah de Blah*... to the 1st bolt then extend the leftwards traverse to a vegetated flake line, above which a line of bolts and incipient crack lead to the top. Try not to think of the shattered pointy blocks below. Belay at abseil point.
[M Boniface 11.88]

▶ **7. Blah de Blah de Blah E4 5c** 30m
A bold start leads into absorbing and better protected climbing on the upper section. Climb to the 1st bolt, Step left around a small corner and ascend to the 2nd bolt. Continue upwards until a right wards rising crack line leads the 3rd bolt. Above this things ease and a shattered crack leads right wards to the top. Fence belay. [M Boniface 11.88]

The next route on the white slab is opposite the end of the promontory. It is best reached by abseil and has a bolt belay at the top; however, gaining this is hairy, and warrants a handrail off the nearby trees.

▶ **8. Damocles HVS 5a** 28m
A crackline is followed to the niche, which is avoided on the left, past some bolts, to regain the crack to the top. [N Walton, M Crook 09.08]

The right of the slab is reached from a scramble up from the end of the promontory. 2/3 up is:

▶ **9. Clippopotamus F6b** ∗ 25m
An enjoyable and highly absorbing romp up the crystalline slate slab. 8 bolts to a 'Crookian' lower-off. [M Crook, N Walton, A Newton 09.08]

*Stevie Haston making an early repeat of **Ride the Wild Surf** E4 6a, Colossus Wall photo: Paul Williams*

Slatehead • Stevie Haston

Stevie Haston is a larger than life character and supremely talented climber who has his roots firmly set in Llanberis. In fact he epitomised the slate scene in the 80s: no money, but bags of time, bottle and attitude; free to mess around like a big kid in a playground. Most of his adventures were seriously serious, climbed onsight with no cleaning and importantly no bolts. Horrors like **Fear of Rejection** (now fallen down), **Lost Castle of my Desires** (Stevie's hardest offwidth route in Wales; perhaps 5.12?, but also now fallen down unfortunately), **Young Men Afraid of Horses** (climbed with the legend of loose rock, Ray Kay) and **Mildly Macho** have rarely, if at all, seen repeat ascents. **Comes the Dervish**, however, has become one of the most popular extremes in Britain, let alone the quarries.

Stevie also spearheaded a fruitful new route campaign in the Glyn Rhonwy Quarries, establishing such classics as **Cracking Up, Gender Bender, Second Coming** and of course the infamous offwidth **Mancer Direct**.

Diary of a Slatehead
Trained Cadres

Climbing training, long since anathema to book hugging aficionados, was by 1984 still largely unfocused nor taken seriously amongst local climbers in Wales and despite once weekly sojourns across Anglesey during long winter's evenings to Llangefni sports centre's rudimentary brick edge cruising indoor wall, even top performers trained less than Livesey had in 1975 before doing *Right Wall*. John Redhead, for example, could hold a conversation whilst hanging holds above his Inglenook fireplace, which he claimed was enough preparation for doing routes on North Stack Wall or Rainbow Slab, even though he usually traversed down after a few minutes before committing to less strenuous moves by reverse manteling into an armchair. Some climbers attended Pat Ingle's stretch classes once a week in Bangor in an effort to improve suppleness, whilst Stevie Haston, Leigh McGinley and Mel Griffiths did pull ups and pushed weights, often in Spartan surroundings with equipment including axles and iron wheels requisitioned from Dinorwic Quarry.

In attempts focussed on overcoming fears about falling, Tommy Jones practiced 'tree lobbing' in Zoe Brown's garden, where ropes suspended at just the correct length, allowed contenders a chance to swarm squirrel like, and incumbent upon a mighty oak's upper branches before launching into ground sweeping plummets, which, although undertaken for different reasons, might be seen as embryonic precursors to bridge, bungee and cable jumping. Tommy Jones also studied Low Gen Kung Fu, and Haston, Andy Shaw and myself trained under the guidance of Al Whittle in Wu Shu Kwan, another Chinese based system. Often this meant travelling away from slatehead psychosis to train at the 'Shaolin Temple', a splendid old church that stood on Manchester's Princess Parkway, and was fully equipped with leather punch bags, sparring equipment and other paraphernalia associated with martial arts. This gave the impression of a gym for holy warriors, though which faith they followed was hard to discern. The 'Temple' was five minutes walk from Mosside, which seemed to form a kind Gulag garrisoned by ethnic soldiers, some of who attended Wu Shu and at times trained with Master Sken or Master Toddy, who's gyms carried awesome reputations built around martial arts prowess, discipline and respect.

Within martial arts culture there exists a strange mix of violence and anti violence, for example, there are axe kicks in which the heel is used to hail down on an opponents head, palm strikes which can take out a nose, jaw or cheekbone and a myriad other techniques including the legendary Di Mak or death touch. All are designed to injure, kill or incapacitate, yet these techniques are rarely followed through in formal combat where stopping a blow after it has clearly penetrated an opponent's guard shows greater skill and control than actually knocking someone out with full force. There is, however, no guarantee that such techniques will always prove overwhelming in a street fight and in most cases martial artists would aim to diffuse a conflict rather than engage in combat since at the very least street brawling is an abhorrence to the martial arts tenet, where style, manner and grace are of the utmost importance.

Such knowledge may be little concerned with climbing skills, yet Kung Fu also encompassed a great number of stretching and breathing exercises designed to retain suppleness in limbs and generally strengthen an individual's constitution, reduce stress and promote spiritual well being - a kind of yoga with attitude you might say. Whether this type of training advantaged us or not is hard to tell, though it at least contributed occasionally to a courteous approach, something which was nowhere more apparent than on the first ascent of *Gender Bender* E3 6b in Film Set Quarry, a slim wet-look slate groove twice the size of *Venom* at Tremadog and equally holdless. Our leader, Stevie Haston had set off after bowing to myself and Andy Newton, who, being unfamiliar with the entering and exiting of Kung Fu gyms, looked slightly puzzled. 'Oos' exhaled Steve after ten feet, before stopping to place a wire.

Surveying our prospective route, it seemed remarkable how many features on slate's unnatural 'crags' broadly resembled those found on their natural counterparts. That said, climbing these slate doppelgangers was largely experimental owing to the medium's favourite signature: i.e. consistent expanses of smoothness between, what we as rock climbers call, 'holds'. On 'normal' cliffs even apparently blank vertical surfaces often provide good frictional properties, having been formed from roughly surfaced rock such as rhyolite or dolerite. Whereas slate's facades are typically less accommodating, even taking into account the recently (this being 1984) introduced Boreal 'sticky boot' rubber.

Diary of a Slatehead

Overhead Stevie's approach seemed in part to represent a kind of scientific research project into the grip fusion axis, where rock meets synthesised acetates, yet by championing an unbending faith in the protocols of pure ascent, Stevie's method went beyond secular concerns, and whilst following no written theological principles, seemed to account for a kind of religious movement in itself. Continuing up, he employed a 'geko shuffle', which when observed from the penitent belayer's position gave little cause for alarm, but much for contemplation. To understand a 'geko shuffle' it is best that onlookers have previously studied reptilian movement on steep terrain. Lizards are of course brilliant climbers; humans generally are not. Stevie however, and who for various reasons was sometimes referred to as Pengo, the creature or the compass, represented some of our best efforts and although at times the ground above became so steep that it threatened to expel him, his armoury also contained a certain zeitgeist, which when present helps overcome seemingly insurmountable difficulties. Some five minutes earlier it had begun to rain, a mere shower by Welsh standards, followed in due course by sunshine beaming through rolling clouds causing light reflected by twisted chromium plated handles on an abandoned pram wedged in a scree shute atop *The Trash Heap Has Spoken* to glow down benignly as if signalling from a secret mirror.

Stevie Haston in a moment of quiet reflection photo: Martin Crook

Rain in this incarnation, even in abandoned quarries, brings a pleasant scent to the earth, whilst barely touching sheltered grooves and alcoves. Nevertheless lesser leaders might call a halt to action under such circumstances since becoming marooned on foot ledges surrounded by wet slate slabs, and contriving a retreat, should the downpour persist or return, is a little celebrated climbing experience and one which is often accompanied by sustained midge attack on high humidity summer evenings. Above us, silhouetted now against blue sky and having forsaken a wide stemming position similar to that illustrating the *Birches Williams* route in Yosemite Climber, our own 'premier corde' continued as if kicking steps in a manner more normally associated with crampon clad ice climbers. This unorthodoxy was quickly extinguished giving way to measured movement with sane talk of holds, though from below their nature remained only speculative despite claims greater than any made previously that 'they were good' and that he had 'nearly done it'. This being the case it remained a second's responsibility, advantaged by a rope, and as if decreed by a loophole in the law, to collude in first ascent fever. Yet what is theoretically desirable is often practically impossible, so that mimicking a leader's performance, in so much as any second can, as he/she covers the same ground must always, despite a free kick at objectivity, be shrouded, cloaked and bound in subjective experience, which during *Gender Bender's* ascent led me to believe the leader had levitated since difficulties up close gave sparse clue as to how they might be overcome. Information on the matter, although interesting, 'use your feet like you're palming' hardly galvanised flurried activity, yet it confirmed a suspected absence in edges on either groove wall and when set in motion, although precarious, allowed adherence, which whilst punishing calves, and eventually attained higher moral ground above the crux — a place revered by both the leader and second since once reached it allows a platform from which pontificating can take place, safe in the knowledge that what lies ahead is at least as worse and probably not harder than what came before.

Augmented by 'Thank Christ' crimps it became possible to canter upwards as if receiving encouragement from an invisible jockey's whip towards an exit strewn with slate shards and surrounded by rusting barbed wire.

Affixed already around chain sawed tree stumps, apparently grown in cement before being sliced to their present size, Stevie prepared to bring up the Newt, whilst I, as unfettered escape officer, probed our perimeter for an easy exit.

Film Set Quarry

The most obvious of the Gideon quarries, Film set lies just above the Clegir road, visible through the fence 100m further on from the recommended parking area. The quarry got its name from its role as the set for the 1983 Michael Mann fantasy film The Keep. With its decaying bridge, weird spires and assorted detritus lobbed over the fence by fly tippers, it certainly feels fairly surreal; Mad Max meets Lord of the Rings.

Whilst it has some quality routes, all require a connoisseur's mentality to even get as far as actually pulling on. The rear of the quarry is separated from the front by the quixotic tower and its accompanying rock wall. Behind this is the Land that God Forgot; which is home to some large boulders, two routes, and the occasionally buried tunnel through to Gideon. The front of the quarry houses 3 towers, or spires, some esoterica, and the Gender Bender Slab.

Conditions: A boggy bottom means midges. Other than that most routes appear to dry fairly quickly, although *Gender Bender* may seep a little. The Gender Bender Slab can get ridiculously hot in summer.

Approach: Once over the 5 bar gate (mentioned in the introduction) follow the track alongside the fence up the hill and beyond the fallen willow tree, until the tarmac path veers off to the left. At this junction circumvent the fence on the right and follow a zigzag track through the trees, and then upwards until you can see into Gideon Quarry itself.

Film Set Quarry is down hill from here. If you scramble to the left of Film Set (looking down hill) you arrive at the old train tracks above *Near Dark*. Here you can abseil into that route, and the Land that God Forgot. For the Gender Bender Slab, continue down that side until a careful descent of a sloping dry stone buttress gains the large tree abseil point.

To gain the scramble in, return the way you came for the *Gideon* approach. 1 level down, a path on the right (looking down hill) side of the quarry brings you down to the road. Just before this is the detached flat top of a prominent buttress, behind which there are some wire telegraph pole anchors. On the right side of this (looking in) is a fairly solid groove which can be scrambled down at about Diff. The most safe descent point is a couple of metres further down hill, by an iron reinforcing rod.

Gender Bender Slab

This impressively blank sweep of light coloured slate is steep (by slate slab standards) and pretty daunting, with a bulging headwall to save your energy for at the top. The rock is fairly soft in places so bury gear deep if you want it to hold.

▶ **10. The Second Coming E4 6c** ✶✶ 36m
A stunning route, similar in nature, but steeper and harder than *Comes the Dervish*. Start up the left hand crack, which is better protected than its neighbour. Get a good rest before assaulting the final fierce crux bulge, or it might give you a good kicking. Scramble through the tree (possible belay) to the abseil point.
[S Haston, M Crook 04.84]

▶ **11. Monsieur Avantski E4 6a** ✶ 36m
The central crack; sustained and spaced (worthwhile) gear, with long spans through the crux head wall. You can belay at a cracked block at the top, or continue leftwards to scramble to the abseil point.
[J Silvester, A Wilkie 10.84]

▶ **12. Gender Bender E3 6b** ✶✶ 36m
The technical pant-splitting groove forms the right side of the slab. Throw shapes up this until a frantic mantel gains the upper groove with its random tree. Pass this to easier, albeit looser, climbing up a chossy groove. Arrange a belay above utilising an oak sapling, or continue along the walkway leftwards to scramble to the abseil point. [S Haston, M Crook, A Newton 04.84]

▶ **13. Marital Aids E5 6b** 40m
The epic girdle of the slab. It follows *Gender Bender* to the mantelshelf, where a crack line leads out left, past *Monsieur Avantski* (gear) to join *The Second Coming*. Follow this to below the headwall, where a skitter to the arête provides a finish to remember. Finish as for *The Second Coming*.
[S Haston, T Downes 18.04.84]

Right of *Gender Bender*, a couple of routes have been ascended up the rubbish shoot.

▶ **14. The Trash Heap Has Spoken E1 5a** 30m
P1 5b 16m Ascend the steep stepped groove immediately right of *Gender Bender* until an exit onto a ledge allows a traverse into the bottom of a large groove full of plants and other detritus.
P2 5a 14m Climb the protectionless groove to a fence post belay, and find a quiet corner to recover. [C Phillips, N Thomas 29.04.84]

▶ **15. The Trash Heap Speaks Again VS 4b** 36m
This takes the bramble covered and fridge strewn corner of the quarry right again from the previous route. Ascend via ledges, grooves, saplings and domestic appliances to the fence.
[C Phillips, M Thompson 02.05.84]

On the opposite side of the quarry to the Gender Bender Slab, between the road and the scramble-in, lies a slender and detached looking flake pinned to the wall with a couple of rusty quarryman's bolts. This is *Layed Back Boys*.

▶ **16. Mental Block VS 4c** 24m
Originally done as a solo by the quarries very own Baron Munchausen, You have been warned. This route starts at the arête left of *Layed Back Boys*; mantel up a series of steps to gain the fiercely vegetated groove, which is battled to the top. [C Phillips 08.04.84]

▶ **17. Layed Back Boys E2 5b** 24m
Layback up the flake with gusto, trying not think of the consequences of the old quarry bolts sheering! [S Haston, P Trower, A Howerd 03.84]

298 Glyn Rhonwy • The Grey Spires • The Land That Time Forgot

The Grey Spires

On the large spire with the ironmongery bolted to its top (i.e. the one nearest the scramble approach) is:

▶ **18. Arse over Tit VS 4c** 15m
Ascend the arête facing the other grey spire with a metal spike as protection to reach the ironmongery on the summit. Scramble down the back.
[C Phillips 02.05.84]

The other grey spire, left of the Gender Bender Slab (when looking from the road), is linked to the side of the quarry by a dolerite rib (providing the 'Col of Conquest') which continues to the quarry lip.

▶ **19. Arrampicata Speiligone E1 5a** 20m
This ascends the tower from the 'Col of Conquest', and apparently has a bolt lower-off somewhere on top. Happy hunting.
[C Philips, M Boniface 1989]

▶ **20. Old Fogies Never Die VS 4b** 30m
This ascends the dolerite rib from the 'Col of Conquest' to exit the quarry. This was originally given VD, but even the VS grade should be taken with a pinch of salt!
[C Philips, P Bagnall 22.02.89]

The Land that God Forgot

A poetic name to a veiled off area of the quarry, it is reached by tunnel, abseil or bad steps. Once the home to a magnificent offwidth called *The Lost Castle of My Desires*, this went the way of many of Stevie Haston's cracks, namely onto the quarry floor. This left the greenish tower standing proud.

▶ **21. Bring me the Head of Don Quixote E2 5a** 25m
Rising like a stick of Brighton rock, this route has adventure written all the way down its core.
Start on the right shoulder of the tower (as seen from the road). Climb the stacked blocks to gain the reddish groove on the *Land that God Forgot* side of the tower. This is followed to a pedestal where the 1st (and last) good bit of protection is found. Move around to the Film Set side of the tower where an exfoliating ledge allows you to gibber back up right and mantel the earth summit. Belay by pulling up one of your ropes and throwing it down the other side for your second to carefully anchor it to the boulders.
[M Dicken, C Neale 2003]

▶ **22. Near Dark (After Dark) E2 5b** * 20m
Spaced bolts keep the tension levels high on this tricky slab route, which is found in the back right corner of the Land that God Forgot side. A couple of bolts show the way up the slab to a steep and cracked headwall. Abseil approach.
[A Newton, K Griffiths 06.05.90]

Gideon Quarry

Gideon Quarry is the showpiece of the Glyn Rhonwy collection. The sheer acreage of rock and the diversity of climbing on offer ensure that there will be something to suit most tastes.

This large hole in the ground is dominated by the majestic sweep of the Gideon Slab, which is nimbly avoided by the route itself. It is also home to the best known off width in the quarries (*Cracking Up*) and the brooding might of the Bone People Buttress; an igneous intrusion guaranteed to get the palms sweating.

There are also the neat and convenient Gideon Terrace routes, which are perfect for a quick evening hit, and the newly developed dry tooling sector.

All that being said, apart from the 'classic' lines there is an awful lot of scabby choss in this quarry, and here 'classic' is used in a similar fashion to how *Mousetrap* is considered 'classic', so you could be in for a bumpy ride...

Conditions: Being much more open than the other quarries on this side, Gideon Quarry is less prone to damp (and midges), however, the top slab of the bone people buttress needs some time to dry, and the *Cracking Up* area can get midgey in the summer after rain.

Approach: Once over the 5 bar gate follow the track alongside the fence up the hill, beyond the fallen willow, until the tarmac path veers off to the left. At this junction circumvent the fence on the right and follow a zigzag track right through the trees, and then upwards until you can see into Gideon Quarry itself.

To gain the *Bone People* abseil, continue up from here via the zigzag on the left (uphill) side of the quarry until a hut is reached above the greenstone wall. Follow the grass along the quarry edge to a small walled enclosure. From here it is possible to scramble (carefully) to the tree abseil point below.

For the other routes follow the path to the right hand side of the quarry where a zigzag goes up to an old quarry hut. Here a cutting leads out to Gideon Terrace. On the left looking out is a short slab bearing a metal quarry spike that is the final *Gideon* belay and main *Gideon* abseil point (you can back it up if you wish). For the Gideon Slab, abseil onto the scree ledge below, and scramble down its bottom edge where another abseil from a jumble of boulders and ironmongery gains the base of the main slab. The *Cracking Up* area is found by continuing around at the same level from the Gideon Terrace to reach a wooded bay at the back of the quarry.

Restrictions: The dry tooling sector and Bone People Buttress has a seasonal bird ban. Please avoid this area between 1st March and June 30th.

Monster Munch Buttress

This is situated below the path on the approach to Gideon Terrace and is clearly visible from the initial col and from above *Bone People*. The much eyed, steep upper tier has some flaky rock, but is quick to dry. Approach is by abseil from the flat boulder above, it may be advisable to leave a rope in place.

▶ **23. Beating the Raine F7b** ∗ 24m
An interesting route which builds up to a hard crux high on the wall. Rising out of the left hand eye socket, this takes a more direct line to a crumbly finish. [C Muskett 13.11.10]

▶ **24. Autocrat F6b** ∗ 25m
A fine wall climb with some intense sections in a position of excellent exposure. The left hand line starts near the edge of the verdant terrace, and wanders near the arête before thrusting up the headwall. [M Raine, E Jones 2008]

Ioan Doyle eyeing the steep finish on **Monsieur Avantski** >
E4 6a, Film Set Quarry photo: Ray Wood

302 Glyn Rhonwy

Mark Dicken and Toen Doyle on the grand sweep of **Giddy Variations on a Theme** E2 5b. photo: Ray Wood

Gideon Slab

A sea of crystals, crunchy loose flakes and ultra fine seams, the Gideon Slab is avoided in general by its parent route *Gideon*. The routes that wade into its depths, however, are reminiscent of the Etive Slabs, with delicate friction moves and mightily spaced gear. It is worth taking an extra rope to pre-place the belay. This is found 10m or so back from the edge, and consists of a round boulder with a subterranean thread, along with a nut in the stack of slate resting against another boulder for good luck.

▶ **25. Wobbly Variations on a Slab E2 5a** 82m
A route that tries to avoid even more of the worthwhile climbing than *Gideon*. Start at the left arête of the *Gideon* slab.
P1 5a 18m Climb the boulder strewn groove until it is possible to exit onto a ledge with a flake crack for the belay.
P2 5a 25m Gain the detached block above (as per *Blue Bottle*) and boldly pad onto the slab to a rusty iron cable. This is the belay.
P3 5a 39m Continue keeping to the edge of the slab until the *Pandora* finish is reached.
[M Boniface, J Webb 1988]

▶ **26. Giddy Variations
on a Theme E2 5b ∗∗** 78m
The best route on the slab, exhilarating and heart stoppingly serious. It starts 6m left of the start of *Gideon* at a little ledge, and thrusts boldly up the centre of the slab. It was originally done solo, and given HVS.
P1 5b 18m Launch up the seam leading right off the ledge until a shothole gives thank God protection in the form of a folded over rock #7 (or a very small tri cam). The slab above gives way to precarious padding to the lower ledge system where a sapling spouting crack gives enough gear to belay off.
P2 5b 60m Climb up the crack you're belayed to, then traverse left 5m along the upper ledge system until before a slim groove, which is right of a larger chossier overlap. Build a nest of micro wires, sky hooks and other articles of faith then commit to the seam until it is possible to pad left to the slab's main overlap via a large erosion pocket. Follow this overlap to a couple of large wires. From here aim for and follow the *Pandora* finish exit, a long way above. The route originally went left around the corner from the *Pandora* finish and scaled the hideous tottering overhang – this is not recommended. [C Phillips 21.02.87]

▶ **27. Gideon HVS 4c ∗** 107m
An historically important route; although not the best line on the slab it does offer a fairly mind bending trip, the highlight being the mildly harrowing traverse on P1.
Starts at the top of the scree cone at the left arête of the main *Gideon* slab.
P1 4c 48m Start in an open right facing groove. This is followed until a scree cornice demands a leftward detour and a ferny ledge at the right arête is gained, where a decaying peg and a nut slot provide a minor security blanket. The long lonely traverse is now undertaken, pausing now and then to kick off the moss or scrape futilely in search of any real protection. At your journeys end, the huge detached block may be a belay site for fans of the ending of Dr Strangelove, but there's a better belay if you carry on until around the edge of the slab.
P2 35m Scramble up the scree and jumbled blocks with due care and attention until below the final slab.
P3 4c 24m From the middle of the slab gain the rising ledge where a meander left along this until it fades and then pad up to freedom. If you're belaying on the terrace then the abseil. spike might help protect your second.
[A Harris, E Penman 07.64]

▶ **27a. Blue Bottle HVS** 30m
A bold variation start to *Gideon*. Start up an indefinite leftward facing groove on the left edge of the Gideon Slab.
P1 20m Climb the groove for 10m until a runner can be placed on a flake on the left. Step left and climb the crack to the ledge. Move right off the ledge and up a short slab to just below the overlap. Traverse right to the detached block and belay.
P2 10m Follow the obvious fault line as per *Gideon*. [R Kane, J Brazinton 10.06.69]

▶ **28. Pandora Plays Sax HVS 4c ∗∗** 75m
More direct than *Gideon* and much better for it. It is also much less serious. Start as for *Gideon*.
P1 4c 18m Follow *Gideon* to the fern and feather strewn ledge and weave a belay.
P2 4c 57m Go left for 2m then surmount the overlap via a rib and follow this up to another crack. Continue to pad up the easy angled slab until just below the top where the slab gives way to a groove of horror choss. A traverse left gains a more solid hanging slab and an exit.
[S Haston, R Kay 03.87]

▶ **29. Pandora Plays Sax
direct start E4 5c/6a ∗** 18m
Near the top of the grade, and gets rather mossy when neglected, but when clean it gives a fine battle. Start a couple of metres left of the arête at the base of a fine crack. Charge directly up the crack, with fear and trembling, to gain the *Pandora* belay. [1987]

▶ **30. Pandora's Box finish HVS 4b**
Offers a direct finish by tackling the horror choss groove right of the tottering arête. You know, if you wanted too... [R Kay, H Falconer 2002]

Gideon Slab • Glyn Rhonwy 305

▶ **31. Ultra Cricket Zone E4 5c/6a** 76m
This tackles the overlap to the right of *Pandora*.
P1 5c/6a 18m As for the direct start to *Pandora*.
P2 5c 58m Go down and right via the loose scree, to a series of cracks rising up the middle of the subsidiary slab. Pad up this to the overlap (gear on the left). Climb through the centre of the overlap, gain and ascend a small rib on the left, as this peters out, trend leftwards into *Pandora*. [T Hodgson, M Wragg, T Jones 05.04.87]

▶ **32. The Climbing Pains
of Adrian Mole HVS 5b** 85m
This starts 8m right of the corner groove of *Gideon* at the base of a scabby rib.
P1 5b 25m Climb the rib until it is possible to gain a crack on the right. This is followed up to a scree bound ledge sporting a large flake.
P2 5b 60m Leave the ledge on the right, following under a slight overlap until a groove system leads back left. This is followed via a tree to a large ledge with a precarious looking boulder on it. From here traverse left into Pandora. Originally the route kept on traversing until it gained the Gideon Terrace, but the *Pandora* finish is more logical.
[T Hodgson, M Hodgson, T Jones 29.03.87]

The top slab of *Gideon* was home to 4 bolted routes. These have been de-bolted as it was felt that they interfered with the top of a historically important route, and that bolts were out of place with the tradition of the slab.

Gideon Terrace
The terrace wall perched above the Gideon Slab provides a series of easy access routes.

▶ **33. The Gnarly SPAR Kid E2 6a** 12m
The short, blocky arête at the start of the terrace provides a forceful little route. Make bouldery moves past the 1st bolt and continue up past a 2nd bolt to an easier, but bold finish (some poor micro wires) and a lower-off.
[T Hughes, G Oldridge 05.09.07]

▶ **34. The Mosquito E5/6 6c** ∗ 12m
Climb up to a protruding slopey triangular hold; technical moves gain better holds leading to the lower-off. No gear but F7b to top rope.
[C Muskett 07.02.10]

▶ **35. The Hand of Morlock E4 6a [F6c+]** ∗14m
The bolted arête is spoilt by an ankle snapping start. Stick clip the 1st bolt for a much better F6c+. Bolt belay over the top on the sloping ledge. [T Hughes, O Cain 22.08.07]

▶ **36. Ladybird Girl/Giddy One E3 6a** ∗ 14m
The open groove line yields a good route. Bolt and small wires protect, bolt belay. Was done originally without fixed pro at around E5.
[S Haston, A Haston 1987/C Parkin, C Ayres 1990]

▶ **37. Kenny's Wall F5+** 18m
Climb the slab to the ledge, to gain the continuation rib, which leads to the bolt belay.
[N Walton, M Crook 09.08]

Cracking Up Area • **Glyn Rhonwy 307**

Cracking Up Area

Beyond the end of the terrace, blocks and boulders give way to a wooded bay. Below these blocks and boulders is a slab, and above the slab a little grubbing around finds the belay/abseil point for:

▶ **38. Uhuru for Mandela E2 5c** 30m
A slightly eliminate line with a hard, but potentially avoidable crux. Start off the ledge at the base of the smooth, but dirty slab directly below a bolt. Ascend to this and struggle up right to a small ledge. Leave this with reluctance and sprint to the overlap where gear and loose rock await. Once past all of this, some bore holes may provide some more protection and the rock does improve towards the top. Belay amongst the boulders. [M Boniface, A Garland 16.06.88]

▶ **39. The Rothwell Incident E2 5b** 24m
Tackle the corner right of *Cracking Up* with some fear, and perhaps a touch of loathing.
[M Reeves, D Rothwell 1999]

▶ **40. Cracking Up E2 5c/6a** ∗∗ 24m
The compelling forked lightning crack rises up the back of the bay. A climb often surrounded by superlatives and expletives. It starts just off fingers and swallows you at the top to provide a difficult and fairly loose exit.
[S Haston, C Phillips 03.84]

▶ **41. Cracked Up HVS 5b** 24m
The off width corner crack on the block's left hand side maintains an air of silent menace.
[S Haston, C Phillips 03.84]

Those seeking a scrambling option down into the base of the quarry may want to investigate the cable snaking through the undergrowth below *Cracking Up*.

◂ Ioan Doyle on the final wide section of **Cracking Up** E2 5c/6a
photo: Ray Wood

Bone People Area

This dramatic dolerite wall is home to some truly spectacular climbs. It gets the evening sun, although all the routes suffer from seepage and need 2 or 3 days of dry weather to dry out. It's worth giving the routes a quick brush on the way down and be sure to take some prussics as a lob may leave you spinning in space. The abseil is long (a 60m rope just reaches the ground) and scary so you may as well break up the journey with a little light gardening to the mossy upper slab (it'll make sense on your way back up). It is also usual to leave your abseil rope in place to ease the final mossy exit. Finally, don't assume that you can move easily from route to route - the ground beneath the wall is pretty sketchy!

Restriction: because of the presence of nesting Choughs and Peregrines all routes in the Bone People Area are subject to an access restriction from 1st March - 30th June. This restriction may be subject to changes - please consult the BMC Regional Access Database for updates.

▶ **42. Synthetic Life F7a+** ★★ 42m ®
An exceptional sport route on granite-esque dolerite with 4 distinct cruxes – a bit like a F7a+ version of *The Plum* at Tremadog.
The route starts at the base of a narrow ramp/groove behind the huge boulder to the left of *The Bone People*. It then forges an intricate and technically sustained line upwards past 14 bolts to reach an abseil station left of the upper section of *The Bone People*. Technical climbing up the ramp/groove leads to a hard move to gain undercuts which lead leftwards across the top of the slab. Pull through the left side of the roof (avoid suspect rock on the left) and traverse back right into a niche. Technical moves up the niche lead to a blind reach to a hidden crimp above the roof. From the crimp make a sideways dyno to a jug on the arete. Move up the rib, and the slab above, to a pair of undercuts in the overlap. Climb with difficulty through this using a layaway on the right wall. Delicate moves lead diagonally left across the upper slab to a rest below the final groove. A final long reach and a stiff pull, or more technical climbing for shorties, ends the difficulties. Take some long extenders for the lower section if climbing on a single rope. There

is an intermediate abseil anchor so it's possible to do it and abseil off with a single 50m rope.
Access: abseil down the line of The Bone People and swing into the base of the route. This requires a 60m rope. [P Harrison, C Parkin 21.05.10]

▶ **43. The Bone People E4 6a ✶✶✶** 51m ®
One of the best E4s in the valley, never mind just the quarries! A route of contrasts: P1 is slabby and serious; P2 is an exercise in extreme, albeit well protected, space walking. The exposed finish is particularly memorable. Start at the back of the amphitheatre slightly right of the 1st bolt.
P1 5c 21m Pass the 1st bolt to go up to a cam #1.5 slot in the overlap above. From here, a rising leftward traverse passes the 2nd bolt and skitters up and out to the rather airy arête, where a confident approach leads up the double bolt belay.
P2 6a 20m Pulling through the bulge on the right dispenses with the crux and leads to a series of awkward moves up across the slab, past 2 more bolts to pull into a steep hanging groove. This is fought with increasing exposure to arrive at the left edge of the mossy summit slab. It is recommended that you belay here at the 2 bolts.
P3 4b 10m Bring up your second, then slither across with extreme care to snag your abseil rope, which eases passage past the treacherous moss. [J Silvester, C Dale 06.88]

▶ **44. The Bridge Across Forever E5 6b ✶✶** 54m ®
Another prize route for the committed slate fanatic. Good but spaced protection, coupled with even more exposure make for a memorable outing.
P1 5c 21m As for The Bone People P1.
P2 6b 33m Follow The Bone People P2 to the 2nd bolt, and then monkey onto the soaring right wall. A sapping traverse past 2 bolts leads down to a sloping foothold at the bottom of a slim groove. Battle up this to the roof, where the crux bars exit to the right arête; a sloping platform allows access to a clean steep groove, and a 'Thank God' jug on the final lip. Exit onto the mossy slab, bolt belay. For an easy life snag the abseil rope to lessen the horrors of the mossy slab. [C Dale, T Hodgson 02.07.88]

▶ **45. Senior Citizen Smith E5/6 6b ✶✶** 25m ®
A wild bolt-free trad line on the right hand side of The Bone People wall with an outrageously steep crack/undercut finale. It follows the eye-catching slabby arête until a flared crack leads left across a very steep wall to connect with a hanging slabby ramp. The initial arête has a bold 5c section, but the real fun begins once the crack is reached. A desperate sequence leads out left on a combination of jams, knee-bars, undercuts and a crucial edge on the upper wall. Although the main section of climbing on the crux traverse is well protected, the final moves do leave the pumped leader in a potentially dangerous position, unless they can remain composed enough

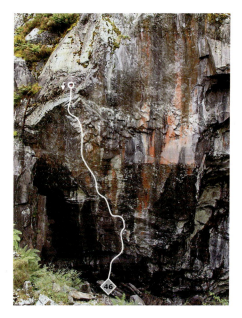

to stuff another cam in. Thereafter the final ramp leads steadily, if boldly, to a lower-off.
The route is best approached from a direct abseil from a small tree just down from the lip of the quarry. Take jumars (to go back up your abseil rope) as the lower-off does not allow access to cliff top. [P Harrison, P Robins 29.06.10]

▶ **46. Chain Wall D8+ ✶✶** 20m ®
If dry tooling is your bag then check out this ridiculously steep line at the left side of the cave/pit at the top left corner of Gideon Quarry, i.e. further right than Senior Citizen Smith. Sustained climbing with some figure of 4s and much precise footwork. Start on top of the boulder with the help of the in situ metal spike and pre-clip the 1st bolt. Approach from the Uhuru for Mandela abseil. [R Marin, M Pritchard 10.10.09]

There are a couple of equipped project lines to the right.

Lee Roberts on the steep and radical **Chain Wall** D8+
photo: Jon Ratcliffe

The Rain Temple (Ddol Quarry)

This is a verdant abyss, located above and left of Gideon Quarry, slightly uphill and left of Wall-in-the-Hole Quarry. All tunnel access to this pit has long since been buried providing quiet seclusion for a wide variety of malevolent flora and fauna.

Conditions: Moss, Midges, Ooze and Ticks! Quite adventurous really.

Approach: Follow the Wall-in-the-Hole description to the metal gate. Don't pass through, but instead follow the fence left until it can be breached. Wander uphill, trending slightly leftwards, and don't fall in. Access to the bottom is by abseil from a pointy little boulder above the route; a 45m+ rope is required.

▶ **47. Cabin Fever F5+** ∗ 37m
The combination of a wet summer, and fervent dog walking produced this jolly outing from some venerable old slateheads. Follow the line of bolts up the surprisingly absorbing slab to a 'Baggy Point' style finish. [M Crook, N Walton 08.08]

Shotgun Quarry (Ffridd Glyn)

This is actually two holes divided more naturally by a thin wall of un-quarried slate. Apart from the aforementioned routes there have been other minor lines climbed and repeated over the years, particularly on the right hand slab of the lower quarry. However, the rock here is stubbornly friable and given to peeling off in big chunks without providing much for gear. Not that appealing really.

Conditions: A sheltered sun trap, it does suffer from midges. A lot.

Approach: Follow the Gideon Quarry approach until the tarmac path leads off left. Follow the path leftwards for a minute or so until you reach a circle of trees fenced off with chain link. Skirt round this on the down hill side, inside or outside the fence, where a cutting brings you to the main terrace. A scramble down via a silver birch will gain the quarry floor.

▶ **48. Clegir Arête HVS 5a** 20m
At the back of the lower/front quarry on the left is an obvious slabby rib rising into a gully at the top. Climb this direct via 3 bolts, a peg and an evil thorn bush (bring secateurs) to a summit tree belay. Originally climbed without the bolts.
[A George, B Lewis, J Banks 17.07.02]

The aforementioned gully is the scramble approach to the rear quarry.

▶ **49. Unnamed E1 8m**
The obvious slab/wall on the right side of the quarry as you enter above the narrow gangway/ledge. Start on the left at a pointy spike which provides a belay of sorts. A crux mantel leads to good holds, gear and easier climbing leading to the top.
[C Watkins, R Greenwood 18.04.09]

The main hole has another bolted line, but the loose appearance of the top would suggest it hasn't been climbed as yet.

Wall-in-the-Hole Quarry • **Glyn Rhonwy 311**

Wall-in-the-Hole Quarry (The Cook Pit)
This is actually a single hole divided by a 20m dry stone wall, which acted as a bridge to carry slates from the cutting sheds to the Ffridd incline. The uphill portion has a little lake and a picturesque waterfall.

Conditions: The walls get afternoon/evening sun and are a little flakey and prone to moss, which affect their drying somewhat. However the quarry is open enough to deter midges.

Approach: It is situated immediately above Gideon Quarry, and is best approached by following a vague path up above the cutting leading to the Gideon Terrace. Tick filled bracken leads to a metal gate in the right hand end of the fence. Beyond the quarry edge the quarry can be seen; a path leads along to the aforementioned 20m dry stone wall. From here it is possible to scramble down the gently banked scree to the lower quarry half.

▶ **50. Twisted Nerve E4 6a/b** 12m
The cleaned slab is the lone attraction hereabouts. 2 bolts lead to the top (still a bit loose) and a wobbly fencepost belay.
[S Neal 06.07.08]

▶ **51. A Big Wall Climb MXS** 20m
Allegedly easy and quite solid climbing up the huge retaining wall at the back of the hole. A good novelty route? [C Muskett, N Malone 09.05.10]

▶ **52. Friendly Argument E2 5b**
Tackle the 1st wall and groove on the left that you come to as you walk down towards the back of the hole. The climb involves yarding on big holds up to a ledge and some gear and then out up the left arete to the top.
[C Muskett, N Malone 09.05.10]

Cefn Du Quarry

This quarry is an explorer's delight. A series of ledges and walkways split by minor bad steps, weave around the open pit, and make it very navigable without recourse to a rope. A lunar landscape of skeletal ridges and fissures, car wrecks and quarry workings - the exploring almost overshadows the climbing.

Conditions: The most open and bereft of vegetation, it is quick drying, non midgey, and the routes get the afternoon/evening sun.

Approach: Take the Ceunant road from Llanrug; drive over the hill until past the mobile phone mast and back into the 30mph speed zone. Turn left at the crossroads sign by the white houses, and continue uphill until you get to the car park at the very top. From here follow the track over towards Llanberis until you can branch off left uphill. At this point Chwarel Fawr is on your left and Cefn Du quarry is on your right. Walk round rightwards, over a 19th century slate stile, the other side of which is the quarry. Walk around it with the edge on your right until at the lowest point of the quarry; here a grassy valley provides an entrance. The routes are found beyond the 1st gallery.

▶ **53. The Reclining Bloon E4 6a** 18m
A hollow start gains the metal spike and the bolted corner. A surprisingly technical route but unfortunately spoiled by flaky and dubious rock, and a big spike between your legs. Lower off.
[M Crook 09.96]

▶ **54. The New Salesman E4 6b** * 18m
This weaves up the striking pillar, right of *The Reclining Bloon*, from its lowest point, the right hand arête. Climb the arete to an overlap, from which great toil gains a ledge up to the left. Return to the arête for a bold finish. Lower off.
[C Parkin 07.90]

▶ **55. Carneddau Flash Goggles E1 5a** 30m
This slab climb, situated up right, involves adventurous padding to a "grimly loose" crest which is followed to safety. Originally done solo.
[M Crook 09.96]

On the opposite side of the quarry is the buttress known as **Mount Doom**; consisting of an igneous band capped with a 'wizarding' hat of slate. The following route commences from the scree on the right, at the start of a gouged out ledge system.

▶ **56. The Wriggler E1 5a** * 50m
This route encapsulates all different aspects of slate climbing from ledge shuffling to tenuous rockovers; it even has a knee bar.
P1 20m Shuffle along the ledge to a bolt belay. Shot holes and the odd cam provide the protection.
P2 5a 30m Delicately step up left out of the igneous band (cam) and back right, ascending to a bolt. A thin section follows, leading to jugs that weave left to a bolt and on to the summit. Bolt belay well over and below the crest.
[M Dicken, I Doyle 30.10.08]

Chwarel Fawr • Glyn Rhonwy

Chwarel Fawr

Chwarel Fawr is the highest of these excavations; it is a charming if slightly inaccessible hole; containing a series of picturesque pools, clumps of alpine plants, and an old boiler. In terms of climbing, however, there is little to attract even the most ardent adventurer. Most of its slopes consist of rubble, and what intact rock there is is mainly vegetated and crumbly. Nevertheless, nestled at its very bottom is a small dolerite promontory providing a refuge of solid and appealing rock.

Conditions: Being a particularly deep hole, the walls are often in shadow and thus have a tendency to be mossy and damp. This is however a very sheltered and serene place which and gets the sun early afternoon.

Approach: Park as for Cefn Du Quarry. From here there are 3 alternatives; option 1 and 2 involve bypassing the fence directly above the car park and following the edge of the hole uphill to the right. Option 1 is the scramble; as the edge levels out briefly, some pine trees will become visible over the edge. There is a faint and perilous path linking these trees to gain a ridge down into the depths. This is dodgy at the best of times, but near-fatally exciting in winter conditions. Option 2 is to continue following the edge to a rusty stake in the far right corner and abseil in. Option 3 is to pack wellies and a head torch and take the 500m tunnel from Cefn Du quarry. The entrance is found in the bottom of the first gallery encountered on the described approach. It is slightly flooded (hence wellies) and is as dangerous as all abandoned slate mine tunnels.

▶ **57. Way Down in the Hole E1 5a** 27m
This takes a rambling journey over the most solid bits of rock, giving an amiable if inane adventure, especially if followed by *The Wriggler* via a trip through the tunnel. Start at the front face of the lower arête. Bolts and slings protect.
P1 5a 5m Tackle the slate pedestal on the right and stretch out to clip the bolt. Climb past this to the top. Chain and thread belay.
Now saunter together across the top of the promontory to arrive at a bollard belay at the base of the continuation dolerite arête,
P2 5a 12m Tackle the airy left arête, via a series of layaways and mantels, to a bolt and thread belay. The remaining rock above is fairly atrocious; abseil off, or take the bad step exit.
P3 4a 10m The bad step exit. Traverse off left with the odd spike for protection. Block and bucket seat belay.
[M Dicken, J Sterling 24.12.08]

Slate Walks and Adventures

Slate Walks and Adventures

The slate quarries are a wonderful place to spend a few hours exploring on a rest day or in bad weather. What follows is a series of walking/scrambling circuits around some of the more interesting and curious sights of the Dinorwig slate quarries. Each route will take an hour or two (or probably three for the more challenging Snakes and Ladders).

There are numerous examples of random art which can be seen as you wander around the quarries. From ambitious sculptures, to tiny paintings or amusing graffiti there is a lot to see, so keep your eyes peeled. The quarries have some remarkable acoustics too; whether it is echoing tunnels or the musical instrument walls peppered with bore holes (if you pat different bore holes with your palm you can get different notes).

All the circuits intersect at various points; these points are highlighted in **bold** In the text, so you can link them up to your heart's content. All these walks start at the kissing gate situated by the old cutting shed close to the popular lookout point. To get there walk in from Bus Stop along the main quarry path. Once you are past the stripped out cutting shed on the left, you arrive at the gate.

Warning: rock fall is a common phenomenon in the quarries; on your travels you may come across fresh rock falls and unstable ground. Use your discretion and tread carefully in these areas. It may also be worth carrying a rope and a few slings to protect the ladder and chain sections, particularly if you are visiting unfamiliar areas. The ladders often have missing or loose rungs and their solidity cannot be guaranteed. A head torch is also useful in some of the tunnels.

1 Tree sculptures built by Andy Parkin during LLAMFF 2004
photo: George Smith

The Path Plus Route

Go through the gate and follow the main quarry path round until it turns right. There is a 5 bar gate here on the left; on the other side of it are the remains of the payroll offices. Behind these there is a covered water reservoir. Water was used throughout the quarries to power hydraulic machinery, hence all the rusting tanks, and miles of pipes. On your right is an old incline that goes up a single level. Ascend this and follow the level round to the right where you encounter **Dali's Wall**. This is a delightful vantage point for observing **Dali's Hole**, the flooded quarry below, with its drowned trees and ever changing water level. Look out for the pattern of paths on the base of the pool.

Dali's Wall is also home to the recently rediscovered **Tunnel to Oz**. This is found between *Dali Express* and *Dali's Dihedral*. Continuing round on this level the tunnels of California Quarry are spotted.

High on the wall, obscured by a tree is the tunnel that is gained by a chain on the other side. At the same level as you are standing the tunnel seen is a dead end, but slip down to the wall below and the main California entrance tunnel is gained, and is worth a visit if you haven't been in before. The path continues down to Dali's Hole, and by staying close to the cliff until the wire fence is gained, the third, most secretive entrance to California is discovered under a tree. This is the **Back Entrance to Hades**, and is often flooded. Staying next to the fence, tramp up the hill until the other side of an incline is reached at Never Never Land. Here is found the Air Vent. The large circular turret is the breathing apparatus of the Electric Mountain; the massive bore hole runs 100m into the mountain itself.

The track on the left runs up to Serengeti, past Hitler's Podium. If you go up the path and turn immediately right onto the butte that rises over the *Peter Pan* wall, you can see what the rock here was like before they quarried it. From here this circuit drops back down and regains the main quarry path. Continue towards Nant Peris, through Watford Gap and past the majesty of Twll Mawr on the left. Beyond Twll Mawr the path turns right and beyond the fence a path contours along to a tunnel through the **Twll Mawr incline**. On the other side is a quiet promontory over looking Nant Peris. Here you will find an engine maintenance shed, complete with maintenance pit, and some quarrymen's bothies, beyond which is the end of the line, where the slate waste was tipped, and this journey ends.

Back Entrance to Hades photo: Mark Dicken 2
Dali's Hole photo: Adrian Trendall 3

Australia Circuit

This Circuit declines to pass through the kissing gate. Instead, gain the concrete slab covered incline rising up the western side of Australia quarry. Originally a series of winding houses and carts ferrying the slate, the incline was put to use in later years as a means of getting power to the workers building the hydroelectric power station housed inside the mountain. Continue up one incline after the first winding house, and cross a fence on your right. Follow this level (the Sidings Level) until it turns left into Australia itself and scramble up the scree and white slate ridge to the Fruitbat Level. If you follow this level to its end you arrive at a fairly intact winding house. Beyond this a short scramble downwards gains the Salt Pans. This alien bog is the end result of lots of lovely Welsh water flowing through the immense Oil Drum Glacier which spills down from the upper levels. The leached mineral salts bleach the rocks white and encourage 'things' to grow in the water. Not somewhere to refill your flask.

Contouring round to the eastern walls of Australia gains the level above Vilcabamba. From here a slippery and mossy incline leads to the first of the Braich ladders, a series of rusting rungs that take you all the way up and out of Australia if you choose to trust them. There are some bolts on the first set of ladders to protect the trickiest section. It is also possible to pick your way up the boulder scree on the left hand side. After the first ladder, a brief diversion to the left end of the level will lead you to an old length of quarryman's rope, still hanging in situ. There are also the remains of an old dump truck, and a hut with some very artistic graffiti.

G'Day Arete Level is reached by a slightly unnerving double ladder situated 50m to the right from the first ladders. Here you will find a much visited and photographed Caban, sometimes referred to as the **coat shed**. Clothes and shoes still remain in the large white building, not returned for when the quarry closed in 1969. Two levels above lies an enormous **rust red water drum**. This powered hydraulic machinery on the levels below, as well as feeding the workshop generators in the adjacent building, which itself contains many gargantuan machines and the remains of an old smithy.

Onwards and upwards; these higher levels were amongst the first to be abandoned and this is evident in the lichen encrusted slates and piles of junked ironmongery. The level above is home to a subterranean winding house. This used to be operated by large ship wheels, behind which you felt like you were sailing the mountain out into the ocean; unfortunately the wheels have long since disappeared. At the level above it is possible to gaze down into an area of Australia known as the Crystal Chasm. This mass of fractured dolerite and quartz was a popular crystal gathering spot in the 80s, until a string of bad luck was attributed to the presence of said crystals in certain people's homes, and collection ceased.

The level above is home to an intact engineering shed and lots of train spotter treasures. It is also the last level to jut out over Nant Peris; a short walk along a grassy path takes you to this most peaceful of spots. The hillside above, leading up to the summit of Elidir is a mass of grass and boulders – a refreshing contrast after so much slate debris.

Loooking down the Australia incline photo: Si Panton

East Braich ladders photo: Mark Dicken

Australia tunnel photo: Si Panton

The coat shed caban with winter snow drifts photo: Si Panton

The rust red water drum photo: Adrain Trendall

The upper half of the Oil Drum Glacier viewed from the Salt Pans photo: Mark Dicken

Cutting shed photo: Mark Dicken

Lost World photo: Mark Dicken

Track of Doom photo: Mark Dicken

Sheds high above the Lost World photo: Adrain Trendall

Go back to the engineering hut and ascend one level. It is now possible to pass along and over the fearsome walls of upper Dinorwig and back into Western Australia, at the Darwin level. This spot is otherwise known as Area 51, due to the large, flooded back entrance to Electric Mountain. Please do not try to enter as there are cameras here. You are now standing above the Oil Drum Glacier. This is a huge spill of excavation waste from the hollowing out of the Electric Mountain, the spilled guts of Elidir, if you like. The adventurous can pick their way down to the Salt Pans and beyond, all the way to the tunnel of Oz, in the Billabong area, directly below Looning the Tube Slab. The tunnel leads out to **Dali's Wall**. The less adventurous can gain the zigzag path leading down the western flank of Australia, which will deposit them at their journey's beginning.

Lost World Circuit

This circuit starts at the base of the **Twll Mawr incline**, at the far end of the main quarry path, before it winds its way down to Nant Peris (which provides an alternative approach). The walk involves a lot of altitude gain so you might as well get started slogging up the incline, avoiding the odd gap and barbed wire barricade. The first curiosity on your way up is the remains of a cutting shed on a sorry looking level jutting out over Twll Mawr itself. The walls are all but gone; however, the workers partitions still jut up like a series of grave stones. Eventually there is respite from the steepness, in the form of a winding house. This level includes a scene reminiscent of Indiana Jones. The partial collapse of the scree into Twll Mawr has left a long section of railway suspended over the brink. This Track of Doom has been walked, but more scree is lost each year and it cannot be recommended. It is possible to gain the other side of the abyss by moving up to the level above and following a hydraulic pipe back down the scree to a cable tower. This is the access to the Khyber Pass, through which a series of decaying ladders takes you into Lost World. Or you could just walk through the adjacent tunnel and view it from above.

Back up at the top of the hydraulic pipe you will encounter the flooded tunnels, and a level further above, the cutting into the Heaven Walls; an ornamental garden of ferns, mosses and rust.

Return to the incline, and approach the quarry citadel, an extensive level, sporting a cutting shed complete with all its machinery. It even had a roof in the 80s until an 'enterprising' and broke local climber harvested the roof slates almost single handed. If you follow this level out towards Dinorwig you will see the **rust red water drum**, mentioned in the Australia Circuit. Also on this lower level, back towards Nant Peris, is a weighing shed, complete with broken scales and truck plate. From here you can continue along the level towards Nant Peris where a rather precarious scramble takes you back through the Heaven's Wall cutting and on to the incline. If that doesn't take your fancy, then retreat to the **coat shed** two levels down on the East Braich of Australia. Here the steps of Cirith Ungol will return you to the Looning the Tube col and the **Dali's Hole** area.

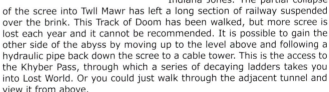

Rainbow Circuit

Follow the main quarry path through the kissing gate and round and down the dip by **Dali's Hole**. Beyond the 5 bar gate on your right a zigzag path leads down towards the Rainbow Slab area. The first sights to encounter are the main waterway, which used to feed off into various hydraulic systems, and the immense slate bridges that cross it. Also here are a few conspicuous blue tarpaulin-clad huts - useful shelters should it rain. The path eventually leads to the Rainbow hut. Originally an electricity generation building, it also housed a small smithy, and in the recent past a series of small raves.

Below the hut, some old cabling and an indistinct path lead down to the Rainbow slab level. If you stay on the right side of the waterway until a decrepit hut is reached a convenient piece of old hydraulic piping provides a precarious bridge across to the rough path on the other side. Once down follow the level past the base of the Bella Lugosi Slab and the impressive Colossus Wall. The stunning **Rainbow Slab** is situated further along the level, just out of sight. This remarkable sheet of slate is the source of much of slate climbing folk lore. Arguably it is best admired from the Cig-Arête Level, which is gained by following the level round until just before a winding house, where a short scramble leads up a set of broken steps.

Once you have gazed enough on the ripples of the Rainbow, follow this level towards Nant Peris, via a bad step, until it merges with the flat plain beyond. This is the Willow Plain, where some of the film Willow was shot, and where wild strawberries flourish in early June. Before climbing the last embankment onto the Willow Plain, be sure to spot the flourishing moss garden on the left. On a sunny winter's day it provides a welcome splash of colour. Staring down at you from the quarry walls above are the Eyes of the Skull, two redundant tunnels puncturing into Twll Mawr. The mouth of the skull is the Twll Mawr tunnel entrance.

Continue past the cones of goat nibbled gorse, towards the Peppermint Tower. As you arrive here a glance back up the scree finds the Alien Spacecraft. A huge slate block thrust into the slope like giant film prop. Continuing along the Willow plain you come to an incline. By climbing two inclines, and moving up the incline on the left, you can find a hut with an intact Caban, complete with stove on the kettle. The incline continues to the main quarry path, at the junction with the **Twll Mawr incline**, and the end of this circuit.

View of Australia from the kissing gate photo: Si Panton 1
The Rainbow hut photo: Si Panton 2
The weighing shed photo: Mark Dicken 3
Wild strawberries photo: Mark Dicken 4
Slate bridge photo: Mark Dicken 5
Moss garden, and above, the Eyes of the Skull photo: Mark Dicken 6
View across Australia to the East Braich photo: Si Panton 7
Rachael Barlow scaling the chain in California photo: Ian Parnell 8
photo: Si Panton 9

Snakes And Ladders (and Tunnels)

Although this route is not a conventional climbing experience, it's roughly equivalent to HVS and provides an unforgettable and deeply atmospheric experience. Needless to say it is sensible/essential to rope up for sections of this.

Start off with the option of the **Back Entrance to Hades**, a tunnel which leads from the east side of Dali's Hole and skirts around the deep echoes of Hades to emerge in California, an impressive arena enclosed by huge walls. The safer/drier option is to walk through the normal tunnels into California. Climb the chain on the left wall leading up to the tunnel at the base of *Esprit de Corpse*. Walk through the tunnel, which exits opposite Dali's Wall where a secret hole at the base of the crag provides the entrance to the bottom of Australia. This is the **Tunnel to Oz**. Scramble up the lower part of Australia's vast Oil Drum Glacier to the Salt Pans Level. Walk across rightwards and climb a series of ladders up to reach the G'Day Arete Level, high up on the East Braich. Walk along the level towards Nant Peris and drop down an obvious steep scree path into a wide cutting. Turn left and follow the cutting along until you are over looking the deep hole of Lost World, a truly forgotten and ethereal place.

A series of abseils and ladders lead down the Heaven Walls to gain the base of the quarry. Walk through a tunnel into the adjacent Mordor and ascend the ladders to the Khyber Pass. Continue up the hillside until the **Twll Mawr incline** on the right leads down to the main track through the quarries.

And now perhaps it's time for a brew or a pint?

320 Addendum

Australia Lower
▶ **Bise-Mon-Cul E2 5c** * 25m
The obvious direct start to *Looning the Tube* is still a bit flakey at present but should clean up into a quality route. There is a bolt belay just right of the start of the route – reach this from below as per the tunnel approach to the lower part of the quarry, or make a short abseil down from the *Looning the Tube* level. Climb up the slab with crux moves around the 3rd bolt, and finish up the original route. [J Kelly, J Redhead 27.03.10]

▶ **Fuck Les Clotures F5b/c** * 17m
The well-cleaned slab right *Gerboa Racer* and left of the unstable pillar. 5 bolts lead to a final few metres common with *Gerboa Racer* and a new lower-off. [J Kelly, J Redhead 27.03.10]

▶ **A Selfish Act of Loonacy E3 6a** * 20m
Follow *Fuck Les Clotures* to its 3rd bolt before making a delicate traverse right (bolt) to small edges on the slab. A series of technical and commiting moves leads up the steep slab above to a further bolt. A worrying move to gain the lower-off adds a sting in the tail! [J Kelly, J Redhead 27.03.10]

Australia Upper
▶ **Rock Yoga F7a** * 18m
The line between *Harri Bach Llanrug* and *Put it on the Slate, Waiter*. Expect thin holds and rock overs with a high stepping and Yoga like crux sequence. Traverse up and left at the top to the *Harri Bach Llanrug* lower-off.
[I Lloyd-Jones, S McGuiness 10.04.11]

▶ **Slabaholics Anonymous F7a+** * 27m
A good intense climb, just to the right of *The Gorbals*. The crux, which is very thin (think finger nails!) is at the top. 8 bolts to a lower-off.
[I Lloyd-Jones 06.06.11]

Australia East Braich
▶ **Not Quite Snakes and Ladders HVS/MXS 4c** 20m
The ominous-looking chimney left of *Where the Green Ants Dream*. [E Russell 25.06.10]

California
▶ **Dwarf Shortage E4/5 6a** ** 57m
A mammoth pitch which packs in everything from baffling groove moves to thin rockovers before a magnificent finish up the final crack of *Central Sadness*. The start is a bit nasty and bold, but the route improves as height is gained. Start 2m right of *Central Sadness* below a line of 7 bolts. Climb up to the little groove (gripping 2nd clip) and continue straight up the spaced line of bolts with a couple of hard moves past the last one to reach a ledge right of the detached spike on *Central Sadness* P2. Finish up the *Central Sadness* P2 crack. 60m ropes will just get you to the belay bolts. [O Barnicott 05.08.10]

Never Never Land
▶ **Release the Kraken! F6b+** * 20m
Fine climbing on the obvious line left of *The Carbon Stage*. Follow interesting slate features up, with the odd small hold, before the rock turns to dolerite and steep moves bar access to the lower-off. [I Lloyd-Jones 18.01.11]

▶ **Zeus F6a/+** * 20m
A good addition taking a direct line up the wall between *The Carbon Stage* and the arête of *Titan*. Steady climbing on surprisingly good edges leads to a tricky crux close to the top; a stretch, a lunge or a smeary layback, the choice is yours. Tall climbers will think F6a; everyone else: F6a+.
[M Hellewell, C Goodey 25.07.10]

▶ **Titan F4b** * 20m
An airy line up the impressive blocky arête. Some loose rock but mostly okay.
[C Goodey, M Hellewell, S Trainer 23.07.10]

Twll Mawr
▶ **Supermassive Black Hole F7a** *** 75m
An awesome 4 pitch slate adventure. Start just left of *Running Scared*.
P1 F7a 25m The obvious well bolted groove. When the holds run out make a rightwards move onto the slab followed by some more technical moves to regain the groove (crux). Belay on the grassy ledge above.
P2 F6b+ 12m This pitch joins the 2 main grooves and has a technical and precarious crux. Continue upwards/rightwards to gain the belay at the base of the 2nd groove.
P3 F6c+ 25m The 2nd groove pitch. As with the 1st groove, when the holds run out, make a rightwards move onto the slab, and then more technical moves to regain the groove (crux). Continue up the groove, which looks desperate, but climbs more easily, to a belay where the groove ends and the dolerite slab begins.
P4 F6b 12m Climb the black dolerite slab via some great quartz pockets to gain the top.
[I Lloyd-Jones, S McGuinness 06.07.11]

▶ **Black Hole Sun F7a+** *** 75m
A scruffy start detracts little from the brilliant upper pitches, P3 being one of the best in the quarries. Start just right of *In the Line of Fire*.
P1 F7a+ 25m Climb up carefully (if you've abbed in pre-clip the 1st bolt) to the blocky ledge to get established in the crackline which gets increasingly difficult the higher you go. Step onto the ledge at the bottom of the clean cut groove and climb this or the arête to a bolt belay at the base of P2.
P2 F7a 25m Follow the line of the arete. Great moves from the ledge passing the final 2 bolts; the vertically challenged may have to jump. Bolt belay.

Addendum

Suncharm Ledge

P3 F7a 25m The superb steep arete, gives funky climbing; all very entertaining and fall-offable. 2 belay bolts on the Fin above. [I Lloyd-Jones, S McGuiness, P Dowthwaite, A Schofield 14.07.2011]

Twll Mawr • Suncharm Ledge

Suncharm Ledge is a neat dolerite wall located up and right of the Golgotha wall (described in the Twll Mawr chapter). A selection of clean problems can be found here. It is quite high so a couple of pads and a spotter are recommended. Descent from the problems is via a traverse off to the left. It is of course possible to make a bold top out on *The Suncharmer* and *Rhinoplasty*.

Approach: From the other side of the fence on the Llanberis side of main quarry path by Twll Mawr scamper to the hut and look over the edge. Take the obvious scramble down.

▶ **1. Flock of Flying Butt Monkeys V1/Font 5**
Tackle the flying arete on the left. [M Dicken 04.10]

▶ **2. The Groove of Smooth V3/Font 6A+** *
The flying groove entered from the left.
[M Dicken 04.10]

▶ **3. Maurice Chevalier V3/Font 6A+** **
The central arête. [M Dicken 04.10]

▶ **4. Observation Groove V0-/Font 4**
The easy central corner. [M Dicken 04.10]

▶ **5. Sunshine Swing V4/Font 6B+**
The impressive right arete taken via its left side with a rockover onto the ledge to traverse off rather than top out. [C Muskett 04.10]

▶ **6. Rhinoplasty V5/Font 6C+** **
The right arete taken head on to finish as for *Sunshine Swing*. [C Muskett 04.10]

▶ **7. The Suncharmer V3/Font 6A+**
The obvious left-to-right girdle linking into the proper highball finish.

Vivian

▶ **Susanna VS 4a** 25m
The corner right of *Dawes of Perception* gives a serious outing. Follow the crack trending right to a ledge at 15m. From here finish up over loose ground to the top. [S Sinfield, G Riley 02.10.96]

Date	First Ascent
1964 Jul	**Gideon** A Harris, E Penman
	The first foray onto slate was inspired by the view across the valley from Al Harris' Dinorwig house, and became popular during the '67 Foot and Mouth crisis. Originally it started from a pillar of stacked boulders; this subsequently fell down (and is now the line of *Pandora Plays Sax Direct*). For a while it was overcome with combined tactics until an alternative start was devised.
1969 June 10	**BlueBottle** R Kane, J Brazinton

1971 Apr 9	**Opening Gambit** J Brown, C Davies, J Smith
	The first exploration of the Dinorwig Quarries, a mere two years after its closure, with Joe making a bee line for the biggest and most adventurous cliff of them all. Claude Davies wrote an article detailing early explorations of Twll Mawr: 'Always a Little Further' appeared in the 1970/71 CC journal.
1971 Apr 10	**Hamadryad** J Brown, C Davies • FFA B Davidson, A Cope 29.10.88
1971 May 1	**Razor's Edge** J Brown, C Davies
	FFA S Haston, T Carruthers 07.82 • *True Finish* C Dale, G McMahon 05.89
	It took four attempts to climb this line! In truth Joe spent many visits to this wall trying to breach its defences, with five out of seven lines eventually reaching the top.
1973	**White Room** R Norcross, J Warburton, M Cox
	The details were lost. *The Gully* was later soloed in the same area by Jon Tombs.
1978	**Legs Akimbo** R Ebbs
1978 Nov	**Vandal** P Trower, C Hudson
1979 Jan	**Butcher** P Trower, C Hudson
1979 Mar 10	**The Poacher** P Jewel, P Williams, M Patterson
1979 Mar 11	**The Hooligan** P Williams, P Jewel
1979 Apr 24	**Deceiver** P Jewel, P Williams
	An early involvement in the development of Nant Peris Quarry failed to convince Paul of slate's worth – his conversion to manic slate fan was still a few years off yet.

∧ Combined tactics on the original start to **Gideon** photo: Derek Wiggett
↓ An early repeat of **Gideon** HVS 4c photo: Derek Wiggett

324 First Ascents • 1980's

1980 Aug	**Wendy Doll** S Haston, N Parker, M Howard • Top pitch M Green, S Kelly 1973	

The best early pitch in the quarry and a debut for one of slate's premier activists who (in contrast to Paul Williams) was inspired by Paul Trower's exploration of Nant Peris Quarry. The stellar top pitch is sadly in the process of falling down.

1980 Aug **Four Wheel Drift** S Haston, N Parker

1981 Feb **Comes the Devish** S Haston
For many climbers this is THE slate route. Cleaned with a knife borrowed from Pete's Eats and well worth its initial E5 6a grade. It has become easier over the years as the gear placements have improved through wear, however the polish on the bold start has worsened – the result of much up and down traffic as climbers 'chicken out' of the run out to the first decent gear placement at 8m. There are some micro wires on this section, and some talk of a crucial nut key placement, but it is better just to not fall off!

1981 Mar **The Mancer** S Haston, L K McGinley • *Direct Start* S Haston, S Downes 09.82

1981 Apr 17 **Scorpion** J Brown, C Davies

1981 May **Hymen Snapper** S Haston, L McGinley

1982 Mar 27 **Bushmaster** J Brown, C Davies

1982 Aug **Sup 1** & **Sup 2** S Haston

1983 **North Wales New Climbs**, Andy Pollitt's 1983 supplement gave the first formal descriptions of slate routes, yet barely hinted at what was about to happen.

1983 **Flashdance** A Pollitt, T Freeman
A bold route that established the ethic for this boltless slab.

1983 **Bong to Lunch** S Haston

1983 **Frustrated Lust** S Haston

1983 Jun **Fear of Rejection** S Haston, M 'Yob' Howard
Sadly the route was rejected and now scatters the floor below.

1983 Jun **Bar of Soap** S Haston, M Crook

1983 Jun **Seamstress** and **Seams the Same** S Haston
Re-discovered by Martin Crook, Andy Newton and Nick Walton some time later. *Seamstress* was to become the most popular route in the quarries.

1983 Sept 2 **Nostromo** M Crook, D Towse

1984 **Nicki's Leap** Nicki Thomas
The infamous 25m pool-jump from the top of the prow in Vivian Quarry. It is a decidedly risky proposition; indeed the list of people who have sported injuries from this mighty plunge is considerable: broken ribs, fractured spines and even colonic irrigation!

1984 Feb **Never Never Land** M Crook, N Walton, A Newton
The start of the major slate boom that was to continue for several years. Cleaned with an ice-axe; the 3 peg runners where later removed and placed elsewhere! There was some controversy over the placing of some bolts on the adjacent *Igam Ogam*, but these have since been moved out of reach.

1984 Mar **Layed Back Boys** S Haston, P J Trower, M Howard

1984 Mar **Cracking Up** S Haston, C Phillips
A striking crackline from the jamming technician.

1984 Mar **Cracked Up** S Haston, C Phillips

1984 Mar 19 **Belldance** J Redhead, D Towse
JR's first new route on slate and the beginning of a colourful campaign from one of the top slateheads.

1984 Mar 20 **Swinging by the Bell** D Towse, M Roberts
The second experienced a very fast traverse of the slab after falling off near the arete!

VIVIAN QUARRY — FLASH DANCE STILL EXISTS!! AP→ -can but its called 'Bell Dance'.

BELL-DANCE E6 · 6B. ✱✱✱

[MAKES FLASH DANCE AN INDEPENDANT ROUTE]

✴ 1. AS FOR 'FLASHDANCE' TO THE JUG ON THE DERVISH — PROTECTION CAN BE ARRANGED HERE. MOVE RT AND UP TO THE OVERLAP (CRUX) — OVER THE OVERLAP AND RT TO AN OBVIOUS CRACKLINE (PROTECTION!) — UP AND LEFT INTO ANOTHER CRACKLINE AND THE TOP. Belay on/w the Dervish. J. REDHEAD.
D. TOWSE   19/3/84

N.B. Although a doctor as a belayer has been suggested, a locksmith as a leader seems more appropriate !!

Vivian Quarry
"Swinging By The Bell" ✱✱ — ~~E5 (44)~~ 6a 150

Starts at the belay of Wendy Doll on the arete right of The Dervish. traverse left for 40ft to the jugs where the Dervish meets Bell/Dance climb the 'Dervish' for 10ft then traverse left to an obvious flat hold move up and left to good holds (crux) underneath the roof then over this and straight up to finish.

D. TOWSE
Mel Roberts
↓
The Bell

Best seconded with a back rope !

20/3/84

326 First Ascents • 1980's

1984 Apr	**Gender Bender** S Haston, M Crook	
	All too easy to get stuck in a position of both hands on one wall and both feet on the other.	
1984 Apr	**The Second Coming** S Haston, M Crook, A Newton	
	Cleaned with a typical lack of concentration - the leader spent the entire ascent pulling off holds and cursing his own impatience.	
1984 Apr 2	**Snap, Crackle & Pop** M Roberts	
1984 Apr 8	**Mental Block** C Phillips	
	A typical probe for slate's Dr Livingstone.	
1984 Apr 10	**Lounge Lizard** I A Jones	
	This route was in an area of Vivian Quarry which is now banned to protect visitors from falling rocks.	
1984 Apr 13	**Stack of Nude Books Meets the Stickman** N Walton, M Crook	
	A stash of porn magazines was discovered near the foot of the route and the stories read to the leader on the first ascent. The peg was lassoed from the ground on the first ascent.	
1984 Apr 18	**Marital Aids** S Haston, T Downes	
1984 Apr 20	**Combat Rock** P Trower, A Howard	
1984 Apr 29	**For Whom the Bell Tolls** A Pollitt, M Crook, J Taylor	
	People know this as the title of a Hemingway novel, but it's also a poem by John Donne which starts "No man is an island..." – a good metaphor for a climbing partnership!	
1984 Apr 29	**The Trash Heap Has Spoken** C Phillips, N Thomas	
1984 May 2	**The Trash Heap Speaks Again** C Phillips, M Thompson	
1984 May 2	**Arse over Tit** C Phillips	
1984 May 4	**Tourmaline; Fellow; Sinhalese; Tuolomne; Gutter Slut Strut** C Phillips	
	All were buried when the large hole at Bus Stop Quarry was 'landscaped'.	
1984 May 8	**So This is Living; Stand to Your Rights; As the Sun Sets in the West** C Phillips	
1984 May 19	**Watford Gap West** C Phillips	
1984 May 20	**Peter Pan** M Crook, C Phillips • *Lost Boys variation* A Kemp, K Scholey 13.11.89	
	After the first ascent bolts appeared then disappeared on this line. During the 2006 re-equipping campaign they were replaced, making the route instantly popular.	
1984 May 20	**Stick's Groove** N Walton	
1984 May 23	**Hole In One; Proless Cliff's Arete** C J Phillips	
1984 May 23	**The Stick Up** N Walton, C Phillips, M Crook, N Thomas	
	In a display of ingenious thrift, rather than placing a bolt or peg (which after all cost money), a slot was cut in the arete by a hacksaw to take a tape sling (albeit badly).	
1984 May 23	**Unsexual** C Phillips, M Crook, N Walton	
1984 May 23	**Andy Pandy** M Roberts, M Crook	
1984 May 24	**Ascent of the Vikings** A Winterbottom, B Cralis	
1984 May 28	**Holy, Holy, Holy** C Phillips	
	A great find, and unusual for the Captain; a route that actually has gear!	
1984 May 28	**Bella Lugosi Is Dead** M Crook, N Walton	
	An early foray into the Rainbow Slab area yielded an excellent and popular route.	
1984 Jun	**The Blind Buddha** M Boater, J Clinton	
	Re-discovered in 1986 by Jon Tombs. A wandering route, *The Blind Mower*, was climbed in this area in 1973 by R Millward, P Kendall; this was the first probing into Vivian and predates almost all of the other slate offerings.	
1984 Jun	**Blades of Green Tara** M Boater	
	The original deep water solo; it was re-discovered in 1986 by Stevie Haston and Michael 'Yob' Howard who walked across the frozen pool to gain the prow. Another early route *Badge* was climbed in this area in 1973 by A Payne, R Norcross.	
1984 Jun	**Binman** M Boater	

1980's • First Ascents 327

1984 Jun 8	**Proliferation Bang On; Neat Arete; Stuck Up Frustuck; Walking Pneumonia** C Phillips
1984 Jun 8	**The Whale's Tail** C Phillips, top rope Years ahead of his time in creating common profanities.
1984 Jun 16	**California Arete** C Phillips A form of extreme protectionless scrambling!
1984 Jun 16	**Classy Situations** C Phillips
1984 Jun 19	**Act Naturally** C Phillips
1984 Jun 19	**Looning the Tube; Tubing the Loon** C Phillips The tube originally spanned out across and up the slab to the level above, it was broke by either vandalism or gravity a couple of years later. *Tubing the Loon* started from the end of the pipe, and was replaced by *Pruning the Tube*.
1984 June	**Red and Yellow and Pink and Green, Orange and Purple and Blue** M Lynden - *The Richard of York Finish* M Lynden, W Lockley 08.07.84 The first route on the Rainbow Slab; soloed and given HVS 4c.
1984 Jun 29	**Cystitis By Proxy** D Towse, J Redhead The first of the big Rainbow Slab routes, picked because it was mistakenly thought to be the easiest of the lines. Originally given E6; some will think Dave got it right!
1984 Jul	**Eros** M Lynden, S Long, J Silvester, D Towse
1984 Jul	**Raped by Affection** J Redhead, D Towse Three skyhooks and a RURP were used as runners to protect the run out to the first bolt at 25m. After the second ascent by Johnny Dawes without the skyhooks, the route was up graded. The route received its first onsight ascent in 1999 by Patch Hammond. The route was also almost 'onsighted' a few years later by Will Perrin until a team of climbers joined him on the slab and caught him working it on a shunt, to which he replied, 'Aww, you've totally blown my onsight now!'

Dave Towse making the first ascent of **Cystitus by Proxy** E5 6b photo: Mark Lynden

"I watched JR leading this. At one point he got the sequence wrong and teetered backwards, but stayed on the rock because a small, sharp spike stuck into his finger and just held him on." - Mark Lynden

1984 Jul	**Poetry Pink** J Redhead, D Towse Calculated bolt placements made this an exciting lead. In the last guidebook the route was downgraded to E4, but the words 'Low in the grade' weren't deleted from the text! The route has been up graded back to E5 as Linford Christie would still be required as a belayer should you blow it by the second bolt. Climbed one handed by Leo Houlding 17.06.98
1984 Jul	**The Rainbow of Recalcitrance** J Silvester, M Lynden A fine effort by a man obsessed and one of the more inspiring lines on slate, with the ultimate 'smear or disappear' move.

"It was really Silv's find – he had been there a lot recceing the Rainbow line. Myself, JR and Towsey were given a guided tour, but sworn to secrecy. The big surprise for everybody was the quality of the climbing on the Rainbow Slab. Okay, the Dervish existed by then, but it was the Rainbow routes that really made people look again at the quarries." - Mark Lynden

| 1984 Jul | **Naked Before the Beast** D Towse, J Redhead • *Direct version* Johnny Dawes 1985 |

328 First Ascents • 1980's

1984 Jul	**Pull My Daisy** M Lynden, J Silvester	

One of the best routes in the quarries.

1984 Aug **Heading the Shot** S Haston, N Walton
Nick had manufactured the hangers at home; these were famously difficult to clip and some folk lamented the re-equipping job in 2006 which left the route as an 'almost' conventional F7a/+ clip up, rather than a spicy E5. In reality the original hangers were more a testament to poverty, than any sort of ethical statement. Nick made initial attempts on the route but soon enlisted the help of Stevie to finish the job off.

1984 Aug 18 **German School Girl** M Crook, N Walton
Martin was rather surprised by the incongruous sight of the aforementioned party traipsing round the quarry.

1984 Oct **Monsieur Avantski** J Silvester, A Wilkie

1984 Oct 26 **OM 69 Runner Bean** C Phillips

1985 Mar **Khubla Khan** M Crook, A Newton • *Variation* M Campbell, I Fox 1985
It is now the norm to climb direct past the bolt at 6b.

1985 May **Menstrual Gossip** J Redhead

1985 May 12 **Last Tango in Paris** M Roberts, C Edwards
How this brilliant line remain unclimbed for so long is a mystery.

1985 May 15 **Biggles Flies Undone** C Phillips

1985 Jun 15 **Horse Latitudes** M Crook, I A Jones, R Drury, D Jones

Horsin' Around finish A Holmes and S Long 20.05.86
The route was retro bolted in 2007 by Neil Dyer – a controversial move which upset some climbers. Needless to say it became very popular once the bolts were in.

1985 Jun 18 **Guillotine** T Taylor, A Whittall

1985 Jun 23 **Wusty Woof** A George, T Taylor

1985 Jun 23 **Solstice** A George, T Taylor

1985 Jun 24 **Fool's Gold** P George, A George
A good find and one of the more popular extremes in the quarries, thus the polish. The crack appears to be widening over the years - hopefully it will survive intact for a few years more.

1985 Jun 24 **Equinox** T Taylor, A George

1985 Jun 28 **Scarlet Runner** W Wayman, P Williams
A new area of rock opened up by the use of sportingly placed bolts.

1985 Jul 3 **Massambula** P Williams, W Wayman
Having previously berated local Slateheads for climbing 'worthless crap', Paul was now a confirmed fan. He produced a landmark article, 'Slate of the Art' in High magazine. This gave a full historical breakdown of recent events along with a set of photo topos of the main areas.

1985 Jul 3 **Virgin on the Ridiculous** W Wayman, P Williams

1985 Jul 31 **Gnat Attack** A Newton, R Newton
Originally started up *Massambula*, a direct start was added later: 04.04.86 J Pitts, S Jones, D Jones.

1985 Aug 8 **Slug Club Special** P Hawkins, R Caves

1985 Aug 31 **The Spark That Set the Flame** R Drury
"I cleaned and led this pitch with a knot in my ab rope for a runner. I didn't want to place a bolt (I don't think any had been placed in Vivian at that time) so I said Moose could have the route if he could lead it without. Moose had a go but unfortunately decked it just after the photo was taken. Fortunately the rope stretch saved him from serious injury but he was quite shaken. How could I then put a bolt in!! Moose retired to lick his wounds and a few days later Bobby Drury came and led the pitch using a sky hook runner. This really pissed Moose off and they fell out for a while, so the Spark that set the Flame was the sky hook." – Mike Raine

The skyhook was dispensed with by Moose on the second ascent and it was soloed on the third ascent by Mark McGowan.

1985 Oct 6	**Good Afternoon Constable**	I Wilson, T Downes
1985 Oct 23	**Dawes of Perception**	J Dawes

On a second ascent attempt John Redhead got level with the bolt then slipped off. His life was saved by Dave Towse jumping out over the pool to take in the slack after the RPs ripped; JR walked away with a mere broken finger!

1985 Oct 24   **Windows of Perception** J Dawes

"On the first ascent day Johnny had problems sorting out the bolt placement for the crux, so he clipped a loop positioned at the same height on the ab rope. It seemed like a fair solution." - Iwan Arfon Jones

NB. Recently a hold on the crux was gauged out by person/s unknown – sadly this has made the legendary move easier. In 2009 the route was flashed in impressive style by both Neil Kershaw and Ryan Pasquill, although it is not known whether the 'new' hold had appeared by then.

1986 Jan 3	**Night of the Hot Knives**	M Crook, D Cuthbertson
1986 Feb 7	**Lone Pine** I A Jones • Direct Finish C Jex, I Lloyd-Jones	
1986 Feb 7	**Snowdon Lady**	I A Jones

Like a magic eye painting - some can see her, others can't. The 'Lady' in question lies on the slopes of Snowdon opposite this route. Have you seen her?

Mike 'Moose' Thomas moments before he decked it from what subsequently became **The Spark That Set the Flame** E5 6b
photo: Mike Raine

Johnny Dawes halfway through the desperate rock over crux on his own route: **Windows of Perception** E6 7a, Serengeti
photo: Iwan Arfon Jones

330 First Ascents • 1980's

1986 Feb 22	**Hot Air Crack** J Tombs, B Jones, N Jones	
1986 Feb 26	**Breaking Wind** J Tombs	
1986 Feb 26	**Road to Nowhere** J Tombs	
1986 Mar 8	**Llechan** J Gladstone, I A Jones	
	Another 'now banned' route in Vivian Quarry.	
1986 Mar 27	**Colossus** P Williams, A Holmes	
	Paul persevered on this previously dismissed wall to unearth a popular slate classic. Now a confirmed Slatehead he was soon touring enthusiastically with a slide show called 'Slate of the Art'! - using the same name as his seminal magazine article from the previous year.	
1986 Apr 2	**Gerbil Abuse** M Thomas, M McGowan	
	Lead onsight after Johnny Dawes, who had cleaned the line, got fed up waiting for a dry day.	
1986 Apr 4	**Purple Haze** P Trower, I Wilson	
1986 Apr 4	**Silly on Slate** N Clacher, T Hodgson	
1986 Apr 5	**Book of Brilliant Things** G Hughes, I A Jones, M Roberts	
	A skyhook was kept in place by judicious use of elastoplast.	
1986 Apr 5	**Splitstream** D Towse, J Redhead • P2 D Towse, A Newton	
1986 Apr 5	**Stiff Syd's Cap** J Redhead, D Towse	
	The first ascent team was listed in the Pete's Eats new routes book as "Stiff Syd's Son and Cap, Dead Uncle Howel's Nephew and Cardigan"	
1986 Apr 6	**Dinorwig Unconquerable** M Raine, J Gladstone	
	A brilliant discovery, considering how well hidden the route is - Yosemite style jamming comes to the quarries.	
1986 Apr 6	**Alive and Kicking** G Hughes, I A Jones	
1986 Apr 6	**Frogs** A Williams, A Popp	
	An unusually amenable addition to the slate canon by Ground Up's designer.	

Looking down on John Gladstone during the first ascent of the classic **Dinorwig Unconquerable** E3 5c, Lost World photo: Mike Raine

John Redhead busy creating another fingery test piece: **Manic Strain** F8a, Vivian Quarry photo: Andy Newton

1986		**Welsh Rock,** an historical celebration of the North Wales scene, was published in early '86 - its memorable front cover shot (taken by Dave Towse) of John Redhead on the first ascent of *Raped by Affection* E7 6c reinforced the importance of the new wave slate routes.
1986 Apr 6		**Great Balls of Fire** P Williams, J Allen, C Chestwig
1986 Apr 9		**Big Greenie** J Silvester, C Dale The opening of the impressive California Wall. In 1994 the route suffered a major rockfall; it was reclimbed and renamed: **Unpaided Bills** J Barton and a certain B Sheen 11.06.94.
1986 Apr 10		**Primal Ice Cream** C Dale, J Silvester
1986 Apr 11		**Slippery People** P Hawkins, D Cuthbertson, J Silvester
1986 Apr 11		**The Madcap Laughs** C Dale, J Silvester
1986 Apr 12		**Espirit de Corps** J Silvester, C Dale
1986 Apr 16		**Greedy Girls** C Dale
1986 Apr 19		**Mad Dog of the West** P Hawkins, J Elliot, R Caves
1986 Apr 20		**Sprint for Print** T Taylor, A Whittal
1986 Apr 20		**Men at Work** P Hawkins, C Parkin
1986 Apr 20		**Goose Creature** A Swann, N Biven, A Jackson, N Yardley
1986 Apr 22		**That Obscure Object of Desire** M Raine
1986 Apr 23		**Ronald Regan Meets Dr Strangelove** L Hardy, M Crook
1986 Apr 24		**Tribal Blow** R Drury, S Britain Originally done with a peg, which was ripped out by a falling Dave Jones. *"The peg reappeared by the time Will Perrin did it but he then removed it afterwards thinking it would go without. He then sent me up on the pretence that there was a good peg to clip, but obviously I didn't find it. I was committed to the crux so I just had to get on with it, with Will pissing himself in the background. Who needs enemies, hey?!"* – Pete Robins
1986 Apr 24		**Loved by a Sneer** R Drury An unintentional onsight solo after bouldering too high. Originally given E7 6b the route was subsequently 'cleaned' into its current state.
1986 Apr 24		**Manic Strain** J Redhead The first F8a on slate, expertly created by the latter-day Michaelangelo. As far as F8a sport routes go it was a few years behind Jerry Moffatt's *Masterclass* ('83) and Ben Moon's *Statement of Youth* ('84) at Pen Trwyn. Nonetheless, F8a was still very much a cutting edge grade in early 1986.
1986 Apr 25		**Ritter Sport** J Redhead, A Newton
1986 Apr 25		**The Gorbals** C Parkin, P Hawkins Originally an ultra bold E5 semi 'chop route', with poor gear behind hollow flakes, and a traverse at mid height to reach the only decent gear. The route was retrobolted in 2006, giving a pleasant E4.
1986 Apr 26		**Hysterectomy** A Swann, D O'Dowd
1986 Apr 26		**Vertigo** T Taylor
1986 Apr 26		**Torrents of Spring** T Taylor
		Wall finish T Taylor 23.05.86. A similar line, **Soda** was climbed by C Phillips in 1985.
1986 Apr 26		**Single Factor** N Biven, A Jackson

332 First Ascents • 1980's

1986 Apr 26	**Genital Persuasion** A Jackson, N Biven	
1986 Apr 26	**Released from Treatment** D Towse, J Redhead, A Newton	
1986 Apr 26	**Ride the Wild Surf** P Williams, D Jones	
	Another tremendous preparatory effort yields a slate classic. Even with the most obvious chipped hold in the quarries the moves passing it are still hard.	
1986 Apr 27	**Cornucopia** T Taylor, A Whittal	
1986 Apr 27	**Senile Delinquent** T Taylor, A Whittal	
1986 Apr 27	**Solvent Abuse** M Crook and a 'cast of thousands'	
	Two spikes were hacked in to offer protection. Redhead seconded the route with the rope attached to his genitals, and Chris Dale followed suit - total commitment!	
1986 May 1	**Digital Delection** L Hardy, G Parfitt	
1986 May 1	**Sanity Fair** C Dale	
1986 May 1	**Sanity Claws** C Dale	
	Soloed, as was *Sanity Fair*, despite the fact that there is some gear.	
1986 May 1	**The Sweetest Taboo** M Raine, J Dawes • Direct start N Gresham, I Lloyd-Jones 28/8/88	
1986 May 1	**Wall of Flame** P Williams, D Lawson	
1986 May 2	**Young and Easy Under the Apple Boughs** J Redhead, M Crook	
1986 May 4	**Heinous Creature** C Dale	
	Another solo from Chris – at least this time the protection is almost non-existent.	
1986 May 5	**Yak Kak** S Haston, R Kay	
	A good example of how innocent exploration can lead to brown trousers.	
1986 May 5	**Youthslayer** L Hardy, G Parfitt, S Anderson	
1986 May 5	**Central Sadness** J Silvester, C Dale	
	One of the great E5s in the quarries.	
1986 May 6	**Binwomen** M Crook	
1986 May 6	**Billy Two Tokes** M Crook, N Craine	
1986 May 6	**Major Headstress** P Williams, C Gilchirst	
1986 May 6	**Down to Zero** C Dale, N Thomas, J Tombs	
1986 May 7	**Love Minus Zero** C Dale	
	Another bold solo.	
1986 May 7	**The Long and Winding Road** M Raine, J Silvester	
	The name refers to the arduous trek in, made all the way from... Llanberis.	
1986 May 10	**Fallout** J Tombs, P Barbier	
1986 May 10	**Sabre Dance; Bungle in the Jungle** C Dale	
1986 May 10	**Is it a Crime?; Never as Good as the First Time** M Raine, C Dale	
	Mike was having a conflict of conscience with regards to the placing of bolts in the quarries. Something he got over in 2006, when he re-equipped his route, placing an extra bolt in *Is it a Crime?* after an old RP placement had worn out. Crime complete?	
1986 May 10	**Wolfhound** P Hawkins, R Deane	
1986 May 10	**Birdman of Cae'r Berllan** R Deane, P Hawkins	
1986 May 10	**Goblin Party** P Williams	
	The end of a busy day for new routes in the quarries.	
1986 May 13	**Ghengis** A Holmes, M Thomas	
	This was subsequently 'altered' when *Short Stories* was climbed, with a bolt low down, and a peg which has subsequently disappeared. Meaning the route is now a bold E5 potential 'chop' route.	
1986 May 14	**Turkey Trot** P Williams	
1986 May 15	**Theftus Maximus** K Strange	
1986 May 16	**Manatese** R Lyon, A Well, M Cluer	
	One of the great slate crack test-pieces. Which gained a much needed lower off in 2006.	

1980's • **First Ascents 333**

1986 May 16	**The Dwarf in the Toilet** J Redhead, M Crook
	Named after a diminutive gentleman offering sexual favours in the toilet of a London Pub.
1986 May 18	**Vivander** C Phillips, P Barbier
1986 May 20	**The Mau Mau** P Williams
	First climbed with two points of aid, and approached by the easier way; it was climbed free and direct after three days of trying. A must do slate crack, captured in Paul Williams' famous photo, captioned: Jim Jewel Versus *The Mau Mau* – No Contest!

1986 May 22	**Feet Apart** M Barnicott
1986 May 22	**A Tourmegamite Experience** C Phillips
1986 May 23	**You Can Dance if You Want To** M Raine
1986 May 23	**Run for Fun** T Taylor
1986 May 25	**Race Against Time** S Britain, P Gilliver
1986 May 25	**Under the Glass** C Phillips
1986 May 27	**The Monster Kitten** S Andrews, S Britain
	Lower-off added during the Foot and Mouth crisis in 2001, which most people now use to top rope the ankle threatening *Ladder Resist*.
1986 May 27	**Green Ernie** M Barnicott
1986 May 27	**Jumping the Gun** M Campbell and party
1986 May 27	**Little Ern** M Barnicott
1986 May 29	**Puff Puff** J Banks, L Naylor
1986 May 30	**Slab and Groove** A Legg, A Milburn
1986 Summer	**Brian Damage** G Hughes
1986 Summer	**Glass Axe** A Woodward
	A desperate (7a!) technical groove which lay undocumented for nearly 25 years! Pete Robins did the probable second ascent in 2009 with protection from the bolts in the adjacent route.
1986 Jun 2	**Child's Play** R Drury
	Originally given E6 6c by Bob.

First Ascents • 1980's

1986 Jun 3	**Pigs in Space** L Hardy, Chief Superintendent J Peck, Detective Constable G Briggs Obviously fans of the Muppets.
1986 Jun 5	**Zambesi** T Taylor Named after Sam Roberts, a local Snowdonia National Park warden.
1986 Jun 5	**Angel on Fire** P Williams, J Dawes
1986 Jun 5	**The Gully** J Tombs A similar route called *The White Room* was climbed somewhere in this area by R Norcross, J Warburton and M Cox in September 1973.
1986 Jun 6	**Celestial Inferno** P Williams, M Barnicott
1986 Jun 6	**Swan Hunter** N Yardley, D O'Dowd, G Smith, P Hawkins, D Hawkins
1986 Jun 8	**Circles are Sound** C Dale
1986 Jun 8	**Cig-Arete** J Dawes, C Dale This route had an extra bolt and a lower off placed in 2006, the extra bolt was needed after a large rockfall raised the ground level by a few metres. Originally given E5 6b by Johnny, Bob Drury downgraded it to E4 6a/b on the second ascent – it is now rated as a tough little F7b!
1986 Jun 9	**Menopausal Discharge** J Redhead Another Redhead sculpture renamed by Paul Williams in the 87 Llanberis guide as *Misogynist's Discharge*. Andy Pollitt also tried to rename the route *Kleinian Envy* after 'eliminating' a traverse to a jug. In the early 90s a super fit Ben Moon flashed the route.
1986 Jun 10	**1000 Tons of Chicken Shite** S Haston Has been re-named *1000 Tonnes of Chicken Shite* due to decimalisation.
1986 Jun 11	**Octopus's Garden** C Dale
1986 Jun 11	**Surfin' USA** C Dale
1986 Jun 14	**Gideon's Way** M Crook, N Craine Named in memory of Gideon Wilson.
1986 Jun 18	**The Illinois Enema Bandit** S Haston, S Andrews A Frank Zappa song title. It commemorates the unusual trademark of a roving American bank robber.
1986 Jun 22	**Jack of Shadows** O Jones, R Whitwell
1986 Jun 25	**Gin Palace** C Smith A line that had repulsed many would-be ascentionists, and still does. Craig originally gave it a grade of: A Struggle 6b!
1986 Jul 3	**Sunk Without a Trace** J Allen, M Stokes Sadly the route has sunk, but there are traces of it all over the levels below.
1986 Jul 3	**Drury Lane** R Drury, J Allen
1986 Jul 4	**DOA** R Drury, J Allen
1986 Jul 4	**Sterling Silver** J Banks, L Naylor, D Clark
1986 Jul 5	**Big Wall Party** J Allen, P Williams

∧ Bob Drury on the first ascent of **Child's Play** F7b, Vivian Quarry photo: Drury collection

∧ Ben Moon making an impressive flash of **Menopausal Discharge** F8a+, Vivian Quarry in '92 photo: Glenn Robbins

1980's • First Ascents 335

1986 Jul 8	**Hooded Cobra** L Hardy, C Parkin	
1986 Jul 9	**The Colour Purple** M Crook, J Dawes	
	The route has been affected by rock fall, meaning the 6c boulder problem start is now no longer feasible.	
1986 Jul 12	**Menai Vice** G Smith, W Rees	
1986 Jul 13	**NE Spur** C Parkin, W Rees	
1986 Jul 13	**Practically Esoteric** N Dixon, A Popp	
	Another climb hits the ground.	
1986 Jul 13	**Slates Slanting Crack** M Raine	
1986 Jul 13	**Lentil in a Stew** P Barbier, R Leishman	
1986 Jul 14	**Fruity Pear in a Veg-Shop Romp** N Dixon, M Crook	
1986 Jul 14	**God Betweens Money** A Williams	
1986 Jul 17	**Light and Darkness** C Dale, N Dixon	
1986 Jul 19	**Freak Yer Beanbag** P Pritchard, P Dowthwaite, S Edmonson	
1986 Jul 24	**Alice Spring** D Holmes, E Wall	
	The first ascentionist was understandably gutted when his only new route in the quarries departed in a fountain of boulders.	
1986 Jul 24	**The Medium** J Dawes	
	Another desperate offering from the king of hard slabs. Johnny rated it as E6/7 7b, but a quick repeat from Tim Clifford saw a down grade to E6 6c/7a- it is now rated F8a. Ryan Pasquill made an impressive flash of the route in 2009.	
1986 Aug 2	**Off the Beaten Track** C Parkin, P Hawkins, G Smith	
	This route was retro bolted in 2006. Originally the route climbed past a RURP to a peg at 20m before climbing up to a bolt. The massive holds on the right were ignored so as not to get in the way of a good dyno for the rail tracks.	
1986 Aug 2	**Here To Stay, Gone Tomorrow** G Smith, C Parkin, P Hawkins	
	A bold offering from Team Railtrack.	
1986 Aug 2	**Above the Line** C Parkin	
1986 Aug 2	**Those who climb clearly marked projects are the kind of people who would steal the chocolate bar from a kid's lunch box - selfish tossers, who owe the bolt fund cash** C Parkin – retrobolted and retronamed in 2008.	
1986 Aug 3	**Red Throated Diver** P Hawkins, R Deane	
1986 Aug 3	**2nd Class Passenger** C Parkin, P Hawkins	
1986 Aug 3	**Watch Me Wallaby Wank, Frank** N Harms, G Alderson	
	The route was re-bolted in the late nineties, the top peg was snapped at around the same time, and was replaced in 2006 by a bolt.	
	"The name was a dare from Paul Pritchard. He reckoned that it was so offensive that either someone would rename it, or it'd never get printed (the new Llanberis guide was in production at the time), or I'd be run out of town or something. In the event the name was abridged, the 'Wank' word being dropped for the Llanberis guide – which sanitised quite a few names." – Nick Harms	
1986 Aug 3	**Stairway to Silence** G Smith, C Parkin	
	George, eager for gear, resorted to snapping an RP and re-knotting the wires to snare a diminutive spike.	
1986 Aug 4	**Between Here and Now** G Smith, P Hawkins, R Deane	
1986 Aug 4	**Waves of Inspiration** C Parkin, P Hawkins, G Smith	
	Another one of slates great E5's. The original ring peg by the lower crux has disappeared (possibly due to a falling climber) and was replaced by a bolt during the first ascent of *The Big Sur*. This was used as a precedent during the re-equipping campaign to replace most pegs with bolts.	

336 First Ascents • 1980's

1986		**Dinorwic Slate Quarries:** The first guide to the quarries was an independent production from Perry Hawkins and George Smith. It was a fairly low key topo guide, but nonetheless it plugged a much needed information gap.
1986 Aug 5		**Gadaffi Duck** R Deane, P Hawkins Originally climbing the overgrown slab to the right, the line now climbs direct to a lower-off. The slab to the right was cleaned and re-bolted as an independent line in 2006.
1986 Aug 10		**The Machine in the Ghost** A Woodward Originally given E7 7a! It was subsequently chipped down to a more mundane 6a.
1986 Aug 12		**Now or Never** G Smith, P Hawkins
1986 Aug 12		**Turn of the Century** P Hawkins, G Smith
1986 Aug 16		**Vermin on the Ridiculous** G Smith Comically undergraded at E4 – current thinking is that it may be F7b/+!
1986 Aug 17		**Big Bendy Buddha** A Whittall and party
1986 Aug 17		**Lesser Mortals** S Siddiqui, I Jones, P Stone
1986 Aug 22		**Wakey, Wakey, Hands off Snakey** P Barbier
1986 Aug 23		**Moving Being** N Harms, J Barbier
1986 Sep 7		**The Toms Approach** R Drury, M Ingle, K Toms
1986 Sep 8		**The Take Over by Dept. C** N Harms, G Hughes The route originally finished by padding up the upper slab.
1986 Sep 8		**Sleight of Hand** M Thomas
1986 Sep 8		**Jaded Passion** M Thomas, S Jones
1986 Sep 9		**Stump Rogers** R Drury, A Amos
1986 Sep 10/11		**The Quarryman** J Dawes, R Drury After falling from the top crux for the third time Johnny was heard to utter: *"For god's sake, are you a foothold or not!?"* Johnny's slate masterpiece became the centre piece of Al Hughes seminal climbing film, Stone Monkey. In 2008 Pete Robins repeated all of the pitches, but not in one day. In 2011 Steve McClure managed a full one day ascent.
1986 Sep 12		**Mud Slide Slim; Breakdance; Blue Horizon** F Ferrero, D King One of these routes has a bolt placed but has sadly been overtaken by vegetation. The use of a bolt on an easy route was a dig at the many VS/HVS lines soloed by some of the top climbers in the quarries. Making the climbing somewhat elitist!
1986 Sep 14		**Shame and Embarrassment** J Dawes, T Hodgson Another route 'stolen'. The story goes that Paul Williams wishing to get the route into the next guidebook told Johnny that Chris Parkin was happy to have him climb the route whilst he was on holiday! *"It really was a tottering pile of shit. I was pulling holds off it all the way up. That's the real reason it got its name!"* - Trev Hodgson
1986 Sep 15		**The Listening and Dancing** T Hodgson, M Thomas *"This is not as serious as when I did the first ascent because you can now clip the bolt on Cig Arete. I did it ground up and it felt pretty ballsy at the time."* - Trev Hodgson
1986 Sep 17		**Where are my Sensible Shoes** M Thomas This route was full equipped as a sport route in 2006.
1986 Sep 21		**Sad Old Red** C Parkin, G Smith
1986 Sep 21		**Simply Peach** G Smith, C Parkin, D O'Dowd
1986 Sep 22		**The Fire Escape** J Dawes

Johnny's hand drawn Quarryman topo from > the Pete's Eats new routes book.

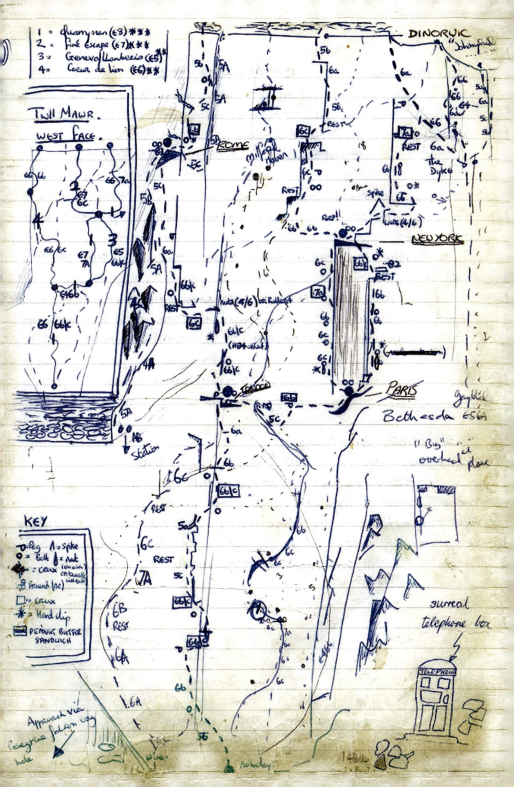

338 First Ascents • 1980's

1986 Sep 29	**Saved by the Whole** C J Phillips	
1986 Sep 29	**Daddy Rabbit** G Smith, A Swann	

Named after the graffiti in the old toilet at the top of the route.

"*I actually saw my own route fall down from Rallt Goch hill in Llanberis!*" - George Smith. The rock fall revealed the line of *The Serpent Vein* which was climbed by James McHaffie in 2007.

1986 Sep 30	**Tongue in Situ** C Phillips
1986 Oct	**Minder** W Wayman, M Barnicott, M Hardwick
1986 Oct	**Arthur Dali** M Barnicott, W Wayman
1986 Oct	**Twm Dre** M Barnicott, W Wayman

The reinforcing rods have since disappeared, and the line was re-climbed totally free by Shane Ohly and S Warren in 2000 at E6 6b and renamed *Charlie Rock'n Roll*.

1986 Oct 6	**John Verybiglongwords** P William, S Howe
1986 Oct 11	**Rock Video** B Wayman, F Crook
1986 Oct 11	**Grandads Rib** F Crook, B Wayman
1986 Oct 11	**Coy Mistress** B Wayman, F Crook
1986 Oct 12	**Salvador; Dali Mirror; Dali Express** B Wayman, F Crook
1986 Oct 12	**Cuts like a Knife** B Wayman, J de Montjoye
1986 Oct 13	**Clap Please** R Drury, A McSherry

An oft-tried problem; the first ascentionist nearly decked out on an early attempt.

1986 Oct 15	**Dangling by the Diddies** C Phillips, N Thomas
1986 Oct 15	**Pain Killer** M Raine, S Howe
1986 Oct 15	**The Barrel of Laughs** M Raine, S Howe
1986 Oct 15	**Her Indoors** M Hardwick, M Barnicott, W Wayman
1986 Oct 28	**Mental Lentils** J Barbier

A very popular climb, which now displays a highly buffed sheen.

1986 Nov 3	**Come off it Arfer** G Barnicott, M Barnicott
1986 Nov 3	**Rycott** M Barnicott, G Barnicott
1986 Nov 3	**Poetry in Motion** P Jiggins, P Dunkley
1986 Nov 3	**Cabbage Man meets the Flying Death Leg** P Pritchard, G Hughes

Paul had great interest in the Brassica family at the time.

1986 Nov 20	**Yuk Hunter** M Barnicott, T Taylor
1986 Dec 6	**Psychodelicate** G Smith, C Parkin

A rock fall at the start appears to have altered the route. It was re-bolted in 2007 to accommodate a new start. It was then re-climbed at F7c by Calum Muskett in April 2010.

"*It's a fantastic route, maybe three stars. I managed it onsight somehow and there seemed to be two distinct crux moves of British 6c. The first crux is between the fourth and fifth bolts and I'm not going to tell anyone how to do it but it's a great problem solving exercise.*" – Calum Muskett

1987	**Resurrection Shuffle** THE Impostor, D Dutton
1987 Jan 1	**Darkness Visible** G Smith, D O'Dowd
1987 Jan 7	**L'Allumette** J Dawes, P Pritchard

A brilliant piece of three dimensional climbing from Johnny.

1987 Jan 29	**When the Wind Blows** P Hawkins, A George
1987 Feb 11	**Long Distance Runner** M Murray, R Austin
1987 Feb 14	**Chewing the Cwd** P Pritchard, T Jones, M Thomas

described in the '92 guide as having "little or no protection in its upper half."

"*This comment is untrue. The route is of a similar nature to the other E5's on this Slab. The only reason Paul Pritchard managed to fall 70' off is, is due to being drunk*" – Adam Wainwright

1987 Feb 16	**Remain in Light** R Austin, R Brookes	
1987 Feb 20	**The Great Curve** R Brookes, R Austin	

This and the previous route had a bolt added below the first that they both share. All other fixed gear was re-equipped in 2006.

1987 Feb 21	**Giddy Variation on a Theme** C Phillips	

The must do line of the slab, hidden for years under a poor one line description. *"Etive slabs come to Llanberis!"* – Mike Raine

1987 Feb 21	**Big Sur** G Smith, C Parkin	

Another stunning addition to the California Wall by Big G - not bad for a man who claims to dislike face climbing!

1987 — **Llanberis:** Paul Williams' classic 1987 Llanberis guide included a large section devoted to the slate quarries. Suddenly Welsh slate was in vogue and visitors flocked to it from all over the UK.

1987 Feb 22	**Return of the Visitor** P Hawkins, G Smith	
1987 Feb 26	**Nifty Wild Ribo** C Phillips, S Andrews	
1987 Feb 27	**The Chiselling** N Harms, M Anthoine	

"People assume that this route is chipped, but it's not. Although a large amount of compacted shite (mud and rubble) was removed from the crack, no chisel was employed. The name is actually a derivation of someone's name who lived in the village." – Nick Harms

1987 Feb 28	**Telescopic Stem Master** N Harms, P Pritchard	

"When I wrote this up, Paul Williams had a bit of a go, saying it was a waste of time (it being so short) I said I'd rather do 20' of perfect climbing than 150' of dull jug pulling, i.e. Colossus!" – Nick Harms

1987 Mar	**Crossville** A Moss, K Neal
1987 Mar	**Pandora Plays Sax** S Haston, R Kay

A return to Gideon's great slab.

1987 Mar 3	**Silver Shadow** R Brookes, M Murray

The ascent of *Rock Dancer's Daughter* at a later date has made the route a different proposition to the one faced by Brookes and Murray, although it is still reasonably wiggy.

1987 Mar 10	**Standby G-L** J Dawes, M Thomas

The right arête of the Quarryman groove, since incorporated into *The Wonderful World of Walt Disney*.

1987 Mar 21	**Making Plans for Nigel** M Crook, J Tombs, M Boniface
1987 Mar 21	**Pitch Two** C Parkin, G Smith
1987 Mar 28	**Coeur De Lion** J Dawes, J Tombs

Another tour de force from Johnny on the Twll Mawr Quarryman Wall.

1987 Mar 29	**The Climbing Pains of Adrian Mole** T Hodgson, M Hodgson, T Jones
1987 Apr	**Geronimo's Cadillac** R Kay, S Haston

Serious territory.

1987 Apr	**Scoop Dragon** J Dawes

Final pitch of *The Wonderful World of Walt Disney*.

1987 Apr	**Johnny Said** M Raine, J Dawes

A sadly departed route that disappeared along with a few thousands tonnes of rock, into the depths of Twll Mawr after a particularly heavy rainstorm.

1987 Apr	**Young Man Afraid of Horses** S Haston, R Kay
1987 Apr	**One Wheel on My Wagon** S Haston, M Raine
1987 Apr	**Split the Dog** S Haston, G Hughes, M Raine
1987 Apr 2	**Laund Arete** N Harms
1987 Apr 2	**Short Stories** S Howe, S Harland

A long reach or a short jump allows the finishing holds to be gained.

340 First Ascents • 1980's

1987 Apr 5	**Ultra Cricket Zone** T Hodgson, M Wagg, T Jones	
1987 Apr 5	**Earwig Ho** M Raine, J Turner	
1987 Apr 11	**The Dyke** J Dawes, M Raine	
1987 Apr 12	**Sombre Music** G Smith, P Hawkins	
1987 Apr 14	**Over the Rainbow** M Raine, M Campbell	
1987 Apr 20	**Faulty Towers** T Dale, C Dale	
1987 Apr 27	**I Ran the Bath** P Pritchard *"Flash it or splash it!"*	
1987 Apr 28	**Fat Lad Exam Failure** N Harms	
	Regular spills of slate fall down this route from above, occasionally followed by the goats and sheep that start them. The route is also in close proximity to a recent large rock fall.	
1987 May 1	**NW Face of the Druid** T Hodgson, S Chesslett	
	An impressive onsight ascent of the imposing wall that rises the full height of the green haven of The Lost World. The poor peg on the first pitch was removed by hand during the ascent of *The Colridge Effect*.	
	"Originally there was a stack of 3 pegs at floor level on the right wall of the first tunnel. I did this all in one pitch and this was pretty much the only runner apart from a poor upside down blade above. I subsequently replaced the 3 pegs with an iron bar when we went back to have some photos taken. On the first ascent I carried loads of pegs, so many in fact that they were pulling my harness off me. But then typically hardly used any of them!" - Trev Hodgson	
1987 May	**Grey Slab** A Grey, C Dale	
	An attempt at introducing easy bolted routes to the quarry was foiled by the easy start falling off.	
1987 May	**Lost Castle of My Desires** S Haston, J Tombs, M Hagler	
	Stevie claimed this super steep route to be the hardest offwidth he'd ever done: *"Without doubt the most shag nasty, brutal mind fucking crack around."* It fell down later that year.	
1987 May	**Ride of the Valkyries** L Hardy, I Stevens, C Ayres	
1987 May	**Mildy Macho** S Haston, G Jones	
1987 May	**My Halo** N Dixon	
	"Originally given E8 6c, I repeated it and downgraded it to E7 6b, about 2 - 3 days after the first ascent I think." – Nick Harms	
	The RP slot by the crux is now perished, a poor skyhook offers little solice. The route was onsighted by Leo Houlding in the late 90s.	
1987 May	**Prometheus Unbound** C Dale, P1 belayed by A Grey, J Silvester seconded the P2.	
	A fine line in an unparalleled situation.	
1987 May 13	**Hollow Heart** R Brooks	
1987 May 20	**Nick the Chisel** T Hodgson	
	"The holds on this have been significantly improved since the first ascent. The porthole is more positive and the borehole above has been altered so that it can be held much lower and is bigger. When I did it you had to slap for a mono at the top of the borehole. Easily the hardest move I've ever done (at least on slate). 7a for sure! I was soloing it too and each time I fell off I'd crunch my ankles." – Trev Hodgson	
	The route has had numerous bolts placed over the years and the line was straightened out in 2006 by retro bolting the top to a new lower-off.	
1987 May 20	**Spider Pants** G Smith, D O'Dowd	
	"A back rope can be fixed from the top of Central Sadness to cheer up the second man." – George Smith	
1987 Jun 4	**Bathtime** P Pritchard	
	"Twice a year whether I need one or not." – Paul Pritchard	
1987 Jun	**Brewing up with Morley Wood** M Crook, G Smith	
	A tribute to the comedy chockstone. Bring your own sheep's head.	

1987 Jun	**Ari Hol Hi** C Waddy, D Crilley
1987 Jun	**The Woodflower** G Smith, M Crook
1987 Jun 20	**'F' Hot** K Hawker
1987 Jun 21	**How Hot is Your Chilli?** S Lumley
1987 Jul	**Buffalo Smashed in Head Jump**
1987 Jul 2	**The Wonderful World of Walt Disney** R Drury, J Dawes, A Popp
1987 Jul 2	**The Gay Blade** J Dawes, R Drury
1987 Jul 24	**Menage a Trois** M Raine
1987 Aug 12	**Midnight Flier** B Wayman, G Landless
1987 Aug 24	**G'Day Arete; Road to Botany Bay** M Turner, C Goodey Another new area investigated and a popular classic unearthed.
1987 Sep 3	**Jack the Ripper** J Jackson
1987 Sep 27	**The Spleenal Flick** N Harms
1987 Sep 27	**Le Cochon** A Maddison, J Martin
1987 Sep 27	**Simion Street** A Maddison, J Martin
1987 Sep 27	**Velvet Walk** A Maddison, J Martin
1987 Oct	**Private Smells** P Pritchard, N Harms • Direct Start P Pritchard 31.12.87 A tough little number that has seen some serious airtime from various leaders.
1987 Oct 3	**Stretch Class** G Landless, B Wayman, M Rudolph, D Kirton
1987 Oct 11	**Geordie War Cry** B Wayman, D Kirton, M Barnicott A very popular route up this wall - something to do with the easy access and bolts perhaps?
1987 Oct 23	**Homicidal Hamster from Hell** P Pritchard A desperate bridging problem – possibly unrepeated?
1987 Oct 26	**On Shite** S Jones, T Kay
1987 Oct 28	**Scare City** T Kay, P Pritchard
1987 Oct 29	**Gay Lightweights and Hetro Stumpies** E Stone, P Johnstone
1987 Oct 30	**Scratching the Beagle** R Deane, P Hawkins
1987 Nov 3	**Golden Shower; Tower of Power** N Harms
1987 Nov 5	**The Shark that Blocked the Drain** S Jones An extremely bold route, originally given E5, but quite possibly E7!
1987 Nov 6	**The Moth to the Flame** A Woodward
1987 Nov 27	**Cure for a Sick Mind** P Pritchard A desperate and bold addition from Paul.
1987 Dec 1	**Prick Up Ureas** N Harms, P Barbier
1987 Dec 3	**Conquistadors** B Wayman, J De Montjoye
1987 Dec 11	**Truffle Hunters Roof** P Johnstone, D J Cuthbertson, K Read One of the finest slate roofs – *one of the only slate roofs* (Ed).
1987 Dec 14	**Memorable Stains** P Pritchard A hold may well have fallen off this route, making the climbing considerably harder, most people now escape left up the groove.
1987 Dec 15	**The Drowning Man** R Deane, P Hawkins This route was retro bolted in 2006, to make a sport route.
1988	**Captain Black and the Mystersons** I A Jones, S Howe
1988	**Wobbly Variations on a Slab** M Boniface, J Webb
1988 Jan	**Sylvester Still-born** P Johnstone
1988 Jan 5	**Zippy's First Acid Trip** I Wallace, M Boniface
1988 Jan 15	**The Turkey Chant** P Johnstone, P Pritchard

342 First Ascents • 1980's

1988 Jan 22	**Soap on a Rope** P Pritchard, P Johnstone
1988 Jan 24	**Boody Building** P Pritchard, P Johnstone
1988 Jan 26	**Booby Building** P Johnstone, P Pritchard
1988 Jan 27	**Sesame St. Comes to Llanberis** P Johnstone, P Pritchard
1988 Jan 31	**Occam's Razor** I A Jones, D Hawkins, S Howe
	'A sad case of a misplaced bolt'- was the comment in the previous guidebook. What would they say now?
1988 Feb 7	**Envy** R Deane, I A Jones
1988 Feb 12	**Emerald Eyes** R Deane
1988 Feb 12	**Pork Torque** R Deane, P hawkins, S Howe
1988 Feb 13	**Walrus Wipeout** I A Jones, R Deanes
1988 Feb 14	**Unchain My Heart** R Deane, P Johnstone, I A Jones
1988 Feb 20	**Another Wasted Journey** P Jenkinson, J McKim, G Howard
	Climbed as a consolation prize after Paul was repeatedly rained off the main prize hereabouts, a line which 20 years later became the ultra classic *Wish You Were Here*.
1988 Feb 23	**Coming up for Air** P Hawkins, E Stone
1988 Mar 1	**Foetal Attraction** E Stone, M Taylor
1988 Mar 23	**Demolition Derby** P Jenkinson, M Boniface
	This climbed a 'Geant' or tottering fin in Bus Stop Quarry, where the only way of was to reverse the blocky horror show. Fortunately it fell down.
1988 Mar 28	**Forsinain Motspur** T Hodgson, S Jones
	A remarkable route, the title taken from the definitions within 'The Meaning of Liff' by Douglas Adams.
	"This was done ground up over a series of visits. The top section was much bolder then as there was one less bolt up there. I took the fall right from the top and I landed about 3m of the deck with Bull level with me!" - Trev Hodgson
1988 Apr	**Brinwell** P Pritchard, S Cheslett
1988 Apr	**Pit and the Pendulum** I A Jones, T Mitchell
1988 Apr 2	**Stay Big** P Hawkins
	A boulder problem on the banned Trango Tower.
1988 Apr 5	**Ancestral Vices** P Williams, N Carson, D Carson, S Kerr
1988 Apr 6	**Jai'a'n** N Harms, J Anthoine
1988 Apr 6	**Artichokes, Artichokes** P Pritchard
1988 Apr 10	**Sucked Away with the Scum** P Pritchard
1988 Apr 11	**The Dyke** J Dawes, M Raine
	"I used a different sequence to Johnny which upset him as I thought the pitch was easier than he found it, so he abbed back in and chipped off the offending hold!" – Mike Raine
1988 Apr 12	**Teliffant** G Hughes, T Kay, C Phillips, N Rice
1988 Apr 12	**The Hong Jagged Route of Death** C Phillips, G Hughes, N Rice
	It is all in the name, if you don't fall off leading, and don't knock any blocks off on your seconds, and if the route doesn't fall on you...you may well survive this epic.
1988 Apr 13	**Bobby's Groove** J Dawes
	After many attempts by Bob Drury, Johnny eventually solved this desperate problem. An undercut was removed in recent years, making the move a little harder, but not impossible. The hold was a mantelpiece ornament for several years.
1988 Apr 13	**Heatseeker** P Hawkins
1988 Apr 19	**Medicine Show** A Newton, K Griffiths, I MacMillan
1988 Apr 20	**Where the Green Ants Dream** E Stone
1988 Apr 21	**The Madness** A Newton, K Griffiths, P Johnstone • Two Tone start A Newton, P Johnstone 05.05.88
1988 Apr 23	**Wishing Well** P Pritchard

1980's • **First Ascents** 343

1988 Apr 23	**Far from the Madding Crowd** P Jenkinson, P Hiscock	
1988 Apr 25	**Beijqueiro** J Dawes	

Quite an undertaking considering its position.

1988 Apr 26	**Phil's Harmonica** J Dawes	
1988 Apr 27	**The Untouchables** J Dawes	

Is this a highball boulder problem? Some suggested it was after it saw its first solo ascent in Oct 2006 by the super talented Neil Dyer.

1988 Apr 27	**A Tourmegamite Experience** C Phillips
1988 Apr 30	**Order of the Bath** P Pritchard, E Stone
1988 May	**Aubergines, Aubergines** M Boniface, I Wallis
1988 May 8	**Psychotherapy** A Newton, P Pritchard
1988 May 8	**Age Concern** C Goodey, S Goodey
1988 May 11	**Imperial Leather** P Pritchard, S Jones, T Kay
1988 May 14	**Working up a Lather** S Jones, P Pritchard, M Thomas, T Kay
1988 May 18	**Pas de Chevre** N Harms

A stunning technical exercise; short but very intense!

"Like the vast majority (nay all) of my routes no one paid any attention to it at the time. It's still a route I'm rather proud of." - Nick Harms

1988 May 22   **Ladder Resist** N Harms, J Anthoine

Originally undergraded, the route's one and only bolt occurs after the crux at ankle snapping height, as some climbers have found out to their cost!

1988 Jun	**Good Crack** G Smith
1988 Jun	**The Bone People** J Silvester, C Dale

A sadly forgotten classic, although recent activity from Pete Harrison in this area looks likely to change that.

1988 Jun 16	**Uhuru for Mandela** M Boniface, A Garland
1988 Jun 18	**Jugs Mawr** G Turner, A Wells, J Wilson
1988 Jun 19	**The Sponge that Walked Away** C Phillips, D Jones
1988 Jul	**Rastaman Vibration** M Boniface, I Wallace
1988 Jul	**Watching the Sin Set** T Kay, S Jones, N Harms
1988 Jul	**Satisfying Frank Bruno** P Pritchard

A brilliant manufactured route with strong echoes of the type of pocketed sport routes that Paul had been doing on his holidays in France!

1988 Jul	**Pocketeering** P Pritchard
1988 Jul 2	**The Bridge Across Forever** C Dale, T Hodgson

"Chris is huge and when he shouted down how to do the moves it didn't make any sense to me as he had at least a foot reach on me." – Trev Hodgson

1988 Jul 8	**Razorback** D Moore
1988 Aug	**Dope on a Rope** T Kay, J Taylor
1988 Aug	**The Moon Head Egg Monster from Allsop** N Smith, A Bond
1988 Aug 3	**Cwms the Dogfish** N Harms

Another excellent hard line from the master of slate clip ups.

"Everyone thought it was chipped, even though it barely had any cleaning done on it at all. I weedled a couple of loose bits of slate out of the slots on the middle slab and it was ready to go." - Nick Harms

1988 Aug 25	**Spread 'Em** C Phillips
1988 Aug 28	**Sweetest Taboo direct start** N Gresham, I Lloyd-Jones
1988 Sep	**Colostomy** G Farquhar, G Ettle
1988 Sep	**Monster Hamburger Eats Alien Baby** N Harms, P Barbier

344 First Ascents • 1980's

∧ Danny Dutton on the first ascent of the super thin **Putting on Ayres** E4 6b, Australia photo: Andy Woodward
Paul Pritchard making an early repeat of **Shazalzabon** E5 6b, Colossus Wall photo: Glenn Robbins ∧

1988 Sep 3	**Tribulation to Bob Marley and Peter Tosh** M Boniface, A Shaw	
1988 Sep 16	**Midnight Drives** J Beasant	
1988 Sep 18	**Tennents Creek; Franzia; Fetzer** I Hassell, J Smithies	
1988 Sep 18	**A Mere Trifle; Fruity Pear Get Just Desserts** N Harms, J Anthoine	
1988 Sep 19	**True Clip** N Harms	
1988 Oct 1	**Harveys Brassed Off Team** A Cummings, M Adams	
1988 Oct 20	**The Coming of Age** P Jenkinson, N Harms	
1988 Nov	**Blah De Blah De Blah** J Webb, M Boniface	
1988 Nov 11	**Scheherazade** N Harms, C Stephenson	
1989	**Arrampicata Speiligone** C Phillips, M Boniface	
1989 Jan 1	**Break Dance** A Wainwright	

A final hard and serious line on this now crowded slab. Repeated by Paul Jenkinson.

"When I first moved to Llanberis in the late 80s I was given the nick name 'Splat' as the older climbers assumed that, sooner or later, that was exactly what would happen to me!" – Adam Wainwright

1989 Jan	**The Time Bandit** P Jiggins
1989 Feb 22	**Old Fogies Never Die** C J Phillips, P Bagnall
1989 Mar 26	**Putting on Ayres** D Dutton, C Stephenson

A gruesomely technical addition that sees regular failures.

1989 Mar 27 **Chitra** N Harms
Yet another ultra classic clip up from Nick. Sadly the start has been filled in by two separate rock falls, although the upper crux section remains intact.

1980's • **First Ascents** 345

1989 Easter	**Spong (is good for you)** N Dixon
	A rare thing indeed - a route that is easier for the short!
1989 Apr 1	**The North Face of the Aga** K Simpson, S Winstanley, C Stephenson, R Pink
1989 Apr 1	**Snoopy** C Stephenson
	That pile of rocks you step over as you emerge onto The Gorbals level!
1989 Apr	**Out of Africa** D Dutton, C Stephenson, S Winstanley
1989 Apr	**Mu Hat Mu Ganja** M Boniface
1989 Apr	**If You Want** A Shaw, M Boniface
1989 Apr 15	**Too Bald to be Bold** K Simpson, S Winstanley
1989 May	**More Bolts Please** R Newcombe, H Walmsley, P Bolger
	The original line of the *Walls Come Tumbling Down* slab
1989 May 6	**Shtimuli** C Dale, A Dale, P Colquohoun
1989 May 9	**Two Bolts or Not To Be** S Scully
1989 Jun	**A Good Slate Roof** R Newcombe, H Walmsley
1989 Jun	**Alsa's Edge** R Newcombe, A Newcombe
	The arête of the *Walls Come Tumbling Down* slab
1989 Jun 18	**Put it on the Slate, Waiter; The Shining; Sprint Finish** C Allen, R Wright
1989 Jun 18	**Up the Garden Path** R Wright, C Allen
1989 jun 25	**Chariots of fire** J Brown, D H Jones
1989 Jul 16	**Shazalzabon** B Gregory, I Barton, D Gregory • P2 by the same team on 22.07.89.
1989 Jul 17	**Wedlock Holiday** G McMahon, C Dale
	A good find to round off the honeymoon. Has since gained quite a reputation for stopping hotshots dead in their tracks.
1989 Aug 3	**Piper at the Gates of Dawn** T Forster
1989 Sep	**Jossypuss** R Kay, J Tombs
1989 Sep	**See Yer Bruce** L Lovatt, M Podd, P Warsop
	Retro bolted in 2006, adding one bolt before the first and one above the previous last bolt. This gave 5 bolts in 25m, so still no sport route!
1989 Sep 17	**Youthanasia** M Podd, L Lovatt
	"Youth is wasted on the young!" - Matt Podd (quoting George Bernard Shaw)
1989 Sep 17	**Dog Day Dogfish** J Tombs, A Shaw
1989 Sep 23	**The Methane Monster** C Davies, M Wells
1989 Sep 24	**Rhyfelwr** I Lloyd-Jones, S Salter
1989 Oct	**Kookaburra Waltz** D Dutton, C Stephenson
	An eliminate line up the slab.
1989 Oct	**Short Staircase to the Stars** D Dutton
1989 Oct	**Lob Scouse** D Dutton, C Stephenson
	The security fence erected in 2009 effectively eliminated the route.
1989 Oct 13	**Second Chance** R Wright
1989 Oct 14	**Immac Groove** C Davies, P Targett, C Stephenson
1989 Oct 21	**The Australian** C Davies, P Targett, M Wells
	For years described incorrectly as being on the level below.
1989 Oct 21	**Laund Arete** C Davies, P Targett, M Wells
	Yet another one – imagination in overdrive! Any more for Anymore?
1989 Oct 21	**M.I.L Arete** P Targett, C Davies
1989 Nov	**Paradise Lost** N Harms, S Young • Direct start C Davies 13.04.91.
1989 Nov	**Solitude Standing** P Targett, C Stephenson, G Oliver, D Dutton
1989 Nov	**Aultimer's Groove** K Goodey, C Goodey
1989 Nov	**Steve Lineman** M Boniface

346 First Ascents • 1980/1990's

1989 Nov 5	**Blue Touch Paper** P Targett	
1989 Nov 25	**Eric the Fruitbat** D Dutton, C Stephenson, G Oliver, P Targett	
1989 Dec 9	**Smokeless Zone** C Davies, M Wells, P Targett, C Stephenson	
1989 Dec 23	**Tentative Decision** C Davies, P Targett	
	The grade of this route seems to cause endless disagreement - what say you?	
1989 Dec 29	**Balance of Power** C Davies, B Davies	

1990	**Llanberis Slate:** In keeping with his mission to populate the quarries with first class sport routes, Nick Harms was the first to produce a guide which included sport grades, even for non-clip up routes.	
1990 Mar	**Fireside Attraction** B Davies	
	Unknown route.	
1990 May	**Near Dark (After Dark)** A Newton, K Griffiths	
1990 May	**Ya Twisting Ma Melon Man** M Boniface, A Shaw	
1990 May	**Giddy One** C Parkin, C Ayres	
	Previously climbed as *Ladybird Girl* S Haston, A Haston some time in 1987.	
1990 May 19	**The Sneaking** J Barton, B Gregory	
1990 May 20	**The Hobbit** B Gregory, J Barton	
	A fine line up a sombre wall, that is now in dire need of a clean.	
1990 Jul 2	**The New Salesman** C Parkin, S Long	
1990 Jul 3	**Arnie Meets the Swamp Monster** C Jex, N Manning	
1990 Jul 3	**Toilet Trouble** N Butterworth, C Jex	
1990 Jul 3	**Stinky Boots** N Manning, N Butterworth	
1990 Jul 3	**The Very Big and the Very Small** J Dawes	
	Johnny's parting shot, before he went to college remains the hardest route in the quarries. Second ascent Steve McClure 1998.	
	"This was originally my project. I'd spent a while working it, eventually doing it with one fall. I had a bunch of projects on the go, some of which were bolted, others just in my head. I got mightily fed up with it, I couldn't get the right shoes, was fed up with the weather and seeing as almost everyone had lost interest in the quarries it was incredibly difficult to get anyone to come up and belay, so in the end I let Johnny do it. I've regretted it ever since." - Nick Harms	
1990 Jul 8	**Wond** C Phillips, P Thornhill	
1990 Jul 23	**Nice Guy** A Evans	
1990 Jul 25	**Wave Out on the Ocean** A Evans, S Bennett	
1990 Sep 13	**Loony Toons** S Puroy, C Fowler, E Thomas	
1990 Oct	**Donald Duck** I Lloyd-Jones	
1990 Oct 7	**Igam Ogam** I Lloyd-Jones, C Davies	
	Once described as altering the top of *Never Never Land*, however there is written evidence that the top of that route used to be home to three pegs! The name is Welsh for 'Zig Zag'.	
1990 Oct 7	**Squashing the Acropods** C Davies, I Lloyd-Jones	
	The easier, more logical way to climb the slab, a hairs breadth left of *Kookaburra Waltz*.	
1990 Nov 20	**Psychic Sidekick; Toad of Toad Hall** P Targett, C Stephenson	
1990 Nov 20	**Crucified By Bolts** C Davies	
1990 Nov 27	**The Dark Half** N Harms	
	Nick produces yet another three star classic sport route. Looking back now he was clearly a man ahead of his time.	

1990's • First Ascents

1990 Dec 11	**Bungles Arete** S Myles	

Another desperate line from a gifted climber. Second ascent Leo Holding 1998.
Sean had a habit of popping up in North Wales and picking off great projects; go and check out *The Ogwen Crack* E7/8/F8a+ on Braich Ty Du and the *Freedwm Roof* E7 6c on Castell Cidwm for further evidence of his talent.

1991 Feb 16	**Genevive; Pontiac Arete; Stretched Limo** C Allen, R Wight
1991 Mar	**The Weetabix Connection** C Jex, L Zablocki

Controversial because of its proximity to *Bobby's Groove*. The bolts were removed but then reappeared. The newly cleaned holds did allow access to a rest from *Bobby's Groove*, however when a local pulled off an undercut from the crux this was no longer an issue.

1991 Easter	**The Wooley (Or Won't He) Jumper** J Webb, M Boniface
1991 Apr 3	**Paradise Lost Direct Start** I Lloyd-Jones, C Davies
1991 Apr 5	**Rodent to Nowhere** N Ratcliffe, A Butchart
1991 Apr 13	**The Dark Destroyer** M Pretty

Slate was definitely in vogue with the top Sheffield climbers during this period. Right on cue Zippy made his mark with a typically excellent route.

1991 Apr 17	**Colditz** S Myles, M Pretty
1991 Apr 20	**Brief Encounter** I Lloyd-Jones, B Llywelyn
1991 Apr 21	**Just For Fun** I Lloyd-Jones, C Davies
1991 Apr 27	**Meltdown** T Taylor, A Barton
1991 May 11	**Walls Come Tumbling Down** C Jex, I Lloyd-Jones

...and they did! The route has suffered a catastrophic collapse, and there threatens to be another one soon, so don't hang around in this area.

1991 May 11	**Y Rybelwr** I Lloyd-Jones
1991 May 14	**Jex's Fumbled Clippin'n Arete** I Lloyd-Jones, C Jex, P Targett

This route appears like it will collapse at some point, and should be avoided. It will not be re-equipped for this reason.

1991 May 20	**Y Gwaedlyd** I Lloyd-Jones, E Jones
1991 May 21	**Silent Home Coming** P Targett, I Lloyd-Jones
1991 Jun 7	**Dalis lemming Ducklings** I Lloyd-Jones
1991 Jun 21	**The Rock Dancer's Daughter** M Delafield, C Goodey, D Goodey

This clip up affected the protection on *Silver Shadow*, the original line up the arete.

Mark Delafield on the first ascent of **The Rock Dancer's Daughter** F7a+, Rainbow Walls Upper photo: Colin Goodey

1991 Jun 29	**The Man Who fell to Earth (From the Planet Zzzoink)** I Lloyd-Jones
1991 Jul 5	**Astroman from the Planet Zzzoink** N Manning
1991 Jul 6	**Planet Zzzoink Arete** I Lloyd-Jones
1991 Jul 6	**No Problem** I Lloyd-Jones
1991 Jul 7	**Diagonal Dilemma** I Lloyd-Jones
1991 Jul 17	**Abus Dangereux** M Mariner, M Nuttal
1991 Jul 19	**Tower of Laughter** I Lloyd-Jones, C Jex
1991 Jul 25	**Karabiner Cruise** P Targett
1991 Aug 8	**The Burning** P Targett, M Turner
1991 Aug 28	**Dried Mouth Frog; Dried Mouth Seasame Seed** K Turner, L Dow
1991 Nov 15	**Caledulwch** P Littlejohn, P Judge

348 First Ascents • 1990's

1991 Dec 20	**The Mark of Thor** N Walton, S Jones	
1992 Jan 1	**Blockhead** A Wainwright, M Thomas	

A fiercely difficult route, which despite making the back cover of the 1999 guide failed to attract a repeat ascent. "This route was never properly documented due to the new routes book being stolen just after Blockhead was written up – which was a shame as it is a brilliant route (should I say so myself)" – Adam Wainwright

1992 **Slate - a climbers guide:** A small black and white production released in '92. The absence of action shots meant it painted a rather dour picture of the quarries.

1992	**Power Tool Resurrection** T Taylor
1992 Jan 19	**The Velociraptor** C McClean and party
1992 Mar 4	**The Manimal** G Sewell, J Cleford
1992 Mar 23	**La Voleur** S Mayers
1992 Apr 23	**Patellaectomy** C Parkin, M Robinson

A references to Chris' ongoing battle with knee injuries!

1992 Apr 26	**Legal Murder** C Parkin, F Ball
1992 Apr 26	**Cyclone B** F Ball, C Parkin

One of the party is a mad scientist, the other just barking!

1992 Apr 29	**The Color Purple; Lethal Injection** C Parkin, J Smallwood
1992 Oct	**The Great and Secret Show** I D Dutton
1993	**In the Line of Fire** S Mayers
1993	**Running Scared** S Mayers

A pair of hard additions from Steve who then claimed, albeit many years later, that he could barely remember what they were, never mind what grade they might be!

1993	**Goodbye Natterjack Toad** T Taylor, A Hughes
1993	**New Rays from an Ancient Sun** J Howel

An extremely serious aid route which features a deadly detached shield of rock. Amazingly it has had three repeats – one by the first ascentionist, one by Andy Kirkpatrick (One of his first aid routes!), and one by Andy Scott who described it as the most lethal route he'd ever experienced!

1993 Jan 28	**Wizz-Bang** C P Smith, P Doyle

An inexplicably popular route lacking any sort of conventional/independent line.

1993 Feb 26	**Fridge** P Doyle, C Smith

Massively mis-graded at F7b in a previous guidebook.

1993 Mar 11	**Anrhefn; Difrod Mawr; Begawnis** I A Jones, R Wightman, J Green

Bolted routes interfering with the historically important final pitch of *Gideon*; the bolts were subsequently removed.

1993 Apr	**Ffa Coffi Pawb** I A Jones, R Wightman

See the comment for the previous three routes.

1993 Apr 6	**Shock the Monkey** I Lloyd-Jones, N Manning
1993 Apr 23	**Rest In Pete's** R Liddle, L Dow
1993 Apr 26	**Snuffler** R Liddle, L Dow, K Turner
1993 Apr 26	**Is Marilyn Monroe Dead?** R Liddle, L Dow, K Turner
1993 Apr 26	**Nothing...** L Dow, R Liddle
1993 Apr 26	**Buxton the Blue Cat** L Dow, K Turner, R Liddle
1993 Jun 1	**Suspension of Disbelief** I Lloyd-Jones
1993 Jun	**Mad on the Metro** C Davies, M Wells

1990's • First Ascents

1993 Jun 5	**Rock Athletes Day Off** M Wells, I Hill, A N Other	
1993 Jun 5	**The Christening of New Boots** A N Other, M Wells, I Hill	
1993 Jun 23	**Sylvanian Waters** M Wells, C Davies	
1993 Jul 6	**Cat Flaps of Perception** R Mirfin, I Davis	
1993 Jul 6	**Home Run** J Bowman, A Bowman	
1993 Aug 10	**Black Daisies for the Bride** P Doyle, C P Smith, B Smith	
	Confusingly the last guidebook placed this route in Gideon Quarry – it is in fact at the top of Australia on the Gorbals slab!	
1993 Sep 9	**Mfecane** D Dutton	
	One of the only Slate roofs and probably the hardest!	
1993 Sep 28	**Men of Leisure** R Tompsett, P Dobbs, T Clements	
	"more than your average new slate route" – first ascentionist comment. To a certain extent they were right in that it climbs some of the better rock in Australia!	
1993 Nov 2	**A Swarm of Green Parrots** S Parker, R Ebbs	
	Ebbs returning to the quarries after putting up *Legs Akimbo* back in 1978!	
1993 Nov 2	**The Dreaming** R Ebbs, S Parker	
	This was re-ascended in the noughties by Mark Reeves, who mistook it for a new line after it was placed in the old guide in the wrong place.	
1994	**Conquistadors of the Useless** M Crook	
	A winter solo of some very loose territory on the intimidating back wall of Australia. The scree was frozen and Martin picked his way up armed with crampons and axes.	
1994 May	**Big Thursday** M Crook, N Walton	
	Another profoundly adventurous trip.	
1994 May 2	**The Muff Affair** L Zablocki, S Harwood	
1994 Jun 11	**Unpaid Bills** J Barton, B Sheen	
1994 Jul 18	**Hasta La Vista Baby** F Haden, M Davies	
1994 Jul 21	**Race Against the Pump** F Haden	
	A fine route, although the bolt on the crux is hard to clip.	
1994 Jul 22	**Scarlet Runner Direct** F Haden, M Davies	
1994 Aug 19	**The Carbon Stage** M Jones	
1995 Apr 4	**Terry's Wall** K Lingiah, J Jones	
1995 Apr 4	**Bring Out the Gimp** K Lingiah, J Jones	
1995 Jun	**The Wall Within** G Smith	
	A stunning addition from the ever prolific and inventive Big G.	
1995 Jun 26	**Full Metal Jack Off** P Pritchard, G Westrupp	
1996 Jun	**Dragon Slayer** D Taylor, P Robertson, M Davies	
1996 Jul 19	**The Porphyry Chair** P Pritchard, A Wainwright, T Leppert	
	"In the Vatican there is a chair with a hole where the Pope must sit to prove he is a man and the Vatican seven come in and say: Oh, yes, he has testicals and they hang well." – Paul Pritchard	
	Also, as George Smith once pointed out, if you say the route name over and over, very quickly it begins to morph into 'Paul Pritchard'.	
1996 Aug 25	**Bonza Crack** N Lowry, T Woodhead	
1996 Sept	**The Reclining Bloon** M Crook, N Walton	
1996 Sept	**Cardeddau Flash Goggles** M Crook, N Walton	
1996 Sept 30	**Journey to the Centre of the Earth** P Pritchard, D Kendal, A Wainwright	
1997 June 6	**Top Gear** C Parkin, K W Robertson	
1998	**The Lost Crack** G Smith	
1998	**The Spirit Level** M Katz	

350 First Ascents • 1990/2000's

1998	**Exploding Goats** M Dicken, a cast of thousands.	

Bolted and claimed as *One for All* in 2008

1998 **Old Farts** D Williams, M Ryan
The first of a trio of aid routes in California.

1998 **Happy Hooking** D Williams, M Ryan, M Hanford

1998 **NYQUIST** D Williams, J Williams, G Middlehurst

1998 Aug 8 **A Small Rusty Nail on a Large Mantlepiece** R Kay, T Hodgson, D Towse
Aid was used to clean the 4th pitch; but it was seconded without at 6a.

1998 Sept **The Wall Without** R Kay, M Crook, J Tombs, N Craine

1998 Sept **Buffer in a Crack House** M Crook, R Kay
A geologically active route, It is no longer "Slate's only true chimney" but a valley of death. Onsight soloed in 2002 by Mark Dicken

1998 Sept 18 **Wild Horses** R Kay, M Crook, D Holmes

1998 Sept 26 **Rosen the Chosen** R Kay, M Crook

1998 Oct **Maupin Rey Route** R Kay, N Peplow, M Crook

1999 **Slate:** An updated version of the '92 Slate guide; beefed up to A5 size and given a splash of much needed colour with an excellent set of action shots from Ray Wood.

1999 The new routes book was lost for this period, as such many of the details of the routes were lost, and information pieced together from area reports in old magazines.

1999 **The Coolridge Effect** M Reeves, L Morris, D Hollingham
Climbed over several days, as the third crux groove pitch remained damp; this pitch was cleaned on abseil prior to an ascent. It subsequently turned out that this pitch had been climbed direct by Paul Jenkinson and Mike Thomas in 1987.

1999 **Lord of the Rings** M Reeves, T Luddington
Cleaned and bolted prior to first ascent, although a crucial handhold pulled off prior to reaching the first bolt on the ascent.

1999 **Lord of the Pies** M Payne, M Reeves

1999 **The Fellowship of the Ring** T Luddington, M Reeves, M Payne

1999 **Song of the Minerals** P Barker
At last one of Paul's project lines actually goes!

1999 **Come Inside** S Sinfield, T Badcock
One of the rare true chimney lines on slate that hasn't fallen down. The chockstones are the nesting site of some protected birds.

1999 **The Rothwell Incident** M Reeves, D Rothwell

2000 **Fruit of the Gloom** W Perrin, D Rudkin
Another of the rare true chimneys, this time with a seriously loose approach.

2000 **Bloodstains** J Weaver, J Gregory, C Dodds

2000 Jan 19 **Il Miglior Fabbro** M Katz
A fierce technical addition from the pocket rocket powerhouse.

2000 May 1 **Two Steps to Heaven, Three Steps to Hell** M Reeves, I Roberts

2000 Jun 6 **667 Neighbour of the Beast** W Perrin, M Reeves

2001 **Geographically Celibate** M Reeves, M Payne

2001 **Glurp** M Jones, L Kathenes, H Owen

2002 **Gerboa Racing** R Mirfin, B Crampton

2002 **Patio Doors of Perception** B Crampton, R Mirfin

2000's • First Ascents

Ray Kay on the first ascent of the **Wall Without** E4 5c, Mordor photo: Noel Craine

Pete Robins re-equipping **Vermin on the Ridiculous** F7b/+, Rainbow Walls Lower photo: Si Panton

2002	**Narcolepsy**	R Mirfin
2002	**The Wicked Box Finish**	R Kay, H Falconer
2002 Feb 2	**Menhir** J Brown, J Lyon	
	The ageing rock star strikes again.	
2002 Feb 2	**Dolmen**	J Brown, J Lyon
2002 Feb 26	**Antiquity**	J Brown, J Lyon
2002 Jun 20	**Buzz Stop**	B Jones, P Trewin
2002 Jul 17	**Clegir Arête**	A George, B Lewis, J Banks
2002 Oct 14	**If You Kill People they Die**	M Dicken
2002 Nov	**Cross Eyed Tammy**	M Dicken
2002 Dec 7	**Waiting on an Angel**	M Dicken L Ford
2003	**Bring Me the Head of Don Quixote** M Dicken, C Neale	
	The first ascent of the principal free standing pillar in Film Set.	
2003	**Green Flash Challenge**	M Dicken
2003 Mar 26	**Snoring Exploring**	B Lillington
2003 Mar 26	**In Between Red and Green**	B Lillington, J Teed
2003 May 11	**Stairlift to Heaven**	M Dicken, C Neale
2003 Jul 5	**... And a Pen Please**	P Woodhouse, K Archer
2003 Jul 5	**Samba Drum**	K Archer, P Woodhouse
2005	**The Mu Mu** A Hocking	
	Talented Lakes expat cleans up a desperate project.	
2005 May 8	**Teenage Kicks**	D Lee, J Warburton

352 First Ascents • 2000's

2006		A comprehensive re-equipping campaign is kick started with the lion's share of the work being carried out by Mark Reeves, Pete Robins and Mark Dicken. Logistical back up from Chris Parkin and financial support from the BMC clinches the deal and soon the once-quiet quarries begin to buzz again.
2006 Aug 17	**Dekophobia** M Dicken, M Turner	
	A return to new routing for Hosey after cratering off *Drowning Man* in 2004.	
2006 Aug 22	**My Hovercraft is Full of Eels** R Mirfin	
2006 Aug 27	**Concorde Dawn** R Mirfin	
	An impressive addition which hinted at what lay ahead in terms of classic 'hard' sport routes; *Rowan* and *The New Slatesman* sit in full view, just above on the next level.	
2006 Sept	**Temple of Boom** M Dicken, R Huws	
2006 Sept	**Sans Chisel variation** P Robins	
2006 Sept	**The Deceptive Dyke** M Reeves, B Wills	
	The first of the New Wave of low grade sport routes.	
2006 Sept	**Sad Man Who's Sane** M Reeves, B Wills	
2006 Sept	**U.B.L.** M Reeves, B Wills	
2006 Oct	**Emerald Dyke** M Dicken	
	Conceived by Mark Reeves, but Hosey knocked the bolts in and soloed it. Soon the rest of the slab would be bolted up with low grade clip ups.	
2006 Nov	**Son of Rabbit** M Dicken	
	Named in homage to the lost route *Daddy Rabbit* and King Kong films.	
2006 Dec 23	**Full Monty; Mister Mister** M Raine, A Newton	
	Two of the original slateheads step back into the fray. Mike had spotted the lines whilst re-equipping his routes on The Conscience Slab.	
2007	**Abattoir Blues** M Dicken	
2007	**The Stream of Obscenity** M Dicken	
	The stream which runs off this level has a habit of spraying back onto the route in high winds.	
2007 Feb 1	**Pas the Duchie...** P Robins	
2007 Feb 14	**Drunken Laughs** M Pugh, M Dicken	
2007 Feb 17	**The Very Old and the Very New** S Beal	
	A radical aid line at the top of Australia, which re-ignited interest in this forgotten area.	
2007 Mar	**Dude in the Orange Hat** N Bradford	
2007 Mar 10	**Catrin** L Morris, M Reeves	
2007 Mar 20	**Gwion's Groove** M Dicken, S Dicken	
2007 Mar 25	**Nik-Arête** P Robins, M Reeves, A Wainwright	
	A route so bad that Adam asked for his name to be left off the FA credits!	
2007 Mar 31	**Easy Routes Can Have Bolts Too** S Beal	
2007 Mar 31	**Wish You Were Here** J Ratcliffe	
	A stunning addition and a serious contender for the best of its grade (F7c/+) in the whole of the quarries.	
2007 Apr	**The Serpent Vein** J McHaffie	
	Yet another mind blowing project falls as the new wave of development picks up pace.	
	"One of the best routes of its type in Britain; an awesome line with some awesome climbing, and as hard as Bungle's Arête." - Caff	
	Originally toyed with by Kristian Clemmow back in the late 90s, it was left to gather dust when Kristian moved to Sheffield.	
2007 Apr 16	**Tambourine Man** P Robins	
	Another brilliant and technical clip up; named in tribute to Will Perrin.	
2007 Apr 18	**Rowan** P Robins, B Bransby	
	"Pete had estimated the line to be about E3, suggesting that myself and Noel Craine	

2000's • First Ascents 353

	pop up for a quick repeat after he'd done it. When we arrived it quickly became apparent that this was of a different order of difficulty altogether; Ben Bransby was aiding the top section!" - Si Panton.
2007 May 4	**My Secret Garden** M Dicken, G Owen
2007 May 5	**Raisin Frumpsnoot** A Wainwright A typically smart move from Adam, picking off a pair of superb routes (including the equally good *Beltane*, climbed at the end of the same month) on a wall that had long since been discounted as having any potential by others.
2007 May 22	**Mini Bus Stop** I Lloyd-Jones, L Body, I Martin
2007 May 26	**Freezer** P Targett
2007 May 23	**Kinder Sport** C Goodey The first of many new additions from an ever-enthusiastic, veteran Welsh climber. Colin quickly became a prime mover in the new wave of low grade sport routes.
2007 May 23	**La Grandmere**. S Goodey, C Goodey
2007 May 30	**Beltane** A Wainwright
2007 May 31	**Le Grandpere** C Goodey S Goodey
2007 Jun 1	**Le Gendre** R Spencer, C Goodey, K Goodey
2007 Jun 4	**Sleeper** I Lloyd-Jones, P Targett
2007 Jun 4	**The Groovy Gang** P Targett
2007 Jun 5	**Mon Amie**. C Goodey, C Wigley
2007 Jun 6	**Tolerance** C Goodey, C Wigley
2007 Jun 6	**Doggy-Style** P Robins Pete's slate campaign continued with this bouldery test piece.
2007 Jun 12	**Pour Tout le Monde** M Simpkins, C Simpkins
2007 Jun 18	**Hawkeye** I Lloyd-Jones, C Goodey
2007 Jun 22	**The Fat Controller** P Targett, I Lloyd-Jones
2007 Jun 22	**Crazy Train** I Lloyd-Jones, P Targett
2007 Jul 6	**XXXposure** I Lloyd-Jones, P Targett
2007 July 19	**Fresh Air** C Goodey, K Goodey A partial retrobolting of a neglected line that had sported a single bolt. Instantly popular.
2007 Aug 5	**One Step Beyond** M Raine, M Reeves
2007 Aug 6	**Technical Hamster** P Targett, T Hughes
2007 Aug 21	**Zzzooming the Tube** I Lloyd-Jones, T Hughes
2007 Aug 22	**The Hand of Morlock** T Hughes, O Cain The high first bolt position and bad landing justified the E grade, but most repeaters chose (sensibly) to stick clip the bolt and take the more appropriate sport grade instead.
2007 Aug 23	**Hyperfly** P Targett I Lloyd-Jones
2007 Aug 23	**Scarface Claw** I Lloyd-Jones, P Targett
2007 Aug 24	**Technical Hamster Dance** Eric T
2007 Aug 27	**Cyber World Sl@te Heads** I Lloyd-Jones, P Targett, T Hughes
2007 Aug 28	**Orangutang Overhang** I Lloyd-Jones, T Hughes, P Targett An excellent addition; perhaps the best of a rash of new sport routes from an increasingly prolific activist.
2007 Sept	**The Missing Link** M Reeves, L Morris
2007 Sept 5	**The Gnarly SPAR Kid** T Hughes G Oldridge
2007 Sept 7	**Maximum Tariff** P Targett, I Lloyd-Jones, P Walley
2007 Sept 7	**Kinder Surprise** I Lloyd-Jones, P Targett
2007 Sept 11	**Surprise Surprise** I Lloyd-Jones
2007 Sept 13	**Shorty's Dyno** I Lloyd-Jones, P Targett

2007 Oct 2	**Sport 4 All** I Lloyd-Jones
2007 Oct 5	**The Punters Retreat** M Dicken, J Byrne
2007 Oct 10	**Le Petit Pois** P Targett I Lloyd-Jones
2007 Oct 13	**Sodor** J Ball The development of the sidings by 10 year old Josie Ball begins (with a little help from her dad, Fraser).
2007 Oct 13	**Polar Express** J Ball
2007 Oct 19	**Tomb Raider** C Goodey, S Goodey, B Williams A multi pitch sport route, adding further novelty to the Never Never Land area.
2007 Oct 29	**362** B Williams, C Goodey
2007 Nov	**'N' Gauge** J Ball
2007 Nov 2	**Last Chance for a Slow Dance** M Dicken
2007 Nov 16	**Slip Not** I Lloyd-Jones
2007 Nov 16	**Why Knot?** I Lloyd-Jones
2007 Dec 13	**Jenga** I Lloyd-Jones
2007 Dec 13	**Bosch Stop Quarry** I Lloyd-Jones
2007 Dec 14	**Bish Bash Bosch** I Lloyd-Jones
2007 Dec 15	**Finatic** I Lloyd-Jones, P Targett
2007 Dec 16	**Thomas the Tank** A Ball Josie's 5 year old brother gets in on the act!
2007 Dec 16	**Rack and Pin** J Ball
2007 Dec 16	**The Mallard** J Ball
2007 Dec 16	**Gordon** A Ball
2008 Jan 27	**Side Line** J Ball
2008 Jan 27	**Derailed** J Ball
2008 Jan 27	**Ivor the Engine** J Ball
2008 Jan 27	**The Level Crossing** J Ball
2008 Jan 27	**Hogwarts Express** J Ball
2008 Feb 15	**The Railway Children** J Ball
2008 Feb 19	**Taith Mawr** M Dicken, J Byrne A very adventurous trip across the back of Twll Mawr.
2008 Feb 25	**The New Slatesman** P Robins "I tried it a bit last year when I wasn't climbing that well, and at the time it felt really hard – in fact I wasn't sure I could do it. This winter I've bouldered a lot, and that gave me the edge I needed." – Pete Robins The crux does involves two consecutive 7a moves, one of which may be the hardest move in the quarries.
2008 Feb 28	**Choo Choo** J Ball
2008 Mar 2	**Aardman productions** P Targett. T Hughes. S McGuiness
2008 Mar 2	**The Big Easy** P Targett
2008 Mar 2	**Steps of Glory** M Chambers, C Roots, I Pagano

Josie Ball on the first ascent of **Sodor** F5c, Australia
Lower photo: Ray Wood

Colin Goodey on the top pitch of **Tomb Raider** F6a/+, Never Never Land photo: Ray Wood

Pete Robins caught mid crux on **The New Slatesman** F8b, Rainbow Walls Lower photo: Gareth Aston

2008 Mar 3	**Sauron** J McHaffie	

When Caff first inspected the line he thought it would make a good F7b+, but closer analysis revealed a much tougher proposition. Luckily he'd been training hard and was able to take the unexpected hike in difficulty in his stride – in fact it only took two sessions before he had nailed the redpoint!

2008 Mar 22	**State of the Heart** M Raine
2008 Apr 14	**In Loving Memory** J Ball
2008 Apr 21	**Hogiau Pen Garret** I Lloyd-Jones, P Targett

The start of a new phase of development up on the remote and neglected levels of the East Braich.

2008 Apr 22	**To Infinity and Beyond!** I Lloyd-Jones, S Beesley
2008 May 2	**The Curious Incident** I Lloyd-Jones, P Targett
2008 May 4	**Atticus Finch** P Targett, I Lloyd-Jones
2008 May 4	**Ride Like the Wind!** I Lloyd-Jones, P Targett
2008 May 5	**All for One** M Goodsmith, C Goodey, D Goodey
2008 May 13	**Birdsong** P Targett I Lloyd-Jones
2008 May 19	**The Koala Brothers** J Ball
2008 May 20	**Cirith Ungol** I Lloyd-Jones, P Targett
2008 May 21	**Jagged Face** M Hurst, B Wedley, T Muller
2008 May 29	**Yossarian** P Targett I Lloyd-Jones
2008 Jun 2	**Walk This Way** I Lloyd-Jones, S Beesley
2008 Jun 2	**Binky Bonk Central** J Widjaya, J Kelly
2008 Jun 6	**Obsession** C Goodey, M Helliwell

The first ascentionist actually had a heart attack attempting this route!

2008 Jun 6	**Don't Look Back in Bangor** J Ratcliffe, S Franklin, A Scott
2008 Jun 10	**The California Express** H Gilbert, S Ratcliffe
2008 Jun 11	**The Faffer** J Ratcliffe

Something of a rarity, a bolt-free, yet physically hard slate trad route. F7b+ on wires!

356 First Ascents • 2000/2010's

2008 Jun 14	**Steps of Escher** P Targett. I Lloyd-Jones	
2008 Jun 14	**A Room With a View** J Ratcliffe, R Lamey	
2008 Jun 15	**My Wife's An Alien**. J Widjaya, J Kelly	
2008 Jun 15	**Over Taken By Department C** I Lloyd-Jones, J Roberts, P White	
2008 Jun 23	**Monkey See Monkey Do** S Beal, A Scott, N Harford	
	The first of a series of new routes that would see the Monkey Bar area of Never Never Land transformed.	
2008 Jun 23	**Captain Slog** J Widjaya, J Kelly	
2008 Jun 24	**Pail Rider** A Scott, J Ratcliffe	
2008 Jun 25	**Beyond the Pail** A Scott, J Ratcliffe	
2008 Jun 25	**A Little Pail** J Ratcliffe, A Scott	
2008 Jun 25	**Dyke Rider** S Beal, A Scott, J Ratcliffe	
2008 Jul	**Slate Arrivals** J Widjaya, J Kelly	
2008 Jul	**The Finger Slicer** C Muskett	
	Unfortunately obliterated by a rock fall shortly after the first ascent.	
2008 Jul	**Unnamed** M Reeves, L Morris	
2008 Jul	**As Yet Unnamed** M Reeves, L Morris	
2008 Jul 6	**Twisted Nerve** S Neal	
2008 Jul 23	**Great Bores of Today** J Ratcliffe	
	An old George Smith project, the blank bottom section of which was solved by the careful positioning of an old metal pipe!	
2008 Aug	**Cabin Fever** M Crook, N Walton	
	Return to action for two of the original 80s slateheads	
2008 Aug 8	**In on the Kill Taker** M Dicken, M Reeves	
	Sportingly bolted; the first ascentionist took the full 8m lob on an early attempt on this 16m climb.	
2008 Aug 14	**The Gargoyle** K Goodey, C Goodey, D Smith	
2008 Aug 22	**The Daddy Club** M Dicken, P Jenkinson, C Muskett	
2008 Aug 27	**1066** P Targett, T Hughes	
2008 Sept	**Kenny's Wall** N Walton, M Crook	
2008 Sept	**Damocles** N Walton, M Crook	
2008 Sept	**Clippopotamus** M Crook, N Walton, A Newton	
2008 Oct 30	**The Wriggler** M Dicken, I Doyle	
2008 Dec 24	**Way Down in the Hole** M Dicken J Sterling	
2009 Jan 29	**Snakes and Ladders** I Lloyd-Jones	
2009 Feb 19	**Ibex** P Harrison	
	A radical dry tooling route manufactured on a steep, blank, and often wet section of rock. It was originally created by Owen Samuel and Rocio Siemens.	
2009 Feb 21	**Wave Rock** I Lloyd-Jones	
2009 Mar 6	**Impact Zone** I Lloyd-Jones, P Targett	
2009 Mar 12	**La Famille** C Goodey, S Goodey	
2009 Mar 16	**Departure Lounge** J Widjaya, J Kelly, C Goodey	
2009 Apr 3	**Gentle LayBack** E Russell	
2009 Apr 3	**Shothole Arete** E Russell	
2009 Apr 3	**Loose Block Corner** E Russell	
2009 Apr 3	**Puffing Billy** C Jordan	
2009 Apr 3	**With a Little Help From a Tree** E Russell	
2009 Apr 15	**Plastic Soldier** I Lloyd-Jones, P Targett, S Beesley	
	The first of a trio of 40m F6a routes on the Skyline Buttress.	

2009 May 14	**Puddy Kat** Jim Kelly, Julia Kelly	
2009 May 28	**Back in the Saddle** C Davies, I Lloyd-Jones	
2009 Jun 9	**The Wow Wow** J Ratcliffe, S Franklin	

A great line. *"Better and longer than The Mau Mau!"* - Jon Ratcliffe

2009 Jun 16	**Ruby Marlee meets Dr Holingsworth** C Davies, I Lloyd-Jones
2009 Jun 16	**Clash of the Titans** I Lloyd-Jones, C Davies
2009 Aug 11	**Septuagenarian** C Goodey, S Goodey, D Kelly
2009 Sept 4	**Slip Sliding Away** C Muskett, J Dawes
2009 Sept 23	**Dark and Scary Stories** C Muskett, T Pearson
2009 Sept 17	**Ziplock** I Lloyd-Jones, P Targett
2009 Sept 24	**Feeling Rusty** I Lloyd-Jones, C Davies
2009 Sept 24	**Indiana Jasmine and the Topple of Doom!** C Davies, I Lloyd Jones
2009 Sept 24	**Pulverised** I Lloyd-Jones
2009 Oct	**Chain Wall** R Marin

A shockingly steep dry tooling route which points the way to future development of the neglected hole at the back of Gideon Quarry.

2009 Oct	**Escape from Coldbits** L Cottle, J Kelly
2009 Oct 1	**The Skyline Club** C Davies, P Targett
2009 Oct 7	**The Beanstalk** C Davies, P Targett
2009 Oct 8	**De Nouement** P Targett, O Jones
2009 Oct 8	**Comfort Zone** C Goodey, S Trainer
2009 Oct 14	**First Stop** C Goodey, S Goodey
2009 Oct 21	**Liquid Armbar** M Dicken, I Holroyd, F Ball

Hosey's obsession with all things of an offwidth nature continued with this fine addition.

2009 Oct 21	**Toe be or not Toe be....** I Lloyd-Jones
2009 Oct 28	**Jepp the Knave** P Targett, C Davies
2009 Nov 12	**Harri Bach Llanrug** I Lloyd-Jones, C Davies
2009 Dec 4	**Slab Rog** I Lloyd-Jones
2009 Dec 18	**Y Rhaffwr** I Lloyd-Jones, C Davies
2010 Feb 6	**Slatebite** C Davies

An excellent line that had been staring everybody in the face.

2010 Feb 7	**The Mosquito** C Muskett
2010 Feb 27	**The Quartz Scoop** C Muskett
2010 Mar 11	**Slabology** I Lloyd-Jones, S Beesley
2010 Mar 16	**Birthday Girl** J Ratcliffe

"The crux moves are as hard as anything on True Clip [a tough F7b+], but the climbing is not as sustained. It might be F7b+ for shorties (i.e. 5.6 and below) but defo no harder than F7b for others, possibly even easier for tall folk as the crux I did would be just a reach to anyone taller." - Jon Ratcliffe

Ramon Marin making the first ascent of the super steep **Chain Wall** D8+, Gideon Quarry photo: Rob Gibson
Jon Ratcliffe on the first ascent of the immaculate **Birthday Girl** F7b/+, Australia East Braich photo: Si Panton

358 First Ascents • 2010's

2010 Mar 27	**Slab Slayer** S Beesley, I Lloyd-Jones, C Davies
2010 Mar 27	**Bise Mon Cul!** J Kelly, J Redhead A surprise return from the old slate master JR.
2010 April 10	**Harold Void** M Dicken, C Muskett
2010 April 10	**Stannah to Hell** C Muskett, M Dicken
2010 April 10	**Mister Blister** I Lloyd-Jones, C Davies
2010 April	**Glasgow Kiss** I Lloyd-Jones *"I'm not sure of the grade as it's more sustained than Pulverised at F7b, I always find it really difficult to grade routes that are 'my style of climbing'..."* Ian Lloyd-Jones The F7a+ grade didn't last long; current thinking places it at F7b+!
2010 April	**Sleazy Rider** G Desroy, S Panton
2010 April	**Exhuming the Tube** M Reeves, M Dicken
2010 April 31	**A Big Wall Climb** C Muskett
2010 April 31	**Friendly Argument** C Muskett
2010 May 1	**Penblwydd Hapus (i Fi)** S Panton, A Scott, G Desroy During some route checking work, the guidebook editor spots an obvious line and sets it up for an ascent on his birthday.
2010 May 7	**Forsinain Motspur direct start** C Muskett
2010 May 8	**Offa's** C Davies, M Williams
2010 May 21	**Synthetic Life** P Harrison, C Parkin A brilliant addition which marked the start of Pete's campaign to develop the long since neglected *Bone People* area of Gideon Quarry. *"Although I'm biased, I don't think it's an exaggeration to say it's one of the best F7a+'s in North Wales."* – Pete Harrison
2010 May 31	**Fuck Les Clotures** Jim Kelly, Julia Kelly, J Redhead
2010 June 5	**A Pair of Six** C Davies, M Williams, I Lloyd-Jones
2010 June 11	**Slabs R Us** I Lloyd-Jones, S McGuiness *"Again not sure of the grade...maybe a grade harder or easier. The crux feels fiercer than most things on Tambourine Man, but less sustained. Having said that I am very familiar with all the moves on Tambourine Man by now!"* – Ian struggles with the grade again, but the clue is in the comparison, a desperate F8a!
2010 June 16	**A Selfish Act of Loonacy** J Kelly, J Redhead
2010 June 16	**Forsinain Motspur Super Direct** C Muskett *"It's probably got the hardest climbing of all the routes on the main wall, maybe F8a, and the direct finish is better than the original finish. Even if I say so myself!"* – Calum Muskett
2010 June 25	**Not Quite Snakes and Ladders** E Russell
2010 June 30	**Senior Citizen Smith** P Harrison, P Robins After Pete had bagged the first ascent, Dr Robins promptly flashed the second ascent in alarmingly casual style. *"I guess that's what happens when you let loose an in-form F8c+ climber on your E6 project! It was like watching Brazil take on Bangor FC!"* – Pete Harrison
2010 July 23	**Titan** C Goodey, M Hellewell, S Trainer

Pete Harrison abseiling in for an attempt on **Senior Citizen Smith** E5/6 6b, Gideon Quarry photo: Si Par

2000/2010's • First Ascents

2010 July 25	**Zeus** M Hellewell, C Goodey, S Trainer
2010 Aug 5	**Dwarf Shortage** O Barnicott
	A whopping 57m pitch!
2010 Aug 16	**Quelle Surprise** C Goodey, S Goodey
2010 Aug 21	**A Grand Day Out** F Ball, A Ball, J Ball
	The Ball family establish a multi pitch excursion in Australia.
2010 Aug 27	**We No Speak Americano!**
	C Lloyd-Jones, T Lloyd-Jones
	Celt and Tesni get to do a new route equipped by their dad.
2010 Sept 20	**Seam Stress** I Lloyd-Jones, S McGuiness
2010 Sept 20	**Gymnastic Fantastic** N Sharpe, G Jones
2010 Oct 10	**Cartoon Lesbians** Jim Killy, Julia Kelly
2010 Oct 19	**The Lost Tomb** M Hellewell, S Trainer
	Clean up and retrobolting of a long forgotten route (*Dog Day Dogfish*) first climbed by John Tombs in 1987.
2010 Nov	**Beating the Raine** C Muskett
	This had been Mike Raine's project – thus the cheeky name.
2010 Nov	**Green Slip** C Muskett
2010 Nov 19	**Slip of the Tongue** P Robins
	Impressive onsight following an invitation to try the route by Calum Muskett who had come close to completing it.
2010 Nov 19	**Split Decision** C Muskett
	Calum saves face by reaching the top of his other project, only to have Pete flash the second ascent of this moments later!
	"I think Split Decision could be the hardest route sans bolts on slate, certainly the most technical. Although Pete thought it was E6 6c (and it probably is) he did have the gear placements handed to him and all of my beta after watching me lead it, still mighty impressive though!" – Calum Muskett
2010 Nov	**Bambi** R Gibson
	Another radical dry tooling route but this time with a run out.

Calum Muskett on the first ascent of **Split Decision** E6 6c, Golgotha, Twll Mawr
photo: Ray Wood

2011 Jan 18	**Release the Kraken** I Lloyd-Jones
2011 March 6	**Swiss Air** T Mueller, I Lloyd-Jones
2011 April 10	**Rock Yoga** I Lloyd-Jones, S McGuiness
2011 May	**King of the Mezz** J Dawes, N Dyer, O Anderson
	A typically flamboyant gesture from the original slate master, leaving his seconds (both formidable climbers in their own right) gasping at the difficulty and boldness of the line.
	"It was desperate, we couldn't really do the moves on the crux. Fair enough we had a sneaky beer on the belay which always takes your edge off, but still, it was so hard and then the run out after the hard bit was outrageous. Johnny clipped the Firé Escape bolts then that was it, all the way to the Blockhead belay!" - Neil Dyer
	"I did it on a whim really. We got to the top of the Quarryman groove and I thought, what can we do? I've done all the existing lines before so I thought I would just go for the traverse line. I got across and suddenly found myself bridging on poor smears, hanging on an edge and having to dyno. At one point I had to sort of layback on the cheek of my face so I could swap hands on a hold. It was very tricky." – Johnny Dawes
2011 May 5	**Saruman** I Lloyd-Jones, S McGuiness
2011 June 6	**Slabaholics Anonymous** I Lloyd-Jones, S McGuiness
	Ian continues his new route campaign, confirming his position as the most prolific new router in the quarries.

And what of the future? Well there is one outstanding project first equipped and tried by Johnny Dawes way back in the mid 80s. *The Meltdown* is a super intense line on *The Quarryman* wall in Twll Mawr.

Al Williams, Ground Up's resident designer, recalls accompanying Johnny on an attempt way back in the day:

"I've seen a bit of Johnny lately, in Sheffield. We reminisce about experiences framed by climbing and flavoured by nostalgia. I remember the day we went up to try The Meltdown, just after he'd cleaned and bolted it. The interveening years shrink to nothing. He was riding high in his mid 80's pomp. I look for a flicker of recognition from Johnny. He can't recall and I realise he's had a thousand days like that. I can recall because I had very few days abseiling into a 1000 foot black hole on a single rope. We laugh and agree, at least, on the horror of that drop. All I can remember is thinking 'what a way to go'. I'm sure Johnny had the same thought in his head, but it meant something different to him. He was visualising success on his climb. He was in his element. I most definitely was not. Anyway I can clearly recall Johnny making significant links. He seemed really close, and even though it was futuristic, he was ahead of his time at that point. It just wouldn't have been a surprise if he'd done it then. Would things have been different if he had? Things are never different, but it would have been a fine distillation of what he was doing at that time; his 'Les Demoiselles d'Avignon' before the cubism took over. I never became what I'd feared that day, and Johnny never climbed The Meltdown. But its nice to see him 25 years later, looking well in his mid 2010's pomp, and who knows..."

The line has been tried by the latest crop of slate masters and the current thinking is that it rates F8c/+. Johnny is also keen for a rematch; his quote speaks volumes about what lies in stall:

"Meltdown is unique, though only 80' high it has two crux traverses of 20' each. Each move is different to any other, tiny slivers of slate as side pulls manifested in spookily appropriate positions, rounded micro mounds for feet, set in natural perfection to limit the sweep of the hand. Clusters of three holds where three are necessary to swap hands. There is a rest before the crux which takes six moves to establish and uses three footholds to enable a heel standing/hands off, possible by starring out your body.

The second crux involves the bronze cap; this will be for six moves. A dyno into a left hand finger pointing layback (fingers straight, hand palm at 90 degrees to them) with right knee resting on top of the left hand. A slap into an undercling and then a flag move where it would be ideal if you could take off your left calf muscle. Then a full foot smear, toe pull and a footless drop down after a low, long slap onto a pinch in front of your face. Extended, a big beautiful slopey foothold comes just within reach, legs and arms all crossed up, a hand off is sequentially possible. A few deft unweightings, a set up and a sideways double dyno (the easiest move on the route) and the Meltdown is complete."

This quote first appeared in an article about the quarries written by Martin Crook for the March 1997 issue of the On The Edge magazine.

James McHaffie attempting **Meltdown** F8c/+? photo: Ian Parnell ʌ

GROUND UP

Ground Up is a grass roots company dedicated to producing beautifully designed and deeply inspiring guidebooks. Here is the roster of books produced so far. On the near horizon we have *Gogarth South*, *North Wales Scrambles* and the 2nd edition of *North Wales Bouldering* lined up.

North Wales Winter Climbing (2011)
The North Wales winter climbing scene has enjoyed a major resurgence in recent years. This visually stunning book provides full definitive coverage of the most popular areas, including: Ysgolion Duon (Black Ladders), Llech Ddu, Cwm Glas Bach, Cwm Lloer, Glyder Fach, Clogwyn Du, Clogwyn y Geifr (Devil's Kitchen), Craig y Rhaeadr and Clogwyn y Garnedd.

"The most awaited guidebook in Welsh history arrived in January to a huge fanfare. And what a great piece of work it is. So well done, it can't fail to be inspirational to anyone interested in winter climbing in Wales, regardless of ability." Tom Hutton, Trek & Mountain Magazine

Recent Developments on Peak Limestone (2010)
Peak limestone guru, Mark 'Zippy' Pretty spills the beans on the latest developments in Peak sport climbing.

North Wales Rock 2nd edition (2009)
An update and significant improvement of this classic guidebook. Better descriptions, more accurate maps and topos, plus significant technical improvements.

Parisella's Cave (2009)
A mini guide to the epicentre of North Wales limestone bouldering.

Main Cliff topo poster (2009)
A dramatic A3 poster showing a full colour topo of the most impressive sheet of rock in North Wales: Main Cliff at Gogarth.

Gogarth North (2008)
The glorious sea cliffs of Gogarth provide a range of exciting traditional routes. This beautifully constructed book covers all of the 'northern' crags including Holyhead Mountain, Upper Tier, Main Cliff, Easter Island Gully, Wen Zawn, Flytrap and North Stack. It also covers the sport climbing crags on the north coast of Anglesey.

"Perhaps the most inspirational definitive climbing guide ever." Steve Crowe of Climbonline.com

North Wales Rock 1st edition (2007)
The first edition of the classic selected climbs guide really put Ground Up on the map and cast the North Wales crags in a new and refreshing light.

"The Ground Up team have raised the bar for North Wales guides and if future definitive guides are half as good then the area has been well served." Ashley Tyler, UKClimbing.com

North Wales Bouldering (2004)
Now out of print, this groundbreaking English-Welsh bilingual guidebook was produced under the Northern Soul title, a forerunner to Ground Up.

"An excellent guidebook, one of the best in the UK."
Mick Ryan, UKClimbing.com

Quarry names

Visitors to the Slate Museum in Gilfach Ddu (next to Vivian Quarry) may notice a mismatch between the modern names used by climbers for the different areas in the quarries and the older names used by the quarrymen.

Some of the disparity can be explained by a desire, amongst early developers, to describe this radical landscape in a humorous and evocative fashion. There was also a degree of confusion over which bits of the quarries were originally known as Australia or California – the result being: the right names, but not always in the right places.

Whatever the truth, the development of the quarries as a climbing venue has produced a collection of colourful, albeit mostly English, names. These have become, through repeated use and appearance in various guidebooks, the accepted terms of reference amongst modern climbers.

Attempts have been made in recent Climbers' Club guides to eliminate crag name mistakes across the North Wales region. Nonetheless, usage of these 'correct' crag names remains sporadic at best. For example, you will struggle to find anybody who refers to Craig y Rhaeadr as Diffwys Ddwr, regardless of what it says in the Llanberis guide, or indeed the Ground Up North Wales Winter Climbing guide. That being said, there appears to be some acceptance of Clogwyn y Tarw over Gribin Facet.

It does seem unlikely that a large scale shift in nomenclature could be successfully instigated in the Llanberis quarries, and none has been attempted in this guide. Nonetheless, the following list makes for interesting reading; in particular the mismatch of California and Rainbow Walls is quite baffling.

Bus Stop = Allt Du
Dali's Hole = Sinc Harriet
California = Sinc Galed
Serengeti = Ponc Morgan
Never Never Land = Dyffryn
Watford Gap = Adwy California
Monkey Bar Level = Sinc Negro
Australia = Garret
Gorbals Level = Ponc Swallow
Skyline Level = Ponc Tophet
Zippy Level = Ponc Abyssinia
Steps of Cirith Ungol = Llwybr Llwynog
Fruit Bat Level = Twll Dwn Dwr
Sidings Level = Upper Penrhydd
Looning the Tube Level = Penrhydd
Darwin Level = Lernion
Level 2 above G'day Arete Level = Ponc Aifft
Far Out Level = Ponc Australia
G'day Arete Level = Ponc Teiliwr
Rainbow Walls = Ponciau California
Trango Tower = Y Ceiliog Mawr
Gideon and Film Set = Glynrhonwy Uchaf
Mancer etc. = Glynrhonwy Isaf
Nant Peris = Chwarel Gallt y Llan
Wall in the Hole quarry = Sinc Cook
Rain Temple = Sinc Ddol

< Looking down from Vivian Quarry to Gilfach Ddu and the Slate Museum photo: Si Panton

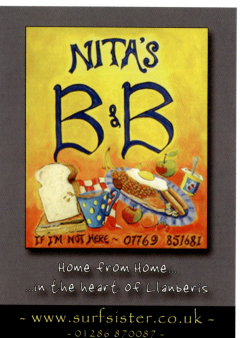

'..Pete's is the place to discover who built and who rocked this cradle of modern climbing...'
Climbing Magazine (USA)

'....probably the best cafe in the world......'
Guardian (UK)

Andy Newton BSc (Hons) P.G.C.E. M.I.C
Mountaineering & Rock Climbing.
Leadership Training.
Technical Consultant.

Min y Don, High Street,
Llanberis, Gwynedd, LL55 4EN

01286 872317
andy@andynewtonmic.org
www.andynewtonmic.org

A - C • Index 365

...and a pen please 72
1000 Tons of Chicken Shit 30
1066 47
2nd Class Passenger 51
362 144
667 Neighbour of the Beast 239
▶ Aardman Productions 111
Abattoir Blues 45
Above the Line 61
Abus Dangereux 273
Act Naturally 77
Age Concern 264
Alice Springs 82
Aliens Stole My Bolt Kit 110
Alive and Kicking 194
All for One 134
Alpen 146
Ancestral Vices 52
Andrei Chertov 106
Andy Pandy 145
Angel on Fire 236
Another Roadside Traction 254
Another Wasted Journey 84
Antiquity 76
Ari Hol Hi 231
Arnie Meets the Swamp Monster 42
Arrampicata Speiligone 299
Arse over TIt 299
Arthur Dali 112
Artichokes, Artichokes 252
Astroman from the Planet Zzzoink 47
As the Sun Sets in the West 36
As Yet Unnamed 81
Atticus Finch 92
At the Cost of a Rope 110
Aubergines, Aubergines 252
Aultimers Groove 118
Autocrat 300
A Big Wall Climb 311
A Good Slate Roof 104
A Grand Day Out 64
A Little Pail 154
A Mere Trifle 234
A Pair of Six 118
A Room With a View 84
A Selfish Act of Loonacy 50, 320
A Swarm of Green Parrots 82
A Tourmegamite Experience 275

▶ Baby Nina Soils Her Pants 273
Back in the Saddle 144
Balance of Power 131
Bambi 152
Bar of Soap 152
Bathtime 253
Beating the Raine 300
Beijqueiro 163
Bella Lugosi is Dead 194
Belldance 267

Beltane 31
Between Here and Now 52
Beyond the Pail 154
Biggles Flies Undone 37
Big Bendy Buddha 230
Big Thursday 56
Big Wall Party 195
Billy Two Tokes 78
Binky Bonk Central 110
Binman 273
Binwomen 78
Birdman of Cae'r Berllan 173
Birdsong 273
Birthday Girl 94
Bise-Mon-Cul 50, 320
Bish Bash Bosch 28
Black Butte 290
Black Daisies for the Bride 81
Black Hole Sun 173, 320
Blades of Green Tara 253
Blockhead 163
Blue Bottle 304
Blue Horizon 35
Blue Touch Paper 250
Bobby's Groove 246
Bong to Lunch 264
Bonza Crack 169, 178
Booby Building 254
Boody Building 254
Bosch Stop Quarry 28
Brain Death 232
Breakdance 34, 267
Brewing up with Morley Wood 282
Brian Damage 232
Brief Encounter 47
Bring me the Head of Don Quixote 299
Bring out the Gimp 230
Brinwell 254
Broken Memories 130
Buffalo Smashed in Head Jump 48
Buffer in a Crack House 97
Bungle's Arête 204
Bushmaster 172
Butcher 284
Buxton the Blue Cat 221
Buzz Stop 34

▶ Cabbage Man meets the Flying Death Leg 203
Cabin Fever 310
Caleduwlch 277
Californian Arête 119
Captain Black and the Mysterons 239
Captain Condom and the
  Mothers of Prevention 82
Captain Slog 110
Carneddau Flash Goggles 312
Cartoon Lesbians 51
Catrin 194
Cat Flaps of Perception 250
Celestial Inferno 236

Central Sadness 121
Chain Wall 309
Chariots of Fire 236
Chewing the Cwd 203
Child's Play 267
Chitra 214
Choo Choo 61
Cig-Arête 217
Circles are Sound 225
Cirith Ungol 92
Clap Please 245
Clash of the Titans 77
Classy Situations 119
Clegir Arête 310
Clippopotamus 292
Coeur De Lion 163
Colditz 264
Colossus 196
Colostomy 196
Combat Rock 159
Comes the Dervish 267
Come Inside 225
Come off it Arfer 112
Comfort Zone 28
Coming up for Air 219
Concorde Dawn 221
Conquistadors of the Useless 56
Con Quista Dors 103
Cornucopia 230
Coy Mistress 102
Cracked Up 307
Cracking Up 307
Crackle 146
Crazy Train 52
Crossville 35
Cross Eyed Tammy 75
Cuts like a Knife 103
Cwms the Dogfish 206
Cyber World Sl@te Heads 57
Cyclone B 160
Cystitis by Proxy 204

▶ Dali's Dihedral 103
Dali's Lemming Ducklings 104
Dali Express 103
Dali Mirror 102
Damocles 292
Dangling by the Diddies 214
Darkness Visible 43
Dark and Scary Stories 145
Dawes of Perception 245
Dekophobia 44
Demolition Derby 31
Departure Lounge 110
Derailed 58
De Nouement 75
Diagonal Dilemma 130
Digital Delectation 76
Dinorwig Unconquerable 187
Dirt 245

DOA 206
Doggy-Style 221
Dog Day Dogfish 277
Dolmen 76
Don't Look Back in Bangor 84
Donald Duck 48
Donkey Rider 154
Dope on a Rope 253
Down to Zero 263
Dragon Slayer 177
Dried Mouth 48
Dried Mouth Sesame Seed 48
Drowning Man 219
Drunken Laughs 160
Dwarf Shortage 120, 320
Dyke Rider 154

▶ Earwig Ho 87 254
Easy Routes Can Have Bolts Too 84
Emerald Dyke 110
Emerald Eyes 220
Envy 220
Equinox 31
Eric the Fruitbat 70
Eros 203
Escape from Coldbitz 106
Esprit de Corpse 121
Exploding Goats 134

▶ Fallout 273
Far from the Madding Crowd 92
Fat Lad Exam Failure 246
Faulty Towers 277
Fear of Rejection 147
Feeling Rusty 73
Feet Apart 263
Fellowship of the Ring 181
Ferrero Roche 28
Fetzer 82
Finatic 28
First and Last 102
First Step 28
Flashdance 267
Flock of Flying Butt Monkeys 321
Flying Death Fin (or is it Dutch?) 82
FM Super Direct 30
Foetal Attraction 268
Fool's Gold 30
Forsinain Motspur 30
Forsinain Motspur Direct 30
For Whom the Bell Tolls 267
Four Wheel Drift 252
Franzia 82
Freak Yer Beanbag 203
Freezer 36
Fresh Air 142
Fridge 36
Friendly Argument 311
Fruity Pear Gets Just Deserts 234
Fruity Pear in a Veg Shop Romp 234

Fruit of the Gloom 122
Frustrated Lust 264
Fuck Les Clotures 50, 320
Full Metal Jack Off 183
F Hot 206
▶ G'Day Arete 93
Gadaffi Duck 48
Gay Lightweights and Hetro Stumpies 187
Gender Bender 297
General Odours 276
Genevive 70
Genital Persuasion 45
Gentle LayBack 58
Geographically Celibate 186
Geordie War Cry 33
Gerbil Abuse 214
Gerboa Racer 51
German School Girl 231
Geronimo's Cadillac 178
Ghengis 145
Giddy One 305
Giddy Variations on a Theme 304
Gideon 304
Gideon's Way 255
Gin Palace 264
Glasgow Kiss 81
Glass Axe 58
Glurp 245
Gnat Attack 35
Goblin Party 82
God Betweens Money 236
Goodbye Natterjack Toad 277
Good Afternoon Constable 76
Good Crack 291
Goose Creature 50
Gordon 61
Grandad's Rib 102
Great Balls of Fire 196
Great Bores of Today 43
Greedy Girls 225
Green Ernie 236
Green Slip 166
Guillotine 30
Gwion's Groove 219
Gymnastic Fantastic 70
▶ Hamadryad 167
Happy Hooking 117
Harold Void 169, 177
Harri Bach Llanrug 78
Harvey's Brassed Off Team 106
Hasta La Vista Baby 33
Hawkeye 142
Heading the Shot 133
Heatseeker 239
Heaven Steps 236
Heinous Creature 246
Hemulin 102
Here to Stay, Gone Tomorrow 52

Her Indoors 112
Hogiau Pen Garret 93
Hogwarts Express 61
Hole in One 127
Hollow Heart 152
Holy, Holy, Holy 106
Home Run 153
Hooded Cobra 206
Horse Latitudes 194
Hot Air Crack 142
How Hot is Your Chilli? 206
Hymen Snapper 267
Hyperfly 48
Hysterectomy 50
▶ Ibex 153
If You Kill People They Die 56
If You Want 282
Igam-Ogam 146
Immac Groove 112
Impact Zone 94
Imperial Leather 246
Indiana Jasmine and the Topple of Doom! 74
In Between Red and Green 159
In Loving Memory 61
In on the Kill Taker 72
In the Line of Fire 173
Is it a Crime? 268
Is Marilyn Monroe Dead? 221
Ivor the Engine 61
I Don't Wanna Pickle 292
I Ran the Bath 253
▶ Jack of Shadows 195
Jack the Ripper 93
Jaded Passion 216
Jagged Face 28
Jai'a'n 206
Jenga 28
Jepp the Knave 72
Jex's Fumble Clipping Arete 104
John Verybiglongwords 105
Joie De Vivre 45
Josy Puss 181
Journey to the Centre of the Earth 183
Jugs Mawr 225
Jumping the Gun 275
Just For Fun 46
▶ Karabiner Cruise 130
Kenny's Wall 305
Khubla Khan 145
Kinder Sport 110
Kinder Surprise 57
King of the Mezz 163
Koala Bare 82
Kookaburra Waltz 146
Kosciusko 55

368 Index • L - O

▶ L'Allumette 232
Ladder Resist 245
Ladybird Girl 305
Last Chance for a Slow Dance 72
Last Tango in Paris 267
Launching Pad 106
Laund Arête 133
Layed Back Boys 297
La Famille 110
La Grandmere 110
Legal Murders 160
Legs Akimbo 263
Legs Together 263
Lentil in a Stew 263
Lesser Mortals 230
Lethal Injection 160
Le Cochon 105
Le Gendre 110
Le Grandpere 110
Le Petit Pois 111
Le Voleur 252
Light and Darkness 195
Lindy Lou 77
Liquid Armbar 290
Little Mo 45
Little Urn 206
Lob Scouse 106
Lone Pine 236
Long Distance Runner 135
Looning the Tube 50
Loony Toons 47
Loose Block Corner 58
Lord of the Pies 178
Lord of the Rings 181
Lost Crack 186
Loved by a Sneer 135
Love Minus Zero 263

▶ M.I.L. Arete 70
Mad Dog of the West 78
Mad on the Metro 51
Major Headstress 196
Making Plans for Nigel 103
Malice in Wonderland 36
Manatese 234
Manic Strain 264
Marital Aids 297
Mark of Thor 134
Massambula 35
Maupin Rey Route 183
Maurice Chevalier 321
Maximum Tariff 48
Medicine Show 113
Meltdown 35
Memorable Stains 204
Menage a Trois 268
Menai Vice 50
Menhir 76
Menopausal Discharge 264
Menstrual 267

Mental Block 297
Mental Lentils 244
Men at Work 80
Men of Leisure 82
Mfecane 112
Midnight Drives 225
Midnight Flier 119
Mildly Macho 33
Minder 112
Mini Bus Stop 36
Mister, Mister 268
Mister Blister 80
Monkey on a Stick 105
Monkey See Monkey Do 153
Monsieur Avantski 297
Monster Hamburger Eats the Alien Baby 232
Mon Amie 110
Moth to the Flame 102
Moving Being 244
Mudslide Slim 28
Mu Hat Mu Ganja 104
My Halo 133
My Hovercraft is Full of Eels 36
My Secret Garden 44
My Wife's an Alien 110

▶ 'N' Gauge 58
N.E. Spur 47
Naked Before the Beast 203
Name Unknown 152
Narcolepsy 55
Nearly but not Quite 194
Near Dark (After Dark) 299
Neat Arête 130
Never as Good as the First Time 268
Never Never Land 145
New Rays from an Ancient Sun 117
Nice Guy 284
Nick the Chisel 127
Nifty Wild Ribo 194
Night of the Hot Knives 273
Nik-Arête 217
North West Face of the Druid 184
Nostrodamus 264
Nostromo 264
Nothing... 221
Not Quite Snakes and Ladders 320
Now or Never Never 52
No Problem 130
NYQUIST 117

▶ Observation Groove 321
Obsession 147
Occam's Razor 236
Octopussy's Garden 232
Offa's 154
Off the Beaten Track 52
Old Farts 117
Old Fogies Never Die 299
OM 69 Runner Bean 196

Caban

Café / Restaurants

Serving Great Mountain Food
– Breakfast, Lunch and Dinner

Two Unique Venues for
Club Dinners & Private Functions

www.caban-cyf.org

Caban - Brynrefail
At the other end of Llyn Padarn
Tel: 01286 685500
Open 7 days a week
 Free WiFi

Caban - Pen y Pass
At the top the Pass
Tel: 01286 870500
Summer 8am - 6pm
Winter 9am - 5pm

One Step Beyond 275
One Wheel on my Wagon 253
On Shite 255
Opening Gambit 167
Orangutang Overhang 57
Order of the Bath 253
Out of Africa 131
Overtaken By Department C 216
Over the Rainbow 206
▶ Pail Rider 154
Pain Killer 187
Pandora's Box finish 304
Pandora Plays Sax 304
Pandora Plays Sax direct start 304
Paradise Lost 236
Pas de Chevre 277
Pas the Duchie... 277
Patellaectomy 154
Patio Door of Perception 51
Penblwydd Hapus 154
Peter Pan 127
Phil's Harmonica 165
Pigs in Space 221
Piper at the Gates of Dawn 145
Pitch Two 119
Pit and the Pendulum 236
Planet Zzzoink Arete 47
Plastic Soldier 77
Pocketeering 220
Poetry in Motion 250
Poetry Pink 204
Polar Express 61
Pontiac Arete 70
Pop 147
Pork Torque 221
Pour Tout le Monde 110
Power Tool Resurrection 277
Practically Esoteric 173
Prick up Urea's 206
Primal Ice Cream 120
Private Smells 276
Private Smells Direct Start 276
Proless Cliff's Arête 133
Proliferation Bang On 133
Prometheus Unbound 177
Pruning the Tube 50
Psychic Sidekick 282
Psychodelicate 52
Psychotherapy 250
Puddy Kat 46
Puffing Billy 58
Puff Puff 275
Pull My Daisy 203
Pulverised 75
Pumping Iron 254
Purple Haze 159
Putting on Ayres 73
Put it on the Slate, Waiter 78

▶ Quelle Surprise 133
▶ Race Against the Pump 33
Rack and Pin 61
Raisin Frumpsnoot 30
Raped by Affection 204
Rastaman Vibration 73
Razorback 73
Red and Yellow and Pink and Green, Orange and Purple and Blue 203
Red Throated Diver 51
Reefer Madness 267
Released from Treatment 203
Release the Kraken! 145, 320
Remain in Light 135
Rest in Pete's Eats 153
Resurrection Shuffle 75
Return of the Visitor 103
Rhinoplasty 321
Rhyfelwr 159
Ride Like the Wind! 92
Ride of the Valkyries 277
Ride the Wild Surf 196
Ringin' in Urea's 204
Ritter Sport 276
Road to Botany Bay 94
Road to Nowhere 144
Rock Athletes Day Off 71
Rock Video 102
Rock Yoga 79, 320
Rodent to Nowhere 144
Ronald Reagan Meets Doctor Strangelove 77
Rosen the Chosen 181
Rowan 221
Ruby Marlee meets Dr Holingsworth 77
Running Scared 173
Run for Fun 230
Rycott 113
▶ Sabre Dance 255
Sad Man Who's Sane 48
Sad Old Red 121
Salvador 102
Sanity Claws 246
Sanity Fair 246
Sans Chisel variation 127
Saruman 187
Satires of Circumstance 275
Satisfying Frank Bruno 220
Sauron 187
Saved by the Whole 219
Scare City 30
Scarface Claw 51
Scarlet Runner 34
Scarlet Runner Direct 34
Scheherezade 145
Schmitt Hammer 113
Scorpion 172
Scratching the Beagle 234
Seamstress 131

Seams the Same 131
Seam Stress 131
Second's Chance 75
Second Thoughts 45
See You Bruce 81
Senile Delinquent 230
Senior Citizen Smith 309
Septuagenarian 28
Sesame Street comes to Llanberis 252
Shame and Embarrassment 150
Shazalzabon 194
Shock the Monkey 152
Shoreline 33
Shorty's Dyno 57
Short Staircase to the Stars 134
Short Stories 145
Shothole Arete 58
Shtimuli 118
Side Line 58
Silent Homecoming 130
Silly on Slate 276
Silver Shadow 231
Silvester Still-born 254
Simion Street 105
Simply Peach 121
Single Factor 45
Skinning the Ladder 230
Slabaholics Anonymous 81, 320
Slabology 81
Slabs 'R' Us 118
Slab Rog 80
Slab Slayer 79
Slate's Slanting Crack 268
Slatebite 71
Slate Arrivals 111
Sleeper 52
Sleight of Hand 217
Slippery People 134
Slip Not 104
Slip of the Tongue 166
Slip Sliding Away 166
Slug Club Special 131
Small Rusty Nail on a Large Mantelpiece 184
Smokeless Zone 269
Snap 146
Snoring Exploring 159
Snowdon Lady 236
Snuffler 221
Soap on a Rope 253
Sodor 61
Solitude Standing 70
Solstice 31
Solvent Abuse 273
Sombre Music 121
Song of the Minerals 225
Son of Rabbit 44
So this is Living 36
Spider Pants 121
Splitstream 204

Split Decision 166
Split the Dog 245
Spong (is good for you) 231
Sport 4 All 57
Spread 'em 246
Sprint Finish 80
Sprint for Print 230
Squashing the Acropods 146
Stack of Nude Books Meets the Stick Man 131
Stairlift to Heaven 150
Stairway to Silence 121
Stand to your Rights 37
Stannah to Hell 150
State of the Heart 143
Steps of Escher 143
Steps of Glory 57
Sterling Silver 31
Steve Lineman 282
Stick's Groove 127
Stiff Syd's Cap 206
Stinky Boots 42
Stretched Limo 70
Stretch Class 103
Stuck up Fruhstuck 127
Stump Rogers 250
Sucked Away with the Scum 253
Sunk Without Trace 230
Sunshine Swing 321
Supermassive Black Hole 173, 320
Sup 1 254
Sup 2 254
Surfin' USA 232
Surprise Surprise 57
Susanna 321
Suspension of Disbelief 152
Swan Hunter 50
Swinging By the Bell 267
Swiss Air 142
Sylvanian Waters 94
Synthetic Life 308

▶ Taith Mawr 172
Tambourine Man 118
Technical Hamster 48
Technical Hamster Dance 48
Teenage Kicks 159
Teliffant 254
Temple of Boom 44
Tennent's Creek 82
Tentative Decisions 134
That Obscure Object of Desire 269
Theftus Maximus 45
The Ascent of the Vikings 145
The Australian 54
The Barrel of Laughs 186
The Beanstalk 72
The Biggest Joke 186
The Big Easy 28
The Big Sur 121
The Blind Buddha 250

The Bone People 309
The Book of Brilliant Things 131
The Bridge Across Forever 309
The Burning 46
The California Express 122
The Carbon Stage 145
The Chiselling 106
The Christening of New Boots 71
The Climbing Pains of Adrian Mole 305
The Coleslaw that Time Forgot 254
The Color Purple 160
The Colour Purple 217
The Coming of Age 232
The Coolidge Effect 184
The Cure for a Sick Mind 204
The Curious Incident 92
The Daddy Club 166
The Dark Destroyer 230
The Dark Half 236
The Deceiver 284
The Deceptive Dyke 47
The Dreaming 77
The Dude in the Orange Hat 102
The Dunlop Green Flash 43
The Dwarf in the Toilet 255
The Dyke 165
The East Face of the Vivian Direct 259
The East Face of the Vivian 259
The East Face Super Charged 259
The East Face Super Direct 259
The Faffer 84
The Fat Controller 51
The Finger Slicer 147
The Firé Escape 165
The Full Monty 268
The Gargoyle 147
The Garret Slide 94
The Gnarly SPAR Kid 305
The Golden Shower 246
The Gorbals 81
The Great Curve 135
The Grey Slab 239
The Groove of Smooth 321
The Groovy Gang 57
The Hand of Morlock 305
The Hobbit 117
The Homicidal Hamster from Hell 214
The Hong Jagged Route of Death 246
The Hooligan 283
The Koala Brothers 93
The Level Crossing 61
The Listening and Dancing 217
The Long and   Winding Road 187
The Lost Tomb 277
The Machine in the Ghost 145
The Madness 276
The Mad Cap Laughs 121
The Mallard 61
The Mancer Direct 291

The Mancer Original Start 291
The Manimal 273
The Man Who Fell to Earth 47
The Master Craftsman (Il Miglior Fabbro) 234
The Mau Mau 230
The Medium 133
The Meltdown 165
The Mere Giggle 186
The Methane Monster 78
The Missing Link 267
The Monster Kitten 244
The Moon Head Egg Monster from Allsup 264
The Mosquito 305
The Muff Affair 246
The Mu Mu 216
The New Salesman 312
The New Slatesman 221
The Niche 282
The North Face of the Aga 80
The Poacher 284
The Porphyry Chair 183
The Punters Retreat 173
The Quarryman 165
The Quartz Scoop 273
The Race Against Time 206
The Railway Children 61
The Rainbow of Recalcitrance 203
The Razors Edge 169
The Reclining Bloon 312
The Richard of York Finish 203
The Rock Dancer's Daughter 231
The Rothwell Incident 307
The Samba Drum 75
The Second Coming 297
The Serpent Vein 97
The Shark that Blocked the Drain 255
The Shining 80
The Skyline Club 76
The Sneaking 117
The Sniggering Smear 186
The Spark that Set the Flame 269
The Spirit Level 135
The Spleenal Flick 214
The Sponge that Walked Away 246
The Stick Up 133
The Stream of Obscenity 55
The Suncharmer 321
The Sweetest Taboo 268
The Take Over by Dept. 216
The Telescopic Stem Master 111
The Toms Approach 52
The Trash Heap Has Spoken 297
The Trash Heap Speaks Again 297
The True Finish 169
The Untouchables 220
The Velociraptor 273
The Very Big and the Very Small 204
The Very Old and the Very New 84
The Wall Within 184

The Wall Without 177
The Weetabix Connection 246
The Wonderful World of Walt Disney 165
The Woodflower 282
The Wooley (or won't he) Jumper 120
The Wow Wow 43
The Wriggler 312
Thomas the Tank 58
Those who climb clearly marked projects... 61
Throttle with Bottle 269
Tick's Groove Project 178
Time Bandit 244
Titan 145, 320
Toad in Toad Hall 113
Toe be or not Toe be…. 78
Toilet Trouble 42
Tolerance 110
Tomb Raider 144
Tongue in Situ 219
Too Bald to be Bold/The Turkey Chant 255
Top Gear 160
Torrents of Spring 230
Tower of Laughter 111
Towse's Project 184
To Infinity and Beyond! 92
Tribal Blow 273
Tribulation of Bob Marley and Peter Tosh 104
True Clip 231
Truffle Hunter's Roof 275
Turkey Trot 82
Turn of the Century 48
Twisted Nerve 311
Twm Dre 105
Two Bolts or Not to Be 246
Two Steps to Heaven, Three Steps to Hell 177
Two Tone 275

▶ U.B.L. 48
Uhuru for Mandela 307
Ultra Cricket Zone 305
Unchain My Heart 220
Under the Glass 273
Unnamed 80, 310
Unpaid Bills 120
Unsexual 127
Up the Garden Path 78

▶ Vandal 284
Velvet Walk 105
Vermin on the Ridiculous 214
Vertigo 230
Virgin on the Ridiculous 34
Vivander 269

▶ Waiting on an Angel 217
Wakey, Wakey, Hands off Snakey 255
Walking Pneumonia 127
Walk This Way 93
Walls come Tumbling Down 234
Wall of Flame 196
Walrus Wipeout 232

Watching the Sin Set 254
Watch Me Wallaby 127
Watch Me Wallaby Wank, Frank 146
Watford Gap West 159
Waves of Inspiration 121
Wave Out on the Ocean 250
Wave Rock 94
Way Down in the Hole 313
Wedlock Holiday 119
Wendy Doll 246, 267
Werp 232
West Face of Australia 65
West Face of Australia Direct 65
West Face of Australia Super Direct 65
We No Speak Americano! 118
When the Wind Blows 113
Where are my Sensible Shoes? 219
Where the Green Ants Dream 97
Whitemate 183
Why Knot? 104
Wild Horses 178
Windows of Perception 133
Wishing Well 253
Wish You Were Here 84
With a Little Help From a Tree 58
Wizz Bang 28
Wobbly Variations on a Slab 304
Wolfhound 173
Womaninstress 234
Wond 36
Working up a Lather 246
Wusty Woof 30

▶ XXXposure 177

▶ Yak Kak 264
Ya Twisting Ma Melon Man 117
Yorkshire VD 130
Yossarian 143
Young and Easy Under the Apple Boughs 264
Young Man Afraid of Horses 178
Youthanasia 81
Youthslayer 78
You can Dance if You Want 269
Yuk Hunter 112
Y Gwaedlyd 130
Y Rhaffwr 55
Y Rybelwr 239

▶ Zambesi 106
Zeus 145, 320
Ziplock 74
Zippies First Acid Trip 74
Zzzooming the Tube 50

Acknowledgements

The biggest thanks go to Pete Robins and Mark Dicken the main authors of the guide and also the key activists who (along with Chris Parkin and Mark Reeves) pushed forward the essential re-equipping campaign – without their commitment and drive the quarries would have likely remained an obscure backwater, instead of the buzzing place that it is now.

Martin Crook deserves extra special thanks for his remarkable Diary of a Slatehead pieces, which provide a fascinating window into the slate climbing scene during its 80s glory days.

Vital feedback and advice has also been drawn from a large pool of climbers; the following 'local experts' have been especially helpful: Jon Ratcliffe, James McHaffie, Noel Craine, Neil Dyer, Adam Wainwright, Rob Wilson, Andy Newton, Chris Davies, Chris Parkin, George Smith, Mark Lynden, Streaky Desroy, Ian Lloyd-Jones, Keith Scarlett, Llion Morris, Mark 'Baggy' Richards, Mike Raine, Nick Davis, Pete Harrison, Phillip Targett, Jim Kelly, Rory Shaw, Tim Neill, Dave Evans, Andy Scott, Tim Badcock, Si Beal, Colin Goodey, Gwion Hughes, Trev Hodgson, Nick Harms, Adam Hocking, Rob Wilson, Zoe Brown, John Silvester, Martin Kocsis, Steve Franklin, Alex Mason, Geoff Bennett, Phil Dowthwaite, Dave Rudkin, Johnny Dawes, Gav Foster and Toby Keep.

The photography contained in this guide is very strong and a real credit to the talented snappers that put forward a whole host of inspiring images. Much of the credit for the visual impact of this book lies with them: Ray Wood, Jethro Kiernan (www.onsight.com), Alex Messenger (www.snowfire.com), David Simmonite, Gareth Aston, Ian Parnell, Jack Geldard, Martin Crook, Al Leary, Graham Desroy, Pete Robins, Rob Wilson, Mike Raine, Si Beal, Dave Kendall, Paul Pritchard, Andy Newton, Glenn Robbins, Chris Davies, Ian Lloyd-Jones, Rob Lamey, Nick Walton, Gareth Hutton, Susan Hatchel, David Atchison-Jones, Iwan Arfon Jones, Mike Raine, George Smith, Claude Davies, Rob Gibson, Tony Kay, Jim Jones, R Pierce and Gill Lovick.

Numerous images from the original Slate of the Art' slideshow, which Paul Williams toured with in the 80s, appear in the guide, especially in the Diary of a Slatehead pieces. Many thanks are due to Mike Raine for obtaining these images from Paul's son, Chris, who is also due a great debt of gratitude for kindly agreed to allow their use in this guide.

Elfyn Jones, the new BMC Cymru Access and Conservation officer deserves many thanks for the sterling work he has done to maintain good relations with First Hydro. Mike Raine (BMC Cymru chair 2005-2010) also deserves credit for his calming presence and willingness to get involved in access discussions over the previous few years.

Ken Latham and Paul Sivyer (Parc Padarn) deserve much credit for helping to maintain 'tolerated' access to Vivian Quarry. Adrienne Stratford from the RSPB has been very helpful too in sorting out the detail of the bird restrictions.

Al Williams, Ground Up's resident designer, has produced some outstanding design work with this guide – he remains a key part of the Ground Up team and someone who never fails to 'come up with the goods'! For that and many other things I am truly thankful.

And finally a very heartfelt thank you to my wife Clare, and my kids, Cadi and Charlie for being there when I need them most.

Simon Panton July 2011

Bibliography

Bibliography

Dinorwig Slate Quarries (Perry Hawkins, George Smith, The Great Arete, 1987)
Llanberis (Paul Williams, Climbers' Club 1987)
Rock Climbing in Snowdonia (Paul Williams, Cicerone, 1990)
Llanberis Slate (Nick Harms, Snowdonia Publishing, 1990)
Slate (Iwan Arfon Jones, Andy Newton, Leigh McGinley, North Wales Slate, 1992)
Slate (Iwan Arfon Jones, North Wales Slate, 1999)
North Wales Rock (Simon Panton, Ground Up, 2006)
North Wales Rock 2nd edition (Simon Panton, Ground Up, 2009)

Advertisers Directory

Ground Up would like to thank all the advertisers who helped to support this guidebook:

The Beacon – page 3
01286 650045
www.beaconclimbing.com

Joe Brown – page 5
01286 870327/01690 720205
www.joebrownsnowdonia.co.uk

MIC – page 6
www.themic.org

DMM – page 17
01286 872222
www.dmmclimbing.com

V12 Outdoor – page 18
01286 871534
www.v12outdoor.com

Moon – page 23
www.moonclimbing.com

High Sports – page 24
01743 231649
www.highsports.co.uk

Eryri Mountaineering – page 62
07711320966 / 07771356229
www.eryri-mountaineering.co.uk

The Indy Climbing Wall – page 63
01248 716058

Awesome Walls - page 108
0151 2982422
www.awesomewalls.co.uk

Plas y Brenin – page 109
01690 720214
www.pyb.co.uk

Slateheads Climbing – page 128
Slateheads1@aol.com

Get High – page 314
www.gethigh.co.uk

Mark 'Baggy' Richards – page 322
www.goclimbingwithbaggy.com

Anita's B&B – page 364
01286 870087 / 07769851681
www.surfsister.co.uk

Pete's Eats – page 364
01286 870117
www.petes-eats.co.uk

Andy Newton – page 364
01286 872317
www.andynewtonmic.org

Caban – page 369
01286 685500
www.caban-cyf.org

---

1 Si Panton on **Combat Rock** E1 5a, Twll Mawr photo: Tim Badcock
2 Pete Robins caught in flight on **Spong** F7c, Rainbow Walls photo: Rob Wilson
3 Martin Crook bouldering in Beddgelert Forest photo: Crook Collection
4 Mark Dicken on **The Take Over by Dept. C** F7a, Rainbow Walls Lower photo: Ray Wood

Ian Lloyd-Jones and Sion McGuiness in Twll Mawr on the Fob top pitch of their magnificent 4 pitch route, **Supermassive Black Hole** F7a photo: Ray Wood